MUSIC AFTER HITLER, 1945–1955

Ganz am äußersten Ende der Künste, ... kommt die Musik, die man, um auf den Grund ihres Wesens zu kommen, ohne Verbindung mit Texten und vollends ohne Verbindung mit der dramatischen Darstellung als Instrumentalmusik betrachten muß.

Wunderbar und rätselhaft ist ihre Stellung. Wenn Poesie, Skulptur und Malerei sich noch immer als Darstellerinnen des erhöhten Menschenlebens geben mögen, so ist die Musik nur ein Gleichnis desselben. Sie ist ein Komet, der das Menschenleben in kolossal weiter und hoher Bahn umkreist, dann aber auf einmal sich wieder so nahe zu demselben herbeiläßt als kaum eine andere Kunst und dem Menschen sein Innerstes deutet. Jetzt ist sie phantastische Mathematik – und jetzt wieder lauter Seele, unendlich fern und doch nahe vertraut.

[At the extreme frontier of the arts ... we find music, which, if we wish to penetrate to the essence of its being, must be taken as instrumental music, detached from words, and above all, separate from dramatic representation.

Its position is wonderful and enigmatic. While poetry, sculpture, and painting can still lay claim to be the representation of a higher aspect of human life, music is only a parable of it. It is like a comet, circling around life in a vastly high and remote orbit, yet suddenly sweeping down closer to it than any other art, and revealing to humanity its innermost feelings. Sometimes it is a mathematics of the imagination – then again pure soul, infinitely distant, yet close and dear.]

Jakob Burckhardt, *Weltgeschichtliche Betrachtungen* (ed. Rudolf Marx, Stuttgart: Alfred Kröner Verlag, 1969)

Music after Hitler, 1945–1955

TOBY THACKER
Cardiff University, UK

ASHGATE

Published by
Ashgate Publishing Limited
Gower House
Croft Road
Aldershot
Hampshire GU11 3HR
England

Ashgate Publishing Company
Suite 420
101 Cherry Street
Burlington, VT 05401-4405
USA

Ashgate website: http://www.ashgate.com

British Library Cataloguing in Publication Data
Thacker, Toby
  Music after Hitler, 1945–1955.
  1. Music – Political aspects – Germany – History - 20th century. 2. Music and state
  - Germany – History - 20th century. 3. Germany – History – 1945-1955. I.Title
  780.9'43'09044

Library of Congress Cataloging-in-Publication Data
Thacker, Toby, 1957–
  Music after Hitler, 1945–1955 / by Toby Thacker.
      p.   cm.
  Includes bibliographical references.
  1. Music – Germany – 20th century – History and criticism. 2. Music and state –
  Germany. 3. Censorship. 4. Germany – Social life and customs – 20th century. I. Title.
  ML275.5.T45 2006
  780.943'0904–dc22   2006005357

ISBN-13: 978-0-7546-5346-2

Printed on acid-free paper

Printed and bound in Great Britain by TJ International Ltd, Padstow, Cornwall.

Contents

Abbreviations

ACA	Allied Control Authority
AFN	American Forces Network
AGWAR	Adjutant General, War Office
BBC	British Broadcasting Corporation
BMI	Bundesministerium des Innern
BSM	Bureau des Spectacles et de la Musique
CCG(BE)	Control Commission for Germany (British Element)
CIA	Central Intelligence Agency
DAS	Deutscher Allgemeiner Sängerbund
DISCC	District Information Services Control Command
DDR	Deutsche Demokratische Republik
DEFA	Deutsche Film-Aktiengesellschaft
DSV	Deutscher Schriftstellerverband
DVV	Deutsche Verwaltung für Volksbildung
ENSA	Entertainment National Services Association
EUCOM	European Command
FDGB	Freier Deutscher Gewerkschaftsbund
FDJ	Freie Deutsche Jugend
GDR	German Democratic Republic
GFCC	Groupe Française du Conseil de Contrôle
GMZF	Gouvernement Militaire de la Zone Française
GMZFO	Gouvernement Militaire de la Zone Française d'Occupation
HA	Hauptabteilung
HJ	Hitlerjugend
IC	Information Control
ICD	Information Control Division
ISCB	Information Services Control Branch
ISCM	International Society for Contemporary Music
ISD	Information Services Division
KPD	Kommunistische Partei Deutschlands
MfK	Ministerium für Kultur
MgF	Ministerium für gesamtdeutsche Fragen
MGG	Musik in Geschichte und Gegenwart
MuG	Musik und Gesellschaft
NSDAP	Nationalsozialistische Deutsche Arbeiterpartei
NWDR	Nordwestdeutscher Rundfunk
OMGB	Office of Military Government, Bavaria

OMGBW	Office of Military Government, Baden-Württemberg
OMGUS	Office of Military Government, United States
OMGUS POLAD	Office of Military Government, United States, Political Adviser
OWI	Office of War Information
PID	Political Intelligence Division
PR/ISC	Public Relations/Information Services Control
PWD	Political Warfare Division
PWE	Political Warfare Executive
RIAS	Rundfunk im amerikanischen Sektor
RKK	Reichskulturkammer
RMK	Reichsmusikkammer
SA	Sturmabteilung
SBZ	Sowjetische Besatzungszone
SED	Sozialistische Einheitspartei Deutschlands
SHAEF	Supreme Headquarters, Allied Expeditionary Force
SKdK	Ständige Konferenz der Kultusminister
SMAD	Sowjetische Militäradministration in Deutschland
SS	Schutzstaffel
Stakuko	Staatliche Kommission für Kunstangelegenheiten
SWF	Südwestfunk
USFET	United States Forces, European Theater
VgC	Verband gemischter Chöre Deutschlands
VDK	Verband Deutscher Komponisten und Musikwissenschaftler
VEB	Volkseigener Betrieb
VKM	Verband Deutscher Komponisten und Musikwissenschaftler
ZK	Zentralkomitee

The following abbreviations are used for archival sources:

ABP	Alan Bush Papers, British Library
AOFC/AC	Centre des Archives de l'Occupation Française en Allemagne et en Autriche à Colmar, Affaires Culturelles
BAB	Bundesarchiv, Außenstelle Berlin
BAB/RKK	Bundesarchiv, Außenstelle Berlin, Reichskulturkammer
BAK/OMGUS	Bundesarchiv, Koblenz, Office of Military Government, United States
BBC/WAC	BBC Written Archives Centre, Caversham

BHA/OMGB	Bayerisches Hauptstaatsarchiv, Munich, Office of Military Government, Bavaria
BHA/MK	Bayerisches Hauptstaatsarchiv, Munich, Ministerium für Kultur und Unterricht
GLAK/OMGWB	Generallandesarchiv, Karlsruhe, Office of Military Government, Württemberg-Baden
IfZ	Institut für Zeitgeschichte, Munich
IfZ/OMGUS	Institut für Zeitgeschichte, Munich, Office of Military Government, United States
NRWA	Nordrhein-Westfälisches Hauptstaatsarchiv, Düsseldorf
SAAdK	Stiftung Archiv der Akademie der Künste, Berlin
SAPMO-BArch	Stiftung Archiv der Parteien und Massenorganisationen der DDR im Bundesarchiv, Berlin
SD	Stadtarchiv, Düsseldorf
SG	Stadtarchiv, Göttingen
TNA/PRO/FO	The National Archive (formerly the Public Record Office, London), Foreign Office Correspondence
WDR/HAC	Westdeutscher-Rundfunk, Historisches-Archiv, Cologne

Introduction

This book explores the connections between music and politics in Germany in the ten-year period between the defeat of Hitler's 'Third Reich' in 1945 and the formal ending of the Allied occupation in 1955. It focuses on efforts to promote or censor music considered to have political meaning or influence, and to favour or disfavour individual musicians on grounds of their political affiliations, real or supposed. The first half of the book deals primarily with music as part of the 're-education' project of the occupiers, and the second half with the evolution of musical culture in a divided Germany. The first half is concerned, therefore, with the intentions of the wartime Allies, and their twofold aspiration of 'denazifying' German music and creating something new in its place. If it overlooks to a significant degree the contribution of Germans themselves to post-war musical culture, this is intended to counter the absence of Allied music officers from existing accounts of music in this period in Germany. The second half restores Germans to centre stage, and places the wartime Allies, now Cold War enemies, in the background.

There is a huge literature on music in post-war Germany, which falls broadly into two significant categories. The first is preoccupied with musical analysis, and rigorously excludes anything outside its self-imposed framework. The second is a literature of memoir and biography. This, for the most part, follows the well-established conventions that separate music from politics, suggesting that to transgress in this area is a sign of poor taste, and somehow irremediably vulgar. Countless biographies and autobiographies of famous composers and performers recount their lives in a studiously apolitical manner. Any reference to politics usually suggests an unworthy contamination of the abstract beauties of music by worldly concerns. This perception is replicated in popular consciousness. Until very recently, even for those involved in and interested in music, the idea that music was politically controlled in Germany after 1945 has often come as a surprise. In the specialist academic literature devoted to 'culture' in post-war Germany, music is typically most present in its absence. Sometimes, an author may point to this, apologetically, but more often than not, there is an unspoken assumption that somehow music, by its very nature, is resistant to political machinations and social currents, and not therefore suited to analysis in the way that literature, theatre, film, or the visual arts are. At one end of the aesthetic scale, purists might concede that popular music can be linked to trends in society,[1] but

---

1   There is in Germany a long tradition of socio-cultural analysis of popular music, stemming in the 1950s from the fear that American popular music was provoking anti-social behaviour, and from earlier discourses on jazz. See Reinhard Fark, *Die mißachtete Botschaft: Publizistische Aspekte des Jazz im soziokulturellen Wandel* (Berlin: Spiess, 1971); Kaspar Maase, *BRAVO Amerika: Erkundungen zur Jugendkultur der Bundesrepublik in den fünfziger Jahren* (Hamburg: Junius, 1992); Uta Poiger, *Jazz, Rock, and Rebels: Cold War Politics and*

at the other is the citadel of abstract artistic integrity: classical instrumental music. In between, certain musical forms, like song and opera, have been included in cultural analysis by being treated as literary texts, but this leaves their recalcitrant musical elements out as fit only for internal structural analysis, or the kind of metaphysical description exemplified by Burckhardt in the nineteenth century.[2]

The result is an imbalance in the treatment of different art forms in Germany after 1945. Music, if referred to, is treated in generalisations, typically couched in an impersonal, passive narrative form. Thus Reiner Pommerin, introducing a recent collection of essays on culture in the Federal German Republic with a survey of the post-war musical scene, says: '[The] music of composers such as Igor Stravinsky, Paul Hindemith and Carl Orff was played again.'[3] Aside from the striking inaccuracy of the statement, which perpetuates the myth of Orff as an anti-Nazi figure when in fact his music was very popular and frequently performed in Nazi Germany, particularly between 1940 and 1944, this style of writing begs many questions. Whose idea was this? Was it a German or an Allied initiative? Who authorised these performances? Where did the actual music come from? As we shall see, all public performances of music in Germany after May 1945 had to be licensed by the

---

American Culture in a Divided Germany (Berkeley, Los Angeles, and London: University of California Press, 2000); Toby Thacker, 'The fifth column: dance music in the early GDR', in Patrick Major and Jonathan Osmond (eds), *The Workers' and Peasants' State: Communism and Society in East Germany under Ulbricht 1945–71* (Manchester: Manchester University Press, 2002), pp. 227–43; and Edward Larkey, 'Postwar German Popular Music: Americanisation, the Cold War, and the Post-Nazi *Heimat*', in Celia Applegate and Pamela Potter (eds), *Music and German National Identity* (Chicago and London: University of Chicago Press, 2002), pp. 234–50.

2   It is revealing that the huge and complex body of work by Adorno on the sociology of music does not directly mention 'music control' in Germany after 1945; nor do critical studies of Adorno's thought on music and politics refer to this (see for example Russel Berman, 'Adorno's Politics', in Nigel Gibson and Andrew Rubin (eds), *Adorno: A Critical Reader* (Oxford: Blackwell, 1992), pp. 110–31, and Max Paddison, 'Immanent Critique or Musical Stocktaking: Adorno and the Problem of Musical Analysis', ibid., pp. 209–33. Paddison explores specifically 'the relation of inner to outer, of the hermetically sealed autonomous work to its social other, and the need for a particular kind of discourse which is able to identify the connections between the two' (p. 210), and refers to Adorno's insistence in *Philosophie der neuen Musik* (1949) on the need for an analysis which went beyond 'mere cultural-humanist stock-taking', but does not relate this demand to the specific situation in Germany at the time Adorno was writing. Nor have I found reference to Adorno in the documentation produced by planners, administrators, and officials involved with the reconstruction of music in Germany between 1945 and 1950. His importance as the champion of a certain modernist school at Darmstadt was greater in the late 1950s and the 1960s. I shall not therefore discuss Adorno, except where, as in 1951, he made a direct intervention in the debate about the political and social position of music in Germany between 1945 and 1955.

3   Reiner Pommerin, 'Some Remarks on the Cultural History of the Federal Republic of Germany', in Reiner Pommerin (ed.), *Culture in the Federal Republic of Germany, 1945– 1995* (Oxford: Berg, 1996), p. 9.

local Military Government: they could not take place as some kind of spontaneous cultural manifestation. At its worst, this general 'cultural history' uses music as a kind of decoration, substituting photographs or other visual images for sustained analysis. Powerful images of musicians performing in ruined buildings, for rapt but subdued audiences, have taken on an iconic role in our imagining of post-war Germany. Cinema has, not surprisingly, exploited music's metaphorical strength in its representations.

In the last few years, a third category of writing on music in post-war Germany has emerged as part of the larger analysis of cultural reconstruction there under Allied control. Much of it is still confined to individual essays in obscure publications, or has reached only a tiny audience, particularly outside Germany. I will comment further on this subsequently. Separately, there is now a large and growing body of academic literature on music in Nazi Germany and in the Soviet Union that explores links with political systems. In so doing, this literature implicitly confirms the idea of music as inherently apolitical, suggesting that this kind of analysis is only possible or worth undertaking as part of a study of dictatorship or totalitarianism. As far as Germany is concerned, this historiography stops at 1945, like the war. By the time music reappears in the cultural histories of Germany after 1945, it has reassumed its apolitical guise as a free-floating art form. It is assumed that there has been some kind of caesura, and, more quickly and easily than the other arts, that German musical culture was able to resume its apolitical course. Music, seen in this way, has proven itself particularly suited to a language of redemption and renewal.

It is a commonplace that after the horrors of Nazism and the shock of total defeat, many German people turned to elements of their cultural past in an effort to salvage something from the ruins of their national inheritance. Nothing was better suited to this than the music of the 'great composers', most of them German. The rapid reconstruction of musical life in Germany after May 1945, its flourishing in the ruins, moral and physical, was from that time held up as a metaphor for the birth of a new Germany which could draw on the best elements of its artistic and spiritual past.[4] This results in an often perfunctory and unsatisfactory treatment. The political divisions amongst the Occupiers, which resulted in 1949 in the partition of Germany into two client states, had consequences for music. In the early 1950s, as the world divided into two ideological blocks, music was part of this wider intellectual and ideological schism. In the East music, like all the arts, was to be owned and produced by the people, for the people. In the West, the idea of music as an abstract art form, resistant to and free from political manipulation, was strongly upheld. In the Federal Republic, these were the 'golden years', when the great German orchestras and performers resumed their former position of supremacy, and radio stations became

---

4   Fred Prieberg courageously made the first serious assault on this vision in 1984, writing: 'Music literature after 1945 is a hotbed of falsehoods.' See '"Nach dem Endsieg" oder Musiker-Mimikry', in Hanns-Werner Heister and Hans-Günter Klein (eds), *Musik und Musikpolitik im faschistischen Deutschland* (Frankfurt-am-Main: Fischer, 1984), pp. 297–305, p. 301.

the pioneers of the avant-garde.[5] From this perspective, music in the East, behind the 'Iron Curtain', was – like the other arts – a prisoner. There was no point in even trying to consider it as something worthy of analysis in its own right. As an art form, it was necessarily debased by political demands and an assumed subservience, or as Wolfgang Geiseler put it, 'obviously in bed with politics'.[6]

This neglect is doubly unfortunate, because music allows so many diverse approaches to aspects of society and politics. In different forms, music reaches almost the entire population. In its most intellectual European forms, as part of a wider religious and literary culture, music is also distinct in that it demands an act of re-creation every time it is performed. The great composers, unlike the great painters, need fresh generations of musicians and singers to bring every note and phrase to life. Each performance, as Burckhardt noted, brings with it a re-interpretation,[7] and this provokes a continuous interaction with contemporary ideas. Any re-interpretation is, furthermore, not just in the hands of an elite body of virtuoso performers and other professionals. In Germany in mid-century, it was something that also extended to amateurs, or lay musicians, from every class and part of society. Music was found in the churches, and as a constituent part of all levels of education. Workplaces and institutions in Germany typically had their own choirs and orchestras. Music was a symbol of village as well as of municipal pride. In an advanced industrial society, engaged after 1945 in a unique historical exercise of forced re-evaluation, music took on symbolic and representative roles of great importance, involving larger ideas about German history and identity, and it is these roles that are the focus of attention here. The goal is to understand those meanings (rather than any current ones), to see where they came from, and what consequences this had.

Quite coincidentally, this ten-year period was also one of rapid and far-reaching technological and stylistic change. In technological terms, it witnessed the introduction of long-playing records, magnetic tape recorders, electronic musical instruments, and transistor radios. As for the music itself, at one end of the cultural scale neo-classicism was supplanted by dodecaphony, by serialism, and by aleatory music. Ideas about musical notation, organisation, and the role of the performer were dramatically changed. At the other end of the scale there were equally rapid changes in popular music. These developments took place not only in the particular context of Germany after the 'Third Reich', but also at a time when the intellectual and artistic confrontation between capitalist and communist ideologies was at its most intense.

---

5   For a detailed, and representative exposition of the 'golden years' theory, see Westdeutscher Rundfunk Köln (ed.), *Zwanzig Jahre Musik im Westdeutschen Rundfunk. Eine Dokumentation der Hauptabteilung Musik 1948–1968* (Cologne: Westdeutscher Rundfunk, 1968). For a more discerning presentation, albeit one which still falls largely within the parameters outlined here, see Wolfgang Geiseler, 'Zwischen Klassik und Moderne', in Hermann Glaser, Lutz von Pufendorf, and Michael Schöneich, (eds), *So viel Anfang war nie: Deutsche Städte 1945–1949* (Berlin: Siedler, 1989), pp. 244–9.

6   Geiseler, 'Zwischen Klassik und Moderne', p. 245.

7   Burckhardt, *Weltgeschichtliche Betrachtungen*, p. 226.

The appearance of music in so many artistic and social forms makes it impossible to treat all of these manifestations with equal depth in an overview. I have thus paid attention here to those forms which appeared most politically charged in Germany between 1945 and 1955, and which, as a consequence, were the subject of most contemporary attention. This results inevitably in a neglect of certain kinds of music, and certain aspects of musical activity, including some which had their origins in the period under consideration here, but which were of greater significance later. One example is that of the cult of Handel in the GDR. The improbable meeting between the cultures of eighteenth-century England and the early German Democratic Republic (GDR), which took shape after the start of the *Händel Festspiele* in Halle in 1952, is a subject of great interest, but took on particular importance only after the Handel anniversary in 1958, when the SED declared work with Britain a focus of its cultural foreign policy.[8] Similarly, the reader will not find here a treatment of military music in the nascent armed forces of either the Federal Republic or the GDR. Adenauer himself in 1954 took a personal interest in the question of what music would be appropriate for the *Bundeswehr*, seeking specialist advice on suitable music that would be martial but not overly nationalist, but both in the Federal Republic and in the GDR, military music was developed largely after 1955.[9] Of greater significance, I do not examine musical education in schools and universities in any detail. This is a large and complex field, which merits study in its own right.

The existing literature on music in the 'Third Reich' has provided intellectual inspiration as well as a wealth of valuable background information that I have relied on in the preparation of this book. Above all, the detailed and nuanced work of Michael Kater should be mentioned.[10] Writers such as Josef Wulf, Fred Prieberg, Michael Meyer, and Erik Levi have also contributed to a broader understanding of music and musicians in the 'Third Reich'.[11] More recently, Willem de Vries, Michael Kaufmann, Pamela Potter, and Anselm Gerhard have illuminated hitherto unexplored

---

8   See Toby Thacker, '"Renovating" Bach and Handel: New Musical Biographies in the German Democratic Republic', in Jolanta Pekacz (ed.), *Musical Biography: Towards New Paradigms* (Aldershot: Ashgate, 2006), pp. 17–42.

9   See Fred Prieberg, *Musik und Macht* (Frankfurt-am-Main: Fischer, 1991), pp. 243ff.

10   Michael Kater, *Different Drummers: Jazz in the Culture of Nazi Germany* (New York and Oxford: Oxford University Press), 1992; *The Twisted Muse: Musicians and their Music in the Third Reich* (New York and Oxford: Oxford University Press, 1997); and *Composers of the Nazi Era: Eight Portraits* (New York and Oxford: Oxford University Press, 2000); see also Michael Kater and Albrecht Riethmüller (eds), *Music and Nazism: Art under Tyranny, 1933–1945* (Laaber: Laaber Verlag, 2003).

11   Josef Wulf, *Musik im Dritten Reich. Eine Dokumentation* (Gütersloh: S. Mohn, 1963); Fred Prieberg, *Musik im NS-Staat* (Frankfurt-am-Main: Fischer, 1982); Michael Meyer, *The Politics of Music in the Third Reich* (New York: Peter Lang, 1991); Erik Levi, *Music in the Third Reich* (Basingstoke: Macmillan, 1994)

areas of German musical culture between 1933 and 1945.[12] Frederic Spotts, historian of the Bayreuth Festival, has put Hitler back into the centre of debate.[13] Music in the 'Third Reich' has thus become an exciting and sophisticated field of historiography. Insofar as a central theme of this body of work has been to suggest continuities in German musical history, and to counter the idea of 1933 as a complete break with the past, this book might be seen as an extension of that literature – one which seeks similar continuities beyond 1945. The literature on music and politics in the Soviet Union has, perhaps surprisingly, been less helpful. This literature covers a much larger chronological span, as the Soviet Union lasted considerably longer than Nazi Germany, but its focus on the Soviet Union has had unfortunate consequences for the study of East and Central European countries after 1945.[14] As one of the Soviet Union's 'satellite' or 'puppet' states, the musical culture of the GDR has only been regarded very recently in the West as worthy of academic attention in its own right. Since the collapse of the Soviet Union, and the opening of many formerly closed archives, a reappraisal has begun. In the last decade, the first serious treatments of music in the early GDR have been published.[15]

This new historiography – returning to the third of the above-mentioned categories of writing about music in post-war Germany – is part of a wider picture. The interest in what is called the 'new cultural history' has coincided with a growth in the study of post-war Germany, helped by the opening of the archives of the Allied Military Governments and High Commissions who governed Germany during 1945–55.

---

12   Willem de Vries, *Sonderstab Musik: Music Confiscations by the Einsatzstab Reichsleiter Rosenberg under the Nazi Occupation of Western Europe* (Amsterdam: Amsterdam University Press, 1996); Michael Kaufmann, *Orgel und Nationalsozialismus. Die ideologische Vereinnahmung des Instruments im "Dritten Reich"* (Kleinblittersdorf: Musikwissenschaftliche Verlags-Gesellschaft, 1997); Pamela Potter, *Most German of the Arts: Musicology and Society from the Weimar Republic to the end of Hitler's Reich* (New Haven and London: Yale University Press, 1998); and Anselm Gerhard, 'Musicology in the "Third Reich": A Preliminary Report', *The Journal of Musicology*, 18:4 (Fall 2001), pp. 517–43.

13   Frederic Spotts, *Hitler and the Power of Aesthetics* (London: Pimlico, 2003)

14   See Boris Schwartz, *Music and Musical Life in Soviet Russia 1917–1970* (London: Barrie and Jenkins, 1972); Alexander Werth, *Musical Uproar in Moscow* (London: Turnstile Press, 1949); Caroline Brooke, *The Development of Soviet Music Policy, 1932–1941*, PhD thesis (University of Cambridge, 1999); and S. Frederick Starr, *Red and Hot: The Fate of Jazz in the Soviet Union 1917–1980* (Oxford: Oxford University Press, 1983).

15   Daniel zur Weihen, *Komponieren in der DDR: Institutionen, Organisationen und die erste Komponistengeneration* (Cologne, Weimar, and Vienna: Böhlau, 1999); Lars Klingberg, *Politisch fest in unseren Händern; musikalische und musikwissenschaftliche Gesellschaften in der DDR* (Kassel, Basle, London, New York, Prague: Bärenreiter, 1997); and Toby Thacker, '"Anleitung und Kontrolle": Stakuko and the Censorship of Music in the GDR, 1951–1953', in Beate Müller (ed.), *Censorship and Cultural Regulation in the Modern Age* (Amsterdam and New York: Rodopi, 2004), pp. 87–110. David Blake, 'The Reception of Schoenberg in the German Democratic Republic', *Perspectives of New Music*, 21 (1982–83), pp. 114–37, is an isolated serious treatment of GDR musical culture during the Cold War.

Unfortunately this historiography, which has just started to consider music, mirrors the post-war division of Germany, and is compartmentalised by the separate Zones of occupation. Norman Naimark has put the study of the Soviet Zone on a serious footing,[16] and now a veritable army of international researchers is encamped in the *Bundesarchiv* in Berlin, studying the most diverse aspects of society and culture in the Soviet Zone, and in the early GDR. Maren Köster's recently published book is the first serious study of music in the Soviet Zone.[17] A separate force is scouring the huge quantities of American material now available on microfilm in archives in southern and western Germany, and in its original form at the National Archives in Maryland. David Monod's recent overview of the American 'denazification' of German music has set an example for others working on this Zone.[18] In northern Germany, and in London, a parallel effort is being conducted on the British occupation; Gabriele Clemens has opened up the area of music there.[19] Isolated detachments of French and German scholars have even started to make inroads into the so-called 'forgotten Zone', working on the French archives in Colmar.[20] In almost all cases, though, the work of these researchers is confined to a single Zone, which is detailed as it if existed in isolation.[21] Berlin is often seen as a further geographical and political sub-division, and is treated separately.[22] This fragmentation is not in itself surprising

---

16   Norman Naimark, *The Russians in Germany: A History of the Soviet Zone of Occupation, 1945–1949* (Cambridge, Massachusetts and London: Harvard University Press, 1995)

17   Maren Köster, *Musik-Zeit-Geschehen. Zu den Musikverhältnissen in der SBZ/DDR 1945 bis 1952* (Saarbrücken: Pfau, 2002)

18   David Monod, *Settling Scores: German Music, Denazification, and the Americans, 1945–1953* (Chapel Hill and London: University of North Carolina Press, 2005) This is unique amongst studies of music in post-war Germany as it presents an overview of developments in a whole zone of occupation, and is based on unpublished archival and oral evidence. An earlier case study from the American Zone that refers to music is Ulrich Bausch, *Die Kulturpolitik der US-amerikanischen Information Control Division in Württemberg-Baden von 1945–1949* (Stuttgart: Klett-Cotta, 1992).

19   Gabriele Clemens, *Britische Kulturpolitik in Deutschland 1945–49. Literatur, Film, Musik und Theater* (Stuttgart: Franz Steiner, 1997)

20   For example, Stefan Martens (ed.), *Vom "Erbfeind" zum "Erneuer": Aspekte und Motive der französischen Deutschlandpolitik nach dem Zweiten Weltkrieg* (Sigmaringen: Thorbecke, 1993). Forty years on, Frank Roy Willis, *The French in Germany 1945–1949* (Stanford: Stanford University Press, 1962), is still the only generally available English language work on the French Zone.

21   One noteworthy effort to overcome this is the collection of essays, including several case studies relating to music, edited by Gabriele Clemens, *Kulturpolitik in besetzten Deutschland 1945–49* (Stuttgart: Franz Steiner, 1994).

22   See, with reference to music, Brewster Chamberlin (ed.), *Kultur auf Trümmern. Berliner Berichte des amerikanischen Information Control Section Juli–Dezember 1945* (Stuttgart: Deutsche Verlags-Anstalt, 1979); and Elizabeth Janik, '"The Golden Hunger Years": Music and Superpower Rivalry in Occupied Berlin', *German History*, 22:1 (2004), pp. 76–100. Wolfgang Schivelbusch's otherwise excellent *In a Cold Crater: Cultural and*

given the difficulties of using the available evidence, and does to an extent reflect the lack of contact between the different Zones following the German capitulation of May 1945. The historiography of 'culture' in occupied Germany similarly follows the structural hierarchies established by the four Military Governments, which had broad similarities. It devotes attention first to education, then to the press, broadcasting, literature, film, theatre, and finally, if at all, to music. This study takes a different route by adopting a comparative approach to 'Music Control' in all four Zones. It resists the tendency to focus on Berlin, and presents a wider picture, looking at developments in other urban cultural centres, and in smaller towns.

The emerging historiography of occupied Germany, with its fourfold zonal division, follows the well-established distinction between work on the Federal Republic and the GDR, which have very largely been treated as two entirely separate entities. The symbolism of the 'Iron Curtain' has played a large part in suggesting that the two Germanys were sealed off from another, and that as societies, they are best treated in isolation. In fact, particularly in the early 1950s, there was an enormous traffic of people, material objects, and ideas between the Federal Republic and the GDR, and not just in Berlin. Musicians, both professional and amateur, had particular freedom to travel; sheet music, scores, and records could be sent through the post, and radio broadcasts from each Germany could reach some parts of the other. Many German citizens had relatives, friends, and contacts living on the other side of the 'Iron Curtain', and they were not to know that the partition would in fact last for another forty years, becoming increasingly impermeable. Culture offers a way to analyse similarities and differences underneath the contrasting and confrontational political and economic systems of the two Germanys after 1949, and this book again departs from established practice by considering the evolving musical cultures of the two post-war German states on equal terms, and asking the same questions of each. It concludes by looking specifically at the musical traffic between the two Germanys between 1949 and 1955, and suggests that it may make more sense to think of this period in terms of two distinctive musical cultures, which nonetheless shared and exchanged far more than has been imagined.

One consequence of the lack of attention to music in post-war cultural histories of Germany, as noted earlier, has been the frequent recourse to an impersonal, passive narrative voice. As far as possible, I try to avoid this, and my approach seeks to establish who was responsible for particular decisions affecting music. Such an approach is informed by a belief in individual agency, conditioned by historical circumstances. The men (and it was largely men) who shaped musical culture in post-war Germany were obviously not free agents. All were products of their environment, education and cultural background. The Allied officers who had responsibility for 'Music Control' in Allied Military Governments between 1945 and 1949 were subject to orders from above, and of course to military discipline. German musicians, cultural administrators, academics, and journalists were driven by the

---

Intellectual Life in Berlin, 1945–1948 (Berkeley, Los Angeles, and London: University of California Press, 1998), specifically excludes music from its treatment.

crudest of imperatives: the need for money, food, and work. After 1949, they had far more freedom and autonomy, but nevertheless worked under great ideological pressure, often generated from outside Germany. Many had personal histories that had to be concealed or denied. Some who found it hard to conform found themselves rejected by both sides. Emigrés, who had been forced to leave their homes and families, returned to Germany with their own burdens. In many senses, the period between 1945 and 1955 in Germany was a particularly difficult one in which to work as a musician, which confirms Kater's conclusion that 'politics and the arts do not good bedfellows make'.[23]

It should finally be stressed that this book is not written from a musicological perspective, and is not concerned with musical analysis *per se*. It is, though, informed by my experience as a practical musician, and therefore addresses many questions that are typically overlooked. To perform music, a choir or orchestra needs parts, and the conductor needs a score. An orchestra needs instruments, strings, and reeds. In order to broadcast music, a radio station needs musicians and recordings as well as microphones, amplifiers, and transmitters. Musical journals and books cannot be produced without paper. In Germany after 1945, most of these commodities were in very short supply, and the different Military Governments controlled access to such limited stocks as did exist. Within those organisations, there were competing demands and priorities. It was therefore one thing for someone to put forward the idea in theory that say, music banned by the Nazis should be played. To carry this out in practice was another matter. As we shall see, musical life in Germany between 1945 and 1955 was frequently characterised by a gap between intentions and achievements.

Michael Kater, whose subtle and painstaking work has provided a model for others who would enter this complex field, did venture into the post-war German musical landscape in the last volume of his trilogy. He had little to say about the GDR, but when he did refer to it, he was damning in his judgement. It was, he said, 'a totalitarian regime, similar in its oppressive nature and censorial intent' to the 'Third Reich'.[24] This obviously stands in complete opposition to the GDR's self-portrayal as the first genuinely anti-fascist German state. Looking at developments in western Germany, Kater concluded with an arresting statement: 'If the muses suffered in the resurrection of the German nation after 1945, that of music, the "magical language of emotion", surely suffered the most.'[25] This is all the more striking coming from one who has such a deep knowledge of and engagement with the subject. It stands in complete contrast to the 'golden years' idea, which has been propagated in the international literature on music for half a century without serious challenge, and to the rosy pictures of socialist musical culture produced by the GDR.

Poised between such contradictory theories, it is difficult to know which one best represents the German musical scene of the post-war period. I hope that this work

---

23   Kater, *Composers*, p. 265.

24   *Ibid.*, p. 110.

25   *Ibid.*, p. 284.

will help by providing an introduction to some of the issues and personalities that dominated that scene, and thus illuminating the huge, and still rather murky, space between Kater's assessments and those of traditional historiography.

A Note on Sources

The difficulties of using the secondary literature on music and musicians to support a political and societal analysis of music have already been mentioned. Much the same applies to the published contemporary literature on music, in particular by the musical press, which strenuously avoided politics. When the German musical press was re-established by the Allies after 1946, it followed this convention. The official journals of the Military Governments and the German-language cultural journals that they sponsored after 1945 have been of more use, particularly in providing evidence of the ways in which the wartime Allies sought to restructure culture in the perceptions of Germany's educated middle classes. The GDR, of course, produced its own highly politicised musical literature, but its usefulness is restricted by its obvious partiality.[26] This study is therefore largely constructed on the basis of unpublished documents, and it may be helpful to comment here on the nature and extent of this material.

Music was not the first priority of the wartime Allies when they embarked on the occupation and re-education of Germany in May 1945. As a result, much of the documentation on 'Music Control' originally produced by Military Governments and High Commissions was not rigorously filed and conserved for posterity. Decisions had to be made about which documents should be brought back to Britain, France, the USA, and the Soviet Union during and after the occupation, and it appears that most of the material relating to music was thrown away. The situation was compounded by material circumstances in Germany after May 1945 in which paper itself was in very short supply. Many documents, particularly in 1945 and 1946, were written or typed on scraps of waste paper, ironically often on stationery originally prepared for Nazi agencies. What survives of these today is fragmentary, and is typically scattered through the files of many different branches of the various occupation agencies. This study necessarily reflects the resulting gaps and fragmentation. The British documents, now in the National Archive in London, are particularly strong on the planning process for 'Music Control', and enable us to reconstruct this process in some detail. Material on the implementation of these plans, even in the larger cities of the British Zone like Hamburg, Cologne, and Düsseldorf, is notably

---

26   The most prominent example is the journal *Musik und Gesellschaft*, published from March 1951. There are also various official histories of music in the GDR published later, and a memorial literature of varying quality. See above all Ernst Hermann Meyer, *Kontraste, Konflikte: Erinnerungen, Gespräche, Kommentare* (Berlin: Verlag Neue Musik, 1979), and Konrad Niemann, *Ernst Hermann Meyer – für Sie porträtiert* (2nd edition, Leipzig: Deutscher Verlag für Musik, 1989); also Karl Laux, *Nachklang: Rückschau auf sechs Jahrzehnte kulturellen Wirkens* (Berlin: Verlag der Nation, 1977).

lacking. In contrast, the American documents now on microfilm in Germany are rich in detail, particularly for the first few months of the occupation. 'Daily reports' from the Music Control Section in Munich in June, July, and August 1945 provide extraordinary insight into the American efforts to restart musical activities there. The French documents, although very fragmentary, make it clear that they had a more sophisticated and ambitious musical programme than the other Allies. Fortunately for the non-Russian reader, the Soviets delegated considerable authority in cultural affairs to German agencies, and many of their papers have been preserved in SED files now open in Berlin.[27] In all four Zones though, the available documentation is incomplete. The general picture may be clear, and it is possible to reconstruct certain developments, at particular times and places, in detail; but much remains obscure.

There is a particular problem with denazification, which is a central theme of this work. This whole process had many dimensions, and was, for all its failings, an extraordinarily far-reaching and complex one, involving many different agencies and mechanisms. A bizarre situation currently exists, where the denazification of Furtwängler has generated a whole literature of its own, and yet the broader denazification of thousands of lesser musicians has hardly been considered.[28] Nor is this area topic illuminated by more general work. This is partly because different domains of civil life in Germany were denazified in different ways. Musicologists in universities were subject to different procedures from performing musicians; there were significant zonal variations, which meant that experience in Baden-Baden was very different from that in Hamburg, Munich, or Dresden. Many musicians were subjected to multiple investigations and judicial processes between 1945 and 1948, carried out by different Allied and German agencies. The main reason that this whole area is still so murky is that many relevant documents have been deliberately withheld or destroyed. Whole record groups are missing from British and American files; all documents relating to individual denazification processes in the French Zone are still classified; many German *Spruchkammer* documents are subject to personal protection laws, which guarantee anonymity until 50 years after the death of the individual concerned. The reasons for this secrecy are not altogether obvious, but will be discussed further. Suffice it to say here that this has been a particularly difficult area to illuminate; the most that I can claim is to have mapped out a terrain, which hopefully will become clearer with further research. As far as possible, I have explored allegations of Nazi association or activity by referring to sources from before May 1945. Readers interested in any of the individuals discussed here will profit from consulting Kater's work, and others previously cited.

---

27   The SED (Socialist Unity Party of Germany) is the acronym given to the amalgamation of the former KPD (Communist Party of Germany) and the SPD (Social Democratic Party of Germany) in the Soviet Zone of Germany, which took place in April 1946. The SED was dominated by German Communists trained in the Soviet Union, and remained the 'leading party' of the GDR until the collapse of the state in 1989.

28   On Furtwängler, see Monod, *Settling Scores*. There has been careful work on some individual musical 'denazifications'. See Kater, *Composers*, and Potter, *Most German of the Arts*.

The second half of this study is constructed very largely from German documents. SED files relating to music are extensive, and have been supplemented by the personal papers of leading SED musicians now at the Academy of the Arts in Berlin. The situation for the early Federal Republic is very different. Government files from the early 1950s, now in the Bundesarchiv in Koblenz, are disorganised, very fragmentary, and have not been catalogued. Control of and responsibility for music was, to a significant extent, devolved to the *Länder* and the towns, and I have supplemented the material in Koblenz with documents found in *Land* and *Stadt* archives. Had time and money permitted, it would have been possible to find more material, particularly of local importance, in almost every *Land* and *Stadt* archive in Germany. The same applies to broadcasting, which was deliberately regionalised by the Allies after 1945. I have used documents from the BBC Written Archive in Caversham, and from the West German Radio archive in Cologne, but there is doubtless further relevant material in other German radio archives. I have also been helped by a habit shared by almost all officials, of whatever nationality, who had responsibility for music – that of collecting relevant contemporary press cuttings. Hundreds of these still exist, scattered through the different archives I have consulted. In translating from German and French into English, I have paid greater attention to conveying the sense of the original text than to producing an idiomatic rendering. Except in quotation, I have used English spellings for German place names (thus Hanover and Munich), and for composers (thus Schoenberg and Handel).

Most of the men and women who actively participated in German musical life between 1945 and 1955 are now dead, or very old, and I have not drawn extensively on oral testimony. Two exceptions are worthy of mention. Jack Bornoff, a British Army Officer appointed in 1945 as the first 'Music Controller' of the NWDR (Northwest German Radio) in Hamburg, spoke to me about his experiences there, in particular about the creation of the NWDR Symphony Orchestra. Georg Knepler, an Austrian musicologist who spent the Nazi years in emigration in Britain, and was after 1949 a leading member of the musical establishment in the GDR, was also kind enough to share his memories with me.

PART 1
Allied Re-Education, 1945–1949

Chapter One

Music and Regeneration

In the early months of 1945, Allied troops fought their way into Germany. From the east, Soviet forces advanced to the river Elbe, encircling Berlin; in the northwest, British soldiers experienced bitter street-fighting in Bremen, and armoured units drove to the Baltic, occupying the historic city of Lübeck. American troops thrust into the centre of Germany, capturing Düsseldorf, Göttingen, and Leipzig, and meeting Soviet troops at Torgau on the Elbe; in the south, they seized Bayreuth and Munich. French troops were urged by De Gaulle to play their part, and occupied Stuttgart and Karlsruhe. When the fighting stopped in early May, Germany was left in a chaotic state: many cities and towns had suffered huge physical damage; transport was entirely disrupted; millions of displaced persons – liberated concentration camp prisoners, former slave labourers, civilian refugees, and soldiers – were on the move, contemplating an uncertain future. Central government had collapsed, and improvised local administrations were left struggling in isolation to maintain order and essential services. Psychologically, the surviving German population was beginning the long and complex process of coming to terms with the past, while facing bereavement, loss, uncertainty, anxiety, and guilt. Many knew that they might face punishment at the hands of the victorious Allies for their actions before the collapse of the 'Third Reich'.

In this confusion, the resurgence of music-making is particularly striking. In Leipzig for example, the Americans, after reassuring themselves that Günther Ramin was not a Nazi Party member, authorised him to perform Bach's *St Matthew Passion* with the *Thomanerchor*. In Dresden, where the city centre had been entirely destroyed by the bombing raids of 13 and 14 February 1945, the Soviet occupiers authorised Gerhart Wiesenhütter to conduct the Philharmonic Orchestra on 6 June, and encouraged Rudolf Mauersberger to direct the surviving members of the city's famous boys choir, the *Kreuzchor*, in a public performance on 1 July.[1] In Hamburg, where large areas of the city were still cordoned off and deserted since the British bombing in June 1943, the British had captured the radio station intact. A former intelligence officer, Jack Bornoff, was charged with the formation of a new symphony orchestra for the station; within weeks of the surrender, a 'Northwest German Radio Symphony Orchestra' was broadcasting performances of Mahler and Mendelssohn.[2]

---

1   Laux, *Nachklang*, pp. 322–3.
2   Jack Bornoff, interview with the author, December 2000.

The Americans set up a 'Music Control' office in Munich in May 1945, and set about interviewing prospective new conductors for the Philharmonic Orchestra. Eugen Jochum, Hans Knappertsbusch, and Richard Strauss were amongst those who offered their services. Jochum was selected, and the Philharmonic performed under his baton on 8 July 1945. The French in Karlsruhe were perhaps the quickest off the mark. Within ten days of the city's capture, they had refurbished the concert hall, and were holding concerts there.[3] In Berlin itself, although the conductor of the Philharmonic Orchestra, Wilhelm Furtwängler, had fled to Switzerland, Leo Borchard directed a rump of surviving members of the orchestra in a performance on 26 May.[4] The Soviets had no intention of allowing a cultural vacuum to develop, and almost as soon as the fighting stopped in Berlin and other large cities they occupied, they set about establishing new cultural organisations. Culture and the arts, the Soviets proclaimed, would play a leading role in pulling Germany out of the abyss into which it had fallen under Hitler. There were two other activities linked with music which took place all over Germany in the immediate aftermath of surrender, and which played a significant role in the post-war period. The first was repressive, the second opportunistic. After years of warfare, and particularly after the harrowing discovery of the concentration camps and of widespread Nazi atrocities in the final weeks of the war, many of the Allied occupation forces were in a vengeful mood. The orgy of rape and looting that took place in areas occupied by the Soviets has been well documented; however, widespread rape by French troops has not received the same attention. British and American soldiers were bound by a strict policy of non-fraternisation, but there were inevitably many instances of abuse, retribution, and theft. As far as music was concerned, all the occupiers intended to carry out a purge of institutions and individuals connected with the Nazi regime. In Wasserburg, near Munich, the Americans immediately disbanded the National Socialist Symphony Orchestra, and confiscated its instruments.[5] In Munich, the Music Control office was brusquely informed that former Nazi musicians would help in the reconstruction 'by contributing their service to the repair of roads and the cultivation of fields'.[6] All over Germany, professional musicians and singers were dismissed from orchestras and operas, often on the basis of denunciations, or hastily gathered information about their past activities and affiliations. Most importantly, all over Germany, it was made clear to the population that the only musical performances that might take place had to be sanctioned by the new military authorities.

Alongside this immediate censorship and exclusion, there was a bizarre and contradictory phenomenon. The thousands of occupying soldiers in Germany, and the rapidly growing military administrations, needed entertainment. This need was

---

3   Bayerisches Hauptstaatsarchiv, Munich, Office of Military Government, Bavaria (hereafter BHA/OMGB) 10/48–1/5, Annex to Weekly Situation Report, Film, Theater, and Music Control Section, 6871st DISCC, 7 August 1945, p. 3.

4   Chamberlin, *Kultur auf Trümmern*, pp. 12ff.

5   BHA/OMGB 10/120–2/8, Van Loon to Ross, 27 June 1945.

6   BHA/OMGB 10/120–2/8, HQ, 6870th DISCC, Kennedy to Vogel, 22 June 1945.

partly met by radio broadcasts, but German musicians frequently supplied live music. While some military agencies were setting about the process of denazification, others were more concerned with the immediate welfare of their troops, and not with the background of German musicians called upon to entertain them. Nowhere did this tension produce a more paradoxical spectacle than in Bayreuth, home of the Nazified cult of Wagner. By July 1945, American soldiers there were being treated to nightly 'Wagner festivals', in which the Festival orchestra played programmes of popular classics to enthusiastic GIs.[7]

During the next four years, these contrasting strands of Allied behaviour were to persist and compete, providing the dominant contours of a resurrection of music-making in Germany. Patronage of high quality professional music went hand in hand with censorship and exclusion. The demand for troop entertainment intersected with both of these. At different times, and in different places around Germany, one or other of these impulses was dominant. At other points they co-existed in a fragile balance. Both contributed significantly to shaping the musical landscape inherited in 1949 by the two new German states founded at the end of the occupation.

Planning for 'Music Control'

The disjointed and inconsistent approaches to music displayed by the Allies in the immediate aftermath of German surrender reflect the different planning processes undertaken in London, Washington, Moscow, and Paris. Understandably, music was not a high priority for the wartime Allies when they envisaged the occupation of a defeated Germany, preoccupied as they were with security, and with political and economic reconstruction. All four Allies recognised, nonetheless, that the restructuring of German cultural life would be an important part of a broader process of 're-education'. Within this, they paid greater attention to the press, cinema, radio, and literature than they did to music. Indeed, nothing testifies more eloquently to the enormous scope of the re-education project than the attention paid, at the end of the planning process, to music.

Wartime planning for 'music control' took place in a number of separate and evolving contexts. Inevitably it reflected the distinct political and musical cultures of each of the individual Allied countries, and their separate wartime experiences, as well as their differing ambitions for post-war Germany. In Britain and America, there was an established liberal tradition that separated the arts from politics, and a central aim of their post-war music control was to enforce this separation in Germany. In the Soviet Union, the arts, including music, had been subjected in the 1930s to the doctrine of 'socialist realism'. Music had thus to play its full part in the consolidation of the workers' revolution and in the building of communism.

Although a more tolerant attitude had developed during the war in the Soviet Union, there was no doubt that all the arts in those parts of Germany occupied

---

7   BHA/OMGB 10/48–1/4, Music Section, Daily Report No.18: Nürnberg Mission, 11 July 1945.

by the Soviet Union would be expected to play a political role. France had been occupied by Germany since 1940. Parts of Alsace were only liberated in February 1945, and 'fortresses' like Dunkirk were held by the Germans until May 1945. Under occupation, the French had been the targets of a German cultural campaign in which music played a significant part, and this experience fed directly into their own post-war occupation of Germany. All four wartime Allies started from a point of reverence for high culture, and for the tradition of 'German music'. None wished to be seen as less committed to high culture than the others, and this resulted after May 1945 in an immediate and intense competition between them as they realised that music played an enormous symbolic role in the public sphere in Germany. The Soviets approached music control with a great confidence in their own national tradition, and in their contemporary revolutionary music. The French similarly had an enormous strength of cultural purpose and achievement, which fed into their post-war programme. The British and Americans, conversely, approached the problem with a sense of musical inferiority. Neither country lacked self-confidence as such, particularly in their recent musical achievements, but both were concerned by the possibility that they would be viewed in Germany as countries without music, or in the case of the Americans, without any high culture at all.

There was a final complicating factor. All four Allies had conflicting views about what had happened to music in Germany under Hitler. One strongly held view, well established in Britain before 1939, was that the great German musical tradition had been almost destroyed by Nazi intolerance and persecution. All four Allied countries had become places of refuge for thousands of exiled German artists and intellectuals, including many distinguished musicians. The Allies knew of the Nazi conception of 'degenerate art', of the Nazi hatred of anything and everything Jewish, and of modern, international music. It was often assumed, particularly by the British and the Americans, that the former high standards of German musical life had been gravely undermined, and that, for instance, any significant new composition of music there had ceased in 1933.[8] The French knew from experience that despite the persecution of Jewish musicians, German orchestras and operas had maintained a very high standard of performance, and that until the final months of the war, Germany still had an extraordinarily active professional musical life. The Soviets, for all their political differences with the Nazis, shared something of the German veneration for great musicians, and this led them to a particularly arbitrary treatment of individual German musicians after 1945, some of whom were punished as 'fascists', while others, like Furtwängler and Abendroth, who had been active in the 'Third Reich', were encouraged to resume their careers.

The idea of 're-educating' Germany was discussed first in Britain. As early as 1940, in a series of radio programmes, Sir Robert Vansittart put forward the idea that

---

8   Adorno, writing in America in March 1945, spoke for many when he described the 'indisputable destruction of German musical culture' under Hitler. Theodor Adorno, 'What National Socialism Has Done to the Arts', *Gesammelte Schriften, Band 20:2, Vermischte Schriften II* (Frankfurt-am-Main: Suhrkamp, 1986), pp. 413–29, p. 414.

Germany would have to undergo some kind of 'spiritual regeneration' if it was not again to become a threat to European security.[9] In 1942, the debate about future Allied policy towards a defeated Germany spread across the Atlantic, and by 1943 there was an emerging Anglo-American consensus that, alongside security measures, and the punishment of war criminals, it would be necessary after the defeat of Nazism to enforce a programme of 're-education' upon the broader German population. In both countries, plans for the future control and restructuring of German media and culture evolved from the wartime conduct of 'psychological warfare'. Understandably, detailed thinking about music was left until very late in the war. When, in early 1945, the British Political Warfare Executive (PWE) did turn its attention to music, it was able though to draw on the practical experience of several years of wartime broadcasting to the German population. The expertise of the BBC German Service, which had consciously used different kinds of music in its propaganda programme, fed directly into the planning for post-war music control.[10]

The BBC German Service was established before the outbreak of war in 1939, and was directly controlled by the Foreign Office. During the war, it had grown in importance as a propaganda weapon. By 1944, the BBC estimated that between 10 and 15 million Germans tuned in daily to its broadcasts, and recent research suggests that these figures may have been 'overly conservative'.[11] The German Service was primarily a spoken word programme, and the conditions in which it operated militated against its suitability for music broadcasting. Nonetheless, from 1940 onwards, it provided 'psychological warriors' in Britain with practical opportunities to think about how different kinds of music might be used for propaganda, and to analyse what kinds of political message might be conveyed by music.

The BBC knew, for example, that jazz and swing were hugely popular, particularly with German troops and young people, but its directors were reluctant to use what they thought of as 'light music' for 'direct propaganda', preferring instead to go for the cultural high ground. The German Service therefore broadcast concerts of classical music, deliberately using exiled German musicians, and performing a wide range of music. It used excerpts from well known classics in spoken word programmes, playing Beethoven for example, to accompany broadcasts about the killing of the Jews in 1942, to contrast the greatness of past German achievement with the moral depths into which the country had now sunk.[12] The BBC commissioned the exiled Russian composer Mischa Spolianski to compose songs with German texts, some of which were apparently very popular in Germany, and in November 1942 even asked

---

9   The text of the programmes was subsequently published. See Robert Vansittart, *Black Record: Germans Past and Present* (London: Hamish Hamilton, 1941), p. 15.

10   See for a fuller discussion Toby Thacker, '"Liberating German musical life": The BBC German Service and planning for Music Control in Occupied Germany, 1944–1949', *'Stimme der Wahrheit': German-language broadcasting by the BBC, Yearbook of the Research Centre for German and Austrian Exile Studies*, 5 (2003), pp. 77–92.

11   Eric Johnson, *The Nazi Terror: Gestapo, Jews, and Ordinary Germans* (London: John Murray, 2002), p. 325.

12   See Johnson, *The Nazi Terror*, pp. 441–50.

him to write a 'Hitler Oratorio', presumably in a spirit of mockery.[13] This plan was not carried through, for reasons that are unclear. It may be that the BBC's directors felt that this overstepped the boundaries of acceptable taste. By 1943, the BBC had evolved a considered musical policy, according to which

> the object of music in propaganda should be ... twofold, firstly to give so notable a projection of British music that our programmes will be listened to on their own rights, and secondly to demonstrate ... that it is from England alone that the forbidden national music or non-Aryan music can be heard, and that it is England which provides not only this artistic and cultural freedom, but also the practical military and political liberation which is connoted by the music we freely play.[14]

In 1944, the BBC began to consider how music broadcasting should be used after the defeat of Germany, commissioning the actor Marius Goring and the exiled composer Berthold Goldschmidt to draft a plan for post-war musical broadcasting. Goring was sent, in November 1944, and again in March 1945, to tour those areas of Germany already occupied by the British to help inform this process. Goring and Goldschmidt proposed a broadcast concert programme with a strong anti-Nazi emphasis. They wanted originally to accompany this with an explanatory commentary, but their superiors displayed a typically British reluctance to mix music and politics in this manner. In January 1945, Steuart Wilson (the Overseas Music Director) summarised the BBC's position: 'It may now be agreed that it is undesirable to have any concerts built with the idea of "direct propaganda".' He added that there should be 'no direct propaganda in Light Music'.[15]

Goring and Goldschmidt therefore devised a concert series in which there would be 'an indirect, rather than a direct, propaganda value'. The programmes would present a wide chronological and geographical range of music, using exiled German performers, and recordings by them. They would include works banned by the Nazis, and modernist works by composers such as Bartok. Here we see what was to be a commonly shared perception in post-war Germany: that international modernist music was a language of anti-fascism. The BBC wanted specifically to include works by Schoenberg for this reason, but was hampered by a lack of available recordings. In addition, Goring argued that broadcasting music of a 'high artistic standard' was itself of propaganda value; this again was to be a common assumption amongst the Allies in post-war Germany after May 1945. Nazi chauvinism, anti-Semitism,

---

13   See BBC Written Archives Centre, Caversham (hereafter BBC/WAC), RCONT1 Mischa Spolianski, Copyright, File 1: 1940–1962.

14   BBC/WAC R27/94/1, European Music Supervisor: Memorandum on European Music. New Schedule, 3 February 1943.

15   BBC/WAC E1/758/2, Post War Music Programmes for Germany, 12 January 1945.

and banality were to be replaced with an understated, but explicit, commitment to internationalism, to modernism, and to the highest musical standards.[16]

By the time this programme was drawn up, it was clear that the end of the war was imminent, and from March 1945 on the planning for post-war broadcasting on the BBC fed into the broader planning undertaken by the British PWE, and in cooperation with the Americans from the Psychological Warfare Department (PWD) at SHAEF in Paris. The American head of the PWD, Brigadier Robert McClure, proposed in February 1945 that the British and Americans should form 'theatre and music sections' to complement other aspects of a larger programme of 'information services control'.[17] He subsequently charged Lieutenant Warren Munsell in Paris with drawing up precise plans for 'music control' in post-war Germany.[18] In London, the complex issue of which music should be censored in Germany was passed to Brigadier van Cutsem of the PWE. Van Cutsem was mindful of the British experience of occupying parts of Germany in the 1920s, when music had been used to articulate nationalism and anti-Allied feeling. Like all those planning for post-war occupation of Germany in 1945, he worked in a situation of great uncertainty, and assumed that there might be considerable resistance to the occupation forces, and a possible resurgence of Nazism.

In a memorandum on 'German Military and Nazi Music', van Cutsem quoted US Draft Directive 13, which prohibited the playing or singing of 'German military music, or of German or Nazi anthems, in public or before any group or gathering', adding: 'During the Control Commission period some of the Germans may become "uppish" and try to gain local reputations by playing military or Nazi music or songs and using them as a rallying point for resistance.' For this reason, van Cutsem suggested 'banning whole categories of music'. He attached an analysis of captured German songbooks, highlighting the sub-genre of anti-British songs like *Wir fahren gegen Engelland* and *Bomben auf Engelland*, and drew attention to particular songs that derided Churchill and other British politicians.[19] Working from captured songbooks, van Cutsem compiled an initial list of 73 'Party Battle Songs' that he considered objectionable.[20] In further discussions in the Foreign Office, British officials argued for a more flexible and pragmatic approach to censorship. They recognised the difficulties inherent in drawing up comprehensive lists of songs,

---

16   BBC/WAC E1/739, M. Goring, Report on preparatory work done for the Post-war Service to Germany, 3 March 1945.

17   The National Archive (formerly the Public Record Office), London, Foreign Office Correspondence (hereafter TNA/PRO/FO) 898/415, untitled memorandum, signed McClure, 14 February 1945.

18   Institut für Zeitgeschichte, Munich, Office of Military Government, United States (hereafter IfZ/OMGUS), 5/243–2/8, SHAEF, PWD, Entertainment Control Section, Semi-monthly progress report, 1–15 March 1945, p. 2.

19   TNA/PRO/FO 1049/71, Van Cutsem, Research Branch, Political Division, German Military and Nazi Music, 3 March 1945.

20   TNA/PRO/FO 1049/71, Van Cutsem, Memorandum for Political Division, 17 March 1945, Appendix A: List of Party Battle Songs.

works, or composers to be banned, and stressed the negative impression that this kind of crude censorship might engender in an occupied population. Ivor Pink at the Foreign Office developed instead the idea, subsequently adopted in the British Zone of Germany, that responsibility for censorship should be turned over instead to German performers and administrators.[21] If they were involved in the performance of pro-Nazi or anti-Allied music, their right to perform would be withdrawn. Faced with such a threat, the Foreign Office reasoned, they would err on the side of caution.

On 21 March 1945, Richard Crossman of the Foreign Office (who also worked for the BBC German Service) chaired a meeting of the PWE in London, at which Warren Munsell represented the Americans. This meeting produced some 'Draft Notes on Music for Germany', which gave a clearer outline of the emerging policy for music control. Censorship would be subtle and pragmatic; a modernist and international repertoire would be reintroduced in Germany; there would be no official promotion of jazz. Crossman's group recognised that 'all Germans can listen to the programme for British or U.S. troops, which will form the greater part of the programme broadcast on German transmitters. This will give them their fill of "light" music and jazz.' It also suggested preparing a collection of records by 'distinguished refugees', of 'German music by well-known British conductors or artists', and of 'ancient music of outstanding merit'. These 'might be useful to any radio station operated in Germany'.[22] Details of the emerging British line were sent to Francis Brown, the Foreign Office representative at SHAEF. He was told that 'it is no use trying to specify what the Germans are not allowed to play or sing'. Rather than draw up complicated lists, the Germans themselves would be required to exercise discretion. They would be 'at liberty to play any music of a non-Nazi, and otherwise inoffensive character'. The occupiers would be clearly in charge though; local Commanders 'should be free to decide what can and cannot be played in their districts'.[23]

Final details were sharpened through further debate between Brown and Munsell. By the end of March, the Americans had a directive on music control ready for their Army Group commanders in the field.[24] Brown confirmed in early April that, in line with other information services, there would be three initial phases during the occupation: First, 'the prohibition of all music'; second, a survey by information control units of 'musical facilities and personnel'; and third, the 'licensing of suitable personnel'. He also noted that the *Deutschlandlied* (the German national anthem) would be banned in schools.[25] In the final weeks of the war, as British and American troops fought their way into Germany, personnel, handbooks, manuals, and directives for Information Control were assembled. McClure was in regular

---

21   TNA/PRO/FO 1049/71, Pink to D.C.(C), 8 March 1945.
22   TNA/PRO/FO 898/415, Draft Notes on Music for Germany.
23   TNA/PRO/FO 1049/71, Pink to Brown, 22 March 1945.
24   IfZ/OMGUS 5/243–2/8, SHAEF, PWD, Semi-monthly progress report, 4 April 1945, p. 20.
25   TNA/PRO/FO 1049/71, untitled memorandum, signed Brown, 2 April 1945.

touch with his British opposite number, Major-General William Bishop, as they prepared for the peace.

In early May 1945, days after the surrender of all German forces, a 'Manual for the Control of German Information Services' was issued by SHAEF. Its tenth chapter contained the results of several months of planning for 'music control', and concerned 'the production and presentation of musical activities, which include: concerts, operas, chamber music, choral music, light music, band music, dance music, recitals, and folk music, the publication and distribution of all types of printed music, and sound recordings'. It stated unequivocally: 'Immediately on occupation by Allied troops all presentation and production of public entertainment will cease' (p. 140). The book described the role of the 'Music Control Officer', who would be responsible for the 'supervision of musical productions and presentations' of 'musical publication', and for the 'manufacture, distribution and sale of sound recordings' (p. 142). It went on to explain how individual Germans who wished to 'create, arrange, or present a concert or musical performance ... must be licensed' (p. 148), and emphasised that all branches of entertainment would be subject to 'post-production scrutiny', which would check for the presence of any 'material likely to create civil disobedience or discontent or produce reactions favourable to nazi ideas, German militarism, or religious or racial discriminations' (p. 149). The Manual had an appendix providing a brief and largely accurate survey of how the Nazi regime had regulated and manipulated musical life in Germany.[26]

Further documents with specific guidance about music, evidently drawn up together, and then altered marginally to suit specific British and American requirements, were issued separately in June 1945. Given the widespread confusion about the nature and extent of British and American musical censorship, it is worth examining them in some detail. Both the British and Americans wished to portray themselves as champions of cultural freedom, while at the same time exercising a subtle, localised control over music. Thus the American 'Draft Guidance on Control of Music' stated: 'It is above all essential that we should not give the impression of trying to regiment culture in the Nazi manner.'[27] The British, in 'The Control of Music', noted: 'We must not give the impression of trying to substitute our system for that of the National Socialist Party.'[28]

The British demanded that 'the German public and musical profession must be brought into contact again with musical tastes and developments from which they have been cut off. Open encouragement should be given to performances of first-class music published outside Germany in the last fifteen years, operatic, instrumental and vocal. It is especially desirable that Germans should appreciate the extent of British musical achievement in these years. ... We should encourage gradually, but without ostentation or comment, performance of works by German composers which were

26   *Manual for the Control of German Information Services*, 12 May 1945.

27   IfZ/OMGUS 5/265–1/2, Draft Guidance on Control of Music, 8 June 1945.

28   TNA/PRO/FO 898/401, Draft, Information Control in the British Occupied Zone of Germany, 18 June 1945, Appendix B, The Control of Music.

prohibited under the National Socialist regime for racial or political reasons (e.g. Mendelssohn, Hindemith, Meyerbeer).' The Americans added: 'We should also encourage the performance of lesser-known works of famous German composers, which have not been accepted as part of the Nazi canon of German national culture, e.g., Haydn's Symphonies, Mozart's piano concertos, Schubert's chamber music.' Appended to the American text was a list of 'Foreign Composers whose works are to be encouraged in Germany'. Britain, France, and Russia were well represented, but the largest group was of thirty-five American composers, including Copland, Piston, Schuman, Barber, and also names more associated with Broadway or even with jazz, such as Kurt Weill, Cole Porter, and Duke Ellington.[29]

On censorship, the two documents were almost identical. The only pieces absolutely prohibited were songs or military marches that had been 'habitually used' by the German Army, the NSDAP, and its affiliated organisations. Similarly, on music 'associated' with the Nazis, both Americans and British devolved wide censorial powers to the 'local music control officer'. Both identified Beethoven's Third Symphony as an example of a work with potential Nazi associations. The Americans also instanced 'Siegfried's Funeral March from the "Twilight of the Gods"', and Richard Strauss's *Heldenleben*. Music was not to be used to celebrate Party and patriotic anniversaries. On living composers, there was unanimity. Strauss and Pfitzner would not be banned, but concerts 'devoted' to their works were to be forbidden. Censorship, as planned by the Americans and British, was to be flexible, and to operate unseen to the greatest extent possible.

It was on their approaches to the use of blacklists for Nazi musicians that the clearest differences emerged. The British noted: 'Germans prominent in musical administration or performance who have shown themselves zealous in carrying out Party functions and policies will be removed.' The Americans demanded similarly that 'only those who have proved themselves to be ardent Nazis, whether by their Party posts in music or by their non-musical political activities, should be actually banned from publication or performance'. The critical divergence between the two, which did have a significant effect on subsequent developments, was on the role of lists. The Americans stated:

> We should therefore, not try to compile a complete index of political music. German musical life must be influenced by positive rather than by negative means, i.e., by encouraging what we think beneficial and crowding out what we think dangerous. This applies in some degree to composers, conductors or artists, though it may be possible to compile a short black list of such people, who must be completely excluded.

The British though were unequivocal: 'It is recommended that no attempt be made to compile a black list of music and composers.'

---

29   IfZ/OMGUS 5/243-2/1, Annex 'A'.

'A New Musical Humanism'

Although these British and American plans were not divorced from wider security considerations, Soviet planning for culture in a post-war Germany was more closely tied to a unified political vision. Culture in the Soviet Union was, after all, owned by the people, and produced by the people; there could be no question in occupied Germany of simply handing it back to its pre-1933 bourgeois owners. The Soviets also differed in their plans to use a group of trained German émigrés to act as their agents, entrusting them from the start of the occupation with wide powers. In the preparation of the 'Ulbricht Group' before May 1945, and in its wider planning for the occupation, the Communist Party leadership gave culture a higher priority than it was accorded in London or Washington. The mobilisation of German intellectuals and artists was at the heart of Soviet thinking. Although initial orders from the Soviet Military Administration in Germany (SMAD) differ little on the surface from British and American directives, with the same commitment to extirpating Nazism and militarism, and to the reintroduction of contemporary international culture, the political context for the implementation of these plans was quite different. In this sense the divisions, which in music only became fully apparent in 1948, can be traced back to the start of the occupation, and further, to the initial planning for a *Kulturbund* (or Cultural League) in Moscow in September 1944.

Two factors helped to conceal the differences between the Soviets and the Western Allies. Firstly, there was during the war years a significant liberalisation of Soviet musical culture, which became far more open to contemporary international developments. The genuine cultural pluralism, particularly in music, of the Soviet Zone after May 1945 surprised the British and Americans, and allowed the Soviets to set a pace that their erstwhile Allies found difficult to match. Secondly, and this was entirely coincidental, the 'Ulbricht group' contained no musicians, and no one who had a particular interest in or knowledge of music. Thus in contrast to other arts, notably literature, the Soviets initially had no politicised German musicians who could give a firm lead in the reorganisation of musical life. The 'Ulbricht group' was able to oversee a reconstruction of music along uncontroversial lines, but it would have to wait for the return of émigrés in 1948 before it could develop a new theory of music in society.

Practical planning for the Soviet occupation of Germany was surprisingly neglected, and as a result, this was initially 'chaotic and uncoordinated'. The local *kommandanturas* that administered parts of Eastern Germany in the spring and summer of 1945 apparently had no specially trained staff, or even handbooks to guide them.[30] It was not until August that control of information media, including music, was centralised in the Propaganda Department under Colonel Sergei Tulpanov. Soviet Order No. 51 of 4 September 1945 called for:

---

30   Naimark, *The Russians*, pp. 12–13.

(a) The full liberation of German art from Nazi, racist, militarist, and other reactionary
    ideas and tendencies;
(b) the active employment of artistic materials in the struggle against Fascism, and for the
    re-education of the German people in a logically consistent democratic manner;
(c) an opening up to the values of international and Russian art.[31]

With the exception of the phrase 'reactionary ideas and tendencies', there is nothing
here that would have been out of place in a contemporary British or American
statement.

Paradoxically, the thinking that would decisively shape the musical culture of
the Soviet Zone, and subsequently the GDR, was going on not in Moscow, but in
England, where the émigré composer Ernst Hermann Meyer was actively developing
a range of Marxist ideas about music. Meyer was one of many German musicians
forced to flee Germany since 1933, but as a committed Communist he brought a
political dimension to his thinking about the future, which was absent from that
of many others. In 1944, he wrote a discussion paper for the émigré Free German
Cultural League in London, in which he argued: 'What will be needed in musical
creative work is realism, no longer flight from the world into cloud-cuckoo land;
simplicity and truth, no longer false sentimentality; clear logical developing of
ideas, no longer opportunism and chaos.'[32] In May 1945, Meyer returned to what
was now an immediate question. For a conference on 'Educational Questions', he
analysed the whole problem historically, identifying tendencies in German music
towards militarism, chauvinism, sentimentality, bulk, pompousness, and the 'sultry
mysticism' of the Wagnerians. He set out a programme 'to lay the foundations of a
new musical humanism, i.e. to tolerance, freedom, to a musical life with the people
and for the people, to realism, to an expression by way of music, of the best emotions
and ideas in human life'. He called for a central 'musical council', and local 'cultural
leagues', and demanded the return of plundered musical instruments, books, and
manuscripts from countries invaded by the Nazis. Meyer also suggested a new
folksong book, to include thirty-five non-German and twenty-five German songs. It
was to include 'at least one or two specially written, expressing the need for active
reconstruction and retribution'.[33] Although Meyer had a considerable reputation
in Britain as a composer, broadcaster, and historian of music, his unconcealed
Communist affiliations precluded any contact between him and the planners in
Whitehall. He had no influence on subsequent events in the British Zone, but it

---

31   Cited in Ministerium für Auswärtige Angelegenheiten der DDR (ed.), *Um ein
antifaschistisch-demokratisches Deutschland. Dokumente aus den Jahren 1945–1949* (Berlin:
Staatsverlag der DDR, 1968), p. 145.

32   Stiftung Archiv der Akademie der Künste, Berlin (hereafter SAAdK) Ernst-
Hermann-Meyer-Archiv, 385, Germany and Music (1944), p. 7.

33   SAAdK Ernst-Hermann-Meyer-Archiv, 386, Music in a Future Germany, May
1945.

is possible to see here the genesis of the distinctive musical culture of the future GDR.[34]

'Une Pénétration Pacifique'

Paradoxically, the French, who were the last to consider the practical problems of occupation, had the most detailed musical policy. Not surprisingly, their planning came after the fact. France itself in early 1945 still had only a provisional government. Another notable feature of cultural policy in the French Zone was the continuity in personnel from planning through to execution. Unlike the other three Zones, where one set of people made plans, and another had to implement them in Germany, French cultural policy was, from the planning stages in 1945 through to the end of Military Government in 1949, determined by the same strong-minded trio, Raymond Schmittlein, who headed the *Direction de l'Education Publique* (Directorate of Public Education), Jean Arnaud at the *Direction de l'Information* (Information Directorate), and René Thimonnier, Head of the *Bureau des Spectacles et de la Musique* (the Office of Drama and Music). It was Thimonnier who was asked to draw up a plan for music, and his 'Principles for a French musical propaganda in occupied Germany'[35] were received enthusiastically by the French government in July 1945.[36] Thimonnier was emphatic that what he called 'positive propaganda' should be the most important part of any musical policy: 'This aspect of our propaganda is the most interesting and the one from which one can expect the best results.'

He had, nonetheless, a clear programme to get rid of Nazi music and musicians, calling for 'a list of artists or of categories of artist whose previous political activity precludes any participation in an artistic performance, whether public or private. … All works which are inspired by Nazi or pan-German ideology … the national anthem, and certain songs which exalt revanchist spirit, are banned.' Going into territory that others had avoided, Thimonnier also suggested banning, at least for the short term, all music written in Germany since 1933, with exceptions only for composers who had been boycotted by the Nazis. Such a prohibition, had it actually been enforced, would have had serious implications for those like Orff, Egk, Fortner, and many lesser colleagues who later represented themselves as anti-fascists, but had

---

34   The Free German Cultural League did write to the Foreign Office to volunteer the active help of its members, including musicians, in the British Zone, but the offer was rejected. TNA/PRO/FO 936/125, Freier Deutscher Kulturbund to Foreign Office, 1 August 1945.

35   Centre des Archives de l'Occupation Française en Allemagne et en Autriche à Colmar, Affaires Culturelles (hereafter AOFC/AC) 528/5, Centre d'Organisation du Gouvernement Militaire en Allemagne, Division Propagande-Information, Section Théâtre, Sous-section Musicale, Projet d'Organisation et de Propagande, Paris, 3 July 1945.

36   AOFC/AC 528/5, Présidence du Gouvernement provisoire de la République Française, Commissariat Général aux Affaires Allemandes et Autrichiennes (signed Schmittlein), to Thimonnier.

enjoyed varying degrees of success with the German public and with the Propaganda Ministry between 1933 and 1945.

The positive side of Thimonnier's plan, which he later described to the French public as 'a peaceful penetration',[37] consisted of an energetic promotion of French music to German audiences, both in live performance by French artists, and through broadcasting. His missionary zeal coincided with the absolute confidence of his superiors, Arnaud and Schmittlein, that France alone possessed the culture that could civilise the Germans. All three were also agreed that the Germans were particularly receptive to high-quality music, and accorded music a higher place than in British, American, or Soviet cultural hierarchies, which ascribed more importance to the word, spoken or written. As a result, the French analysed more carefully than their Allies the role played by different kinds of music, and fashioned their policies accordingly. The clearest exposition of French musical intentions in occupied Germany was drawn up by Jean Arnaud, in a report written after two years of French cultural propaganda in Germany:[38]

> It is the German soul which must be attacked, it is the mentality of the old, and above all of the young which must be reformed, it is democracy which must be made to live in hearts and minds, it is a humane and humanist culture which must be promoted. (p. 9)

Who was best qualified for this task? Arnaud was quite clear on this:

> France, the country of moderation, of good sense, of taste, of finesse, the country both of the Revolution and of the rights of man, the country which exports humanist values, is now the appointed antidote for the German soul. (p. 10)

Throughout, Arnaud highlighted the particular role of music in this civilising process, and conversely, its previous links with Nazism. Arguing that radio had 'not only the task of distracting', but 'a determining role on mentalities', he singled out a problem with 'music, which because of its colossal dimensions encourages too much the German pretension to be the only ones to penetrate to mystical-musical depths' (p. 35). Arnaud believed that the Nazi sense of racial superiority was founded partly on a conviction that Germans were the 'the only really musical people'. To challenge this was to attack the roots of Nazism: 'If one can be brought to think that music is no longer a German monopoly, one of the fundamental premises of racist and pan-Germanist philosophy collapses'. (p. 48)

This perception underlay the censorship of not only Wagner and Strauss, but also other music of 'colossal dimensions' such as that of Bruckner, in the French Zone. In addition, the French, alone amongst the occupiers, extended their analysis to popular

---

37   AOFC/AC 528/5, Texte de l'interview donnée par Monsieur Thimonnier pour la Radio Française, 11 July 1947, p. 1. The term was earlier used during the French occupation of the Rhineland after 1918.

38   *La France en Allemagne, Numéro Special: Information et Action Culturelle*, August 1947. Page references are given in the text.

music. In place of Wagnerian mysticism and Nazi banality, in their broadcasting there was a conscious internationalism:

> From the musical point of view a special place is reserved for those composers like Hindemith, Debussy, Roussel, Ravel, Honegger, Darius Milhaud, and for all those excluded by the Hitler regime on racial grounds (like Mendelssohn). American jazz has been introduced and maintained despite numerous protests, in contrast to the march music and the sentimental light music which was too complacently exploited by German stations. (p. 35)

Describing Thimonnier's 'Office of Drama and Music', Arnaud wrote:

> Its endeavour is carried above all by music, not only because this is a kind of international language, but also because it is the means of expression which responds best to the most profound aspirations of the Germanic soul. (p. 46)

Evidently, the French saw a happy coincidence here between their cultural chauvinism, the German love of music, and the potential of different musical forms to carry anti-Nazi meanings. It is also clear that culture was higher in the French scale of priorities than elsewhere. As we shall see, this meant that Schmittlein, Arnaud, and Thimonnier had greater authority in the French Military Government than their counterparts, particularly in the British and American Zones.

Music in Post-war Germany

> The floor of the church on the Old Market was still littered with rubble and debris; the bare walls towered forbiddingly, the empty windows gaped, but already the doves congregated peacefully in the apertures. Nearly three thousand people had gathered, standing on heaps of stone, sitting on half-burnt broken beams, for a musical experience that they would never forget: the first performance of Rudolf Mauersberger's *Funeral Ode on the Destruction of Dresden*, with a text from Jeremiah's Lament, which might have been written in 1945, here in these ruins: 'How desolate lies the city, which was so full of people.'[39]

If it was one thing to make plans in wartime capitals, it was quite another to try to implement them in the extraordinary physical and psychological conditions in Germany after the surrender in May 1945. Existing antagonisms were heightened by the bitter fighting experienced by all four Allies as Germany itself was invaded in the final weeks of the war, and by the discovery of the concentration camps. For the German population, many of the worst nightmares of Goebbels' propaganda became a harsh reality. Paradoxically, the immediate experience of occupation by the two Powers most committed to a cultural programme in Germany, France and the Soviet Union, was characterised frequently by rape. Looting and intimidation

---

39   Laux, *Nachklang*, pp. 322–3.

were commonplace all over Germany. British and American troops were strictly forbidden to fraternise, initially even with German children.

Music might have been perceived as a frivolous irrelevance in this situation, but it almost immediately assumed an importance far exceeding anything the planners had imagined. For a shocked and overwhelmed German population, music offered a locus of refuge, a space for contemplation and consolation. Bach and Beethoven above all seemed important at this time, a lifeline to another Germany and to eternal values. It became immediately apparent that music would serve as a public symbol of the occupiers' intentions, and of their commitment to high culture. With incredible rapidity, a sense of competition emerged between the four wartime Allies, and there was an unseemly scramble for the cultural high ground. This competition was literally played out in front of the German public, and resulted in the quick revival of concerts in cities and towns all over Germany. Supported by Military Governments, occupation personnel, and the German people, an incredibly rich musical life developed alongside conditions of appalling hardship.

From the first, differences between the Allies were apparent. Speaking for the Americans and British, Brigadier-General McClure gave a press conference in May 1945. He spoke of the 'long term task of attempting to reorient the German mind', and announced: 'There will be music in Germany, but its character will be closely supervised. ... No music will be permitted which propagates militaristic ideas, or which is associated with the Nazi Party, Fascism, Pan-Germanism, or the German Army.'[40] All areas of Germany under British and American control were bound by SHAEF's Law No. 191 Amended (1), which stated that 'except as directed or otherwise authorized, all music is prohibited'. To publish music, produce sound recordings, or present a concert, required a licence, which could only be given to individuals who registered with the military authorities. Responsibility for the suitability of any music subsequently played rested with these individuals. Public performance of music was permitted in churches, where it was 'incidental to services of a religious character'.[41] These regulations were publicly displayed on posters in the American and British Zones.[42]

In Göttingen, post-war music started as early as 28 April 1945 under American occupation, when the *Stadtkantorei* inaugurated a series of Saturday cantatas in the *Johanniskirche*.[43] In Marburg, another virtually undamaged university town, the Americans allowed a performance of Bach on 16 June in the *Elisabethkirche*.[44] In Leipzig, initially occupied by the Americans, the local commander allowed the

---

40   IfZ/OMGUS 5/243–2/17, Text of Press Release, Berlin, 25 May 1945, p. 6.

41   TNA/PRO/FO 1056/151; see also IfZ/OMGUS 5/243–2/8.

42   See IfZ/OMGUS 5/347–3/27, Nachrichtenkontrolle Anweisung Nr. 1.

43   Roderich Schmidt (ed.), *Ludwig Doorman: Ein Leben für die Kirchenmusik. Erinnerungen, Gespräche, Briefe, Berichte* (Göttingen: Deuerlich'sche Buchhandlung, 1988), p. 29.

44   Generallandesarchiv, Karlsruhe, Office of Military Government, Württemberg-Baden (hereafter GLAK/OMGWB) 12/91–1/7, Weekly Situation Report of the Film, Theater, and Music Control Section, 6871st DISCC, 16 June 1945.

Thomanerchor to perform some Bach motets. In June, the choir was allowed to perform Bach's *St Matthew Passion*. Even performances in churches came under suspicion though, and very quickly the Americans acted to prevent concerts being given where they were not part of a genuine religious service. Thus, in Hanau they intervened after two Bach concerts were held in a church.[45] In July, the Music Control Section in Munich reported similar problems in Erlangen and Nuremberg.[46]

In areas occupied by the British, SHAEF's prohibition on performance was less rigidly enforced, not least because Information Control Units were slow to arrive and desperately undermanned. Not until 10 July did Major-General William Bishop and a team of officers arrive to take charge of the situation on the ground in Germany. They met immediately with McClure to coordinate policy. In contrast to the Americans, whose Information Control Division (ICD) had a staff of 1700 men with their own transportation, including aircraft, the British Public Relations and Information Services Control Branch (PR/ISC) was under-resourced, with only 16 officers.[47] When they finally entered Berlin in early July, the British had only one Information Control officer available, and had to ask infantry officers to improvise until qualified staff could be sent in.[48] The British also established Information Control Units in Düsseldorf, Hanover, and Hamburg, but these had to arrange accommodation, secretarial facilities, food, and transport before they could do anything about music. One of Bishop's first reports gives a sense of the *ad hoc* nature of the early British efforts: 'My IC team in Berlin has now risen to six officers. None of them knows anything at all about newspapers, theatres, film, radio, etc., but they are doing their best.'[49]

In this situation, local Army commanders took the initial decisions about whether or not to allow concerts in British occupied areas. Although the British had started the occupation in an angry mood, shaken by the revelations of Belsen and by the bitter fighting in the final stages of the war, after only weeks of occupation there was a notable softening in the tone of officers and soldiers actually in northern Germany. Many were struck above all by the overwhelming and apathetic suffering of the civilian population, and keenly aware that in the longer term, they had to create favourable conditions for some kind of re-education. As early as 7 June, the commander in Hanover asked whether it was possible to start up plays, concerts, and operas.[50] The

---

45   IfZ/OMGUS 10/18–1/6, HQ 12 Army Group, Publicity and Psychological Warfare, Illegal Entertainment activities in Hanau, 16 June 1945.

46   BHA/OMGB 10/48–1/5, Music Section, Daily Report No. 18, Nürnberg Mission, 11 July 1945.

47   TNA/PRO/FO 898/401, Lockhart, PWE, to Harvey, Foreign Office, 10 July 1945.

48   TNA/PRO/FO 898/401, D.D.G to D.G, 15 July 1945.

49   TNA/PRO/FO 1005/1803, Bishop to IC Services, CCG (BE), 22 July 1945. This is a useful corrective to Schivelbusch's account, which presents a much more assured and dignified image of the British cultural arrival in Berlin. See *In a Cold Crater*, pp. 30–31.

50   TNA/PRO/FO 1030/379, Col. Brown, Military Government Detachment, Hanover Region, to Military Government 30 Corps, 7 June 1945.

Hamburg Philharmonic played on 2 July.[51] Sir William Strang, the senior Foreign Office official advising the British Army on the occupation of Germany, argued in early July that the time had come to 'allow more concerts'.[52] Information Control in Berlin was told to encourage concerts, particularly of previously banned music. As for Wagner, the advice was not to ban it, and not to encourage it.[53]

By the end of July Information Services was able to issue its first Directive, which noted: 'Music, opera and ballet will be given preference over other forms of entertainment, as providing fewer opportunities for subversive propaganda.' Not that Bishop, who wrote this, was given to high flights of cultural-political fantasy. His reasons for the re-establishment of music were prosaic, 'to combat idleness, boredom, and fear of the future.'[54] Already, though, a sharp distinction between this kind of pragmatism in occupied Germany and public opinion in Britain was clear. A population shocked by newsreel images of British troops burying thousands of corpses in Belsen was not sympathetic to the idea that the Germans should have opera, or symphonic concerts. Word that the opera house in Brunswick had been reopened in June 1945 evidently reached Britain and provoked a hostile article in the *Daily Mirror*.[55]

American Information Control units were quicker to get into Germany and to take control of the media. In some places, like Munich, they arrived before the front-line troops. Munsell's team, which had been training music control staff through March and April, was quick to get into the major cities of the future American Zone; in the first week of May they were in Wiesbaden and Frankfurt.[56] Munsell himself appears to have acted as a roving adviser to the British as well. In June, he visited Hanover, Bremen, Hamburg, Kassel, Erlangen, and Munich to help with the initial licensing of German musicians.[57] Nonetheless, tensions arose immediately between Information Control directives and the demands of local commanders mindful of morale in their own units. In Munich, the medium-wave radio transmitter, once repaired by the Americans, was immediately used to relay 'AFN [American Forces Network] programs for troop entertainment'.[58] It is little wonder that Bavarian prejudices about America being synonymous with jazz were strengthened.

Another problem in many cities occupied by the Americans was the use of German orchestras and singers to provide music for their troops. Local commanders

---

51   Glaser et al., *So viel Anfang*, p. 101.

52   TNA/PRO/FO 898/401, Strang, Office of the Political Adviser to the C-in-C, British Forces of Occupation, to Secretary-of-State, 11 July 1945, p. 4.

53   TNA/PRO/FO 898/401, Draft letter to Commandant, British Sector, Berlin.

54   TNA/PRO/FO 1056/20, ICSB, Directive No.1, 20 July 1945.

55   TNA/PRO/FO 1030/379, Subject: Newspaper Article, 3 July 1945.

56   GLAK/OMGWB 12/91–1/7, Activity Report, HQ 6871st DISCC, 2 May 1945, and Daily Activity Reports, 7–11 May 1945.

57   IfZ/OMGUS 5/243–1/4, SHAEF, PWD, Semi-monthly Progress Report, 1 July 1945, p. 14.

58   IfZ/OMGUS 5/243–1/4, SHAEF, PWD, Semi-monthly Progress Report, 15 June 1945, p. 8.

were often uninterested in licensing procedures, and appeared unconcerned about any potential Nazi affiliations of the musicians they were employing. German musicians were also quick to offer their services to their new masters. These ranged from the sublime to the ridiculous. In Munich, Hans Swarowsky offered to put on an unfinished opera by Richard Strauss for the Americans.[59] Strauss himself innocently offered to conduct for them.[60] By contrast in Nuremberg, 'Variety Shows' were put on by the municipal opera, led by former SA *Sturmführer* Hans Dressel, while 'Wagner Festivals' were laid on for the GIs in Bayreuth.[61] The need for entertainment was damaging in other ways. In Kassel, for example, 'requisitions' of musical instruments, lighting, and costumes by American troops, with the sanction of local commanders, were apparently 'completely out of hand', and prevented any concerts from being held.[62]

Conscious that they were lagging behind the other occupiers, the Americans decided to stage a symphonic concert in Munich, their chosen cultural capital. The Philharmonic was chosen as the less Nazified of the city's two main orchestras and ordered to prepare, using instruments confiscated from the National Socialist Symphony Orchestra.[63] The city council agreed to pay a small stipend to a limited number of musicians,[64] and a hasty process of denazification was initiated. Lieutenant Arthur Vogel of the Music Control Section was ordered to draw up a blacklist.[65] The Americans attached great importance to finding a conductor with an international reputation who was not tarnished politically. Adolf Mennerich, the Philharmonic's current conductor, was summarily dismissed. Captain Ross, head of Theater and Music Control in Munich, was told to go to Mennerich's house, or if necessary to a rehearsal, to inform him of his removal, and to find his deputy Edenhofer to continue the rehearsals.[66]

There was no shortage of candidates putting themselves forward to replace Mennerich. Hans Knappertsbusch, the idol of the Munich public, was working hard to convince the Americans that he had been an opponent of Hitler. Eugen Jochum, previously conductor of the Hamburg Philharmonic, presented himself at Vogel's office, where he amused the Americans by declaring his readiness to conduct for

59   IfZ/OMGUS 10/18–1/7, Plans and Operations Section, 6870th DISCC, Summary of Daily Diaries for half-week ending 25 May 1945, 28 May 1945, p. 1.

60   IfZ/OMGUS 10/18–1/7, Report on Mission No. 5 (3 to 5 June, 1945), 9 June 1945, pp. 1-2.

61   BHA/OMGB 10/48–1/4, Music Section, Daily Report No. 18: Nürnberg Mission, 11 July 1945.

62   GLAK/OMGWB 12/91–1/7, Weekly Situation Report of the Film, Theater, and Music Control Section, 6871st DISCC, 30 June 1945, p. 5.

63   BHA/OMGB 10/120–2/8, Van Loon to Ross, 27 June 1945.

64   BHA/OMGB 10/18–1/7, Plans and Operations Section, 6870th DISCC, Summary of Daily Diaries for half-week ending 25 May 1945, 28 May 1945, p. 2.

65   BHA/OMGB 10/120–2/8, HQ, 6870th DISCC, Kennedy to Vogel, 22 June 1945.

66   BHA/OMGB 10/120–2/8, 6870th DISCC, Van Loon to Ross, 27 June 1945.

'the enemies'.[67] Eventually, Jochum was chosen. Presumably, having conducted in Paris during the war on Hitler's birthday,[68] he was used to performances that also had a propaganda function. The concert was held on 8 July for American troops, and immediately repeated for the German public; it was also broadcast. The programme, Mendelssohn's *Overture to a Midsummer Night's Dream*, Mozart's 40th Symphony, and Tchaikovsky's Fourth Symphony, reflected the symbolism of similar inaugural post-war concerts all over Germany.[69]

The situation was altogether different in the East. In Berlin itself, the survivors were 'ordered' to play music in the midst of a continuing orgy of rape and looting.[70] The Soviet Commandant met with artists on 14 May. The previous evening, a chamber orchestra led by Hans von Benda had performed; on 18 May a surviving rump of the orchestra of the Municipal Opera played. On the 26th, the Berlin Philharmonic performed for the first time since the war, under Leo Borchard.[71] The Soviets were also quick to restore German broadcasting. Within days, they restarted transmissions from *Berlin Radio* in Masurenallee, combining high culture and entertainment. The renamed *Radio-Berlin-Tanzorchester* (Radio Berlin Dance Orchestra), which had previously broadcast jazz for Goebbels, was back at work within a fortnight of Hitler's death.[72] A British Intelligence report of June 1945 noted that the Soviets were broadcasting a full programme, including music, 'apparently run by the Germans'.[73] The American magazine *Stars and Stripes* noted at the same time how quickly and effectively Radio Berlin was being used by the Soviets, broadcasting 'plenty of jazz'.[74] In other cities, the Soviets gave similar encouragement to the renewal of musical life at the same time as they dismantled industry. The first orchestral concert in Dresden took place on 6 June.[75]

The Soviets also took advantage of the few weeks before the arrival of the Western Allies in Berlin to establish authorities run by Germans. The 'Ulbricht group' was brought in to the city on 2 May 1945, and culture was an area it quickly colonised with new organisations run by Communists or their chosen nominees.[76] The most important of these was the Cultural League for the Democratic Renewal of Germany (*Kulturbund zur demokratischen Erneuerung Deutschlands*), which

67   BHA/OMGB 10/48–1/5, Music Section, Munich, Daily Activities, 28 June 1945.

68   AOFC/AC 28/2, Haut-Commissariat de la République Française en Allemagne, Note, 19 October 1951.

69   BHA/OMGB 10/48–1/5, Barricelli to Vogel, 4 July 1945.

70   See Curt Riess, *Berlin Berlin 1945–1953* (Berlin: Non stop-Bücherei, 1953), pp. 11–15. On rape see Naimark, *The Russians*, pp. 69–140.

71   Chamberlin, *Kultur auf Trümmern*, pp. 12ff.

72   See the references to the *Deutsche Tanz- und Unterhaltungsorchester* in Kater, *Different Drummers*.

73   TNA/PRO/FO 898/401, Russian Policy in Occupied Germany, 18 June 1945.

74   *The Stars and Stripes Magazine – Weekly Supplement*, 1:4 (23 June 1945), p. v.

75   Laux, *Nachklang*, p. 323.

76   See the classic account by Wolfgang Leonhard, *Die Revolution entläßt ihre Kinder* (Cologne: Kiepenheuer and Witsch, 1955).

posed as a non-party group for all artists and intellectuals. Its initially reluctant Chairman was the poet Johannes R. Becher, who was flown into Berlin on 10 June. He was given permission to organise the *Kulturbund* by the Soviet Commandant.[77] The organisation was formally inaugurated at a hastily convened ceremony in early July. Appropriately, the Berlin Philharmonic graced the occasion, with music by Beethoven and Tchaikovsky.[78] At this stage, though, the *Kulturbund* had no clear musical orientation. Becher himself appears to have had no great feeling for music. His later Deputy Minister for Culture in the GDR, the harpsichordist Hans Pischner, subsequently confirmed that Becher did not like opera, but that he did (rather in the way all SED leaders were said to) love Bach and German folk music.[79] Although the musicologist Bernhard Bennedik was amongst the *Kulturbund*'s founding members, and gave the opening speech at the inaugural ceremony, he never emerged as a decisive or influential figure; nor did music feature in the generalised terms of the *Kulturbund*'s manifesto.[80] The first plans for the *Kulturbund*'s Presidential Council included literary and theatrical representatives, but no painters or musicians. These, apparently, were still to be chosen.[81]

Other shadowy administrations proliferated in the ruins of Berlin. The newly formed City Council had a Department for Culture and People's Education, headed by another of the Ulbricht group, Otto Winzer. Even before the Allies met at Potsdam, this office was constructing grandiose schemes for the renewal of choral life.[82] A body called the Chamber of Artists (*Kammer der Kunstschaffenden*), a title eerily reminiscent of Goebbels, operated out of the former headquarters of the Reich Chamber of Culture in Schlüterstrasse. Its pretensions to control cultural life in and beyond Berlin were tolerated by the Allies for a year or so, and it was allowed to play a significant role in denazification. However, its influence on music was limited, perhaps because the first head of its music section, Erich Fincke, had to resign after it was discovered that he had joined the SA in 1934.[83]

---

77   Stiftung Archiv der Parteien und Massenorganisationen der DDR im Bundesarchiv, Berlin (hereafter SAPMO-BArch) DY 27/841, Jelissarow, Chef der Garnison und Militärkommandant der Stadt Berlin, to Becher, 25 June 1945.

78   *Berliner Zeitung*, 5 July 1945

79   SAAdK Hans-Pischner-Archiv, 1118, Meine Jahre im MfK, p. 8.

80   *Manifest des Kulturbundes zur demokratischen Erneuerung Deutschlands* (Berlin: Aufbau-Verlag, 1945)

81   SAPMO-BArch DY 27/2751, Organisations-Schema des Kulturbundes; and Gründungskomitee des Kulturbundes zur demokratischen Erneuerung Deutschlands, 28 June 1945.

82   SAAdK Heinz-Tiessen-Archiv, Korrespondenz, Kulturbund, Richtlinien für den Aufbau von Laienchören, Amt für Volksbildung, Magistrat der Stadt Berlin, 16 July 1945.

83   Most histories of culture in post-war Berlin are vague about the *Kammer der Kunstschaffenden*, which was also headed by Otto Winzer. See IfZ/OMGUS 5/348-2/13, Some Informal Notes on the Kammer der Kunstschaffenden, 5 October 1945; and Bericht über die Präsidialsitzung am 8. Januar 1946, p. 9. See also Monod, *Settling Scores*, pp. 72–7.

Another distinctive feature of musical reconstruction in the Soviet Zone was apparent from the start: a completely arbitrary approach to denazification. Acting in the spirit of Stalin's rejection of collective guilt, in those cases where the Soviets valued a German musician as an important artist, any institutional or personal associations with Nazism were totally overlooked. Others that they regarded as dispensable might find themselves very harshly treated. Thus, in Dresden, Rudolf Mauersberger, an NSDAP member since 1933,[84] was immediately encouraged to resume work with the *Kreuzchor*, eleven of whose members had been killed in the British and American attack on the city in February.[85]

In areas occupied by the French, there was a similar contradiction between barbaric behaviour and cultural pretensions.[86] Baden-Baden was occupied on 13 April 1945, and even in this genteel and undamaged spa there was looting. Musical instruments were tempting prizes for soldiers in the early days of the occupation, and many were stolen before some order was restored.[87] Initially De Gaulle, who had urged the seizure of Stuttgart and Karlsruhe, was hoping to retain control of these larger cultural centres.[88] In the brief period before they reluctantly had to abandon both cities to the Americans, the French set about the re-establishment of music, theatre, and broadcasting there. In Karlsruhe, according to an American report: 'Under the French occupation, the concert hall was repaired in short order, all the artists chipping in and working along. Ten days from the time they started they had the first concert.' When the French left the city, they took the stage sets of the Baden State Theatre with them to use in Baden-Baden.[89]

A strange situation arose in Stuttgart, which had the added attraction of one of very few opera houses left intact in post-war Germany. The French used the Philharmonic to stage orchestral concerts here in June for 'mixed' audiences of German citizens and French troops, and also managed to stir up local anti-Americanism to fever pitch. Before the handover of the city, an American report spoke of the 'already prevalent rumour that the Americans will not allow any entertainment in retaliation for atrocities, or that there will be no Festivals or Philharmonic because the Americans

---

84   See p. 68, fn. 142.

85   Laux, *Nachklang*, p. 323.

86   On rape see 'Ein schwieriges Erbe: VerGEWALTigungen bei Kriegsende' in Annemarie Hopp and Berndt Warneken (eds), *Feinde, Freunde, Fremde. Erinnerungen an die Tübinger Franzosenzeit* (Tübingen: Universitätsstadt Tübingen, Kulturamt, 1995), pp. 57–62; also Edgar Wolfrum, 'Das Bild der "Düsteren Franzosenzeit": Alltagsnot, Meinungsklima und Demokratisierungspolitik in der französischen Besatzungszone nach 1945', Martens, *Vom "Erbfeind" zum "Erneuerer"*, pp. 87–114.

87   The violinists Kiskemper and Templer of the *Kurhausorchester*, for example, had their instruments seized 'without compensation' in April 1945. AOFC/AC 519/2, Chef du Bureau des Spectacles et de la Musique to Parodin, Délégué pour le Cercle de Baden-Baden, 16 July 1946.

88   Willis, *The French*, pp. 17ff.

89   BHA/OMGB 10/48–1/5, Annex to Weekly Situation Report, Film, Theater, and Music Control Section, 6871st DISCC, 7 August 1945, p. 3.

are cultural barbarians. ... Some intellectuals and artists have a strong suspicion that intellectual life under American occupation would be severely handicapped. Some of the musical programs of our radio stations seem to have confirmed this opinion.'[90]The theatrical determination with which the Americans prepared their takeover, seeking to counter these fears, shows the significance that music had already taken on in the rivalry between the Allies. The US 100th Division formally took over Stuttgart at 12.00am on 8 July. At 12.01 a prepared license to perform music was presented to a municipal official, and at precisely 12.02 Schubert's Trout Quintet was performed. At 5.00pm, the Philharmonic gave a concert, and in case anyone had not yet taken the point, a recording of this was broadcast at 10.00pm.[91]

The loss of Stuttgart was a blow to the French, leaving them without a radio station, or any musical institution of international renown in their Zone. Undaunted, they turned back to Baden-Baden, where they found suitable tools for their cultural propaganda. The Spa Orchestra was ideal for their serious music programme, and alongside it they took over 'un orchestre de danse et de hot'.[92] Although the *Generalmusikdirektor* in Baden-Baden, Gotthold-Ephraim Lessing, had been sent to the front in 1944 and captured, he was quickly released from a POW camp in Clermont-Ferrand to resume his old post.[93] French engineers were brought in to construct a radio transmitter from scratch.[94] These were the origins of the *Südwestfunk* (Southwest Radio, or SWF) and its orchestra, soon to be internationally known for the promotion of progressive music.

The early experience of occupation showed that the ideas of the planners had, in some senses, been completely eclipsed. Nowhere was the performance of Nazi or militarist music by 'uppish' Germans a problem; rather the reverse. Musicians all over Germany were keen to work for their new masters, and besieged music officers with offers. Göttingen bandleader William Lustig, who claimed to have been previously imprisoned by the Gestapo, and now tried to get work with the British in May 1945, will serve as an example.[95] Municipal authorities were also eager to cooperate by rebuilding halls and continuing to finance orchestras and opera companies. On the other hand, it was clear that denazification would be far more complex than had been previously envisaged. As Allied intelligence officers probed the institutional structures of German music before 1945, they discovered that it had

---

90 GLAK/OMGWB 12/91-1/7, Weekly Situation Report of the Film, Theater, and Music Control Section, 6871st DISCC, 30 June 1945, pp. 2–4.

91 GLAK/OMGWB 12/91–1/7, Weekly Situation Report of the Film, Theater, and Music Control Section, 6871st DISCC, 14 July 1945, p. 2.

92 'Une réalisation française: les services de la radiodiffusion en Allemagne occupée', *Revue de la Zone Française*, April/May 1946, pp. 8–10.

93 AOFC/AC 501/3, Le Directeur des Services de l'Information, 24 July 1945, and Note de Service, 10 September 1945.

94 AOFC/AC 526/2, Rapport sur l'activité des Services de l'Information (1945–1949), 15 June 1949, p. 13.

95 TNA/PRO/FO 1030/379, Lustig to Commander, Military Government, Göttingen, 25 May 1945, and to Allied Radio-Sender Hamburg, 30 May 1945.

been intensively Nazified. An unusually high proportion of professional musicians were Nazi Party members.[96] The Reich Music Chamber, with its different branches, had officials throughout Germany. All professional performers had been required to hold membership. Musical education, at school and university levels, was riddled with enthusiasts and opportunists who had written Nazi music and taken up Party membership to further their careers in the enforced absence of Jewish colleagues. Organisations like the SS and the HJ had their own music schools and ensembles, employing thousands of musicians. Publishers, many of international importance like Schotts of Mainz, had censored their catalogues, and printed nationalist and racist songbooks.[97] When the Allies enquired into these matters, they found that apparently all German musicians were anti-fascists or strictly apolitical professionals, who had acted under duress. Allied investigations gave the culture of denunciation that had thrived under Hitler a new impetus, as ex-Nazis went into denial, and old scores were settled. In the office of the Music Control Section in Munich, German musicians competing for favour came to blows, and had to be forcibly removed.[98] In the straitened circumstances of post-war Germany, a job with a municipal orchestra licensed by the Allies, or with one of their radio stations, was worth lying for.

The Allies also found that their plans to introduce contemporary international music would be difficult to implement. The music libraries of many orchestras and conservatories were surprisingly well preserved, and old copies of Mendelssohn overtures and Tchaikovsky symphonies could be easily recovered. The campaign to root out 'degenerate music' had not been without effect though: there was virtually no music written outside Germany since 1933, and very little modernist music from the 1920s, actually available to use. The underlying attitudes that had contributed to this state of affairs would prove depressingly resilient.

---

96   Often, the Allies found that more than 50 per cent of the musicians in professional orchestras were Party members, as in the Baden-Baden *Kurhausorchester* (AOFC/AC 600/5, Liste der Orchestermitglieder, 28 March 1946). By comparison, 44.8 per cent of doctors, another highly Nazified profession, were NSDAP members. See Michael Kater, *Doctors Under Hitler* (Chapel Hill and London: University of North Carolina Press, 1989), p. 56.

97   See AOFC/AC 490/8, *Vollständiges Verzeichnis Herbst 1940, Edition Schott*, which lists no Mendelssohn, but many titles like *HJ singt, Das neue Soldaten-Liederbuch I/III*, and individual songs like *Bomben auf Engelland*.

98   BHA/OMGB 10/48–1/5, Music Section, Munich, Daily Report, 26 July 1945.

Chapter Two

Denazification

All four wartime Allies occupied Germany with a commitment to getting rid of Nazi, militarist, and pan-German music from the repertoire. To a greater or lesser extent, they were also all committed to the exclusion of former Nazis from musical activities in the public sphere. Both goals were fraught with complications, which, more than half a century later, are still unresolved. The recent academic interest in the relationship between music, musicians, and Nazism has served more to heighten awareness of the complexity of these relationships and of the moral issues which arise from them, than to produce any consensus on some of the most contested cases. The debate on whether Carlf Orff's *Carmina Burana*, by far the most significant single musical work composed during the 'Third Reich', is 'Nazi music' (or in more recent terms, has 'fascistoid traits'[1]) continues, as do popular performances of the work itself, in and outside Germany. Arguments about whether Furtwängler and Strauss were collaborators or resisters are still highly polarised. Attitudes towards the nature and role of Wagner's anti-Semitism, and the extent to which it is embodied in his music are still very divided. When we try to analyse the multi-faceted processes in Germany that are subsumed under the heading of 'denazification', we encounter further difficulties.

The documentary record on denazification is scattered in many different archives, and unlike most of the material relating to the occupation of Germany, much of the material relating to the denazification of musicians is still classified. Many professional musicians in Germany after 1945 had practical reasons to deny, conceal, or misrepresent aspects of their behaviour before and during the 'Third Reich', and frequently it suited one or other of the occupiers to collude with this. After 1948, when denazification petered out, there was a general sense of dissatisfaction and embarrassment about the whole process, and it appears to have suited all involved to draw a veil over it. The analysis here will focus first on the Allied effort to pursue a collective policy on denazification in music, and then proceed to consider in greater depth the policies pursued separately in individual Zones of occupation. As we shall see, this was an area where none of the Allies was prepared to renounce its jurisdiction within the area of Germany it controlled.

In accordance with wartime plans, the Allies in 1945 established an 'Allied Control Council' in Berlin, which took over executive authority in Germany from the government of the 'Third Reich'. For the next three years, this council provided a forum in which the Soviets, Americans, British, and French were represented, and in

---

1   See Kater, *Composers*, p. 128.

which, with growing difficulty, they attempted to create a common legal framework for all Zones of occupation. Laws passed by the Control Council were published from October 1945, and were intended to have binding authority in all Zones. During late 1945 and early 1946, the Control Council grew, spawning committees and sub-committees dealing with individual issues. As far as the media – or 'information services' as they were called by all the occupiers – and the arts were concerned, it was the Americans who showed the greatest commitment to Four-Power coordination, and it was largely at the instigation of McClure that an Information Services Directorate was set up within the Control Council in April 1946, following which, a Theatre and Music sub-committee was also created. In the process, McClure brought to Germany a figure who would play a number of different roles in later years, the émigré Russian composer Nicolas Nabokov. Nabokov was brought to Berlin in 1945 specifically to coordinate Allied approaches to music control. It was felt that he would be helped in this by his command of English, French, Russian, and German.

McClure's most pressing concern in music control was with the denazification of musicians, and with securing a common Allied approach to this. He was a dedicated anti-Nazi, and he viewed the purging of Nazis from German cultural life as a mission, believing that a higher standard should prevail there than in other areas of public life. McClure, and others in the American ICD, viewed the public performance of music as an act of great ritual significance, and they did not want to see former Nazis, regardless of the music they played, being applauded by German audiences. They went further than the other Allies in wishing, also, to exclude many who had been professionally successful under Hitler, arguing that they were compromised solely because of this. The other occupiers balanced their fierce hostility to former Nazis with a pragmatic desire to employ gifted and popular musicians in their own Zones, and all were sensitive to the enormous benefits that might accrue from allowing them to perform in public. The Americans also realised one implication of this, the opprobrium that would fall on them if they were perceived to be harsher than other occupiers, particularly when intervening in the hallowed area of 'German music'. Very soon after the cessation of hostilities, the Americans started what was to be a long experience with major musical figures, excluded from work in the American Zone, who then went to other Zones to take up prestigious appointments. The first high-profile case of this sort was that of Eugen Jochum, who as we have seen, was in Munich in May and June 1945.

Jochum had conducted the Hamburg Philharmonic during the war, with great success, earning ever-larger sums in the process. He was profiled in a wartime documentary film, and conducted in occupied France as a representative of the 'Third Reich'. In July 1945, Jochum was invited by the British, who had no sense that he might be compromised, to return to his former post in Hamburg. Jack Bornoff, the 'Music Controller' of the NWDR, travelled to Munich, where he met Jochum; together they went on to Linz, where Bornoff also recruited a number of musicians from the now disbanded Reich Bruckner Orchestra, previously conducted by Jochum's brother Hans. Bornoff, Eugen Jochum, and the musicians from Linz returned to Hamburg to help in the British-sponsored musical reconstruction there.

The subsequent dispute over Jochum between the British and the Americans will be explored later, but at bottom there was a difference of perception. The Americans felt that Jochum had been a beneficiary of Nazism. The British regarded him first and foremost as a very talented conductor inspired by a deep Roman Catholicism.

The debates about music in the Four-Power Information Directorate followed a consistent pattern. The agenda was set by the Americans, who could usually count on support from the British, reluctant acquiescence from the French, and, after much quibbling, some kind of formal Soviet agreement. All sides jealously guarded their exclusive jurisdiction in their own Zones, and were often unwilling to reveal too clearly what policies they were pursuing there. There are points in the minutes of the Directorate's meetings where individual 'Allies' misrepresented what was going on in their Zones, or represented the situation in such an obscure way that their statements were misleading or even contradictory. Under a veneer of diplomatic courtesy, each occupier went its own way, following first and foremost its own interests in the area of Germany it controlled. At a lower level, there was, between 1945 and 1949, considerable cooperation between the Americans and the British, rather less between these two and the French, and very little between these three and the Soviets.

The Control Council did concern itself with the prohibition and destruction of Nazi and militarist music. Its Order No. 4, 'Confiscation of Literature and Material of a Nazi and Militarist Nature', specifically referred to 'song and music books', held by 'circulating libraries, bookshops, bookstores and publishing houses'; it ordered directors of all educational institutions to remove 'from libraries in their charge' all 'Nazi and military literature', and deliver this to 'specially allocated places'.[2] It seems that, by 1946, this order was hardly necessary. All over Germany, as the hostilities drew to an end, Nazi literature of all kinds, including music, was thrown away and destroyed by Germans themselves. Typically, for whatever reasons, libraries, schools, universities, publishers, and bookshops collected all the most obviously incriminating material they could find on their premises, and put it out to be pulped or destroyed. Most of those who had been involved in producing this material, if they survived the war, were keen to cooperate in this act of self-censorship, and to get rid of potentially compromising evidence. The cantatas glorifying Hitler, the 'heroic festive music' of the 'Third Reich', and the hundreds of Nazi songs written before 1945, all largely disappeared. What remained was a larger spectrum of material with less obvious Nazi connotations and connections, much of which proved harder to judge.

There was virtually no problem created by the continued performance of Nazi music. There is no known example of professional musicians gathering publicly, or even privately, with the intention of performing Nazi music as some kind of gesture. Doubtless, individuals hummed to themselves the tunes they had learnt and sung before 1945. Groups may, in maudlin reflection, have sung together the *Horst-*

---

2   IfZ/OMGUS 5/347–3/2, Action of the Coordinating Committee, Control Council to Order No. 4, 13 May 1946.

Wessel-Lied, or the Hitler Youth's favourite song, *Es zittern die morschen Knocken* (*The Brittle Bones are Shaking*), while they remembered torch lit parades, campfires, and evenings of alcoholic comradeship, but there are only isolated instances of this being done in a consciously oppositional manner. Music was not used, as Van Cutsem had feared, to rally resistance, or to mobilise a resurgent Nazism.

Just as with printed material, there remained a problem with the censorship of live music that had potential Nazi, militarist, or nationalist connotations, but this was not something that the Control Council or its Information Directorate attempted to rule on. It did, repeatedly and on American insistence, debate the denazification of musicians. The legal framework for the Allied denazification of civil society in post-war Germany was provided by Control Council Directive No. 24, 'Removal from Office and from Positions of Responsibility of Nazis and of Persons Hostile to Allied Purposes', which was not ready until January 1946 and was only published in March 1946. Had this Directive been rigorously and consistently implemented, many of those who ended up playing a significant role in post-war German musical life would have been prevented from doing so. Paragraph 10 of the Directive specified several 'Compulsory removal and exclusion categories' from positions of responsibility in public life. Amongst those to be removed and excluded, it specified all NSDAP members who joined before 1937, 'all officials at any time' of the 'Reichskulturkammer and subsidiary bodies', and 'persons who have denounced or contributed to the seizure of opponents of the Nazi regime'. The Directive also allowed for 'discretionary removals or exclusions'. Paragraph 12, which gave advice on how to judge whether an individual was more than a 'nominal' Nazi, had several sections that might relate to musicians. Membership of the German Christian Movement (*Deutsche Christenbewegung*) or the German Faith Movement (*Deutsche Glaubensbewegung*), for example, raised 'strong presumption of Nazi sympathy'. Paragraph 12 also identified 'Persons who have received financial favoritism from the Nazis', and stated that this might constitute grounds for exclusion.[3]

The Directive thus left the Allies with wide discretion. It also raised several other problems, which were left to individual tribunals and investigators to resolve. The requirement that all who had joined the NSDAP before 1937 be excluded, however, was clear and unequivocal. Given that the Americans, in 1945, had captured virtually intact the NSDAP membership card index, it was even, in theory, enforceable. We know now, though, that the circumstances in which individuals joined the Nazi Party, and their motivations for so doing, before and after 1937, were enormously varied, and that party membership alone was not necessarily proof of any particular commitment to Nazism. Nor did the Directive define what was meant by a 'position of responsibility'. Did this include conductors or choirmasters? What of other professional musicians and singers, or teachers of music, many of whom worked privately? Additionally, the Allies in 1945 and 1946 did not state precisely for how long any exclusions were to last. It soon became clear that exclusions would be

---

3   *Official Gazette of the Control Council for Germany*, 5 (31 March 1946), pp. 98–114.

impossible to maintain for an indefinite period, and arguments therefore developed around how quickly various musicians might be readmitted to their former professional careers.

One individual case, which was discussed by the Information Directorate, and exemplifies many subsequent problems, was that of Hermann Abendroth. Like Jochum, Abendroth was a high-profile figure, revered in Germany, and identified not primarily as a Nazi, but as a great interpreter of the German classical tradition. He had conducted the Leipzig Gewandhaus Orchestra ever since the Nazis had forcibly hounded out its Jewish conductor, Bruno Walter, in April 1933. Like most prominent musicians in Hitler's Germany, Abendroth had held office in the Reich Music Chamber, where he served as director of musical education. He had also conducted at a number of Nazi ceremonial occasions. After the war, Abendroth surfaced in Weimar, where the Soviets sanctioned his appointment as conductor of the Philharmonic Orchestra, just as they encouraged other potentially compromised virtuosi in their Zone. It is not clear when Abendroth learned that he had been blacklisted by the Americans, but it is reasonable to assume that he must have known. His was a much-discussed case, along with those of Furtwängler, Jochum, Knappertsbusch, Krauss, Konwitschny, and other famous conductors. Abendroth, indeed, has the very rare distinction of appearing on blacklists held by all four occupiers. That he is included on a rather brief, and scrappy copy of a 'Soviet black list' in the French archive in Colmar suggests that the Soviets did accept that he was compromised, and at least considered his exclusion.[4] Abendroth was very successful in Weimar, and was favoured by the Soviets and the German communists they propelled into power in the years after 1945. He was the first conductor from Germany allowed to tour the Soviet Union itself after the war, and subsequently received many public honours in the GDR.

In May 1946, McClure took up Abendroth's case in the Information Directorate, arguing that he should not be allowed to conduct in Weimar. The Soviet response was evasive: they argued that they were 'not aware' of problems with Abendroth, and that 'extenuating circumstances in Control Council Directive No. 24 could be applied'. He had been 'thoroughly investigated', and, conceding that he was in some way tainted, the Soviets pointed out that they had moved him from Leipzig to a less prestigious position in Weimar. Although the Soviets refused to give way over Abendroth, they agreed with the other Powers that blacklists of musicians should be exchanged between them, and that if any one Power wanted to employ a musician on these lists, it would notify the others.[5] Subsequent efforts to implement these ideas became increasingly farcical. In July 1946, the British even denied that there was an official blacklist in their Zone, something flatly contradicted by the evidence.[6] The French, who in practice had no such lists to exchange, were equally unhelpful.

---

4   AOFC/AC 596/1, Liste noire URSS, undated.

5   TNA/PRO/FO 1005/831, ACA, Political Directorate, Information Committee, Minutes of the Fourth Meeting, 27 May 1946, pp. 14–16.

6   TNA/PRO/FO 1005/831, ACA, Political Directorate, Information Committee, Minutes of the Sixth Meeting, 2 July 1946, p. 2.

By January 1947 there had still been no quadripartite action on blacklists, and the Americans again demanded a higher standard in Information Control than in other fields.[7] It was agreed to draw up a 'binding' blacklist.[8] Apparently, by June 1947, by which time the lists had become largely redundant in all four Zones, only the French and Americans had produced copies; the British and the Soviets were still providing nothing more than good intentions.[9] The Americans, who undoubtedly attached the most importance to these lists, appear to have been the only ones to have acted with anything approaching good faith here. Clearly there was great mistrust on all sides; none of the Allies was prepared to relinquish its right to final jurisdiction in the areas it controlled.

A bizarre footnote to this failed effort was the parallel attempt to abolish militaristic and nationalistic titles in German musical life. This idea, again American-inspired,[10] surfaced in the Theatre and Music Working Party, which reported in December 1946: 'In line with the decentralization of cultural life in Germany and the re-education programme, the Germans should be shown how unnecessary and somewhat ridiculous such titles sound in a democratic set-up.'[11] In March 1947 it was 'generally agreed that quasi-militaristic titles such as "Generalmusikdirektor", "Generalintendant", etc., are unwarranted'.[12] By May, the Information Committee had accepted that 'German artists must be discouraged from calling their officials by titles, and use their surnames instead.'[13] The discussion rambled on, but without many tangible results, even though the Americans apparently ran a press and radio campaign to try to convince the Germans to drop these usages. A brief and rather puzzled report in the Soviet-licensed *Nacht-Express* provides evidence that, in the British Zone at least, the campaign had some effect. Apparently the conductor Günter Wand had asked the Cologne administration to change his title of 'Generalmusikdirektor' to 'Gürzenich-Kapellmeister'.[14] Further commentary is provided by an anecdote from the late 1950s, when the occasionally eccentric Otto Klemperer returned to Germany. Politely addressed by an orchestral musician as

---

7   TNA/PRO/FO 1005/832, ACA, Political Directorate, Information Committee, Minutes of the Fourteenth Meeting, 14 January 1947, p. 6.

8   AOFC Berlin, GFCC, Caisse 131/p. 5, ACA, Political Directorate, Information Committee, Report from Theatre and Music Working Party, 9 January 1947, Appendix B.

9   AOFC Berlin, GFCC, Caisse 131/p. 5, Autorité Alliée de Contrôle, Directoire Politique, Comité de l'Information, Rapport du Groupe de Travail "Théâtre et Musique", 27 June 1947. The French relied on American lists, and it is probable that they supplied copies of these, rather than lists they had independently compiled.

10   See IfZ/OMGUS 5/265–1/2, Frank to Powell, 25 January 1946.

11   IfZ/OMGUS 5/347–3/2, Minutes of Theatre and Music Working Party (Quadripartite), 19 December 1946, p. 11.

12   IfZ/OMGUS 5/348–2/7, Working Party, Theatre and Music, on 11 and 17 March 1947.

13   AOFC Berlin, GFCC, Caisse 131/p. 5, ACA, Political Directorate, Information Committee, Report from Theatre and Music Working Party, 19 May 1947, p. 1.

14   'Generalmusikdirektor abgeschafft', *Nacht-Express*, 15 August 1947.

'Herr Generalmusikdirektor', Klemperer replied: 'I am not in command of an army, nor am I the director of a bank. My name is Klemperer.'[15]

'Outright Stinkers' and 'Parade Horses'

The American commitment to denazification in music brought them frustration, and the profound hostility of the German population in their Zone. Those carrying out the purges were criticised by their own press, and faced constant obstruction from the newly created German authorities. That procedures in other Zones were 'so much more superficial, disorganized, and haphazard'[16] was small consolation to US music officers, who had to live with the spectacle of musicians they were trying to punish basking in public acclaim there. The Americans arrived in Germany with a sense of righteous anger, greatly intensified by the discovery of concentration camps at Ohrdruf, Nordhausen, Buchenwald, Dachau, and elsewhere in April 1945. They were determined to reform all aspects of civilian life in Germany, and were not disposed to argue the finer points of individual cases.

Young and completely inexperienced officers had responsibility for immediately vetting the personnel of probably the most highly developed musical culture in the world, and censoring its repertoire. These men knew that music had been inextricably linked with Nazism, and that it played a significant role in public life in Germany. They objected particularly to the appearance in public of musicians who had been popular under the Nazis, even if there was no clear proof that they had been Nazi sympathisers. Unfortunately this became confused with the punishment of ex-Nazis, and often fostered the impression that American policy was driven by vindictiveness and a lack of cultural understanding.[17]

This confusion was particularly apparent in the 'discouragement' of certain kinds of music. Wagner was singled out, not because the Americans thought it was Nazi music, but because the Nazis had liked it so much. By the same token, Beethoven or Bruckner might have been 'crowded out', but were not. No performances of Wagner were permitted in the American Zone once the early confusion at Bayreuth had been sorted out; the Festival there did not resume until 1951. The situation at Bayreuth in May 1945 was particularly ironic, since the manager of the Festival Hall, Raymond Lutz, was actually an American citizen. Through the summer, performances by unlicensed German orchestras to US troops in Bayreuth vexed the Music Control

---

15   Peter Heyworth, *Otto Klemperer: His Life and Times* (Cambridge: Cambridge University Press, 1996), **II**, p. 277. The American intention to abolish these titles is best understood as part of the larger concern with the reform of the German language itself, and specifically with civilian titles perceived to have Nazi and militaristic connotations. See for an extended discussion Dirk Deissler, *Die entnazifizierte Sprache: Sprachpolitik und Sprachregelung in der Besatzungszeit* (Frankfurt-am-Main: Peter Lang, 2004), pp. 77–85.

16   John Herz, 'The Fiasco of denazification in Germany', *Political Science Quarterly*, 63:4 (December 1948), pp. 569–94, fn. 3.

17   For a detailed treatment of American denazification see Monod, *Settling Scores.*

Section in Munich.[18] Not until September did denazification begin in earnest. The Bayreuth Symphony Orchestra had to close down temporarily because so many of its members were excluded.[19] Lutz himself was dismissed because of his wartime work in Posen and Gablonz.[20] Symbolically, the first official performance of Wagner was given by an American singer, Marjorie Lawrence, in Berlin in December 1946, and this served as a clear signal of a relaxation of the existing policy.[21] In quick succession, *Tannhäuser* was performed in Coburg, *Die Walküre* in Munich, and *Parsival* in Regensburg.[22] The audience in Munich made its feelings clear by continuing its applause after *Die Walküre* for a full thirty minutes.[23]

There was equal confusion in the censorship of music by living composers. The Bavarian State Opera was told in December 1945 that performance of Wolf-Ferrari's *Secret of Suzanne* was 'not desirable at this time', although it was 'itself quite innocent'. Apparently it was 'too early to produce an opera ... of someone as prominently involved with the Nazis as this composer'.[24] Wolf-Ferrari had been named as a popular composer in the 'Third Reich' in the *Germany – Basic Handbook*, produced by the Americans during the war, as had Hans Pfitzner. Ironically, pieces by Pfitzner were included in the first concerts allowed by the Americans in Frankfurt and in Bremen,[25] but by May 1946 they were concerned about Soviet plans to broadcast a Pfitzner series, and by an invitation for him to appear in Düsseldorf, in the British Zone.[26] After two concerts in Munich that Pfitzner attended in person turned into a public display of support for the blacklisted local composer, performance of his music there was banned.[27] In a gesture certain to provoke comment, Joseph Haas, Director of the Music Academy, was 'advised' not to include any pieces by Pfitzner in a commemorative centenary concert of the Academy in Munich in October 1946.[28]

---

18   See BHA/OMGB 10/48–1/5, Music Section, Daily Report, 11 July 1945, and Music Section, Elimination of Nazi musicians, 24 July 1945.

19   BHA/OMGB 10/48–1/5, HQ, 6870th DISCC, Summary of activities for week ending 28th September 1945, 29 September 1945, and HQ, 6870th DISCC, Weekly Report, Film, Theater, and Music Control Section, 21 November 1945.

20   BHA/OMGB 10/48–1/5, OMGB, ICD, Weekly Report, Film, Theater, and Music Control Section, 21 January 1946, p. 3.

21   Lucius Clay, *Decision in Germany*, (London: Heinemann, 1950), p. 284.

22   BHA/OMGB 10/48–1/4, OMGB, ICD, Yearly Report of Music Control in Bavaria, July 1946 to July 1947, p. 2.

23   BHA/OMGB 10/66–1/45, OMGB, ICD, Statistical and analytical report covering period 1 May-31 May 1947.

24   BHA/OMGB 10/48–1/5, Munich Detachment, 6870th DISCC, Weekly Report, 12 December 1945.

25   GLAK/OMGWB 12/91–1/7, Annex C, 2 June 1945, and Weekly Situation report of the Film, Theater, and Music Section, 6871st DISCC, 22 September 1945, p. 2.

26   BHA/OMGB 10/48–1/5, OMGB, ICD, Music Weekly Report, 18 May 1946, p. 2.

27   BHA/OMGB 10/48–1/5, Weekly Report to Chief, Film, Theater and Music, 6 July 1946.

28   BHA/OMGB 10/48–1/5, Music Section, Weekly Report, 20 September 1946. This begs the question of why Haas himself was left in charge of the Academy. He was one of the

The Americans had moved a long way from their earlier position of not wanting to be seen 'to regiment culture'.

The exclusion of performers from professional life by the Americans was taken much further than their censorship of music, and challenges any assumption that denazification of musicians was lenient or superficial. We can distinguish here four phases before the Americans reluctantly abandoned their effort in 1948. In the early weeks of the occupation, they were concerned to restart concerts in major cities. This meant finding local officials who could be licensed to produce concerts, and then carrying out a quick purge of selected ensembles before they could perform in public and on radio. All over the American Zone, music officers were instructed to draw up blacklists of musicians, and to send these to McClure's headquarters at Bad Homburg. The Americans relied at this stage on locally captured documents, or on information received from Germans, which might or might not be reliable. This explains why they initially employed a number of musicians, such as Jochum and Knappertsbusch, who were subsequently blacklisted, and by November 1945 described as 'Nazi parade horses'.[29] Inevitably, the early purges appeared arbitrary and unfair. Already, tensions between different branches of the Military Government were apparent. The Intelligence Branch of ICD, headed by Colonel Alfred Toombs, demanded that all NSDAP members be excluded.[30] Music officers were aware that were this to be enforced, few orchestras would be able to play. In July 1945, Arthur Vogel in Munich protested: 'The recent wholesale dismissal of Nazi party members from the State Opera, and the paralysing effects this policy will have on musical life if pursued throughout Bavaria, force me to state my opinion of this policy.'[31] Three days later he wrote: 'Schmitt and Altmann of the Philharmonic dropped in, visibly trembling lest we should fall on the 19 Nazis in their orchestra ... I sent a note over to Captain Busey telling him this office favors retention of all musicians save the outright stinkers and trouble-makers.'[32] From papers drawn up by the orchestra, it would appear that sixteen of its musicians were dismissed.[33] Vogel subsequently reported that if all who had been NSDAP members prior to 1 May 1937 were excluded, there would be no orchestras left in Nuremberg, Bayreuth, Augsburg, or

---

most popular contemporary composers in Germany during the war, and had been involved with music in the HJ. His oratorio *Das Lied von der Mutter* (1940) apparently included the line 'Nazi-Deutschland hat gesiegt'. See the correspondence on this between the *Collegium Musicum Verdau* and the *Kulturbund* in SAPMO-BArch DY 27/249.

29   BHA/OMGB 10/48–1/5, HQ, 6870th DISCC, Weekly Report, 28 November 1945.

30   Toombs had been in the first American IC unit to work in Germany, in Aachen, in September 1944, and it is significant that he was involved in the investigation into the Buchenwald concentration camp in April 1945.

31   BHA/OMGB 10/48–1/5, Music Section, Daily Report No. 22, 16 July 1945.

32   BHA/OMGB 10/48–1/5, Music Section, Daily Report No. 25, 19 July 1945.

33   BHA/OMGB 10/120–2/8, Tätigkeit der Münchener Philharmoniker seit Kriegsende, Mai 1945–1.Februar 1946.

Regensburg, and that in Munich, the orchestra of the Bavarian State Opera would have to merge with the Philharmonic.[34]

This situation was mirrored in cities all over the American Zone. In Karlsruhe, provisional screening of the Symphony Orchestra resulted in 'several severe musical losses'.[35] In Stuttgart, the Americans began a long struggle with the municipal authorities to denazify the Opera and the Philharmonic.[36] In Bremen, which the Americans took over from the British in June 1945, a preliminary survey noted:

> Music and Theatre activities in Bremen and the Enclave are less advanced than in any other of the key cities selected as initial targets. This is a very critical area, since the adjoining areas, under British control, are extremely active, and the contrast results in comparisons highly unfavorable to the American occupation and control agencies.

The report went on to state that if Party members in the Bremen Philharmonic were excluded, the orchestra would be temporarily crippled, and argued that they should be retained, particularly as in surrounding areas – under British control – nominal Nazis were permitted to work 'in subordinate positions'.[37]

Surviving blacklists drawn up by American officers in southern and central Germany in this first phase of occupation give a vivid picture of the chaotic situation prevailing then. They are hastily typed, and whole pages are now illegible. This first phase of American denazification was draconian, inevitably arbitrary, and partial. It left hundreds of professional musicians out of work, and facing an uncertain future.

A second, intensified phase began in October 1945 with the completion of the first post-war 'Black, Grey, and White lists' for the whole of the American Zone. Alongside hundreds of lesser musicians, the leading lights of German musical life, including Furtwängler, Knappertsbusch, and Gieseking, were named as Nazi collaborators, causing widespread comment.[38] The Americans were now using the Reich Chamber of Culture files held by the British, and in the next few months were

---

34   BHA/OMGB 10/48–1/5, Music Section, Elimination of Nazi Musicians, 24 July 1945. This proposed merger was vehemently rejected by the two ensembles, which had a political rivalry going back to before 1933. The Philharmonic prided itself on being less 'nazified', and was keen to exploit the advantages this gave it with the Americans after 1945.

35   GLAK/OMGWB 12/91–1/7, Weekly Situation report of the Film, Theater, and Music Control Section, 6871st DISCC, 1 October 1945, p. 5.

36   See IfZ/OMGUS 5/237–3/3, Dilemma of ICD, 28 November 1946, for a summary.

37   GLAK/OMGWB 12/91–1/7, Weekly Situation report of the Film, Theater, and Music Control Section, 6871st DISCC, 8 September 1945, pp. 4–5.

38   See for example the *Regensburger Post*, 23 October 1945, quoted in *Les Nouvelles d'Allemagne*, 35 (29 November 1945), pp. 9–10. PWD at SHAEF had drawn up provisional blacklists in November 1944, which included some thirty musicians, mostly known to the Americans from German press and broadcasting. IfZ/OMGUS 5/246–2/5, Black and Grey Information Personnel, PWD, 18 November 1944.

thus able to extend their purges.[39] Analysis of these lists is complicated by changes in the way they were drawn up between 1944 and 1947. As well as three categories defined by colour, there were further subdivisions. On the first post-war lists, there were distinctions between white 'A' and 'B', and black 'D' and 'E'. Later lists dropped these distinctions, but introduced a new one, between grey 'acceptable' and 'unacceptable'. As Ulrich Bausch has pointed out, there were many discrepancies between lists drawn up by ICD centrally, and by detachments in individual areas.[40] Changing directives from McClure's headquarters further undermined any hope music officers might have had of achieving consistency.

The new climate in the autumn of 1945 was heralded in Munich by the dismissal of Knappertsbusch. Behind the scenes, his case also revealed difficulties with communication. Knappertsbusch, after 'exhaustive investigation' by the Intelligence Branch, had been appointed temporary *Intendant* at the Bavarian State Opera, and allowed to direct the Munich Philharmonic.[41] He even conducted a Beethoven piano concerto in September, in which Edward Kilenyi, an American music officer, played the solo part.[42] Evidently Toombs, the head of the ICD's Intelligence Branch, had heard that Knappertsbusch was conducting in public again, and he angrily demanded that the Munich detachment should carry out its responsibilities with more urgency.[43] Knappertsbusch was 'summarily dismissed'.[44] Vogel and Kilenyi in Munich were apparently unaware at the time that he had been blacklisted, claiming to have learnt this only later from the magazine *Stars and Stripes*.[45] The case was widely reported, and discussed all over Germany.[46] The effect was calamitous, and not just in Munich. Fragile relationships between music officers and German musicians were undermined, and the exodus of musicians from the American Zone gathered pace.

Nor was Knappertsbusch an isolated example. Between October 1945 and March 1946, orchestras and choirs that had resumed performance were scrutinised again, and hundreds more individuals excluded; Intelligence Branch extended the purge to smaller towns, which had previously escaped attention. The American assessment of the staff of the Coburg *Landestheater* is illustrative. In the October 1945 'Black, Grey, and White Lists', 35 of its musicians and singers, including the principal

---

39   IfZ/OMGUS 5/243–2/17, Minutes of General McClure's meeting, 19 September 1945, p. 2.

40   Bausch, *Die Kulturpolitik*, pp. 120–122.

41   IfZ/OMGUS 5/265–1/2, Ross, ISCC Munich Detachment, to Roland, 19 July 1945.

42   IfZ/OMGUS 5/348–1/15, Hagen, Deputy Chief Music Control, Report on Mission to Munich, 14–23 Sept., 29 September 1945, p. 5.

43   IfZ/OMGUS 5/270–3/4, Toombs to Powell, 17 October 1945.

44   IfZ/OMGUS 5/270–3/4, Hills (for Chief ICD), to CO 6870th DISCC, 19 October 1945.

45   BHA/OMGB 10/48–1/5, HQ, 6870th DISCC, Weekly Report, 26 October 1945.

46   See *British Zone Review*, 1:5 (24 November 1945), p. 12; also TNA/PRO/FO 371/55798, Information Services Control Branch Summary for Period Ending 13 March 1946, p. 20.

conductor Walter Talk, were on the 'Grey List – Classification C', defined as 'Party members without a record of Nazi or nationalistic convictions, or small non-Party opportunists. Cannot be employed in policy-making or creative capacity or executive position or as a personnel officer'. A 'Refreshment Room Clerk', stage and lighting technicians, and hairdressers were also on this 'Grey List'. A further 19 musicians and singers, the chief cashier, the chief costumier, and a porter were on the 'Black List – Classification D', 'not to be employed at present'. The many names on the 'Black List – Classification E – Possible security menace, not to be employed' are illegible.[47] New lists, each longer than the last, were issued in December 1945, and in April 1946.

A third phase was inaugurated by the Law for the Liberation from National Socialism and Militarism of March 1946, which transferred the responsibility for denazification to local German tribunals, or *Spruchkammern*. This law restricted nominal Nazis to 'ordinary labor', and the Americans found themselves caught up in torturous judgements as to which musicians fell into this category. The extremists in the Intelligence Branch argued that although orchestral musicians might be performing 'ordinary labor', they appeared in public, and therefore a higher standard of denazification should apply to them. Toombs demanded that 'first bench players' and 'principal soloists' be excluded if they had been NSDAP members. He and McClure also refused to accept a large number of ex-Nazis appearing together in any one ensemble.[48] In May 1946 McClure intervened personally, to demand that 'the party members in the Stuttgart Symphony be eliminated', after hearing from the Intelligence Branch that 25 per cent of the orchestra's musicians were former NSDAP members.[49] *Spruchkammern* were slow to deal with the thousands of cases presented in each locality, and the Americans carried on with their own exclusionary processes, frequently overriding German decisions. By this time musicians were caught up in a 'paper war';[50] to perform in public they had to satisfy potentially several different branches of the US Military Government, to complete a *Fragebogen*, and appear before a *Spruchkammer* if they had any Nazi Party connections. Many lied about these, but were caught: as already mentioned, the Americans, as well as having access to the Reich Chamber of Culture files, had from 1947 the entire NSDAP card index to refer to. Musicians caught falsifying their *Fragebogen* were subject to further punishments.

The Americans also established a German *Prüfungsausschuss*, or scrutiny committee, in every locality, and this vetted performing musicians. Their own Information Control offices retained the right to overrule the decisions made by *Spruchkammern* or *Prüfungsausschüsse* by issuing *Spielverbote*, or performance bans. These prevented named musicians from appearing in public, without giving

---

47   IfZ/OMGUS 11/47–3/24, List No. 3. Black, Grey, and White Lists for IC Purposes [10 October 1945].

48   IfZ/OMGUS 5/347–3/25, Toombs to Clarke, 23 May 1946.

49   IfZ/OMGUS 5/347–3/27, McClure, 23 May 1946.

50   Bausch, *Die Kulturpolitik*, p. 120.

reasons, and had no date of expiry.[51] Between March and November 1946, 52
performance bans were issued in Ulm, and 75 in Karlsruhe;[52] in Württemberg-
Baden, 224 had been issued by August 1946.[53] William Castello, Music Control
Officer in Stuttgart, gave as reasons for issuing performance bans 'falsification of
Fragebogen', 'violation of regulations', and 'bad behaviour'.[54]

Through 1946, the Americans took the purge into the smallest villages of their
Zone. Dozens of musicians were banned from performing in rural communities
like Füssen, Göggingen, and Illertissen.[55] Foreign nationals were not exempted.
The American violinist Guila Bustabo, who had stayed in Germany during the
war, performing with great success there and in occupied France, was blacklisted.[56]
Denazification was given priority over reconstruction, even in Munich, which the
Americans were trying to turn into the cultural centre of their Zone. In June 1946,
the Bulgarian conductor Zankov, who had worked in Germany during the war,
was prevented from performing only thirty minutes before the start of a concert
at the State Opera;[57] in August, a concert by the Munich Chamber Orchestra was
cancelled: 'too many of its members were at one time or another members of the
Nazi Party'.[58]

Using captured files, the Intelligence Branch of ICD drew up ever longer 'White,
Grey, and Black Lists for Information Control Purposes' in 1946, and these served
to inform decisions about who was to be excluded, irrespective of decisions reached
by other tribunals or branches of the Military Government. There has been much
inaccurate and vague comment about 'blacklists', so it worth examining them in
some detail. Those issued in 1946 had a preamble which explained the categories
used, and the first, in April 1946, had a detailed guide to help Intelligence officers
place musicians, actors, journalists, and radio technicians into the appropriate
category. The lists look like small telephone directories, and it is instructive to track
a few individuals through them during 1946. The April list is just over a hundred
pages long. Most of the musicians listed in it were then resident in the American
Zone. A number of well-known individual musicians, working, or attempting to
work, in other Zones, or in Austria, are also listed. On the Black List, 'not suitable
for employment in any Information Control Media', amongst hundreds of other
musicians, the following appear:

---

51   See the sample in IfZ/OMGUS 5/347–3/27.

52   GLAK/OMGWB 12/91–2/7, untitled paper. See also GLAK/OMGWB 12/91–2/10,
Sherman, Theater and Music Control Officer, Karlsruhe Outpost, to Jenkins, 19 November
1946.

53   IfZ/OMGUS 5/347–3/27, Activities Report from 5 to 11 August 1946, Chief
Theater and Music Section, ICD, OMGWB.

54   GLAK/OMGWB 12/91–2/10, Castello to Jenkins, 14 November 1946.

55   See the lists in BHA/OMGB 10/76–1/5.

56   IfZ/OMGUS 5/265-1/16, Peeples (for Director IC) to Jack Bustabo, Chicago, 21
November 1946.

57   BHA/OMGB 10/48–1/5, Music Weekly Report, 15 June 1946.

58   BHA/OMGB 10/48–1/5, Music Weekly Report, 16 August 1946.

Hermann Abendroth, Franz Adam, Hans von Benda, Karl Boehm, Cesar Bresgen, Werner Egk, Karl Elmendorff, Wilhelm Furtwängler, Walter Gieseking, Franz Grothe, Gustav Havemann, Robert Heger, Eugen Jochum, Otto Jochum, Herbert von Karajan, Josef Keilberth, Hans Knappertsbusch, Franz Konwitschny, Clemens Krauss, Georg Kulenkampf, Gottfried Mueller, Elly Ney, Hans Pfitzner, Michael Raucheisen, Norbert Schulze, Paul Sixt, Heinrich Spitta, Fritz Stein, Richard Strauss, Bruno Stuermer, Heinz Tietjen, Richard Trunk, and Georg Winkler.[59]

In June 1946, a 'Supplement' added another fifty pages of names. Added to the 'Black' list were Johann Nepomuk David, Helmut Degen, Ernst von Dohnanyi, Wolfgang Fortner, Ottmar Gerster, Paul Hoeffer, Wilhelm Kempff, Clemens Schmalstich, and Elisabeth Schwarzkopf. Only one of the musicians above categorised as 'Black' in April had been reclassified. Bruno Stuermer, described tersely as 'Music Director for KDF' in the April list, was reclassified as 'Grey – unacceptable' in June, and therefore judged suitable for 'Ordinary Labor only'.[60] In August 1946, a new list, now nearly two hundred pages long, was issued. Guila Bustabo was added to the 'Black' section.[61] A 'Supplement' was issued in November, and this represented the high-water mark of American denazification. Of some 10,000 people working in 'Film, Theater, and Music' now listed by the ICD, only four musicians were in the category 'White A'. Bruno Stuermer was moved back to the 'Black' section.[62] The American public was clearly informed about this rigid programme: the composer Virgil Thomson, critic of the *New York Herald Tribune*, reported in September 1946 that less than one percent of musicians in the American Zone were officially 'available for employment'.[63]

It was immensely difficult for McClure and Toombs to maintain this hard line. The Soviets, French, and British all employed prestigious musicians excluded from employment in the American Zone, and the very public case of Furtwängler served to highlight this. Individual German musicians struggled against the restrictions placed upon them, and frequently managed to contravene these, even in the American Zone. There was little support for McClure and Toombs from higher or lower levels of the American Military Government. As we have seen, Music Control officers often acted upon their orders to purge musicians only with reluctance,

---

59   Bundesarchiv, Koblenz, Office of Military Government, United States (hereafter BAK/OMGUS), 11/47–1/17, White, Grey, and Black list for Information Control Purposes, 1 April 1946.

60   BAK/OMGUS 11/47–3/25, White, Grey, and Black list for Information Control Purposes, 1 June 1946, Supplement 1 to list of April 1946. The 'KDF' was an acronym for *Kraft durch Freude* (Strength through Joy), a Nazi Party organization intended to bring cultural activities to workers.

61   BAK/OMGUS 11/47–3/26, White, Grey, and Black list for Information Control Purposes, 1 August 1946, superseding list 1 April 1946 and Supplement No.1 thereto.

62   IfZ/OMGUS 5/242–1/48, White, Grey, and Black list for Information Control Purposes, 1 November 1946, Supplement 1 to list of 1 August 1946.

63   Virgil Thomson, 'German Culture and Army Rule', *New York Herald Tribune* (Paris Edition), 22 September 1946.

and by the end of 1946 it was clear that Lucius Clay, the officer commanding the American Military Government in Germany, was weakening in his resolve. Earlier in the year, he had threatened that German *Spruchkammern* would be replaced with American tribunals if they continued to be over-lenient, but he had not carried out this threat.[64] In November 1946, McClure informed all his subordinates that future decisions on the licensing and registration of musicians and artists would not need clearance from the Intelligence Branch,[65] and in January 1947 Music officers were told that the 'authority granted Information Control to apply a higher standard than Spruchkammer, or similar clearances ... will not apply to conductors, artists and musicians'.[66] After this, excluded musicians in the American Zone were able, one by one, to resume their former way of life.

The clearance of Furtwängler, who had from the start acted as a symbol, marked the beginning of a final phase. Against the express wishes of most of the German music-loving public, and of the Soviets, the French, and even his own music officers, McClure had insisted that Furtwängler be excluded until his case had been properly investigated.[67] When Furtwängler was cleared by a denazification tribunal in Austria in February 1946, McClure took the unusual step of issuing a personal statement:

> It is an undisputable fact that through his activities Furtwängler was prominently identified with Nazi Germany. By allowing himself to become a tool of the party, he lent an aura of respectability to the circle of men who are now on trial in Nuremberg for crimes against humanity ... It is inconceivable that he should be allowed to occupy a leading position in Germany at a time when we are trying to wipe out every trace of Nazism.[68]

Furtwängler returned to Berlin in March, and was cleared by the *Kulturbund*'s *Prüfungsausschuss* in June 1946. Initially, McClure refused to accept this decision, and Furtwängler returned to Switzerland. In December 1946, his case was heard by the Berlin Denazification Commission for Artists, a body approved by all four Powers, but no judgement was rendered until April 1947, when Furtwängler was cleared.

By this time, Toombs and McClure had left Germany, and the American effort to purge German musical life of former Nazis had almost come to an end. Only

---

64   Herz, 'The Fiasco', p. 573.

65   IfZ/OMGUS 5/265–1/16, McClure, Director IC, to all IC Divisions, 31 October 1946.

66   GLAK/OMGWB 12/90–3/8, Jenkins, Acting Chief, Theater and Music Control Branch, to All Outposts, 9 January 1947.

67   IfZ/OMGUS 5/243–1/4, HQ, USFET, ICD, Semi-monthly progress report for period 16–30 September 1945, p. 8. Not all Germans supported Furtwängler. In the Radio Stuttgart series *The public voice speaks*, broadcast in July 1945, the opinion 'of a prominent high school director' was read out: 'It is shameful that an artist with the distinction of Furtwängler allowed himself, as a conductor, to appear apparently on behalf of Nazi culture, both at home and abroad.' Historisches Archiv des (ehemaligen) Südfunks, Stuttgart, Programmnachweis v., 30 July 1945. I am grateful to Dirk Deissler for this reference.

68   IfZ/OMGUS 5/270–3/4, OMGUS Public Relations Service, 20 February 1946.

composers, who could be 'considered to exert influence in the forming of public opinion', were still to be blacklisted. A new, much smaller list was produced in March 1947 to replace those of 1946, which had read like directories of German musical life. Nonetheless, some thirty composers, including Strauss, Orff, Gerster, Degen, David, Stuermer, Schmalstich, Schulze, and Fortner, remained proscribed, in various categories of black and grey, along with the jazz pianist Hans Grothe.[69]

McClure, and other hardliners at the ICD had to grit their teeth as the Nazis' favourite performers and composers returned to the public arena, usually to great acclaim. Knappertsbusch made his reappearance in Bamberg in January 1947;[70] Gieseking was taken off the blacklist at the same time. He and Furtwängler gave hugely acclaimed return concerts in April and in May. Werner Egk was cleared by a *Spruchkammer* in October 1947; Strauss was cleared in June 1948; even Elly Ney, one of the most enthusiastic Nazis amongst Germany's leading musicians, reappeared. American advice to concert managers not to give 'such great publicity' to her 'comeback' was ignored.[71]

Although the collapse of the Furtwängler case, and Clay's decision that *Spruchkammer* verdicts had to be accepted, can be seen as the end of the American denazification in music, the machinery they had set up ground on for much longer. Musicians still had to present themselves before *Prüfungsausschüsse*, and to submit *Fragebögen*. Some who had escaped American jurisdiction were pursued. The ICD reported to the British in October 1947 that Lothar Gruenberg, a musician licensed on the understanding that he was only previously a member of the Berlin SA Choir, was in fact in 1934 the choir's director, and asked what action the British proposed to take about this.[72] A plan to bring the exiled Hindemith to Germany was postponed in September 1947, apparently in deference to American public opinion, because there was 'considerable evidence that Hindemith's connections with the Nazi Party were closer than had been supposed in the early days'.[73] Only in October 1948 were American music officers instructed that 'political vetting' of musicians was to end altogether.[74]

The American denazification programme has been roundly condemned. Typically, the criticism has been sharpest when linked to individual cases. Anti-American clichés of lack of cultural understanding and naivety, or simple accusations of

---

69   IfZ/OMGUS 5/428—3/9, Black, Grey, and White Lists for Information Control Purposes, March 1947.

70   BHA/OMGB 10/66—1/45, OMGB, Statistical and analytical Report covering period 1 January to 31 January 1947, p. 3.

71   BHA/OMGB 10/48–1/3, OMGB, Cultural Affairs Branch, Music Office, Monthly Summaries for Period from 1 August 1948 through 31 August 1948, 2 September 48, p. 3.

72   IfZ/OMGUS 5/265–1/16, Adler (for Director ICD) to Sely, Intelligence Section, PR/ISC, 1 October 1947.

73   IfZ/OMGUS AG47/20/2, AGWAR to OMGUS for ICD, 27 August 1947, and OMGUS to AGWAR, 2 September 1947.

74   IfZ/OMGUS 5/364–2/38, Agreement between Education and Cultural Relations and ICD on Theater-Music Licensing Procedure, 19 October 1948.

vindictiveness have set the tone. Most recently, the Americans have been criticised for double standards:

> where the bogeyman of Nazism was raised, [America's cultural Cold Warriors] campaigned vigorously for the separation of art and politics; but where dealing with Communism, they were unwilling to make such a distinction. This egregious illogicality had first surfaced back in the late 1940s, during the 'denazification' of Germany. Then, whilst Furtwängler had been rewarded with high-profile concerts alongside Yehudi Menuhin, Bertolt Brecht was ridiculed by Melvin Lasky in *Der Monat*.[75]

It is difficult to imagine that Furtwängler, or any of the thousands of other musicians, actors, and writers blacklisted by the Americans between 1945 and 1948, would have felt themselves 'rewarded' by the Americans at this time.

'If People like Papen, Schacht, and Fritzsche Get off, then there Can Be no Reason for Condemning Furtwängler.'[76]

The record on denazification in the British Zone is paradoxical. On the one hand the British supported the Americans on Furtwängler, and worked closely with them on many lesser musicians, but on the other, their Zone was considered lenient by comparison. In large measure, this was because public opinion in Britain was reluctant to accept a clear connection between politics and music. There was consensus on the prosecution and punishment of murderers and torturers, but not of musicians. William Beveridge toured the British Zone in 1946 and reported that a 'common-sense step would be to reconsider the denazification policy'.[77] Sydney Jacobsen, reporting for *Picture Post* in August 1946, called for 'an amnesty for all except known criminals'.[78] Even members of the British occupation forces were uncomfortable with the denazification of musicians. Georgiana Melrose speaks for many: 'Sometimes the conscientious weeding out of Nazis was carried to absurd extremes; a second violin in the radio symphony orchestra barred because it had been discovered he'd held a job as a minor clerk in the Party'.[79] Information Control officers typically reflected a similar ambivalence:

---

75   Frances Stonor Saunders, *Who Paid the Piper? The CIA and the Cultural Cold War* (London: Granta, 1999), p. 227.

76   Reported answer from a German civil servant to a question about denazification in the arts, TNA/PRO/FO 1010/45, PR/ISC Regional Staff, Hanover Region, Reaction Report, October 1946, p. 15. Papen, Schacht, and Fritzsche had recently been acquitted of all charges by the International Military Tribunal at Nuremberg.

77   William Beveridge, *An Urgent Message from Germany* (London: Pilot Press, 1946), p. 19.

78   'Europe cannot afford this Germany', *Picture Post*, 32:9 (31 August 1946).

79   Georgiana Melrose, *A Strange Occupation* (Ilfracombe: Stockwell, 1988), p. 72.

All Corps Districts report that the party membership of great artists is felt to be a matter of no importance. The Hannover public bemoans the exclusion of Gieseking and Knappertsbusch from the world of music. ... In Hamburg (and in fact throughout the British Zone) l'affaire Furtwaengler is being hotly contested.[80]

Although the documentary record on British denazification in music is fragmentary, we do have the gossipy memoir of George Clare, who worked for the Intelligence Branch of PR/ISC. One chapter, typically balanced, is dedicated to Furtwängler, but Clare's account is noteworthy for its absence of comment on the denazification of ordinary musicians, and for its profound scepticism. He paints a memorable portrait of Britain's equivalent of Al Toombs, Colonel Kaye Sely, born Kurt Seltz in Munich. Sely was the head of the Intelligence Branch, and worked from the old office of Hans Hinkel, executive secretary of the Reich Chamber of Culture. From Clare's memoir, it appears that the work of the Intelligence Branch consisted mainly in catching artists and journalists who had falsified their *Fragebogen*. Punishments could be severe. Leopold Ludwig, conductor of the Municipal Opera in Berlin, was sentenced to one year's imprisonment by a Military Government Court for this.[81] By April 1948, 2,326,257 Germans in the British Zone had completed *Fragebögen*; 358,466 had been suspended from employment, and another 2,456 prosecuted for falsification.[82] Conversely, musicians who had been Party members, or had held office in the Reich Chamber of Culture, and who admitted this, were far more likely to be licensed than in the American Zone.

Such British lenience originated in the decision, taken in June 1945, to allow the German population 'entertainments' as a matter of priority. Unless musicians had worked for the SS or HJ, Party membership or success under the Nazis was overlooked. The British even recruited from other Zones. Arthur Vogel in Munich wrote despairingly in July 1945: 'Major Lambert [the British Music Officer in Hamburg] doesn't help us very much when he paints very rosy pictures to people like Hans Hotter about the ease and wealth of musical life in Hamburg, where no one is being removed from positions of responsibility because of past political connections.'[83] Jack Bornoff, the first Music Controller of the NWDR, was allowed in June 1945 to recruit Hans Schmidt-Isserstedt to conduct the orchestra he was creating for the NWDR. Together these two travelled across Germany and into Austria, recruiting musicians from POW camps, and from other orchestras, including the Berlin Philharmonic, and the Reich Bruckner Orchestra in Linz. No questions

---

80   TNA/PRO/FO 371/55798, ISCB Summary for Period Ending 13 March 1946, p. 20.

81   George Clare, *Berlin Days 1946–47* (London: Macmillan, 1989); on Ludwig, see p. 105.

82   TNA/PRO/FO 1056/268, Denazification and Categorisation Statistics, 20 May 1948.

83   BHA/OMGB 10/48–1/5, Music Section, Daily Report No. 21, 15 July 1945.

were asked about the political backgrounds of the musicians selected; their suitability was judged on purely musical grounds.[84]

As American denazification became more systematic, the British were dragged along behind them. There was close coordination on particular cases. The conductor Hans Konwitschny, former SA and NSDAP member, who went on to a distinguished career in the GDR, was blacklisted by the Americans in Frankfurt in November 1945, but managed to direct a number of concerts in Hanover before the British were informed by the Americans about his past.[85] However, the disagreement over Eugen Jochum, wartime conductor of the Hamburg Philharmonic, illustrates particularly well the difference in approach between the Americans and the British. The Americans, who had initially cleared Jochum, agreed in July 1945 to allow him to work in Hamburg under the British, on the condition that he would return to Munich.[86] While he was away, the Americans found out more about his popularity and success under the Nazis, and he was blacklisted. Much to the dismay of the American ICD, the British found no fault with Jochum. He was not a Party member, but was a convinced Roman Catholic, and had in their eyes not compromised his artistic integrity. In December 1945, McClure wrote personally to Bishop to argue that Jochum should not be employed in Hamburg. In an extraordinary letter, McClure described Jochum as an opportunist who had made good under the Nazis. He had performed in private gatherings in front of Hitler, had pushed his annual earnings up to 100,000 RM, and appeared in a propaganda film. His brothers had been fanatical Nazis, and Jochum had used his success and connections to act as a 'god-father' of the Nazi musical world.[87] Bishop replied, stressing his desire to cooperate, but also politely insisting on a different interpretation of the available evidence. Jochum remained in the 'Black' category on American lists until December 1946, before being reclassified as 'Grey Acceptable'.[88] In the meantime he continued to conduct the Hamburg Philharmonic. As late as January 1948 the Americans were checking NSDAP records for evidence of Jochum's past affiliations. They found that he had not been a member of the NSDAP, SA, or SS.[89] The essence of the American case, and this was indisputable, was that Jochum had done exceptionally well under the Nazis. The British, while accepting that Jochum had prospered, did not accept that he had been in any sense an active Nazi.

This high-level disagreement over Jochum was something of an exception. In many more cases, the British followed the American lead. Having reluctantly supported the Americans on Furtwängler, the British in September 1946 led the

---

84   Jack Bornoff, interview with the author, December 2000.

85   AOFC/AC 508/5, Rapport No. 16 de l'Officier Britannique de Liaison ICD, 17 January 1946, p. 3. See also the correspondence in Bundesarchiv, Außenstelle Berlin, Reichskulturkammer (hereafter BAB/RKK) 2703/0127/27.

86   BAB/RKK 2703/0108/08, Memorandum on Eugen Jochum, 7 December 1945.

87   BAB/RKK 2703/0108/08, McClure to Bishop, 19 December 1945.

88   BAB/RKK 2703/0108/08, Rehabilitation of persons on I.S.C. Black-list, 5 December 1946.

89   BAB/RKK 2702/0006/12, BS I C BR, 7 January 1948.

criticism of the French when they heard that he had been invited to conduct in Baden-Baden.[90] Eventually, the British reversed their wartime commitment not to blacklist musicians and drew up lists. In a way that perhaps reflects the British embarrassment about the whole process, none survive in the British National Archive, but there are some copies in American files. Unlike the Americans, who employed different categories, the British approach was unsubtle. List No. 11, of March 1946, stated: 'Persons on this list may not be employed in any capacity'. It named 103 musicians, with 'reasons' for their inclusion.[91] A supplement added six weeks later included another twenty-six.[92] Although most were ordinary musicians and singers, there were also some prominent individuals, like Robert Heger, who was briefly considered as a replacement for Furtwängler at the Berlin Philharmonic in September 1945, before being rejected by the Americans.[93] There was evidently a purge in Hamburg, where *Generalintendant* Noller, and orchestra leaders Müller-Lamptertz, Gotthardt, and Sosen were removed, along with Ernst Klussman, the Director of the Musical Academy, and dozens of ordinary musicians. Most were blacklisted because they had joined the NSDAP before 1937. Many had been officials in the SA or the HJ. In a few cases, more specific objections were recorded. Several had played in SS ensembles. Berlin conductor Hans von Benda's name was accompanied by the terse note: 'Kampfbund der Kultur. Political activities.' Norbert Schultze, who had written *Bomben auf Engelland*, was described as 'composer of anti-British songs'. In two cases, those of Abendroth and Gieseking, the reason given was their appearance on a US blacklist. Their inclusion only points up the arbitrary nature of the list: why were the hundreds of other musicians also on American lists not included? More curious is the geographical spread of the addresses given. Almost all were from Berlin or Hamburg, with a few from Hanover and from towns in Schleswig-Holstein. A conductor from Detmold and an opera singer from Bonn appeared in isolation, and there was no one from Cologne or Düsseldorf. A second supplement was drawn up in July 1946, and suggests that the British were gradually extending their understanding of music in the NSDAP. Fritz Stege, music critic of the *Völkischer Beobachter*, was listed, as were Maximilian Sternitzki, 'Chief of HJ musical college in Cracow', the violinist Gustav Havemann, 'Kampfbund für deutsche Kultur. Founder of RMK', and Gottfried Wolters, 'Composer of songs and music for HJ'. The culture of denunciation that thrived in this climate is evident. Hans Doberitz was 'Voted out by the Advisory Council N.W.D.R. as an objectionable Nazi'. A unique case was that

---

90   AOFC Berlin, GFCC, Caisse 131/5, Acting Chief PR/ISC to Theatre and Music Control, Control Council (French Element), 5 September 1946.

91   IfZ/OMGUS 5/244–1/11, ISCB, List of persons dismissed, rejected, or refused employment in the British Zone, No.11, 1 March 1946.

92   IfZ/OMGUS 5/244–1/11, Addendum No.1 to ISC/2043 of 1st March 1946, 15 April 1946.

93   Chamberlin, *Kultur auf Trümmern*, pp. 122 and 177.

of Anni Lebedebur, who was denounced as a 'propagator of Nazi ideologies after the war'.[94]

The British also took the lead in licensing German musical organisations. In January 1947, they agreed to the formation of the German General League of Singers (*Deutscher Allgemeiner Sängerbund* or DAS). Although they were concerned that this might be a resurrection of the Nazi *Deutscher Sängerbund*,[95] the British need not have worried: the DAS threw itself into the denazification of music in schools, drawing up ambitious schemes for new songbooks, curricula, and guidelines for music teachers.[96] In 1948, the British licensed an Association of Orchestral Directors, which quickly developed similar supra-zonal pretensions.[97] More controversial was the Society for Music Research (*Gesellschaft für Musikforschung* or GfM), which later operated in both the Federal Republic and the GDR. The GfM's President, Friedrich Blume, had chaired the conference that accompanied the 'Degenerate Music' exhibition in Düsseldorf in 1938, giving the keynote speech on 'Music and Race'. The Vice-President, Walther Vetter, had used the same occasion to vent his anti-Semitism and to praise the ideas of Rosenberg, who in the 'Third Reich' had led the campaign for ideological purity in the arts . It has been assumed that the British were so lenient about denazification that they were willing to overlook the Nazi associations of many of the GfM's members, from Blume downwards, or even that they were so naïve as to have been unaware of them. Neither of these assumptions is accurate. In fact, the British knew a great deal about Blume, and within the Intelligence Section of the ISC, there were grave suspicions about him. The participation of ex-Nazis like Müller-Blattau in the GfM was further cause for concern. In the American Zone, Newell Jenkins, the music officer for Württemberg-Baden, received many complaints from German academics about the involvement of compromised colleagues like Besseler and Müller-Blattau in the GfM. Jenkins questioned whether this should be tolerated.[98] It is reasonable to presume that these concerns were put to the British, who sent an Intelligence Officer to observe the inaugural meeting of the GfM in Göttingen in April 1947. A strategic decision was then taken to allow the GfM to operate. Interestingly, the Society's journal, *Die*

---

94   IfZ/OMGUS 5/244–1/11, Addendum No. 2 to ISC/2043 of 1st March 1946, 20 July 1946. The *Kampfbund für deutsche Kultur* was a Nazi cultural organisation founded in 1928. Involvement with this body was taken by the British as evidence of early Nazi affiliation.

95   TNA/PRO/FO 1056/65, PR/ISC Report for period ending 7 April1948.

96   Bayerisches Hauptstaatsarchiv, Munich, Ministerium für Kultus und Unterricht (hereafter BHA/MK) 51335, DAS to all Kultusministerien, 6 September 1947; see also Sonderbeilage zum Protokoll über die 1. Tagung des Künstlerischen Beirats des Deutschen Allgemeinen Sängerbundes am 3–4.4.1948.

97   BHA/MK 51340, Kapellmeister-Union to Bayerisches Staatsministerium für Unterricht und Kultur, 22 February 1950.

98   GLAK/OMGWB 12/90–3/1, Jenkins to Clarke, 8 March 1947, and 1 April 1947. On Blume, Besseler, Müller-Blattau, and other musicologists, see Potter, *Most German of the Arts*.

Musikforschung, was not licensed in the British Zone, but was published in Kassel – in the American Zone.

Blume went on to play a dominating role in post-war German musicology, and not just as editor of *Die Musikforschung* and the huge encyclopedia *Musik in Geschichte und Gegenwart* (or *MGG* as it is known to librarians). Chameleon-like, he appears to have been involved in almost every significant musical and musicological project, not just of the Nazi period, but also in the Federal Republic, and even in some in the GDR. Recent researchers have found it difficult to trace his connections and activities in precise detail, and frequently refer to him with frustration. All are agreed that he was not an NSDAP member. De Vries describes him as an 'outside specialist' for the NSDAP's *Hauptstelle Musik*, which was part of Rosenberg's organisation; hc does not establish a clear link between Blume and the *Sonderstab Musik*. He devotes several pages to a discussion of the wartime origins of *MGG*, and suggests that the project may have originated not with Blume, but with Rosenberg's favoured musicologist, Herbert Gerigk. De Vries sceptically quotes Blume's post-war explanation that *MGG* was an initiative from the Bärenreiter publishing house in 1943, and raises the disturbing suspicion that some of the archival material used for *MGG* may have been looted during the war by the *Sonderstab Musik*. 'After the war', de Vries writes, 'Friedrich Blume quickly erased his role from German musicology'. He concludes that 'the emergence of *Musik in Geschichte und Gegenwart* merits closer investigation'.[99]

Pamela Potter similarly refers frequently to Blume. She has scrutinised his many published works during the Nazi period, and suggests that he was an ideological master of disguise. She refers specifically to the example of his speech on 'Music and Race' at the Reich Music Festival in 1938, suggesting that he managed to display 'obsequiousness toward the prevailing ideology', while simultaneously appearing to criticise aspects of Nazi methodology, and 'the interference of nonspecialists in the realm of musicology'.[100] Potter subsequently describes how Blume acted as the spokesman for an apolitical German musicology after 1945, but again raises the spectre of his association with more sinister aspects of Nazi musicology. Analysing Blume's post-war writings, she adds: 'needless to say, he did not mention the extracurricular pursuits carried out under the aegis of the Propaganda Ministry, the SS, and the Rosenberg Bureau'.[101]

She notes how under Blume's leadership, the GfM distanced itself from Nazism and anti-Semitism by refusing to review Moser's book, *Die Musik der deutschen Stämme* (1957), and gives an interesting hint that Blume's denazification started unusually early. She refers to an article in the British journal *Music and Letters* in 1947, which referred to Ernest Newman, who had in 1938 defended Blume's work on 'Music and Race'. This was a 'noble and daring attempt to replace the race nonsense of the Nazis by a sober and scientific analysis of the facts'. Evidently Blume had

---

99   De Vries, *Sonderstab Musik*, pp. 79–84.
100   Potter, *Most German of the Arts*, p. 79.
101   *Ibid.*, p. 238.

some well-placed allies in British academic life. This post-war view of him as a cunning resister again suggests the image of the chameleon: 'He had to camouflage the true meaning of his words with a certain amount of current phraseology.'[102] Potter is particularly scathing about British denazification. It was, she says, 'known to be the most lenient'. At universities in the British Zone, 'denazification appeared to be very congenial and problem free'.[103] In a recent article for the *New Grove*, Potter writes: 'After the war, Blume evaded the complexities of denazification'.[104]

In fact, although Blume's denazification was congenial, he may have escaped more closely than either he or Potter realised. When the British made their first investigations of Kiel University in 1945, Blume, no doubt remembering his successful pre-war contacts in England, went out of his way to be helpful. He was one of the staff cleared to restart lectures when the university, temporarily based in hulks in Kiel harbour, re-opened in the autumn.[105] In the summer of 1947, Blume was invited back to Oxford University; as we know, he was at this time portrayed by the musical press in Britain as an anti-Nazi. Behind the scenes, the visit to Oxford provoked new enquiries. The Intelligence Section in Hamburg sent a letter in March 1947 about Blume to Information Services Control in Berlin. In September, it wrote again to express concern about Blume's new role as chairman of the GfM, noting the involvement in the society of ex-Nazis like Müller-Blattau, and pointing out that Blume had written *Das Rasseproblem in der Musik* (1938), and 'some articles of a similar strain'.[106] In October 1947, the Licensing Control Section in Lower Saxony renewed its concerns about Blume's invitation to Oxford, and the publicity given to the visit in the *British Zone Review*. On this letter there is what appears to be a conclusive handwritten addition, which states 'Blume OK. File. 21/1/1948'.[107]

Would Blume's contacts in Britain have been so well disposed towards him, either before or after the war, if they had known that his visit there in 1939, which further strengthened his credentials as an anti-Nazi, was financed by the Reich Research Council at the request of the NSDAP's *Hauptstelle Musik*?[108] Would the Intelligence Section in the British Zone, or the University Control Officer in Kiel,

---

102   *Ibid.*, pp. 253–6.

103   *Ibid.*, p. 245.

104   Pamela Potter, 'Blume, Friedrich', *New Grove Dictionary of Music and Musicians* (London, 2001), 3, pp. 739–41, quote on p. 740.

105   TNA/PRO/FO 1050/1370, *Christian-Albrechts-Universität Kiel. Personal- und Vorlesungsverzeichnis. Sommersemester 1945* (Kiel, 1945); see also the handwritten notes referring to Blume in this file.

106   BAB/RKK 2703/0020/33, Subject – Musicologists conference at Goettingen, IS, ISC(HE) Hamburg, to IS PRISC Branch, HQ Mil Gov, British Troops Berlin, 11 September 1947.

107   BAB/RKK 2703/0020/33, Licensing Control Section, PR/ISC Regional Staff, Land Niedersachsen, 6 October 1947.

108   See Blume's *Reichsforschungsrat* file in the Bundesarchiv, Berlin. On the place of the *Hauptstelle Musik* in the Nazi party apparatus see de Vries, *Sonderstab Musik*, pp. 39–48.

have taken a different view? These will remain hypothetical questions. As for certain other notorious Nazi musicologists, who were quickly reinstated in the British Zone, like Fellerer in Cologne, and Gerber in Göttingen, we must presume that the British were unaware of the full extent of their wartime activities.[109]

The complexity of each individual case makes generalisation unwise, and suggests that any summary judgements must be cautious. To imagine denazification, in the British Zone – or any other – as lenient, congenial, or problem-free is not exactly inaccurate. It does suggest, though, that the occupiers could not be bothered, and this is to misread the situation altogether. It also underestimates the extent of the task. None of the Allies could employ suitably skilled personnel in anything like the numbers needed to reconstruct the career of each individual musician or musicologist. Clearly, it was more important to the British to refashion intellectual life in Germany than to persecute individual scholars, just as it was more important to have high quality musical performance in the public sphere than to persecute individual musicians.

A symbolic moment in the rehabilitation of German music came in October 1947, with the return of Richard Strauss to London, where he received a hero's welcome, although his denazification in the American Zone was still pending. Prior to this, his music had already been broadcast by the newly established BBC Third Programme, and played at the Promenade concerts in London in 1946.[110] By this time, in the British Zone, almost all the musicians formerly excluded from employment were back at work. In 1948, the British, with varying degrees of dissatisfaction, turned the process of denazification over to the Germans, creating committees to license theatre and music personnel.[111] This devolution of authority to regional bodies representing different interest groups was in line with overall British policy in local government, education, and broadcasting. Brian Dunn was responsible for overseeing these committees. On paper, he was demanding, referring to conductors in particular. The committees were 'to prevent persons who were politically undesirable from gaining positions of influence in the theatrical and musical world'. Conductors, in particular, 'must be individuals of the highest political integrity'.[112] Dunn's report on a conference in Cologne to coordinate the work of these committees revealed though

---

109   Gerber was cleared as early as January 1946. TNA/PRO/FO 1050/337, Murray (for Director, Education Branch) to Rektor, Göttingen University, 19 January 1946, Appendix E.

110   Humphrey Carpenter, *The Envy of the World: Fifty Years of the BBC Third Programme and Radio 3 1946–1996* (London: Weidenfeld and Nicolson, 1996), pp. 48–9. As late as December 1946, the Home Office and the Ministry of Labour ruled that possibly compromised German musicians were not welcome in Britain. See BBC/WAC R27/68, Hynd, Control Office for Germany and Austria, to Haley, 28 September 1946, and 23 December 1946.

111   TNA/PRO/FO 1056/151, Military Government – Germany, British Zone of Control, Ordinance No. 107.

112
TNA/PRO/FO 1056/147, Directive to Land Niedersachsen Theatre and Music Committee, February 1948.

a different approach in practice: 'I carefully avoided any discussion of denazification as I felt this beyond my terms of reference.'[113]

The Intelligence Branch carried through a final purge of German press and radio in the British Zone in 1947 and 1948, but was put under increasing pressure to leave things be. Sely was told in 1948 that he had no authority to interfere in denazification processes.[114] He put up a committed rearguard action, but denazification in music was effectively over. As the immediate reality of the war faded, British attitudes became more cynical. By 1949, a senior licensing official could write to his superior: 'It is generally accepted that denazification in the British Zone has become a pure farce.'[115]

'Une Véritable Révolution'?

Surviving documentation on denazification in the French Zone is limited; all individual files are still classified. From the fragmentary material that can be examined, it is clear that the French were profoundly sceptical about the idea of denazifying individual German musicians, but were determined to restructure the musical repertoire. A report on denazification compiled by Jean Arnaud in January 1947 made clear these different priorities.[116] He had little to say on individual musicians, beyond noting the high numbers of Party members in professional orchestras all over Germany, and observing that even the Americans had abandoned their early commitment to excluding them. Admitting that the showpiece orchestra of the French Zone, the *Grande Orchestre du SWF*, still had 30 ex-Nazis amongst its 95 members, Arnaud argued that this reflected no more than the 30 per cent proportion accepted in other Zones (pp. 13–14). He had more to say on its repertoire. Proceeding from a recognition of 'the considerable influence of music on the German character', he reported that the French had carried out 'a veritable revolution'. The performance of Wagner had not been permitted, and as far as possible, nor had symphonic music, which encouraged the vanity and pretension of the Germans, Bruckner being an example.[117] Even the imitators of Wagner and Strauss had been banned. Arguing that 'certain traditional German music doubtless had some responsibility for German

---

113   TNA/PRO/FO 1056/147, Report on Conference with Länder Kulturreferenten on the implementation of Ordinance 107, June 1948.

114   TNA/PRO/FO 1056/268, Gibson, Deputy Regional Commissioner, Hansestadt Hamburg, to IS Regional Staff, 1948.

115   TNA/PRO/FO 1056/268, Licensing Adviser, Zonal Offices of Information Services, to Deputy Chief, ISD, 9 March 1949.

116   AOFC/AC 857/5, Rapport sur l'oeuvre de démilitarisation, dénazification et de démocratisation entreprise par la Direction de l'Information, 8 January 1947. Page references are given in the text.

117   Curiously, when tackled by the Bruckner Gesellschaft in Vienna in July 1947 about the censorship of Bruckner in the French Zone, Thimonnier denied that this had occurred. AOFC/AC 519/2, Chef du BSM to President, Bruckner Gesellschaft, 23 September 1947.

nationalism and militarism', Arnaud explained why contemporary composers like Müller, Trunk, and Kilpinen, were censored: 'We are trying to eliminate from our programmes musicians compromised spiritually by Germanic pride.'[118] Similar considerations had been applied to light music: 'All popular songs and chants disseminated under the Third Reich, as well as all productions in public concerts organised by Goebbels which are falsely sentimental and in bad taste, have been banned.' (pp. 16–17)

The French put the demands of their broader cultural programme before denazification. This was particularly apparent in publishing. Intensely conscious that, compared to other Zones, they had limited musical resources, the French quickly made a special investigation of the music publishers, Schotts, in Mainz. Early in November 1945, General Bouley reported on interviews conducted with its directors, the brothers Ludwig and Willy Strecker. Apparently, although the firm's presses were partly damaged, all of its stocks of music had been preserved. Bouley reckoned that with 30 tons of paper, production could be quickly restarted, and reach 70 per cent of pre-war output by the end of the year. The Strecker brothers had made a favourable impression, and appeared to be good anti-fascists with an international outlook; both spoke perfect French.[119] Schmittlein confirmed that Schotts should be revived as quickly as possible, to facilitate the distribution of French music in Germany, and to compensate for shortages in sheet music in the French Zone. The necessary paper would be supplied; 75 percent of new production and 50 per cent of existing stocks would be reserved for the French Zone.[120] The French could have taken a different view. Schotts had been a major publisher of Nazi and militarist music, as must have been evident from even a cursory examination of their catalogues. The Strecker brothers may have spoken excellent French, but they had not made Schotts Germany's largest music publisher before 1945 by resisting the Nazis. Ludwig was apparently a Party member, and Willy had written enthusiastically about the Nazis to Stravinsky in April 1933: 'This movement has so much that is healthy and positive about it ... a welcome cleaning-up has been undertaken ... in an attempt to restore decency and order'.[121] In 1947, Schotts restarted publication of the journal *Melos*, which quickly resumed its pre-1933 position as the leading voice of the avant-garde in Germany.

French denazification of musicians was also linked with the experience of collaboration in Occupied France between 1940 and 1944. Alone amongst the Allies, the French had experience of denazifying their own musicians before they arrived in Germany. They appear to have been more punitive with their own collaborators in

---

118　Müller, Trunk, and Kilpinen were all composers popular with the Nazis. Kilpinen was a Finnish national.

119　AOFC/AC 490/8, Bouley, Délégué Supérieure pour le Gouvernement Militaire de Hesse-Palatinat, to l'Administrateur Adjoint pour le GMZFO, 3 November 1945.

120　AOFC/AC 490/8, Schmittlein to Bouley, 26 November 1945.

121　Cited in Robert Craft, *Stravinsky: Selected Correspondence*, (London and Boston: Faber, 1985), **3**, p. 218.

France than they were with ex-Nazis in Germany.[122] By August 1945, the Provisional Government had drawn up lists of French musicians who had worked for Radio Paris during the war. Those judged to have collaborated for political reasons were banned from further broadcasting for life; the many who had merely taken part in broadcast musical performances were excluded for 15 days per broadcast.[123] By May 1946 many new names had been added to these lists, which were sent to Baden-Baden, to prevent these excluded French musicians from getting work in Germany.[124] Curiously though, almost a year into their occupation, the French had produced no parallel lists of compromised German musicians, and were reliant on American lists.[125] Possession of the American lists did not mean that they acted upon them. An internal report, quoting a German priest, compared the French approach with the American one: 'In contrast, the Americans, with their extensive methods of purging, their inhuman bureaucracy, and the work of their police, are starting to create … sentiments of bitter hatred and resistance.'[126]

Almost as soon as they decently could, the French turned over responsibility for vetting musicians to local committees, which included officers from the Office of Drama and Music and representatives from German cultural circles. From surviving documents it is clear that these committees were concerned first and foremost with artistic standards, and only marginally with political issues. The punishment of ex-Nazis was devolved to *Spruchkammern*, which could be expected to err on the side of leniency. Thimonnier recommended to Schmittlein as early as April 1946 that denazification in theatre and music should be handed over to the Germans.[127] Significantly, French *Fragebögen*, unlike the British and American ones, did not list the Reich Chamber of Culture, or any of its branches as Nazi Party organisations.[128]

French pragmatism is clearly shown in their treatment of the SWF orchestra. A list of its members in March 1946 shows that 27 out of 51 were ex-Nazis. To turn this into an acceptable proportion, the French simply added other non-Nazis. By the end of June, the orchestra had 90 members; of the 27 former Nazis, only two, Willi Maurer and Hermann Schober, were no longer employed.[129] In other individual cases

122   This whole area has only recently attracted historiographical attention in France. See 'La Vie Musicale sous l'Occupation', *Journal du Vingtième Siècle* (February 2000), pp. 142–3.

123   AOFC/AC 596/1, Ministère de l'Information, Republique Française, Note de Service No. 114, 8 August 1945.

124   AOFC/AC 596/1, Liste à Jour, 1 May 1946.

125   See AOFC/AC 490/8, Bouley, Délégué Supérieur pour le Gouvernement Militaire de Hesse-Palatinat to l'Administrateur Général Adjoint pour le GMZFO, 11 February 1946.

126   *GMZF, Commandement en chef Français en Allemagne, Témoignages et Interrogatoires*, 17 (December 1945), p. 6.

127   AOFC/AC 524/2, Chef du BSM to Directeur de l'Education Publique, 13 May 1946, p. 3.

128   See the examples in AOFC/AC 519/2.

129   AOFC/AC 600/5, Liste der Orchestermitglieder, 28 March 1946, and Liste des Orchesters, 22 June 1946.

the demands of cultural propaganda were clearly paramount. Phillip Wüst, former Musical Director of the Stuttgart Theatre, was blacklisted by the Americans and the Soviets, but found employment with the French as the director of the *Musique Philharmonique Sarrois*. The French considered the Saar such an important area, and were so short of talented conductors, that they insisted on retaining him, even though the Americans complained.[130] Likewise, they made a determined effort to get Furtwängler to conduct in Baden-Baden in July 1946, even though the Americans and British still objected to his appearing in public.[131]

No case highlights the complexities of denazification in the French Zone better than that of Heinrich Strobel, now remembered as a champion of modernism in the 1920s, and 'high priest of the music scene'[132] in West Germany after 1945. Strobel was an early biographer of Hindemith, and the editor of *Melos* in the Weimar Republic. As a champion of modernism and of the international avant-garde, he was publicly identified by the Nazis as a 'cultural bolshevist'. Strobel also had a Jewish wife. He left Germany after 1933, and found refuge in Paris. From 1940, he worked as musical correspondent for the *Pariser Zeitung*, a newspaper published for the German community in Occupied France. Most of Strobel's contributions were studiously neutral in tone, and he was able to write about music with greater latitude than he would have enjoyed in Germany itself.

The *Pariser Zeitung*, though, was a mouthpiece for an Occupying Power, which regarded French music as decadent and racially inferior; its columns were filled with crude Nazi propaganda. It was constantly anti-Semitic, anti-Bolshevik, anti-British, and anti-American. It paid homage to the personality cult of the *Führer*. Strobel's articles sit alongside other contributions of a decidedly less civilised nature. Thus in June 1944, a piece of his on Richard Strauss appeared in the same issue as an article on 'Jewish Invasion Societies' in London.[133] On occasion, Strobel was drawn into Nazi and pan-German discourse. In May 1942, he went to Vienna to report on a festival of contemporary music dedicated to the memory of HJ composers who had died in action, like Bräutigam and Jörns. He paid fulsome tribute to them in the *Pariser Zeitung*.[134] In June 1944, as the Allies fought to consolidate the Normandy beachhead, Strobel rhapsodised about the recent European tour of the Berlin Philharmonic, which had demonstrated 'the inviolable heights of German artistic practice, and the ethical power of German music which spans a continent'. [135] In

---

130   AOFC/AC 508/5, Colombet, French Liaison ICD, USFET, to Acting Chief ICD, 3 January 1946, and AOFC/AC 519/2, Le Commissaire Principal, Chef du Service Régional des Renseignements Généraux, 4 April 1946.

131   See AOFC Berlin, GFCC, caisse 131/5, Extintor Vienne to Contrôle Berlin, Section Information, 19 July 1946 and 20 July 1946; also AOFC/AC 519/2, Strobel to Furtwängler, 5 August 1946.

132   Hans-Werner Henze, *Music and Politics: Collected writings 1953-81* (trans. Labanyi, London: Faber, 1982), p. 37.

133   *Pariser Zeitung*, 10/11 June 1944.

134   *Pariser Zeitung*, 6 May 1942.

135   *Pariser Zeitung*, 14 June 1944.

August 1945, the French, determined to use radio for the diffusion of French culture and international modernism, appointed Strobel Artistic Director at the SWF in Baden-Baden. In the end, they were more concerned with the promotion of their own music, and with building good relationships in Germany, than in the punishment of individuals such as Strobel, whose transgressions were perhaps deemed minor.

A consequence of their stance was sporadic criticism by the Americans and the British, and on occasion the French were embarrassed. One such instance was that of Franz Grothe, who, after falsifying his *Fragebogen*, had left the American Zone to work in the more congenial climate in Baden-Baden.[136] Grothe was a talented jazz pianist and film music composer who had worked closely with Goebbels, particularly after 1941, in creating jazz music for propaganda broadcasts to Britain. This might be considered trivial, but when one considers the anti-Semitic content of some of these broadcasts, and the genuine attitude of the Nazis towards jazz, it can be seen as a particularly disgraceful kind of musical prostitution. Another example prompted a personal intervention from General Koenig, the French C-in-C in Germany. The French had been particularly energetic in rebuilding musical education, opening 'conservatories' and 'high schools' throughout their Zone.[137] They were particularly pleased that these attracted students from all over Germany, noting that they were 'excellent auxiliaries of our cultural propaganda'.[138] Although Thimonnier had urged that the teaching staff in these institutions be closely vetted,[139] it was embarrassing to have the British point out that Ernst von Knorr, a professor at the Trossingen Academy, had been a writer of Nazi songs.[140]

'The Most Tolerant (with Artists) are the Russians'[141]

If the French were occasionally embarrassed, and felt at least some residual obligation to the Americans and the British, the Soviets did not. They were not prepared to take lectures on denazification from the capitalists, and blithely went their own way. To an extent they shared the German veneration for artists and were prepared to treat them differently from other mortals. Even more than the French, the Soviets

---

136   AOFC Berlin , GFCC caisse 131/3, Peeples (for Director ICD) to Silbert, Chief of Information Section, Political Division, GFCC, 12 September 1946, p. 3.

137   AOFC/AC 526/2, Rapport sur l'Activité des Services de l'Information (1945-1949), 15 June 1949, p. 20.

138   AOFC/AC 526/2, Rapport sur l'Activité de la Division de l'Information pendant le mois d'Octobre 1948, 8 November 1948, p. 4.

139   AOFC/AC 519/2, Chef du BSM to le Directeur de l'Education Publique, 26 September 1947.

140   AOFC/AC 519/2, Koenig to le Délégué Supérieure pour le Gouvernement Militaire du Würtemberg, 6 January 1948; also BAB/RKK 2703/0122/45, Clare to Général Hombourger, 17 December 1947.

141   SAAdK, Hans-Heinz-Stuckenschmidt-Archiv, Korrespondenz, 473, Stuckenschmidt to Gurlitt, 18 December 1947.

overlooked previous Nazi associations in those cases where they wanted the services of prestigious German musicians for cultural reconstruction. All over the Soviet Zone after May 1945, compromised musicians were surprised to find that they were treated with courtesy, and invited to resume public concerts. In Weimar, Abendroth was able to take up the baton. In Dresden and Leipzig, surviving members of the *Kreuzchor* and *Thomanerchor* had to get rid of their HJ uniforms, but were able to carry on their music-making without interruption. Rudolf Mauersberger was allowed to lead the *Kreuzchor* in a performance of his *Funeral Ode on the Destruction of Dresden* on 4 August 1945.[142] Josef Keilberth had conducted in Prague during the war, and served as 'Leader' (*Landesleiter*) of the Reich Music Chamber in the 'Protectorate' of Bohemia-Moravia.[143] In July 1945, he was appointed to conduct the Dresden State Orchestra, an initiative of the KPD leader in Saxony, Hermann Matern – a move that was sanctioned by Captain Peresvetov, the Soviet cultural officer in Dresden.[144] In Berlin, Furtwängler was invited to direct the State Opera. In February 1946, the *Kulturbund*'s journal *Aufbau* published an article defending his record under the Nazis.[145] The Soviets were also keen to mobilise less exalted German intellectuals. The first issue of the *Kulturbund*'s internal newsletter, *Die Aussprache*, opened a debate on whether nominal Nazis should be admitted to the *Kulturbund*, arguing that the time had come for forgiveness. Former NSDAP members were allowed to join after March 1947. SMAD Order No. 201, in August 1947, allowed ex-Nazis to enter many previously restricted occupations.

This does not mean that there was no denazification of musicians in the Soviet Zone. Individuals with a dubious record who were regarded as dispensable, or who fell foul of local Soviet authorities, or local KPD (and later SED) officials, might find themselves harshly treated. One such was the renowned Bach scholar and former

---

142   The record on Mauersberger is contradictory, and illustrates the difficulties faced by all investigations into individual musicians and their record under Hitler. One representation is that he was a non-political director, dedicated to his choir and to sacred music – see Erna Hofmann and Ingo Zimmerman (eds), *Begegnungen mit Rudolf Mauersberger* (Berlin: Evangelische Verlagsanstalt, 1964). According to a contemporary West German publication, Mauersberger joined the NSDAP in 1933, and was given membership No. 2,451,659 – see Untersuchungsausschuß Freiheitlicher Juristen (ed.), *Ehemalige Nationalsozialisten in Pankows Diensten* (Berlin: no publisher given, 1965), p. 297. A British educationalist in Germany noted that, in 1947, Mauersberger refused to conduct his choir in West Berlin for fear that he would be arrested by the Americans – see Edith Davis, 'British Policy and the Schools', Arthur Hearnden (ed.), *The British in Germany: Educational Reconstruction after 1945* (London: Hamilton, 1978), pp. 95–107. When this author enquired at the Bundesarchiv in Berlin for the Reich Chamber of Culture files on Mauersberger, he was told that there were none available. Mauersberger's *Funeral Ode* is still performed annually on the anniversary of the RAF attack.

143   *Karlsbader Tages Zeitung*, 20 July 1941.

144   Laux, *Nachklang*, pp. 313ff.

145   Erwin Kroll, 'Wilhelm Furtwängler zum 60. Geburtstag', *Aufbau*, 1946/2, pp. 213–14.

Thomaskantor Karl Straube. He had indeed been an NSDAP *Altgardist*, and had taken the *Thomanerchor* into the HJ, where it played an important ceremonial role. Straube directed the choir in front of the assembled Reich leadership of the HJ and BDM in Brunswick in May 1939.[146] Although retired since 1940, Straube was denied his pension after 1945, despite protests from many quarters. Even after his death in 1950, his wife was denied the pension.[147] An obscure Leipzig composer, Theodor Blumer, is an example from among the many lesser musicians who suffered. He had been an NSDAP member, and despite joining the SED in 1946, remained until October 1948 on a list of 'banned composers and conductors',[148] and was accordingly prevented from resuming work with the radio in Dresden and Leipzig. Blumer wrote repeatedly to the government in Saxony, to the SED authorities in Berlin, and later to Otto Grotewohl, protesting about this. His wife Hildegard Ostkamp-Blumer, an opera singer, felt she was also being persecuted because of her husband's past sins, and wrote to Justice Minister Rolf Liebler in 1950: 'My husband was a small representative in the composers' section of the Reich Music Chamber, and that seems to have been a crime. Professor Abendroth was a section leader in the Reich Music Chamber.'[149] Their protests were to no avail. Both felt persecuted by local SED official Rudolf Hartig, who had been working in Leipzig when their troubles commenced. Ostkamp-Blumer wrote bitterly to him in 1952: 'You have denied my husband an existence since '45, and now it is also finally the same with me.'[150]

Blumer was not an isolated example. Well into the early 1950s, by which time ex-Nazi musicians were being comfortably reintegrated into West German society, individuals looking for work in the GDR were being rejected on the grounds of their past activities and affiliations. The pianist Friedrich Wührer, recommended for an academy teaching post by the conductor Heinz Bongartz in 1952, was turned down as a former leading Nazi in Austria.[151]

Particularly in Berlin, where the Soviets had to, in some measure, cooperate with their former Allies, ex-Nazis faced lengthy proceedings. The Chamber of Artists, established with Soviet permission directly after the surrender in May 1945, was allowed by the Allies to constitute a 'Berlin Denazification Commission for Artists'. This body, chaired by Alex Vogel, prepared individual cases, and Wolfgang Schmidt acted as the public prosecutor.[152] The experience of Max Butting in Berlin illustrates the particular difficulties faced by musicians there. Butting, a socialist who made a name for himself as a composer for radio in the 1920s, appears today as a nominal

---

146 Kaufmann, *Orgel und Nationalsozialismus*, p. 118.

147 See the correspondence on Straube in SAPMO-BArch DY 27/1568.

148 SAPMO-Barch DR 1/154, Sekretariat Otto Grotewohls, 22 July 1950. I have not seen a copy of this list.

149 SAPMO-Barch DR 1/154, Ostkamp-Blumer to Liebler, 20 April 1950.

150 SAPMO-Barch DR 1/154, Ostkamp-Blumer to Hartig, 7 February 1952.

151 See SAPMO-BArch DR 1/286, Bongartz to Hartig, 30 May 1952, and Knepler to Hartig, 20 June 1952.

152 On Vogel, Schmidt, and the *Kammer der Kunstschaffenden*, see Schivelbusch, *Cold Crater*, pp. 39ff, and Clare, *Berlin Days*, pp. 73ff.

Nazi, and an example of musical inner emigration. He was the last artist elected to the Prussian Academy of the Arts before the Nazis came to power, and his music was entirely shunned after 1933. Unlike other composers who were suspect to the the Nazis on racial, political, or aesthetic grounds, but who nonetheless succeeded in getting their music performed, published, and broadcast in Germany between 1933 and 1945; and unlike so many compromised by the content of their music, or by appearance at Party ceremonies, Butting withdrew altogether from musical life. For reasons that are still unclear, he joined the NSDAP in 1940, and was therefore called before the Denazification Commission. Butting was fortunate in that friends, including fellow composers Heinz Tiessen and Joseph Haas, provided testimony supporting his claim to have maintained an anti-fascist stance throughout the Nazi years. Walther Stehr described how Butting had taken considerable risks in helping him after he was arrested and sentenced to death in the final weeks of the war; without Butting's help, he argued, he might well have been executed. Not until April 1947 was Butting cleared; he immediately joined the *Kulturbund*'s Music Commission, and subsequently played a leading role in the musical culture of the GDR.[153]

'White, Grey, and Black'

In the last twenty years, in a sequence that recalls on a larger scale events in Michael Verhoeven's film *Das schreckliche Mädchen* (1989), the 'brown history' of Germany's musicians, and with it the failures of denazification, have been painfully revealed. After Josef Wulf's controversial documentation of 1963, it was not until 1982 that Fred Prieberg's groundbreaking work reopened the question of collaboration between Nazism and the musical professions. In 1992, Michael Kater revealed how some of Germany's leading jazzmen worked with Goebbels, and he has since turned an equally unsparing searchlight on the collaboration of other musicians. The way in which Germany's Protestant church musicians allowed their movements for renewal and purification to be taken over by Nazism after 1933 has been controversially explored by Günther Hartmann, and more recently by Michael Kaufmann, who has explored the links between the 'Organ Movement' of the 1920s and music in the rituals of the Nazi Party and Hitler Youth.[154] The scandal of Göttingen musicologist Wolfgang Boetticher, exposed by Willem de Vries as having worked for Rosenberg's *Sonderstab Musik*[155], has been rapidly overtaken by Pamela Potter's larger investigation of continuities in German musicology before 1933 and

---

153   SAAdK Max-Butting-Archiv, Korrespondenz Mappe 1, 1920–1945, Stehr to Butting, 28 September 1945, and Haas to Butting, 12 December 1945; SAAdK Heinz-Tiessen-Archiv, Korrespondenz Max Butting, Tiessen to Butting, 7 May 1947. See also the documents in BAB/RKK 2701/0003/11. Butting provided a less than full account in his memoir *Musikgeschichte, die ich miterlebte* (Berlin: Henschelverlag, 1955).

154   Günther Hartmann, *Karl Straube und seine Schule: "das Ganze ist ein Mythos"* (Bonn: Verlag für Systematische Musikwissenschaft, 1991)

155   See De Vries, *Sonderstab Musik*, pp. 181–202.

after 1945. This body of work has not overcome the reluctance of some German individuals and institutions to face up to the past, as is evidenced by the difficulties these researchers have faced. It is still more comfortable for many to believe that music, like religion, was an area of refuge, somehow untainted by Nazism.

One could argue that denazification in music was actually very successful, in that Nazism in musicological analysis, in composition, and in performance either stopped in 1945, or was driven into such disguised pathways as to be hidden from all but the most alert and inquisitive eyes and ears. Only a single piece of music written and celebrated in Nazi Germany has maintained its place in the repertoire of choirs and orchestras world-wide, and is currently reaching ever wider audiences because of its use in commercial advertising, in public ceremonies, and in television programmes: Carl Orff's *Carmina Burana*. Judging from the excerpts typically used by advertisers and programmers, it appears to be an elemental, dramatic excitement that Orff articulated so successfully, presumably what the *Völkischer Beobachter*'s reviewer had in mind in 1940 when he described *Carmina Burana* as 'the music, clear, storming, and indeed always more disciplined in its stance, that our time is longing for'.[156] It would be more difficult to argue that this is 'Nazi music', and that the emotions it stirs in millions of people from different cultures are Nazi emotions. On the whole, though, and perhaps fortunately, tastes and fashions in popular music have changed since the 1930s, and the tuneful Nazi songs that millions obviously enjoyed then seem curiously dated today. Even amongst skinheads and neo-Nazis, marching songs like the *Horst-Wessel-Lied* do not have anything like the enormous suggestive power they had in Nazi Germany.

From other perspectives, it is clear, though, that denazification was a failure. In all Zones, and after 1949 in the East as well as the West, there were composers, conductors, performers, and musicologists who resumed their careers and flourished, despite extensive involvement with Nazism. Given that in almost all cases they appear, though, to have abandoned Nazism as a political creed, and instead seem to have adopted historical materialism, a pro-Western liberalism, or an Olympian detachment from politics, we have to ask whether this issue of their pasts mattered at all. Should it concern us today that some music academies in post-war Germany were headed by men who had written Nazi music, or that university departments were dominated by scholars who had previously argued that Jewish, Negro, or Slavic composers could not achieve greatness because of their racial origins? Should we even be surprised that writers of Hitler Youth songs turned after 1945 to writing songs for the 'Free German Youth' in the GDR, or for schoolchildren in the Federal Republic? These continuities do matter, on a number of levels.

Firstly, there is the matter of the falsification of history involved. No conscientious researcher can rest content with the way in which post-war historiography has misrepresented aspects of German music under Nazism. It will no longer do to pretend that Protestant church music was solely a place of shelter or protection from

---

156   *Völkischer Beobachter*, 7 October 1940, cited in an advertisement for Schotts Söhne, *Zeitschrift für Musik*, December 1940, p. 803.

Nazism between 1933 and 1945.[157] Texts set by Handel were falsified to support Nazi racism and the cult of the *Führer*. Church composers and priests adapted liturgical music to the pagan rituals of the Nazi Party, and Germany's elite church choirs were incorporated into the Hitler Youth.[158] At a more general level, *Musik in Geschichte und Gegenwart*, published between 1949 and 1986, is still used as a standard reference all over the world. It is not only worrying that many contributors, from the editor downward, were compromised, but also that so many individual articles deliberately misrepresented musical history by omission and selection. This kind of work stands at the critical interface between academic research and popular consciousness. Its entries on German music, in particular, have found their way into countless publications in English, not least into *MGG*'s English language analogue, the *New Grove Encyclopedia of Music and Musicians*. How many programme notes, record and CD sleeves, and radio programmes have distilled material from *MGG* for a wider public since its publication!

One can argue that a more effective denazification might have prevented this. Without invoking the need for a crude academic censorship, one can question the integrity of German universities, which could apparently rest easily with scholars who could so dramatically trim their sails to suit the political needs of the time. How can we respect academics who shifted so quickly from a concern with 'music and race' to Marxism, or to the place of music 'in the development of the Occidental spirit'? Or a journalist who was prepared to propagate the Zhdanov decree in Germany in 1948, but who ten years' previously had asked publicly whether the modernist composer Boris Blacher was 'degenerate or not degenerate?'[159] Similar suspicions are aroused from an artistic perspective. How do we judge composers who found themselves in tune with the vulgarity of Nazi aesthetics, and expressed agreement with its racially oriented hostility to modernism, but subsequently altered their compositional style to pose as twelve-toners, serialists, or social realists? What does it say about German music academies that so many teachers of composition had demonstrated their own

---

157   See Oskar Söhngen, *Die Wiedergeburt der Kirchenmusik* (Kassel: Bärenreiter, 1953), and *Kämpfende Kirchenmusik* (Kassel: Bärenreiter, 1954), for early post-war examples of this tendency. Söhngen, before and after 1945 was a leading figure in German Protestant church music. His post-war accounts should be read alongside some of his offerings from the 1930s, like 'Zum 50. Geburtstag des Führers', *Kirchenmusikalische Mitteilungen*, Ausgabe A, 15/16, March/April 1939, pp. 267–9. This contains, amongst paragraphs of obsequious flattery of Hitler, the statement 'The Führer … should know that the German Protestant Church in all its branches, with its whole priesthood and all its congregations, declares its allegiance, never to be destroyed, to him and his work.' (p. 268)

158   See the exploration of certain facets of this relationship by Doris Bergen, 'Hosanna or "Hilf, O Herr Uns": National Identity, the German Christian Movement, and the "Dejudaization" of Sacred Music in the Third Reich', Applegate and Potter, *Music and German National Identity*, pp. 205–17.

159   See *Leipziger Neueste Nachrichten*, 26 May 1938, cited in Henrich Heribert (ed.), *Blacher Boris, 1903–1975: Dokumente zu Leben und Werk* (Berlin: Henschel, 1993), p. 79.

prowess by writing Hitler Youth songs or festive Nazi music? Should they have been allowed to resume positions of educational influence?

In the final analysis, the answer to these questions must hinge on the nature of any such links with Nazism. It has been argued that most of these kinds of collaboration were essentially harmless. We are, after all, not speaking here of executioners who pulled triggers, or doctors, lawyers, or policemen who were accomplices to murder. We can accept that many of the musical collaborators, including most of those individually named here, were not fervent Nazis. Typically, far more prominent in their intellectual and political make-ups were nationalism, militarism, and anti-Communism. In many cases they were men who found their German national conservatism sympathetic to large areas of Nazi ideology, and turned a blind eye to the paganism, intellectual sterility, aesthetic banality, and the criminality of Nazism. To argue that by doing so they contributed to and were linked with the worst excesses of Nazism, is not to make a case for some kind of German exceptionalism, but rather to suggest the role of individual and collective agency in the evolution of culture. Music in Germany between 1933 and 1945 can no more be separated from Nazism than religion, law, or medicine.

The Americans have been particularly criticised for their denazification programme. We should bear in mind that between 1945 and 1948, they had much to gain from a relaxation of their purges. Denazification in music brought them no commercial advantages. By pretending that musicians were apolitical, they could have won popularity with the German population, and by employing musicians who had been successful under the Nazis, they could have given much needed impetus to their own cultural propaganda. What is striking now is the number of musicians with Nazi connections being belatedly 'exposed' by contemporary researchers who had been, between 1945 and 1947, listed by the Americans as 'Black', or 'Grey – Unacceptable'. McClure and his colleagues deserve some credit for attempting, however unsuccessfully, to argue that artists had a wider social responsibility, and that those who had consorted with, profited from, and given cultural legitimacy to a criminal movement should be confronted with this. Mass murder, enslavement, and conquest had been accompanied by professional musicians playing Beethoven and Wagner, and by youthful singing that exalted racism and violence. The Americans alone demanded that the German people should face these unpalatable truths.

Chapter Three

Anti-Fascism and Music

New musical languages were needed in Germany after May 1945, and here there was a happy coincidence of Allied and German self-interest. German musicians were, on the whole, happy to be in contact again with international music culture; employment as a musician, whether at a municipal opera house or an Allied radio station, was, in the first few months after the war, a comparatively happy situation. The shattered population was eager to find some refuge in music, and people often walked for miles to get to concerts in partially repaired halls. Before the currency reform of 1948, tickets for concerts were virtually free in the black market economy. For a brief period, concert-going was not restricted to the better off. Almost immediately, three currents asserted themselves. Firstly there was a return to the classics. All over Germany, inaugural post-war concerts included works by Beethoven, Mozart, and in churches, by Bach. These composers could be accepted by the Allies as artists who had spoken for all of humanity, and by Germans as representatives of their nation whose greatness transcended the horror of Nazism. Within months of the surrender, the cycles of Beethoven and Brahms symphonies which dominated post-war concert programmes in Germany had begun. Photographs of pensive listeners in shattered buildings listening to Beethoven have taken on an iconic status in representations of post-war German cultural history.

Almost as uncontroversial was the reinstatement of those composers banned by the Nazis purely on racial grounds – above all Mendelssohn, Tchaikovsky, and, to a lesser degree, Mahler. In the summer of 1945, to perform or broadcast a Mendelssohn overture or a Tchaikovsky symphony was to make an anti-fascist statement, one whose content was so obvious as to render further elaboration unnecessary. William Strang's report on the British Zone in July 1945 has already been referred to. In a long document, concerned mainly with what appeared almost insuperable economic and political problems, this passage stands out:

> In one studio we witnessed the German musical director, the German conductor, and the British control officer listening with great pride and pleasure to the first recording of a Mahler symphony, and it was very evident that in this sphere at least there are no political barriers to the closest cooperation between ourselves and the Germans.[1]

The situation was apparently less harmonious in Munich. Early in August, the Americans reported:

---

1   TNA/PRO/FO 898/401, Strang to Secretary of State, 11 July 1945, p. 17.

The first concert of the Staatsorchester ... appeared to be aimed at us, or their rivals the Philharmonic ... the program consisted of "parade" pieces which were probably played countless times under the Nazis ... From now on, Mr. Roland's suggestion will be enforced, that every program contain at least one number "verboten" under Hitler.[2]

It seems, though, that Germans orchestras were already wise to this, and now simply started all concerts with a Mendelssohn overture, typically pieces greatly missed since 1933. The Munich Detachment wrote: 'the Mendelssohn situation has become critical, ridiculous, and urgent.'[3] Nonetheless Mendelssohn, above all, continued to serve as a symbol of anti-fascism in the post-war period. In July 1945 Yehudi Menuhin toured the British Zone with Benjamin Britten, playing in Belsen and other camps for 'displaced persons'. During a brief stay in Hamburg, he broadcast a performance of the Mendelssohn Violin Concerto.

The promotion of modernism was more controversial. Although it served more strongly than Mendelssohn's essentially Protestant music as a symbolic anti-Nazi language, most modernist music was far less popular with the German public. It was also more obviously recognisable as Allied cultural propaganda, particularly where it intersected with the promotion of individual national composers. The early delight at hearing previously censored or unknown music – a sense of tasting forbidden fruit – could soon give way to weary tolerance, and even frustration with newly imposed orthodoxies. In any case, at the beginning, to espouse modernism was to demonstrate anti-fascist commitment, and military governments, new German municipal and regional authorities, as well as composers and conductors, rushed to demonstrate their avant-gardism. In Munich, not previously noted as a progressive musical city, the new Bavarian government often found its conservative inclinations in conflict with American 'reorientation' efforts. In education, there were constant confrontations. The Americans were frustrated in their attempts to avoid the politicisation of regional theatrical and cultural life. The censorship of Egk's *Abraxas* by the Bavarian authorities in 1948 might be seen as a symbol of American failure in this whole programme.[4]

In this context, the relationship between the Bavarian Government and the composer Karl Amadeus Hartmann is noteworthy. Hartmann had been interviewed by the Americans in Munich in June 1945. They found him to be of 'utmost integrity' and possessed of an 'astonishingly sound and fresh musical outlook',[5] and seized on his willingness to help implement their musical programme. In October 1945, under the patronage of the Bavarian State Opera, Hartmann started a series of modernist concerts, the *Musica Viva*, in the *Prinzregententheater*. Although typically portrayed

---

2   BHA/OMGB 10/48–1/5, Munich Detachment, 6870th DISCC, 5 August 1945. Will Roland was Chief of Film, Theater, and Music Control, 6870th DISCC.

3   BHA/OMGB 10/48–1/5, Munich Detachment, 6870th DISCC, Report, 10 August 1945. (Emphasis in the original)

4   Egk's ballet was censored because of a particular dance; the music was not an issue, and it will therefore not be discussed here. See Monod, *Settling Scores*, pp. 195–6.

5   BHA/OMGB 10/48–1/5, Music Section, Daily Report No. 3, 15 June 1945.

now as a landmark series, quintessentially representative of the changed artistic atmosphere in post-war Germany, it is clear from contemporary documents that Hartmann had great difficulty with the conservative Munich public. An early American assessment of his concerts spoke of poor attendances, and a chilly atmosphere.[6] The French noted sceptically, quoting the *Neue Zeitung* of 25 January 1946: 'The public is not used to this fare after the privation of these last years, and finds it to difficult to understand.'[7] A year later, Hartmann himself expressed similar sentiments to his long-time colleague, Hermann Scherchen.[8] The Bavarian Government, though, did not doubt the importance of the *Musica Viva*. Early in 1947, Culture Minister Alois Hundhammer was invited to serve as Patron of the series. Hundhammer, who agreed to this, was advised by State Secretary Sattler in convoluted and tautological prose:

> I believe that the support of contemporary music is of the greatest importance for our cultural politics. … The programme includes the most important works of modern music and doubtless presents an extraordinarily effective cultural propaganda for a progressive Bavarian cultural politics.[9]

These political alliances could also be reversed. While a conservative Bavarian government presumably felt that sponsorship of modern music was a relatively cheap gesture which could help its standing, others had to face more directly the effect this music had on audiences. The Association of those persecuted by the Nazi Regime in Bad Godesberg wrote in 1947 to the *Kulturbund* in Berlin asking for suggestions for a series of anti-fascist concerts. They had a problem though: Nazi sympathies were still strong in the area, and they asked the *Kulturbund* not to suggest Schoenberg or Hindemith, or anything that sounded like 'degenerate art'.[10]

These ironies were most apparent at the two places that have since become internationally recognised symbols of cultural freedom, Donaueschingen and Darmstadt, although this is not a theme that the huge literature on the musical avant-garde there explores. The French gave permission for the Donaueschingen Festival to resume in the summer of 1946, and it seems typical of their approach to denazification that they allowed its earlier director, the composer Hugo Herrmann, to resume his old functions. Under the Nazis, Donaueschingen had been turned into a celebration of Germanic festive and folk music. By 1937, Herrmann had so far

---

6   BHA/OMGB 10/48–1/5, HQ, 6870th DISCC, Weekly Report, 26 October 1945.

7   GMZFO, Direction de l'Information, *Les Nouvelles d'Allemagne*, 46 (9 March 1946).

8   Hartmann to Scherchen, 28 January 1947, cited in Bayerisches Staatsbibliothek (ed.), *Karl Amadeus Hartmann und die Musica Viva: Essays, bisher unveröffentliche Briefe an Hartmann, Katalog* (Munich: Piper, 1980), p. 316.

9   BHA/MK 50129, Sattler to Hartmann, 22 April 1947; Sattler, Veranstaltungen von zeitgenössischer Musik, 17 April 1947.

10   SAPMO-BArch DY 27/249, VVN-Ortsvereinigung Bad Godesberg to Kulturbund, 17 September 1947. Interestingly, the *Kulturbund* suggested asking the British-licensed radio in Cologne for help.

abandoned the ideals of the 1920s as to conduct the National Socialist Symphony Orchestra there, in a brown dinner jacket. In 1946 Herrmann put on the programme local composers like von Knorr, older friends like Joseph Haas, though making the appropriate gestures by also featuring Shostakovich and Piston. In 1947, his programme was worse than parochial. The German composers whose works were played, von Knorr, Gerster, Degen, Herrmann himself, were all compromised. The lone international representative was the Swiss composer Sutermeister, who had also worked in Germany during the war, achieving great popularity.[11] After this, the festival was stopped, reappearing in 1950, in different hands, and in changed circumstances.

More surprising is how this was mirrored in the American Zone. The origins of the Darmstadt Summer School are strangely unclear. A recent four-volume study says that 'only little is known about the founding of the Darmstadt Summer School'.[12] It reports, and dismisses, Wolfgang Fortner's claim in 1981 to have suggested the outline of the summer school to the Darmstadt *Kulturreferent*, Wolfgang Steinecke. It says virtually nothing about the involvement of American Military Government and Radio Frankfurt. What is particularly odd is that Fortner and Hermann Heiss, who led the composition classes at Darmstadt in the early post-war years, were both blacklisted by the Americans, and were not carrying out there what Toombs or McClure would have accepted as 'ordinary labor', but were rather in a public educational role. Heiss had written, in 1940, a 'fighter pilots' march', *Kein Tor der Welt ist uns zu hoch*, and his *Flieger-Fanfare* was on an American blacklist of songs.[13] Fortner had earlier written a song called *Tag der Machtübernahme*; he specialised in 'festive music' for the HJ, and conducted the HJ orchestra in Heidelberg. As we have seen, he was blacklisted well into 1947.[14] How ironic, then, that Steinecke's introduction

---

11   Even the French were concerned about Sutermeister. In July 1947, Thimonnier was asked to investigate his involvement with Goebbels' Propaganda Ministry during the war – see AOFC/AC 600/4, Ponnelle, Chef de la Section Radio, to Thimonnier, 11 July 1947. For details of programmes and performers at Donaueschingen see Josef Häusler, *Spiegel der neuen Musik, Donaueschingen: Chronik, Tendenzen, Werkbesprechungen* (Kassel: Bärenreiter, 1996), and Max Rieple, *Musik in Donaueschingen* (Constance: Rosgarten, 1959).

12   Gianmario Borio and Hermann Danuser (eds), *Im Zenit der Moderne – Die internationalen Ferienkurse für Neue Musik Darmstadt 1946–1966* (Freiburg im Breisgau: Rombach, 1997), **I**, p. 67.

13   GLAK/OMGWB 12/91–2/10, Blacklist of Songs, p. 1. Heiss, a former student of Hauer, was not a Nazi. By his own admission though, he had written a number of 'soldiers' songs', as well as 'commissions for the *Luftwaffe*', and other military compositions. See BAB/RKK 2341/0065/32, Fragebogen betr. Spende "künstlerdank", 22 June 1940. This was an application for a grant from a fund for artists, and it is clear from it that by this time Heiss was experiencing economic hardship.

14   Fortner's political history was revealed by Prieberg in 1984. By this time, his alibi had developed to the point where he was represented as an 'internal emigrant'. See 'Nach dem 'Endsieg' oder Musiker-Mimikry', Hanns-Werner Heister and Hans-Günter Klein (eds), *Musik und Musikpolitik im faschistischen Deutschland* (Frankfurt-am-Main: Fischer, 1984), pp. 297–305. In a job reference in 1937, Fortner was described by a Heidelberg HJ leader

to the 1946 Darmstadt Summer School explicitly positioned it in opposition to Nazi musical culture, in which 'march songs and festive music were seen as the highest ideals'.[15] Heiss was the first in post-war Germany to write extensively about twelve-tone music. At Darmstadt in 1946, he declared: 'We have today a unique opportunity, with our experience and knowledge, to preserve young people from wrong turnings and detours.'[16]

Fortner also turned rapidly to twelve-tone music. Alongside Heiss and Fortner, many of the composers whose music was played at Darmstadt in 1946 were compromised, such as Degen, Pepping, Distler, and Höffer. The piano class was taken in 1946 and 1947 by former NSDAP member Udo Dammert, who was certainly *persona non grata* with the Americans, having falsified his *Fragebogen*. In December 1946, an American report had said: 'Udo Dammert, pianist, gave a concert in Berchtesgaden after having been told not to perform in public. The case was not quite definite enough to jail him, but he is recommended for the black list and received explicit warning.'[17]

In 1947, Bruno Stürmer joined Fortner and the 'twelve tone apostle' Heiss at Darmstadt to take classes on chamber music,[18] despite having been moved by the Americans from 'Grey – Unacceptable' to 'Black' on their lists.[19] It has been asserted that the participants at the first Summer School were asked to fill in a form that asked 'Did you belong to the NSDAP or to one of its branches?'[20] If this was so, presumably Fortner, Dammert, and Stürmer simply denied their previous Nazi affiliations when they were first engaged to work at Darmstadt. One can only presume also that the Intelligence Branch of the ICD did not know about Darmstadt in any detail in either 1946 or 1947, and that it was not kept informed by either the Education Branch in Hesse, or by Radio Frankfurt, which sponsored the first courses. It is unthinkable that Toombs and McClure would have sanctioned blacklisted composers and soloists

---

as one who 'had fitted in splendidly with the community of the Hitler Youth'. BAB/RKK 2338/0015/06, NSDAP Gauleitung Berlin, Gau-Dozentenbundführer to Pg. Prof. Dr. Drissen, 18 December 1937. This suggests that he was more than a 'nominal' or unwilling participant in the HJ, as does his composition of 'festive string music' for the HJ in 1938. See *Hofmeisters Jahresverzeichnis*, **87**, 1938 (1939), p. 32.

15   'Einleitung zu den Kursen 1946', reprinted in Borio and Danuser, *Im Zenit der Moderne*, pp. 24–5.

16   Cited in *Ibid.*, p. 71.

17   BHA/OMGB 10/48–1/5, Munich Detachment, 6870th DISCC, Weekly Report, 12 December 1945. See also BAB/RKK 2703/0037/31.

18   Hans-Heinz Stuckenschmidt, 'Kranichstein, das Schloß der Neutöner', *Neue Zeitung*, 8 August 1947.

19   IfZ/OMGUS 5/242–1/48, White, Grey and Black List for Information Control Purposes, 1 November 1946, Supplement 1 to list of 1 August 1946, p. 8. Stürmer had been active with the *Kraft durch Freude* (Strength through Joy) organisation between 1933 and 1945.

20   Berndt Leukert, 'Musik aus Trümmern. Darmstadt um 1949', *Musik-Texte: Zeitschrift für neue Musik*, 45 (July 1992), pp. 20–28, quote on p. 21.

to work in position such as these, even if it made good cultural propaganda. By the summer of 1948 though, McClure had left, blacklisting was ended, and the Darmstadt courses, newly styled as the 'International Summer School', were taking on a new political significance. Another myth about post-war German music was in the process of construction.

'Une Cascade de Spectacles'

For Allied military governments, the promotion of modernism was linked with their national music. The French were most committed to the use of music as a propaganda tool, and they alone were prepared to introduce their own musicians and composers into Germany almost immediately after the war ended. A further advantage was their willingness to contemplate performers appearing before mixed audiences of German civilians and French soldiers. This happened in Karlsruhe and Stuttgart immediately after French occupation, and a similar situation developed in Baden-Baden once the French settled on this as their cultural capital. 'Mixed performances' were officially authorised 'for French propaganda' as early as August 1945, and quickly became the norm.[21] In September and October 1945, the first French artists gave concerts in Baden-Baden, and as Thimonnier's Office of Drama and Music was established, tours were quickly organised throughout the French Zone. In December 1945, Thimonnier reported proudly on the appearance of the choir of Strasbourg Cathedral, on the 'explosive success' of Marie-Aimée Warrot, a 14-concert tour by the Calvet Quartet, and the appearance of Francis Poulenc and Pierre Bernac in Baden-Baden.[22]

The cultural programme was lavishly financed, the Office of Drama and Music needing a monthly budget of 2 million francs at this early stage.[23] Schmittlein, Arnaud, and Thimonnier were given more authority than their counterparts in British, and particularly American, Information Control. Arbitrary use by French troops of German concert halls and theatres was stopped so that there would be no interference with the cultural programme.[24] The 'requisitioning' of musical instruments was forbidden.[25] Throughout the Zone, there was an absolute insistence on high artistic standards. The Third Division in Neustadt was reprimanded for putting on a mediocre production of *Carmen* for German audiences.[26] In Baden-

---

21   AOFC/AC 486/3, Laffon to Gouvernements Militaires de la Sarre, du Palatinat, du Württemberg, et du Pays de Bade; see also Koenig, Commandemant en Chef, Décision No. 7, 10 May 1946.

22   AOFC/AC 486/3, Rapport Mensuel, Période du 25 Novembre au 25 Décembre 1945, and BSM, Rapport Mensuel, 23 January 1946.

23   AOFC/AC 486/3, Projet de Budget Mensuel du BSM, 21 September 1945.

24   AOFC/AC 486/3, Schmittlein to Gilbert, 27 March 1946.

25   AOFC/AC 490/8, Bouley, Note de Service, 6 October 1945.

26   AOFC/AC 486/3, Rapport sur une tournée d'inspection en Hesse-Palatinat et Rhénanie, 8 March 1946.

Baden, Thimonnier demanded extra patrols late at night to guarantee the security of concertgoers as they returned to their homes or hotels.[27]

In September 1945, French engineers arrived to build a radio station in Baden-Baden, which started transmission in March 1946. From its inception, SWF transmitted the weekly series *Music of the World*, 'dedicated to international new pieces',[28] and presented live broadcasts of French artists touring the Zone. The former spa orchestra had a new role:

> The most important part of the musical broadcasts is the series of concerts by the Grand Symphony Orchestra of the Südwestfunk, which is aimed above all at introducing the great works prohibited under the Nazi regime, those of the best composers, amongst whom the names of Mahler, Hindemith, Mendelssohn, and those of Roussel, Ravel, Honegger, Debussy, and Darius Milhaud frequently recur.[29]

The French also planned to use jazz as a symbol of freedom, and this meant more than just playing American records. In August 1946, they proudly reported on 'three excellent concerts of symphonic jazz given by the celebrated Jacques Hélian ensemble of Radio France.'[30]

The French were supremely confident in both their performers and their composers. Conscious of the deteriorating material conditions in the Zone, they were also aware of the tensions between their lavish cultural policy and the near-starvation conditions prevailing in their Zone.[31] 'Culture and democracy are no replacement for calories' was how Arnaud put it.[32] They were confident, though, that even in intensely depressed physical conditions, the German population would respond to music of quality. They also consciously aimed to reach more than the musically literate: 'We are not concerned simply to maintain the prestige of French art with an elite, but to propagate this thought and this art to the working masses, who show themselves to be extraordinarily receptive.'[33]

They were sure that their performers, from large ensembles to talented soloists like Monique de la Bruchollerie, Monique Haas, André Navarra, Ginette Neveu,

---

27   AOFC/AC 490/7, Thimonnier to Colonel Boucher, Chef de la Section des Beaux-Arts, 15 September 1945. Thimonnier specifically demanded that assaults by Moroccan soldiers be prevented, giving examples of previous incidents.

28   AOFC/AC 600/4, Composition des programmes du "Südwestfunk", 19 September 1945.

29   'Une réalisation française: les services de la radiodiffusion en Allemagne occupée', *Revue de la Zone Française*, April/May 1946, pp. 8–10.

30   *La France en Allemagne*, 2 (August 1946), p. 59

31   This is a recurrent theme in the historiography of the French Zone. See Hopp and Warneken, *Feinde, Freunde, Fremde*; and Martens, *Vom "Erbfeind" zum "Erneuerer"*.

32   *La France en Allemagne, Numéro Special: Information et Action Culturelle*, August 1947, p. 61.

33   AOFC/AC 525/2, Laffon to Koenig, 20 September 1947.

Henry Merckel, later even the 'partisan of collaboration', Pierre Fournier,[34] and international stars like Dinu Lipatti, would be able to communicate with the Germans. The French Military Government journal stated: 'If attendance at French plays implies a very good knowledge of the language, this is not the same with music, where there will always be a sufficiently large audience in Germany if the concert is of high quality.'[35]

In attempting to reshape the German repertoire, the French were sustained by a belief that their own music had a similarly unbroken tradition, one that reached into diverse musical forms. From Josquin and Dufay, to Lully, Couperin, and Rameau, they had a series of older models to look to. Even in the nineteenth century, which loomed so large in terms of German dominance, the French could claim a symphonic giant in Berlioz. As for organ music, so important in the German tradition, had not the Nazis had to try to claim Franck as one of their own?[36] Fauré, Debussy, and Ravel, as modernists, had achieved the respect and popularity with both specialist and lay audiences that had eluded their German contemporaries. Contemporary French composition was vibrant, and in Messiaen they had someone at the cutting edge. This was the canon the French introduced to Germany after 1945, and pursued into the 1950s.[37]

Although French performers and composers were given the greatest exposure, the music of the other Allies was also promoted. In December 1945, the French asked the Soviets to supply them with recordings of Russian music for use at SWF.[38] A Festival of international new music was held in Constance in June 1946, including separate days for contemporary music from Britain, America, and the Soviet Union. Johannes Becher, President of the *Kulturbund*, was invited to speak.[39] When Britten's *Peter Grimes* was made available for production in Germany, the French quickly arranged a performance in Baden-Baden. In June 1946, they were the first to allow one of the great musical émigrés to return to Germany, giving special permission for Otto Klemperer to conduct in Baden-Baden.[40] They were the first to license German

---

34   Philippe Burrin, *Living with Defeat: France under the German Occupation 1940–1944* (London: Arnold, 1996), p. 351.

35   *L'oeuvre culturelle française en Allemagne* (1947), p. 45.

36   In 1941, German local music officials were ordered to show Franck's 'German origin' by referring to him in all programmes as Caesar August Franck, rather than as César Franck. *Reichsmusikkammer, Amt für Konzertwesen, Rundschreiben Nr. 16*, 10 April 1941. See also Kaufmann, *Orgel und Nationalsozialismus*, pp. 105ff.

37   An early report also lists Nicolas de Grigny, Daquin, Roussel and Ibert. 'Chronique de la Zone Française', *La Revue de la Zone Française*, 6/7 (April/May 1946), pp. 42–53, p. 47.

38   AOFC/AC 600/4, Peronnet, Chef de la Section Radio, to Viwikichko, 5 December 1945.

39   'La Quinzaine Culturelle de Constance', *La France en Allemagne*, 1 (July 1946), pp. 20–24.

40   AOFC/AC 600/5, Message téléphoné par le cabinet du Général Koenig, 29 June 1946. See also Heyworth, *Klemperer*, **II**, p. 146.

musical journals. Herbert Graf, the pre-war editor of *Melos*, and Walter Harth, were licensed to publish the *Berliner Musikbericht* in February 1947,[41] and *Melos* itself, 'intended particularly for the avant-garde public' was restarted in August 1947.[42] Strobel, its editor, was also head of music at SWF, which gave him enormous powers of patronage.

Attendance at concerts, the ratio of German to French listeners present, and their reactions to French performers and music were all carefully recorded. During 1946, 29 French musical tours gave over 250 concerts in the Zone. Chamber music was central: 'The Calvet Quartet, the Moise Trio, and the Jamet Quintet have always received an enthusiastic welcome, and the proportion of German listeners at the concerts (80.2%) proves that French music is greatly appreciated.'[43] Thimmonier claimed that French musicians had attracted over half a million spectators in Germany by December 1946.[44] Soon, the French Zone was able to claim a cultural life superior to that of metropolitan France. The concert season in Baden-Baden outshone that in Paris, and attracted many visitors from France. The military government of the Saar reported that 'in France, no provincial town could pride itself on such a cascade of performances'.[45]

How successful was the French programme in meeting its stated goals? Was it effective in turning people into democrats, or did it merely serve to broaden the cultural horizons of few unrepentant ex-Nazis? The key men involved, Schmittlein, Arnaud, and Thimmonier, were obviously concerned to portray their programmes in a positive light, and to justify their operations. They also really believed in their work. Thimmonier argued in March 1947: 'I am convinced that in the last two hundred years, no similar opportunity has been given to us to promote French culture in Germany and to develop appreciation there for what we do best, to make our writers and artists known.'[46] In a radio interview he told the French public that 'the French Zone is currently the only one which is interested in cultural propaganda through live performances'.[47] In 1949, Arnaud wrote:

The Americans and the English have copied the model of the French organisation of performances and have, two years later, made a similar effort, but of a lower standard.

---

41   AOFC/AC 919/3, Harth to BSM, undated.

42   AOFC/AC 919/4, Strobel to Arnaud, 28 July 1947. See also Hemmerlé, Chef de la Section Presse, to Melos, Zeitschrift für neue Musik, 20 August 1947.

43   *L'oeuvre culturelle française*, p. 45.

44   AOFC/AC 528/5, Activité du BSM du 1er Août 1945 au 31 Décembre 1946, 13 February 1947, p. 2.

45   AOFC/AC 526/2, Gouvernement Militaire de la Sarre, Rapport, Février 1947.

46   AOFC 524/2, Chef du BSM, 3 March 1947.

47   AOFC/AC 528/5, Texte de l'Interview donnée par Monsieur Thimmonier pour la Radio Française, 11 July 1947, p. 4.

Even though their resources are greater, they do not have an equally varied repertoire or equally qualified performers.[48]

British and American officers referred to the French programme in glowing terms, typically when they were arguing the case for upgrading their own. As early as December 1945, Bishop, in charge of British Information Control, had heard that the French were bringing in their own musicians, and was vainly suggesting to Tulpanov and McClure the formation of a common policy on their own respective artists appearing in Germany.[49] The Americans suffered particularly in cities like Stuttgart and Karlsruhe, which had been initially occupied by the French. A performance in Stuttgart by the pianist Monique de la Bruchollerie was organised in July 1946 by the American Music Control Office, but when she arrived she was told she could not play, and abruptly ordered out.[50] In early 1947, she was allowed to play in Stuttgart, but was rudely treated by American soldiers, and denied food. Apparently, she was fed by German music lovers. A French complaint about this was forwarded to the American Governor of Württemberg-Baden with the following comments:

> The Germans told her that the Americans were very mechanical people, who had no conception of the finer arts of life. ... They intimated that two cultured nations like the French and the Germans were much more fitted to cooperate on artistic matters than the somewhat uncouth Americans.[51]

By 1948, the American Cultural Affairs Branch reported that the French musical programme, now spreading into Bavaria, was winning unbounded admiration.[52] In similar vein, an article in the British journal *Foreign Affairs* criticised the British effort, describing the German population as 'highly appreciative of the French cultural programme'.[53]

Regional French reports paint a different picture, suggesting that some 'spectacles' were poorly attended. From Constance, an officer attempted to explain this: 'The month of December is not one for going out, and, it must be said, there is in part of the population a sharp antipathy to French performances in particular, and to the French in general.'[54] From the Saar, the Fine Arts Section reported in February 1947

---

48   AOFC/AC 526/2, Rapport sur l'Activité des Services de l'Information (1945–1949), 15 June 1949, p. 22.

49   TNA/PRO/FO 1049/485, Bishop to Tulpanov, McClure, and Hoffet, 18 December 1945; AOFC Berlin, GFCC Caisse 131/p5, Hoffet to Bishop, 21 December 1945.

50   IfZ/OMGUS 5/348–2/7, Jenkins to Clarke, 8 July 1946.

51   AOFC/AC 524/2, Robertson, Director Allied Liaison Division, to Sewall, 3 February 1947.

52   BHA/OMGB 10/48–1/3, Monthly Summaries for Period from 1 June through 30 June 1948, p. 5.

53   Paul Bidwell, 'Reeducation in Germany: Emphasis on Culture in the French Zone', *Foreign Affairs*, 27:1 (October 1948), pp. 78–85, p. 85.

54   AOFC/AC 526/2, Constance, Rapport mensuel, Beaux Arts, 28 December 1946, p. 3.

that concerts were poorly attended because of general hostility to the French, and at bottom, because of the desperate shortage of food. Without irony, the Section suggested that effort should be focused on the 4–10 year old age group; thousands of children had seen the recent tour of a puppet show.[55]

German accounts and reactions are decidedly mixed. Hans-Heinz Stuckenschmidt praised the 'intelligent cultural politics' of the French after seeing the Calvet Quartet in Berlin. Their performance, he wrote, displayed 'a richness of colour of incredible strength and variety'.[56] A young student in post-war Berlin, drinking up the varied cultural offerings of the Allies in the 'hunger years', who later went on to a distinguished academic career, recently described the French programme as 'pure cultural imperialism'.[57]

'Finally, Real Schoenberg'

The Soviets were equally keen to be identified with modernism. As they tried, after the disastrous early weeks of the occupation to rein in the worst excesses of their troops, and to win the trust of the civilian population, culture was consciously used as a bridge.[58] There was no repression of the avant-garde, or of jazz, but rather the opposite. Their greatest asset was Shostakovich, who, as a *Kulturbund* writer noted, was 'still fully unknown to us. Extraordinary things are reported of him. But not one of his nine or ten symphonies has yet been heard in Berlin.'[59] His reputation had been established in Britain and the USA before 1939, and in the wartime enthusiasm there for everything Russian, it had grown enormously. His 'Leningrad' Symphony was a potent symbol; special flights had taken parts to New York and London for performances there in 1942. *Pravda*'s condemnation of 1936 was well in the past, and Shostakovich was ideally placed, after 1945, to be held up as a representative of Soviet culture. It was an added advantage that Shostakovich was, above all, a symphonist. His greatest works demanded large orchestras, halls, and audiences for their consummation, and were thus particularly appropriate for grand celebrations and demonstrations. The Soviets also benefited from British and American enthusiasm for Shostakovich and other contemporary Soviet composers. In October 1945, the Communist Party in Frankfurt reported on its close collaboration with the town's orchestras, and asked for scores and parts for the 'Leningrad' Symphony.[60] A

---

55   AOFC/AC 526/2, Gouvernement Militaire de la Sarre, Rapport, Février 1947.

56   'Hohe Musizierkultur', *Neue Zeitung*, 15 March 1947.

57   Werner Kanzog, in conversation with the author, September 2000.

58   See Maren Köster, *Musik-Zeit-Geschehen. Zu den Musikverhältnissen in der SBZ/ DDR 1945 bis 1952* (Saarbrücken: Pfau, 2002).

59   Friedrich Herzfeld, 'Deutsches Musikleben auf neuen Bahnen', *Aufbau*, 1946/2, pp. 177–187, p. 180. The confusion over how many symphonies Shostakovich had written is revealing.

60   SAPMO-BArch DY 27/1404, Kommunistische Partei Frankfurt, Abt. Kultur und Volksbildung, Bericht über die bisherige Tätigkeit, 7 October 1945, p. 9.

performance of Shostakovich's Fifth Symphony in Munich in June 1946 was a huge success.[61] Khachachurian, Shostakovich, and Kabalevsky are prominent on lists of music sent from Britain to Germany for Information Services in 1946 and 1947.[62] In 1947, the Berlin Philharmonic, conducted by American music officer John Bitter, played Shostakovich's First Symphony. The score was printed in America.[63]

Most concert managers in the Soviet Zone, professional and amateur, understood the changed situation after May 1945, and included plenty of Russian and Soviet music on their programmes. The 1947 programme of the Leipzig Gewandhaus Orchestra, the most prestigious in the Zone, included, alongside Mendelssohn and Mahler, Shostakovich's Eighth and Ninth Symphonies, Prokofiev's Fifth Symphony, and the Khachachurian Piano Concerto.[64] Where this understanding about including Soviet music was lacking, programmers were quickly put right by local Soviet authorities. In Stadtroda, the *Kulturbund* was bluntly told that unless more Russian music was performed, no concerts would be allowed.[65] The Soviets were slower to introduce their own musicians. It was unthinkable that their artists should entertain the defeated Fascists immediately after the war. Not until October 1946, a year after the French, but before the British or Americans, could Tulpanov inform his Allied colleagues at the Information Committee of the arrival in Berlin of a Soviet choir, a string quartet, and the pianist Nina Emilianova.[66]

The Soviets' greatest difficulty was in finding progressive German musicians to work for them. There was no Hartmann in their Zone, and it was not surprising that German composers were wary of Soviet intentions. The Communist émigrés, Eisler, Dessau, Toch, and Meyer, were not yet willing or able to return. In Dresden, the Soviets enrolled the services of the bourgeois critic Karl Laux.[67] Within the *Kulturbund*, Laux established in Dresden a 'New Music Section', which, between 1946 and 1948, presented concerts of international chamber music, and hosted performances by Soviet musicians and singers. A high point of the programme

---

61   BHA/OMGB 10/48–1/5, Music Weekly Report, 22 June 1946.

62   See the reports in TNA/PRO/FO 946/30.

63   Laux, *Nachklang*, p. 397.

64   Fritz Hennenberg, *The Leipzig Gewandhaus Orchestra* (Leipzig: VEB Edition, 1962), p. 65ff.

65   SAPMO-BArch DY 27/213, Vorsitzender, Kreisvorstand Stadroda, to Wirkungsgruppe des Kreises Stadtroda, 11 December 1947.

66   AOFC Berlin, GFCC Caisse 131/p5, ACA, Political Directorate, Information Committee, Minutes of the Tenth Meeting, 10 October 1946.

67   SAAdK, Hans-Heinz-Stuckenschmidt-Archiv, 477, Laux to Stuckenschmidt, 17 September 1946. Laux had been involved with the 'new music' scene of the 1920s, notably in Donaueschingen and in Baden-Baden, and had suffered under the Nazis after 1933. He had compromised himself by contributing an essay on Werner Egk, then head of the composers' section of the Reich Music Chamber to a wartime volume celebrating the musical culture of Nazi Germany. See Karl Laux, 'Werner Egk', in Hellmuth von Hase (ed.), *Jahrbuch der deutschen Musik 1943* (Leipzig: Breitkopf und Härtel, 1943), pp. 122–8.

was a concert given by the Moscow State People's Folksong Choir.[68] In Berlin, the Soviets were desperately short of a suitable representative who would run a progressive music programme. The only composers there were all, to a degree, compromised, and after years of isolation, out of touch with developments. In the circumstances, the Soviets drew on a group of now obscure Berlin composers who had survived, with varying fortunes, under the Nazis – above all Heinz Tiessen, who had built a reputation as a progressive in the 1920s.[69] Although no Communist, of the available musicians in Berlin, Tiessen came closest to the Soviet ideal of 'good comrade, good artist'.[70] In July 1945, he was asked by the City Council to supervise the reconstruction of Berlin's choral life, placing an emphasis on schools and the workplace.[71] In December, he was asked to form a 'Music Commission' to coordinate the musical work of the *Kulturbund*.[72] Tiessen gathered for this purpose the composers Paul Höffer, Joseph Rufer, and Boris Blacher, the critics Herbert Graf and Walther Harth, and Alfred Berner, Music Adviser at the City Council. Höffer and Blacher also worked for the International Music Institute in the American Sector; Harth wrote for the French-licensed *Kurier*, and together with Graf, later edited the *Berliner Musikbericht*. Max Butting joined the group in April 1947; he was the only member who could be identified as a Communist. There is a striking parallel, in both membership and purpose, between the Music Commission, and the musicians of the 'November group' between 1922 and 1927.[73]

The Music Commission also had a specific objective: to stage a monthly series of contemporary chamber concerts. By this time the French programme was well under way, as was Hartmann's *Musica Viva* in Munich. Tiessen and his colleagues were almost pathetically out of touch, and there was a risk that without outside help, their concerts might descend into embarrassing mediocrity. They did little until, ironically, the Americans brought Hans-Heinz Stuckenschmidt back to Berlin. Stuckenschmidt's career has remarkable parallels with that of Strobel. Like Strobel, he had been exiled under the Nazis – in his case to Prague, and later to Romania, where he had worked as a critic. Stuckenschmidt ended the war in American captivity, but was released in 1946, to work for them in Berlin.

68　SAPMO-BArch DR 27/46, Aufstellung der Veranstaltungen des Kulturbundes zur demokratischen Erneuerung Deutschlands, Ortsgruppe Dresden, Anfang April 1946 bis März 1947.

69　See Tiessen's memoir, *Wege eines Komponisten* (Berlin: Akademie der Künste, 1962), pp. 34–55, for an account of his involvement with the International Society for Contemporary Music, and the Deutscher Arbeiter Sängerbund in the 1920s.

70　See the commentary on this slogan in David Pike, *The Politics of Culture in Soviet Occupied Germany 1945–1949* (Stanford: Stanford University Press, 1992), p. 127.

71　SAAdK Heinz-Tiessen-Archiv, Korrespondenz, Kulturbund, Wallner-Basté, Amt für Volksbildung, Magistrat der Stadt Berlin, to Tiessen, 19 July 1945.

72　SAAdK Heinz-Tiessen-Archiv, Korrespondenz, Kulturbund, 'Der Komponist nach der großen Pause'.

73　See Elizabeth Janik, '"The Golden Hunger Years": Music and Superpower Rivalry in Occupied Berlin', *German History*, 22:1 (2004), pp. 76–100.

The Soviets had stolen a march in the battle for Germany's airwaves by seizing Radio Berlin in May 1945; they had not relinquished it since, and after months of fruitless negotiation, the other Allies realised that if they wanted transmitters in Berlin, they would have to build them. The Americans created a radio station, initially using telephone lines, hence the name *Drahtfunk im amerikanischen Sektor*, later altered to *Rundfunk im amerikanischen Sektor*, or RIAS (Radio in the American Sector).[74] The 'necessity for the Drahtfunk to stand out as a cultural instrument'[75] demanded a commitment to modernism, and Stuckenschmidt was invited to head a 'Studio for new music'. Tiessen immediately asked him also to help with the Music Commission's concerts as well.[76] Stuckenschmidt brought to the Commission the knowledge that Tiessen and his colleagues had been isolated from: with his range of contacts he could get hold of printed music that was otherwise unobtainable in post-war Berlin, and draw in those rare musicians who could perform technically challenging works. Under his guidance, the *Kulturbund*'s monthly 'Evenings of Contemporary Music', which started in December 1946 and ran until the founding of the GDR in 1949, became a showcase for international new music.

At this stage, the *Kulturbund* did not have a distinctly Communist musical agenda. Höffer wrote, uncontroversially, that the task of the Music Commission was to present 'the new music of all countries', and to bridge the gap between artists and listeners.[77] The first 'Evening of Contemporary Music' presented pieces by Prokofiev, Britten, Hindemith, Copland, and Milhaud. The second highlighted the Second Viennese School, with works by Berg, Eisler, Schoenberg, and Webern. The third presented music by the British communist composer Alan Bush, and works by Messiaen, Tippett, and Sessions. The fourth presented contemporary Berlin composers, Blacher, Höffer, Noetel, Pepping, and Tiessen himself. Through 1947, this internationalism was maintained, and anything that might be interpreted as support for the Soviets was balanced by similar gestures towards the other Allies. Thus, September's concert was dedicated to the 30th anniversary of the Soviet Union, and highlighted contemporary Soviet composers, Miaskovsky, Kabalevsky, and Prokofiev; the next focused on American music, featuring Porter, Copland, and Piston.[78]

In this climate, Schoenberg represented the most progressive and unambiguous political statement that modern music could offer, as the Soviet licensed *Nacht-Express* recognised. Under the heading 'Finally, real Schoenberg' it wrote: 'The

---

74   See Schivelbusch, *Cold Crater*, pp. 107ff, on radio politics.

75   IfZ/OMGUS 5/265–1/2, Lewis (for Director ICD) to Radio Network Control, OMGUS, 23 August 1946.

76   SAAdK Hans-Heinz-Stuckenschmidt-Archiv, Korrespondenz, 33, Tiessen to Stuckenschmidt, 19 June 1946; see also Stuckenschmidt's memoir *Zum Hören Geboren: Ein Leben mit der Musik unserer Zeit* (Munich: Piper, 1979), pp. 177ff.

77   Paul Höffer, 'Musik auf neuen Wegen', *Die Aussprache*, 1946/4, November, p. 2.

78   Programmes for the series are in SAPMO-BArch DY 27/433, and DY 27/249.

Kulturbund has the task of presenting the real, unfalsified Schoenberg'.[79] In similarly progressive spirit, *Berlin am Mittag* praised the synthesis with jazz in Stravinsky's music.[80] This pluralism was also evident in the *Kulturbund*'s journal *Aufbau*, which, in an early issue, wrote enthusiastically about contemporary British music, introducing its readers to Vaughan Williams, Bliss, Lambert, Walton, and Britten.[81] Stuckenschmidt also wrote for *Aufbau*, notably on Schoenberg in December 1946.[82] Allied cooperation was symbolised by John Bitter's talk on musical internationalism, in German, at the *Kulturbund* clubhouse in Jägerstrasse in March 1947, an event favourably reviewed in the Soviet-licensed press.[83]

'We Shall Be Judged in Germany very much by the Standards We Have in Music, in the Theatre, and in Science.'[84]

It is ironic that the *Land ohne Musik* achieved its greatest success in post-war Germany with opera, a musical form not always associated with Britain, but one that had far greater importance in Germany. The whole 'Projection of Britain' was intended to focus on the modern and contemporary, to counter images of Britain as a decadent relic of former greatness. It could not, therefore, rely on the music of the 16th and 17th centuries, any more than English literature could be represented solely by Shakespeare and Marlowe. Broadly, it does appear that few Germans in 1945 were aware of any modern British music, apart from jazz. Music officers often used this fact to justify their programme, but it should be qualified. Better-informed Germans had taken notice of Elgar, and as recently as 1938, Britten's *Frank Bridge Variations*, performed by the Boyd Neel Orchestra, had caused a stir at the Salzburg Festival. Purcell was well known in Germany, as were many of the madrigalists. Bizarrely, music by William Byrd was even performed to representatives of the NSDAP and Reich Youth Leadership in Freiburg in 1938.[85] In 1946, IC officers sampled the reaction in the British Zone to the idea of British musicians appearing, and asked, 'What works of British music would the public like to hear?' Some of the replies suggested a detailed knowledge of British music: 'church music, particularly

79   This was not the first Schoenberg played in post-war Berlin. Wolfgang Hohensee earlier directed Schoenberg's op. 26 Wind Quintet, and Eisler's *14 Arten, den Regen zu beschreiben* at the High School in Charlottenberg. Zur Weihen, *Komponieren*, p. 394.

80   'Friedenschluß mit dem Jazz', *Berlin am Mittag*, 28 April 47.

81   *Aufbau*, 1945/2 (August), pp. 198-199.

82   Hans-Heinz Stuckenschmidt, 'Arnold Schönberg', *Aufbau*, 1946/12, pp. 1240–1245.

83   SAPMO-BArch DY 27/249, Vortrag von John Bitter im Klubhaus Jägerstrasse, 3 March 1947.

84   TNA/PRO/FO 898/401, D.D.G., 28 August 1945.

85   Kaufmann, *Orgel und Nationalsozialismus*, pp. 77–81.

choral, and madrigals were mentioned in all Corps Districts'.[86] Germany was more fertile soil for a musical projection of Britain than we might imagine

The British were able to take the lead in music broadcasting. They not only took over a radio station in Hamburg, intact and complete with staff, but they had the wartime experience of the BBC German Service to draw upon. In one of the opening moves of the Cold War, after May 1945, the German Service continued with precisely the same objectives, directed now to the Soviet Zone rather than Nazi Germany. Other BBC stations, notably the British Forces Network, and after 1946 the Third Programme, had many listeners in Germany. Post-war broadcasting in Germany began on 4 May 1945, with *God Save the King*, followed by the words: 'This is Hamburg, a station of the Allied Military Government'.[87] An Intelligence Officer, Jack Bornoff, was appointed 'Music Controller' of the renamed Northwest German Radio (NWDR) in May 1945. He 'insisted on a proportion of British music', and immediately re-introduced Jewish music. Bornoff created a new orchestra 'in the image of the BBC Symphony Orchestra', which performed Mahler's First Symphony, and played the Mendelssohn Concerto with Yehudi Menuhin in July 1945.

Hans Schmidt-Isserstedt, who until the surrender had conducted the Municipal Opera in Berlin, was evidently happy to be allowed to conduct the new orchestra, and enthusiastically took up the modern, international repertoire that Bornoff suggested. They used the former radio orchestra as a nucleus, but added many first-class musicians they collected from around Germany and Austria.[88] In this way, the NWDR provided the model for other Allied radio stations in Germany. Soon, none could afford to be without its own symphony orchestra and supporting choirs, chamber groups, and dance bands. All felt compelled to display a commitment to new music, to sponsor compositions, and to give first performances. By September 1945, the British were able to restore a transmitter in Cologne, and Captain Ken Bartlett was sent there as 'Music Supervisor'. Like the other Allied stations, *NWDR-Köln* was soon employing hundreds of musicians in its own orchestras and ensembles.[89] These included Herbert Eimert, who in 1953 opened Germany's first electronic music studio there.[90] The NWDR was the main route into Germany for British music, and Schmidt-Isserstedt became its personal champion, subsequently performing Tippett in many other countries.

Following the instructions in Bishop's first directive, the British paid particular attention to opera, encouraging municipal authorities across their Zone to rebuild shattered opera houses, and to re-form dispersed companies of singers and

---

86   TNA/PRO/FO 371/55798, ISCB Summary for period ending 4 July 1946, pp. 32–3.

87   Hans Bausch (ed.), *Rundfunk in Deutschland, Band 3, Rundfunkpolitik nach 1945. Erster Teil 1945–1962* (Munich: Deutscher Taschenbuch Verlag, 1980), p. 43.

88   Jack Bornoff, interview with the author, December 2000.

89   Westdeutscher-Rundfunk, Historisches-Archiv, Cologne (hereafter WDR/HAC) 9454, Bartlett to Musikabteilung, 21 June 1946, and Poston to Heycook, 9 April 1946.

90   WDR/HAC D1471, Stockhausen to Höller, 1 November 1990.

instrumentalists. In Berlin, the Municipal Opera in the British Sector was quickly reopened. In the summer of 1946, Karl Ebert, its former conductor, who during his exile in Britain had started the Glyndebourne series, was brought out to supervise the reconstruction of opera.[91] By this time, twenty-two municipal operas were up and running in the British Zone.[92] Inevitably, repertoires were to an extent predictable and conservative, but the drive to import twentieth-century British opera was remarkably successful. British-licensed newspapers and journals were used to publicise the new works and composers, but they also received good publicity in other parts of Germany.[93] In March 1946, Vaughan Williams' *Shepherd of the Delectable Mountains* was produced in Brunswick, meeting with a 'favourable reception'.[94]

It is ironic that the two composers the British championed most strongly as representatives of their own modern music had both had such unhelpful wartime records. Benjamin Britten and Michael Tippett had both been involved with the pacifist movement in the 1930s, and were registered as conscientious objectors during the war. Britten had stayed in the USA during the 'finest hour', and Tippett, a former Communist Party member, was even briefly imprisoned in 1943 for failing to comply with the terms of his registration.[95] The two were, though, after 1945 celebrated as creators of a new British opera. This only underscores the apolitical nature of the British view of music. It did not occur to policy-makers to challenge the promotion of Britten and Tippett because of their pacifism.

In September 1946, Tippett's *Child of our Time* was performed by the NWDR Orchestra, with Walter Goehr from the BBC conducting.[96] Britten's *Peter Grimes* was premiered in Hamburg in March 1947. The *British Zone Review* wrote that 'thunderous applause again and again called the actors to the curtain', although it noted that some Germans in the audience were rather more reserved.[97] *Die Welt*'s critic heralded the first significant English opera since Purcell's *Dido and Aeneas*.[98] The *Monthly Report* was even more fulsome about the Berlin premiere in May:

---

91   TNA/PRO/FO 946/30, Monthly Report for August 1946 on the ex-PID sections, p. 2.

92   Stadtarchiv, Göttingen (hereafter SG) III B 146, Ergebnis einer Rundfrage des Städtetags über die Musikpflege in den Stadtkreisen der britischen Zone, 53/1947 – Theater in Stadtkreisen.

93   See *Aufbau*, 1945/2 (October), pp. 198–9, which reprinted information on British composers from *Ausblick*, August 1945. *Neue Auslese*, 1946/1 (January), which was distributed in the British and American Zones, ran an article on *Peter Grimes*.

94   TNA/PRO/FO 371/55798, ISCB Summary for period ending 18 March 1946, p. 19; also *British Zone Review*, 1:14 (30 March 1946), p. 14.

95   On Britten see Donald Mitchell, *Britten and Auden in the Thirties: The Year 1936* (London: Faber, 1981), and Humphrey Carpenter, *Benjamin Britten: A Biography* (London: Faber, 1992); on Tippett's imprisonment see his autobiography, *Those Twentieth Century Blues* (London: Pimlico, 1991), pp. 142–58.

96   TNA/PRO/FO 1056/65, Dunn to Deputy Chief PR/ISC, 25 August 1946.

97   *British Zone Review*, 1:40 (29 March 1947), p. 2.

98   'Peter Grimes', *Die Welt*, 25 March 1947

'The cast received thirty-three curtain calls at the conclusion and the opera may now be said to be firmly established in the German repertoire.'[99] Great care was taken to provide scores and parts (in German) for *Peter Grimes*, which was already signed up for Hanover, Cologne, Frankfurt, Stuttgart, Mannheim, Baden-Baden, Munich, Leipzig, Dresden, and Halle.[100] In Düsseldorf, home of the Nazi Reich Music Festival in 1938 and 1939, the opera house had survived the war intact. Here, though, Information Control had enormous difficulties getting allocations of the opera house for performances for German civilians. The local Army Corps held out against 'mixed audiences',[101] and not until July 1947 was the building released to the municipal authorities. In a highly symbolic gesture, Berg's *Wozzeck* was produced there in July 1948.[102]

Cultural Priorities

Nobody needed the cultural credibility that modernist music could provide in post-war Germany more than the Americans, who were all too aware that they were stereotypically imagined there as not only without music, but without any real culture. In the American Zone though, the priorities of the French were reversed, and music officers had to carry through an anti-fascist and pro-American programme, in conditions that seem extraordinary today. In addition to the difficulties imposed by their far more rigorous denazification, American music officers faced several other distinct obstacles.

Throughout the Zone, priority in the allocation of concert halls was given to 'troop entertainment'. Typically, German audiences were only allowed one concert, perhaps on a Sunday afternoon, while for the rest of the week the Red Cross and Special Services provided films, variety shows, and concerts for GIs and invited German guests. These were, as the Mayor of Karlsruhe observed in February 1946, 'probably, in the first instance girls'.[103] Often German audiences were rudely ejected at the limited times allowed them – even during religious services or specifically anti-fascist events. This is one of many reported examples:

> On March 10th a memorial program for the "Victims of Fascism" was given in the theater in Landsberg/Lech under Military Government Information Control License No.1037. The local Military Governor, Capt. Mott had also given his approval. The house was jammed to capacity, 500 odd seats, when, during the second number Third Army soldiers

---

99   *Monthly Report of the Control Council for Germany (BE)*, 2:6 (May 1947), p. 42.

100   AOFC/AC 519/2, Theatre and Music Adviser to ICUs, 21 August 1946.

101   TNA/PRO/FO 1013/1895, Chief of Staff, 1 Corps District to No. 1 ICU, 29 April 1946.

102   TNA/PRO/FO 1013/1904, Information Services Department, Land North Rhine/Westphalia, Draft, July 1948.

103   GLAK 481/398, Oberbürgermeister der Stadt Karlsruhe an den Herrn Präsident der Bad. Landesverwaltung, 27 February 1946.

cleared the house and took over the theater for the presentation of a movie for some 35 GI's.[104]

Appeals from music officers for greater sensitivity, and demands by McClure for parity of treatment between the ICD's cultural programme and 'troop entertainment' were ignored. Virgil Thomson was allowed to tour the Zone in August 1946, and publicly argued for a more enlightened approach:

> The [Stuttgart] Opera House, which is intact, has been requisitioned by the Army for movies, USO shows and a Red Cross club, complete with barber shops and shoe shines. It can be used for opera only at moments that do not inconvenience our military. The situation in Nuremberg and Wiesbaden, where opera houses are also still usable, is even graver, because the military will not even lend them to the local opera company. In the latter city our Air Force continues to give movies in the opera house while the opera company performs in a movie theater. The Army movies are not well attended anywhere. I counted in Stuttgart's Opera House about 100 people though the place seats 1,400. Our military is fearful of releasing all such properties lest the GI newspapers editorialise unfavorably. The pampering of our soldiers is considered everywhere to take precedence over the reconstruction of German cultural life, even where this has been thoroughly de-Nazified.[105]

German opera houses were turned into microcosms of the American entertainment scene. The Red Cross, Special Services, and the American Forces Network unwittingly set one of the Cold War's strongest weapons running as they introduced a generation of Germans to American popular music.

Music officers trying to establish an anti-fascist programme faced a chronic shortage of contemporary sheet music, and the raw materials that sustain musical performance, such as reeds, strings, and paper, soon ran low. Efforts to get the firm of Pirazzi in Offenbach to start producing strings again failed 'owing to a lack of understanding on the part of Military Government',[106] and no paper whatsoever was allocated to the fourteen music publishers in the Zone.[107] These might appear to be trivialities, but by early 1947 music making in the American Zone was literally grinding to a halt.[108] Increasingly desperate pleas from music officers for a more positive policy went unheeded. When invited, at a cost of 20,000 RM, to stage an American day in the French-sponsored Festival in Constance in 1946, Newell

---

104   IfZ/OMGUS 5/348–1/8, Weekly Report of Theater and Music Section for period 1 May to 8 May, 1946, 8 May 1946, p .2.

105   Thomson, 'German Culture and Army Rule'.

106   IfZ/OMGUS 5/348–1/8, Weekly Report of Theatre and Music Section for period April 19 to 24 1946, 24 April 46, p. 2a.

107   IfZ/OMGUS 5/348–3/4, Frank to Clarke, 15 April 1947.

108   It is easy to underestimate the materials needed for an orchestra. The French estimated that the SWF orchestra needed 1600 new strings annually. AOFC/AC 600/5, Demande de Cordes pour le Grand-Orchestre, 24 July 1946.

Jenkins, the music officer in Württemberg-Baden, was informed that the ICD was not prepared to ask the State Department for the money.[109]

There was undoubtedly plenty of jazz around in Germany after May 1945, but there appears to have been no American art music available at all. Frankfurt, where 'all the classics including Mendelssohn, and plenty of French and Russian composers' were available, was typical.[110] The process of getting American music over was incredibly slow. Not only did the State Department have to clear pieces, one by one, for use in Germany, but in most cases they were then microfilmed, and sent over in this form. Microfilms were obviously useless for performance, though, and they had to be reproduced and enlarged in Munich. In October 1945, music officers were even told to prepare to make arrangements for 'handwritten copies' of American works.[111] While this might conceivably have been a practical way to prepare a solo recital or even perhaps a chamber concert, the mind boggles at the difficulties involved in copying by hand a large scale work. The set of parts circulated in Germany for *Peter Grimes* came to 15,000 printed pages weighing some 200 kilograms.[112] The slow workings of the American machine are all the more incomprehensible since American composers, like other artists there, had for years been working closely with the Government and the Armed Forces.[113] The State Department certainly took the whole question of American music in Germany very seriously, requesting detailed reports on each performance, including numbers attending, as well as public and press reaction.[114] In January 1946, music officers were finally told of the first group of five American works 'cleared for performance in Germany'.[115] The first scores were sent out in February, at the same time as lists of American works cleared for broadcast.

With such a desperate shortage of music, lending libraries were particularly important. It was on the initiative of Nabokov that the Americans put forward the idea of an Inter-Allied Music Library in Berlin.[116] At the first meeting of the Four-

109   GLAK/OMGWB 12/91–2/10, Kulturdezernat des Stadtkreises Konstanz to Jenkins, 9 March 1946, and 8 April 1946, and GLAK/OMGWB 12/90–3/1, Coleman (for Director ICD) to OMGWB, ICD, 22 May 1946,

110   GLAK/OMGWB 12/91–1/7, Weekly Situation Report of the Film, Theater, and Music Control Section, 6871st DISCC, 9 June 1945, Annex C.

111   GLAK/OMGWB 12/90–3/1, Preliminary Meeting of Theater-Music Officers, 20 October 1945.

112   AOFC/AC 519/2, Theatre and Music Adviser to ICUs, 21 August 1946.

113   See the chapter 'American Music and World War II' in Barbara Zuck, *A History of Musical Americanism* (Ann Arbor: UMI Research Press, 1980).

114   IfZ/OMGUS 5/265–1/2, Peeples (for Director ICD) to Chief, Theater and Music Branch, OMGWB, 21 March 1946.

115   IfZ/OMGUS 5/265–1/2, Hills (for Director ICD) to OMGB, Information Control Branch, 9 January 1946.

116   GLAK/OMGWB 12/90–3/1, Preliminary Meeting of Theater-Music Officers, 20 October 1945, p. 2.

Power Information Committee, this was enthusiastically taken up.[117] Through 1946, scores, parts, and books about music were assembled, and the Music Library, housed in the State Library in Berlin, was opened with a fanfare of publicity in September.[118] The American contribution appeared thin in comparison with those from Britain and the Soviet Union. By June, when preparations for the opening of the Library were well advanced, the Americans had a mere 80 works ready, compared to 200 Soviet, and some 500–600 British works.[119] In addition, the American music was all on microfilm, and as late as May 1947 was not actually available for use.[120] By this time, the music of the other Allies was being frequently loaned out – the Soviet music in particular. Shostakovich was apparently the most popular single composer.[121]

Another problem was that Military Government regulations controlled entry to the American Zone, and prevented American artists and other Allied musicians from performing for German audiences. One exception to this came in August 1945, when the Berlin Section of the ICD was put in a sudden quandary by the accidental killing of Leo Borchard, who had replaced Furtwängler with the American-licensed Berlin Philharmonic. The Americans had been very content with Borchard, entrusting him with the development of Germany's most prestigious orchestra, which had settled in their Sector. Borchard though was accidentally shot and killed by a guard at a roadblock in August, leaving the Americans with the difficult task of finding a suitable replacement. Before settling on the Romanian Sergiu Celibidache, they succeeded in getting the black conductor Rudolph Dunbar, who had worked with the London Philharmonic during the war, to perform twice with the Berlin Philharmonic, and pushing the challenge to racism further, to conduct William Grant Still's *Afro-American Symphony*. Dunbar's appearance apparently caused 'great excitement'.[122]

Following this, McClure in May 1946 argued that 'the time will soon come when U.S. artists can make an important contribution to the democratic reorientation of Germany. Appearance of a careful selection of such artists in the U.S. Zone would disprove the belief, constantly fed by Nazi propaganda, that Americans have no understanding for the arts.' Having heard that 'by summer French, Russian, and British artists will be performing in other Zones of Germany and will also seek permission to perform in the U.S. Zone', McClure suggested that some twenty American musicians be brought over to tour the major cities, and to make broadcasts in the American Zone: 'The overall program should show ... the high technical

---

117   TNA/PRO/FO 1005/831, ACA, Minutes of the First Meeting of the Information Committee, Political Directorate, 9 April 1946.

118   'The Future of Music in Germany', *British Zone Review*, 1:28 (12 October 1946), p. 8.

119   IfZ/OMGUS 5/348–1/8, Weekly Report of Theater and Music Section for period April 10 to 17, 1946, 17 April 1946.

120   IfZ/OMGUS 5/348–3/4, Staff Meeting, 6 May 1947, p. 3.

121   'Sowjetische Musik in Berlin stark gefragt', *Melos*, March 1948, p. 89.

122   Chamberlin, *Kultur auf Trümmern*, p. 142; see also pp. 122 and 127. Celibidache had been educated in Germany during the war. The Americans classed him as 'White B'. See IfZ/OMGUS 11/47–3/26, White, Grey, and Black List for IC Purposes, 1 August 1946.

and artistic standards of American performers. Emphasis should be laid on recent American works.' McClure explicitly recommended including 'negro' artists.[123] Presumably by presenting black American musicians alongside whites, McClure intended to project a vision of a multi-racial America in which distinction was open to all of merit. Similarly, a later plan from Information Control highlighted 'the great importance of having top-rank American Negro vocalists give concerts in Germany'. Marian Anderson and Dorothy Maynor were named.[124] The Americans doubtless remembered that Marian Anderson had been prevented from singing in Germany in 1936 'because of the colour of her skin'.[125]

The idea of using black musicians to represent America in Germany was primarily an anti-fascist statement, but should also be understood in the context of particular American sensitivities there. Ironically, racial discrimination in the American music industry reflected broader patterns in society, and was only opened as an issue for public debate in America in November 1947 by Leonard Bernstein's article 'The Negro in Music' in *The New York Times*. McClure and his colleagues were aware that racism in America was frequently commented on in the licensed German press after 1945, and were conscious of Soviet charges that US cultural policy was racist.[126] Virgil Thomson went furthest in his scathing critique:

> Our general disdain, however, for honest German citizens ... is in every way deplorable. We treat them very much as we do Negroes in the United States. We expect them to work hard and to be very grateful to us. But we refer to them as "krauts" and do not eat with them in public.[127]

McClure's plan appears to have been vetoed by Robert Murphy, the Political Adviser to the American Military Government in Germany. He was undoubtedly responsive to American public opinion, which was for a 'hard peace'. The use of Federal taxes to support American musicians performing to German audiences was not a vote-catching idea. Through 1946, music officers called for American musicians, but their ideas were rejected. Eric Clarke, Chief of Film, Theater, and Music Branch, complained bitterly to McClure in early 1946 about Murphy's unwillingness to support visits by 'top-line performers' to Germany.[128] Some of America's most distinguished musicians were brushed off when they tried to help. Serge Koussevitzky wrote to Murphy in November 1946, expressing his interest in the whole project of musical reorientation, and asked if a French colleague could be

---

123   TNA/PRO/FO 946/57, untitled memorandum signed McClure, 14 May 1946.

124   IfZ/OMGUS 5/348–3/4, Report of Meeting on 15 February 1947.

125   Kater, *Different Drummers*, p. 30.

126   See Alexander Dymschitz, 'Totalitäre Kulturpolitik im Westen', *Tägliche Rundschau*, 28 September 1947. Dymschitz, a Soviet cultural officer, criticised US censorship of literature and drama, asking why books like Richard Wright's *Native Son* were not translated for use in Germany, and explicitly compared American racism with Nazi anti-Semitism.

127   Thomson, 'German Culture and Army Rule'

128   IfZ/OMGUS 5/265–1/2, Clarke to Director IC, 29 March 1946.

allowed into the American Zone to get some first-hand impressions. Murphy's reply was polite, but placed a host of difficulties in Koussevitsky's way.[129] Newell Jenkins was told in February 1947 that Leonard Bernstein 'was not to be considered for performances in Germany'.[130]

In the circumstances, it seems remarkable that music officers were able to achieve as much as they did. Tentative programmes like the *Musica Viva* were developed in the larger cities, and a Festival was held at Schwetzingen in the summer of 1946. Hartmann's work has received most attention, but in the first years after the war, the conductor Hans Rosbaud, who worked very closely with the Americans in Munich, was undoubtedly the most influential single figure in bringing modern music to wider audiences. He started a 'Studio for new Music' series in 1946, with American support. Hartmann and Rosbaud jointly refounded a German Branch of the International Society for Contemporary Music in early 1946.[131] Initially, the few performances of American concert music were isolated events, sometimes unconnected with the ICD. In Wiesbaden in March 1946, Ezra Laderman conducted the Spa Orchestra in the premiere of his *Leipzig Symphony* at the 'Red Cross Eagle Club'.[132] Piston's suite *The Incredible Flutist* was played in Mannheim in March,[133] and Randall Thompson's Third Symphony in Frankfurt in April.[134] The first American piece performed in Bavaria was Schuman's Second String Quartet, in a *Musica Viva* concert in May, alongside Shostakovich's Fifth String Quartet. Apparently the Shostakovich was very well received, but there was less enthusiasm for the Schuman, which the music officer John Evarts regretfully described as a 'difficult' work for the audience.[135] Not until January 1947, when Piston's Second Symphony was played in Nuremberg, did Bavarians get an opportunity to attend a performance of American symphonic music.[136] One piece introduced to Germany at this time obviously made an impact then, and has stayed in the repertoire: Barber's *Adagio*, which was played by Celibidache and the Berlin Philharmonic, first in Berlin in April 1946, and then in Leipzig.[137]

---

129   See IfZ/OMGUS POLAD 459/9, Koussevitzsky to Murphy, 30 November 1946, and Murphy's reply, 16 December 1946.

130   GLAK/OMGWB 12/91–2/7, Hinrichsen to Jenkins, 26 February 1947.

131   BHA/OMGB 10/48–1/5, Music Weekly Report, 4 February 1946.

132   *Wiesbaden Post*, 1:4 (7 March 1946)

133   GLAK/OMGWB 12/91–1/9, ICD, Heidelberg Detachment, Weekly Report, 2 March 1946.

134   IfZ/OMGUS 5/348–1/8, Weekly Report of Theater and Music Section for period April 3 to 10, 1946, 10 April 1946.

135   BHA/OMGB 10/48–1/5, Music Weekly Report, 31 May 1946.

136   BHA/OMGB 10/48–1/5, Music Weekly Report, 18 January 1947.

137   Peter Muck, *Einhundert Jahre Berlin Philharmonisches Orchester: Darstellung in Dokumenten* (Tutzing: H. Schneider, 1982), **II**, p. 198.

Lucius Clay finally agreed, in August 1946, to the trial appearance of an American musician.[138] Marjorie Lawrence, 'courageous in her wheelchair', sang a 'Wagnerian selection' in Berlin in December.[139] Belatedly, the Americans were recognising the importance of good cultural propaganda. In February 1947, the composer Harrison Kerr was appointed to the Reorientation Branch of the War Department in Washington to coordinate a new programme. He immediately travelled to Berlin to discuss 'U.S. artists, U.S. Art Exhibits, and urgently needed U.S. music' with McClure.[140]

---

138   IfZ/OMGUS 5/347-3/27, Laurence, Executive Manager, Ballet Theatre New York, to Pastene, Theater and Music Officer for Northern Baden, 21 October 1946.

139   Clay, *Decision in Germany*, p. 284.

140   IfZ/OMGUS 5/348–1/8, Weekly report of Theatre & Music Section for Period 11 to 18 February 1947, p. 1.

Chapter Four

'Cultural Freedom' or 'Contemporary Realism'?

The political tensions that led to the collapse of the Allied Control Council, the Berlin blockade, and the emergence of two German states in 1949 have been frequently charted. The complex relationship between the cultural programme of the SED and the evolution of Zhdanovism in the Soviet Union itself after 1946 has also been carefully traced, not least by David Pike. Attention has, though, focused on literature and theatre, and to a lesser extent on the visual arts. Music was, in fact, distinctly out of step with the other arts, and held out for longer the chimerical hope that in one cultural field at least, harmony might reign, and German unity might be preserved.

Most commentators have identified 1947 as the year of division, when landmark events like the Writers' Congress in Berlin in October made it clear that artists had to choose which side they were on. The banning of the *Kulturbund* in the American and British Sectors of Berlin, and its ejection from the old Reich Chamber of Culture building by the British in November, was seen by many at the time as a cultural declaration of war.[1] Certainly, throughout the year, the tone of Soviet press commentaries on the arts had become increasingly strident, starting with reviews by the Soviet cultural officers Tulpanov and Dymschitz of the All-German Art Exhibition held in Dresden in September 1946, and proceeding to wide-ranging attacks on Western literature and drama, particularly French existentialism. No one reading the Soviet-licensed *Tägliche Rundschau* or the *Kulturbund* journal *Aufbau*, in 1947, could imagine any longer that the arts in the Soviet Zone would remain impervious to the demands of the formalism/realism dichotomy that had been reasserted in the Soviet Union.[2] By the same token, 1947 was the year during which the Americans woke up to the importance of culture in the Cold War, and started to redirect the work of their Information Control Division in Germany from anti-fascism to anti-communism. It saw also the foundation of the CIA and the first hearings of the House Un-American Activities Committee. As the western Zones of Germany moved towards economic and political unity, so too the Americans and British began the reintegration of their

---

1   The letter to the *Kulturbund*, from Brigadier Hynde, which told them to move out, is written with a glacial formality, which fully matches some of the SED memorialists' colonial images of the British in Germany. SAPMO-BArch DY 27/841, Hynde, Deputy Director Military Government, 8 November 1947.

2   The *Tägliche Rundschau* was the mouthpiece of the Soviet Military Government in Germany. Its German staff was carefully vetted for political suitability before employment.

cultural economy with that of Western Europe and North America. The French had been doing this for two years, but strengthened their efforts. In all parts of Germany, the memory of the Nazi years was still potent, and attempts to control culture, or to impose censorship of any kind, invited comparison with Nazism. Both East and West used this as the ultimate insult against their opponents, and conversely used the phrase 'cultural freedom' to characterise their own policies.

Given the climate of developing hostility in 1947, it is striking how the rebuilding of German music actually went against the grain. In March, the British Military Government journal reported: 'Russian and French liaison with us in the fields of theatre and music has become closer during the past few months.'[3] The American officer in charge of Theater and Music at ICD, Benno Frank, was even more enthusiastic: 'In spite of all existing political differences between the East and the West, it is felt that in the field of Theatre and Music complete understanding can be reached with the Russians.'[4] As late as November 1947, as the erstwhile Allies locked horns over the status of the *Kulturbund* in Berlin, the Foreign Office in London noted: 'Communists, like the Nazis, have shown an understandable reluctance to demand politico-musical composition, and they have provided no parallel to the Nazi prohibition of "Jewish" and discouragement of "modern" music.'[5]

At the Information Committee, where through 1946, Bishop, McClure, Tulpanov, Dymschitz, and various French representatives met regularly,[6] proceedings became increasingly fractious, and were dominated by accusations of misrepresentation in various zonal newspapers. Music provided the last remaining area for cooperation, and symbolically, this ill-fated body in January 1948 finished where it had begun: with the Inter-Allied Music Library. Almost its final act was to agree on an additional annual subsidy of RM 12,000 for the Library,[7] which by this time was providing music to all parts of Germany, charging orchestras according to their status. Those in Group A, such as the Berlin Philharmonic, and the Leipzig Gewandhaus Orchestra, had to pay more than their less illustrious colleagues in Group B, like the Weimar State Orchestra, or in Group D, including the orchestras of Wesermünde, Zwickau, Rudolstadt, or Koblenz. The register of 102 orchestras held by the Library made no distinction between the four Zones. It constitutes a unique record of the post-war

---

3   *Monthly Report of the Control Council for Germany (BE)*, 2:2 (February 1947), p. 49.

4   IfZ/OMGUS 5/348–3/4, Frank to Clarke, Implications of the Stuttgart Theatre Convention, 5 March 1947.

5   TNA/PRO/FO 945/217, Research Department, Foreign Office, Supplement to "Germany: Weekly Background Notes No. 115", Cultural Policy in the Soviet Zone of Germany, 6 November 1947, p. 5.

6   The senior figures in French 'information control', Schmittlein, Arnaud, and Thimonnier, worked in Baden-Baden, and did not travel to Berlin. They were represented at the Information Committee by officers from the Section Information, Berlin, like Colonel Hoffet.

7   IfZ/OMGUS 2/96–2/8, Extract from Minutes of Meeting of Dpol held on 26 January 1948.

cooperation that might have been, and embodies a genuine sense of that over-used term, 'cultural freedom'. It is a map of an imagined Germany.[8]

'DM Reorientation'

By the time that ICD's 'intensified mission' was announced to American music officers in November 1947,[9] there was considerable goodwill between them and their colleagues in other Zones. A sign of this was the freedom given to German musicians to travel between Zones, and between Sectors in Berlin. A ubiquitous figure was Stuckenschmidt, whose work with the media in different Zones is in itself revealing. He contributed to *Aufbau*, and gave introductory talks at the *Kulturbund*'s 'Evenings of Contemporary Music'. He wrote for the French-licensed press, and for the paper regarded by the Soviets as the most important American propaganda sheet, *Die Neue Zeitung*.[10] He presented new music for RIAS. He managed to attend the Summer School in Darmstadt in 1946 and 1947. From November 1947, the Americans licensed Stuckenschmidt to produce his own music journal, *Stimmen* (*Voices*), its very name signifying pluralism. Stuckenschmidt's contacts made sure that this was not as parochial as some of the journals now emerging in Berlin. Amongst early contributors were Aaron Copland, Wilhelm Furtwängler, Bertha Geissmar, Ernst Krenek, Thomas Mann, Olivier Messaien, Sergei Prokofiev, Humphrey Searle, Hermann Scherchen and Arnold Schoenberg.

In this light, it is not surprising that the different tone and language that appears in American documents in 1947 derives not from music officers in Germany, but from the State Department. An obscure note in the files of ICD's Theater and Music Branch suggests that some of its officers had been briefed in Washington. One line stands out: 'Fear of being subjected to Red-baiting has an increasingly restrictive influence on the work of the Branch.'[11] The surviving internal correspondence of American music officers in Germany never expresses this kind of anti-Communism, or uses language like 'Red-baiting'. The one exception was Nabokov, that unique swashbuckler of Cold War cultural history. Nabokov, the archetypal aristocratic Russian émigré, had close links with Stravinsky, and was like him a fervent anti-Bolshevik. We should still treat with some scepticism his later claim that he decided 'to stay in Germany with the American Occupation Government as an anti-Stalinist

---

8   GLAK/OMGWB 12/91–2/7, Bezugsklassenverzeichnis der deutschen Orchester.

9   IfZ/OMGUS 5/348–3/4, Clarke, Special Facilities needed for IC, 1 November 1947.

10   *Die Neue Zeitung* differed from other American-licensed newspapers in Germany, in that it was intended to be entirely like an American newspaper format, tone and style. See Jessica Gienow-Hecht, *Transmission Impossible: American Journalism as Cultural Diplomacy in Postwar Germany 1945–1955* (Baton Rouge: Louisiana State University Press, 1999).

11   IfZ/OMGUS 5/348–1/5, Report on conversation with officials in Reorientation Branch and in State Dept., Washington D.C., February 5—19, 1947, 22 February 1947.

and stay precisely for that single purpose'.[12] In any case, Nabokov returned to America in 1946, and did not return to Europe to work for the CIA until 1950.[13]

A more significant figure left Germany in 1947. McClure, who had made such an important contribution to the cultural climate of post-war Germany, was replaced in May 1947 by Colonel Gordon Textor. The latter's appointment was accompanied by a pronounced shift in the whole balance of ICD's work, towards 'reorientation'. Textor's brief was specific, calling for the creation of twenty 'Information Centers' in the American Zone, and for the 'importation of top-ranking artists to portray and exhibit fine American music to the German people', to be paid for by private individuals and institutions.[14] In practice, Washington's new priorities merely allowed music officers in Germany to do more of the things they had vainly suggested in 1945 and 1946. At last there was some actual American music to play from and broadcast. In 1947, programmes of new music were performed in Frankfurt and Stuttgart, as well as at the now established events in Munich, Darmstadt, and Schwetzingen.[15] In February 1947, the Americans agreed to allow French musicians to tour their Zone, as did the British.[16] Over the next two years the cultural policies of the three western Zones were allowed to seep from one to the other. Their journals and newspapers were allowed to circulate, and were available in greater numbers. As ever, the French led the way. Their cultural journal *Die Quelle* (*The Source*) was started in April 1947. By July, 6,000 copies of each issue were going to the French Zone, 7,000 to the American, and 8,000 to the British. Another 1,000 copies were sent to Berlin, and 250 to the Soviet Zone.[17] The French were no strangers to what the Americans later called 'DM reorientation'. By March 1948, *Die Quelle* was running up a monthly deficit of 155,000 francs.[18] Gradually, following the French example, networks of British and American 'Information Centres' were extended across the larger cities of what became the Federal Republic. They were ideal venues for concerts and discussion groups, and their libraries held scores and books about music. In the years before the 'economic miracle', a *Schallplattenabend* (an evening of music on records) in an information centre was an effective way to introduce new music to German audiences. A whole generation often had its first contact with

---

12   Nicolas Nabokov, *Bagázh: Memoirs of a Russian cosmopolitan* (London: Secker and Warburg, 1975), p. 224.

13   Saunders, *Who paid the Piper?*, pp. 74–75.

14   IfZ/OMGUS 3/428-3/12, Textor, The Mission and Status of the ICD Program, 2nd half of 1947, pp. 8–10.

15   See GLAK/OMGWB 12/91–2/10 for programmes of the Woche für Neue Musik in Frankfurt, the Zeitgenössische Musiktage in Stuttgart, and the Schwetzingen Festival in June 1947.

16   IfZ/OMGUS 5/348–2/13, Frank to Clarke, 1 March 1947.

17   AOFC/AC 939/4, Johannes Asmus Verlag to Maréchal, 2 July 1947.

18   AOFC/AC 939/4, Thimonnier to Monsieur le Contrôleur Général Rohmer, 4 March 1948.

British, American, French, and other international composers in these centres.[19] The French, who had opened their first centre in Constance in July 1945, had 51 others in Germany by August 1947.[20] By May 1949, there were 16 'British relations centres' in Lower Saxony alone, with a combined projected annual budget of DM 757,000.[21]

The Americans, particularly, faced considerable prejudice. Evarts reported from Munich that one concert of American chamber music was 'rather a dismal failure'.[22] Previously, at a talk he had given on American music in Regensburg, he had found his young audience very patronising 'towards jazz and American culture in general'.[23] The Americans also had difficulties when it came to larger spectacles. Yehudi Menuhin, who had briefly toured DP camps in the British Zone in the summer of 1945, was keen to play in Germany again as a gesture of reconciliation, and particularly to perform with Furtwängler, whom he greatly admired as a conductor. The Americans in Germany, still smarting from the failure to have Furtwängler excluded, were clear about their opposition to this idea: 'OMGUS would be glad to sponsor Menuhin as part of reorientation program of Germans but under no conditions would sponsor Furtwängler.'[24]

Evidently, OMGUS was overruled by Washington, and in September 1947, Menuhin arrived in Berlin, where he also played at the State Opera in a concert arranged by the Soviets. The centrepiece of his visit from the American point of view was the concert with Furtwängler and the Berlin Philharmonic at the *Titaniapalast*, described as 'one of the most important steps thus far undertaken in Berlin by the War Department in connection with the reorientation policy'. It was 'marred by a number of incidents for which Military Police and Special Services officials were responsible, thus making it appear in the eyes of the Germans that Americans are not sincerely appreciative in cultural activities'. Apparently, the audience was allowed to enter only in single file, so that all 'passes' could be checked; this delayed the start of the concert by over an hour, and 'many ... prominent Germans', including music critics, 'were not permitted to take their seats'. People were still coming in during the first two pieces; 'during the playing of the Beethoven Concerto MP's walked up and down the aisles asking for passes from Germans and Allies. Persons

---

19   An example is the GDR composer Reiner Bredemeyer, who later recounted how he first heard the music of Charles Ives and Anton Webern at the *Amerika Haus* in Munich. See Mathias Hansen (ed.), *Komponieren zur Zeit: Gespräche mit Komponisten der DDR* (Leipzig: Deutscher Verlag für Musik, 1988), p. 10.

20   *La France en Allemagne, Numéro Special: Information et Action Culturelle*, August 1947, p. 53.

21   TNA/PRO/FO 1049/1877, Report of Land Niedersachsen Regional Commissioner, 14 May 1949, Appendix B, Estimated Costs of British Relations Centres in Niedersachsen, 1949/1950.

22   BHA/OMGB 10/48–1/5, Semi-monthly summary for period from 26 July 1947 through 9 August 1947.

23   BHA/OMGB 10/48–1/5, Music Weekly Report, 22 December 1946.

24   IfZ/OMGUS 5/270–3/4, Kinard, Deputy Director GSC, to Staff Secretary ICD, 5 May 1947.

without passes were ejected. This not only disturbed the audience and Mr. Menuhin but completely nullified the effect the concert was supposed to make.'[25]

Only days previously, a memorial festival, sponsored by the French, had been held in the State Opera.

> By invitation, all four powers participated. The Russians offered dances and music by their famous soldier chorus. The British offered a concert by a famous Scottish bagpipe band. The United States Special Services supplied a small jazz band and a parody skit on 'Carmen' in which four soldiers participated. The inappropriateness of the American offering for this event was cause for comment by representatives of various Allied Military Governments present.

This report concluded by demanding that in future, Information Control should be consulted for such occasions 'in view of the effect that these performances have, not only upon our Allies, but upon the Germans witnessing such performances'.[26] Clearly the ill-coordinated and under-resourced American musical programme was being reassessed at the highest level. Several weeks before Melvin Lasky's better-known letter to Clay, demanding a more active cultural policy in Germany,[27] Carolyn Gray, one of the disgraced performers at the State Opera, was corresponding with Kenneth Royall, Secretary for War, about this. Germany, she wrote, 'offers a fertile field for propaganda to an art-loving and art-hungry nation, who are convinced that we are a culturally undeveloped country unable to produce anything but jazz and be-bop'.[28] Clay's 'intensified mission' undoubtedly followed these discussions. In 1948, a 'Visiting Artists Program' was started, and the public in the American Zone could at last see some impressive American performers. Leonard Bernstein's visit to Munich in May was a huge success. Cheering crowds surrounded his car after his appearance at the *Prinzregententheater*.[29] After the currency reform in June 1948, though, the flourishing concert life of the Western Zones came to an abrupt halt. Tickets, formerly almost worthless on the black market, became an expensive luxury. Audience figures collapsed, and only the most popular programmes were financially viable. Left to the free market, the fragile institutional supports for new, international, or experimental music in the American Zone would have collapsed altogether.

Carlos Moseley, who had taken over from John Evarts in Bavaria in March 1948, warned that the *Musica Viva* 'must now be abandoned', unless fresh funds

---

25   IfZ/OMGUS 5/267–3/4, Howley to Commanding Officer, Berlin Command, OMGUS, 1 October 1947. See Humphrey Burton, *Menuhin: a life* (London: Faber, 2000), for a fuller account.

26   IfZ/OMGUS 5/267–3/4, Brigadier-General Gailey, Chief of Staff GSC, to Major-General White, Deputy Chief of Staff, EUCOM, 22 October 1947.

27   Saunders, *Who Paid the Piper?*, pp. 28–9.

28   IfZ/OMGUS 5/267–3/4, Gray to Royall, 13 November 1947.

29   BHA/OMGB 10/48–1/3, OMGB, ICD, Monthly Summary for Period 1 May 1948 through 31 May 1948, p. 4.

were provided to support it.[30] By the end of the year Moseley was receiving nearly 10,000 DM a month to prop up the *Musica Viva*,[31] and Reorientation Projects 707c, -d and -e: respectively an 'American Music Project', a 'Munich Youth Music Project', and a 'Contemporary Music for German Youth' programme.[32] In Hesse, the newly appointed Everett Helm was likewise able to channel funds to the renamed International Summer School in Darmstadt in 1948 and 1949.[33] To support concerts and talks in America Houses, blocks of free tickets were given to selected groups such as music students.[34]

At the same time, the Americans had to represent themselves as champions of freedom. In June 1948, all branches of ICD were told to drop the word 'control' from their official titles.[35] In August, Theatre and Music were transferred to 'Cultural Affairs Branch, Education and Cultural Relations Division'.[36] This was apparently to lose 'the odium of control', and 'to permit them to be exploited as purely cultural media'.[37] Similar moves followed in the British Zone, where the occupiers proposed only to exert 'cultural influence' through the maintenance of an 'Information Services Division' in Germany.[38] Not that everyone was taken in by these verbal sleights of hand. The director of the Bavarian State Conservatory in Würzburg wrote a helpful and courteous letter to Moseley in which he quite innocently described the American concerts there as 'propaganda'.[39]

'Important Cultural-Political Tasks'

It was in Berlin, above all, that differences in the occupiers' understandings of music became apparent during 1948. Here, debate about the arts was at its most intense, as the former Allies displayed their cultural wares to one another, to the licensed German press, and to the public. For the western Allies it was sufficient to show

---

30   BHA/OMGB 10/48–1/9, Reorientation Funds for Music Activities, 15 September 1948.

31   BHA/OMGB 10/48–1/9, Music Projects, Reorientation Funds, November 1 1948 to January 30 1949.

32   BHA/OMGB 10/48–1/9, Music DM Reorientation Projects.

33   See Amy Beal, 'Negotiating Cultural Allies: American Music in Darmstadt, 1946–1956', *Journal of the American Musicological Society*, 53:1 (2000), pp. 105-139.

34   BHA/OMGB 10/48–1/9, Music and Theater DM Reorientation Projects 1948, 21 October 1948.

35   IfZ/OMGUS 5/347–3/25, ICD Memo to all Branch Chiefs, 11 June 1948.

36   IfZ/OMGUS 5/348–3/10, Establishment of Cultural Affairs Branch, Education and Cultural Relations Division, 12 August 1948.

37   IfZ/OMGUS 5/348–3/10, Cessation of Licensing by Theater and Music Branch, Education and Cultural Relations Division, 15 October 1948.

38   *Monthly Report of the Control Council for Germany (BE)*, 4:1 (January 1949), p. 14.

39   BHA/OMGB 10/48–1/9, Direktor, Bayerisches Staatskonservatorium der Musik, to Moseley, 3 February 1949.

a commitment to 'cultural freedom', and to maintain a cultural presence in Berlin during the blockade. There was no need to develop any new political perspective; indeed they could and did make a virtue out of this. Ironically, only five years earlier, the Americans had noted as characteristic of Nazi Germany that 'propaganda use is made of foreign tours by such orchestras as the Berlin Philharmonic'.[40] In blockaded Berlin, the Americans found themselves masters of the orchestra, and were drawn into similar manoeuvres. Although Murphy and Clay allowed the orchestra to play in the Soviet Zone in October 1948, they agreed not to let it broadcast on the Soviet-licensed Radio Berlin, as this, in their eyes, amounted to propaganda.[41] In the standard German documentation of the orchestra, this is represented as retaliation for the Soviet banning of newspapers from West Berlin in their Sector.[42] In fact, the Soviets and the SED were well aware of the folly of relying on the Americans for the Berlin Philharmonic. The DEFA film company had already asked for permission to form its own orchestra, so it did not have to hire the Berlin Philharmonic at great cost for film music.[43] In March 1949, the Americans handed the Soviets a much-needed propaganda opportunity by preventing the Amsterdam String Quartet from performing for the *Kulturbund* in the Soviet Sector.[44]

French cultural politics were also tied to propaganda. Franco-Soviet relations had been very good in occupied Germany, as both found themselves outside the strong Anglo-American axis. During 1947, French artists and thinkers had though been singled out for criticism by Soviet ideologues, particularly those on the left, like Sartre and Gide, 'this Pétain of literature'.[45] As we shall see, when Zhdanovism reached the Soviet Zone in the form of vicious personal attacks on individual musicians, it was typically directed first at French-speaking composers. Whether this was because the Soviets really did perceive Messiaen and Honegger as particularly insidious, or, as is more likely, the attacks were an extension of their general hostility towards French dramatists, writers, and painters, is not clear. Walther Harth, who wrote for the French-licensed *Der Kurier*, was also a member of the *Kulturbund*'s Music Commission, and knew which way the wind was blowing. In November 1947, he warned that composers in the Soviet Union were expected to write music that was 'folksy, optimistic, and realistic'.[46] He resigned from the Commission a year later, and made the political orientation of his musical journal, the *Berliner Musikbericht*, very clear. After April 1948, in blockaded Berlin, to produce a journal at all that most scarce of raw materials, paper, was needed. The Western Allies had to airlift this in, when cargo capacity was desperately needed for essentials like food and coal. Harth's rationale in asking for a further 500 kilogram allocation of paper from the French

---

40   *Germany – Basic Handbook, Part II Administration* (1944), p. 340.

41   IfZ/OMGUS POLAD/461/53, Murphy to Clarke, 9 October 1948.

42   Muck, *Einhundert Jahre*, **II**, pp. 216–17.

43   SAPMO-BArch DY 30/IV 2/9.06/202, Monatsbericht der Musik-Produktion, Monat April 1947.

44   *Nacht-Express*, 17 March 1949, and 22 March 1949.

45   Dymschitz, 'Totalitäre Kulturpolitik im Westen'.

46   'Kühle Leidenschaft', *Der Kurier*, 18 November 1947.

authorities in early 1949 was direct: 'The journal (*Musikbericht*) fulfils important cultural-political tasks and, in the current situation can contribute particularly to strengthening the position of western culture in Berlin and the Eastern Zone, and to upholding the connection between Berlin and the other Zones of Germany.'[47] Harth was granted the paper.[48]

The British were equally aware of the importance of culture in Berlin. In April 1948, some embarrassment was caused by rumours that all of the British music had been removed from the Inter-Allied Music Library and taken to Hamburg for safe keeping. Brian Dunn, the British Head of Theatre and Music, quickly reassured his superiors that only some of the music had been moved. Nonetheless the senior Information Control Officer in Berlin complained bitterly about this, concerned not with the loss of the actual music, but with the impression potentially given that the British were not confident that they would be staying in Berlin: 'There are at stake in Berlin issues in comparison with which the cessation of ALL music activities in the British Zone would be of no significance, and the move could not have been more ill-timed.'[49] Robert Birley, the public school headmaster entrusted with reshaping education in the British Zone, wrote anxiously from Berlin to call for a heightened cultural presence there. From London, Birley was reassured that this need was fully appreciated, and as the blockade unfolded, the British made a number of gestures 'to steady and encourage Berlin opinion, and persuade Berliners we mean to stay here'.[50] In April 1948, a new Information Centre was opened, and in August an Elizabethan Festival was held, apparently on the initiative of the Foreign Secretary.[51] Whether the performances in blockaded Berlin of the Cambridge University Marlowe Society and Madrigal Singers, had the desired effect of steadying morale amongst Berliners is not known.[52]

Harth's warning about music in 'the land of collectivism' must have appeared an understatement when, in February 1948, the Communist Party of the Soviet Union denounced its own leading composers in a published decree. Not only was the 'historic decree' (as it became known in the Soviet Union) on music more intemperate in its language than the earlier decrees on literature, theatre, and film that had been issued in 1946, it was commented on in the Soviet Zone much more rapidly, sparking off a heated debate amongst musicians. From this point on, it was clear that even music would be politically divided. Although some individuals would try to keep a foot in both camps for some time yet, all would be forced, in the end, to decide which side they were on.

---

47   AOFC/AC 919/13, Harth to BSM.

48   AOFC/AC 919/13, Hemmerlé to Sous Directeur, Chef du BSM, 14 March 1949.

49   TNA/PRO/FO 1056/65, Bell to Deputy Director PR/ISC and to Director ICSB, 8 April 1948.

50   TNA/PRO/FO 371/70706, Berlin to Foreign Office, 30 June 1948.

51   See the Festival Programme, and the many related documents in TNA/PRO/FO 1012/166.

52   See Noel Annan's account of the Festival in *Changing Enemies*, (London: HarperCollins, 1995), pp. 237–9.

There has been much analysis of the implications of the decree for Soviet musicians; the debate on Shostakovich's relationship with the Party grinds on.[53] Its precise significance in occupied Germany in 1948, and subsequently in the GDR, has not been examined, though. Firstly, we should be clear that it was seen in the context of remembered Nazism. Inevitably, its central demands, that music should be melodic, understandable, and derive from the people, appeared similar to Nazi requirements. Its condemnation of dissonance, unusual rhythms, and abstraction echoed the Nazi categorisation of 'degenerate music'. Zhdanov's ideas, though, were originally cast in the context of Russian music, not German, and their transmission in occupied Germany required considerable adaptation. A fully developed Marxist-Leninist theory of music would only emerge in the GDR in 1951.

Soviet diatribes against formalism and cosmopolitanism in 1948 were directed primarily against their own contemporary composers, and also very largely against the neo-classicists of the early twentieth century, who were associated with White Russian counter-revolutionaries. Many of those personally abused were, by 1948, looking distinctly old-fashioned, or 'regressive' as Adorno would have it, and were not controversial in Germany, amongst either Germans, or their various occupiers. Shostakovich and Prokofiev were particularly popular, and there was no one in Germany who added to the criticism of them developing in the Soviet Union itself. Schoenberg, Berg and Webern were represented in the Soviet Union as alien imports, but in Germany they had indelibly marked the musical culture of the years before 1933, and the current generation of active musicians had an entirely different relationship with their complex legacy. The most famous identifiably 'communist' German composer was Eisler, a pupil of Schoenberg. In addition, the exaggerated hostility of Soviet language of music criticism hardly invited serious theoretical analysis. A new German vocabulary had to be gradually constructed to try to define terms like 'realism', 'formalism', and 'cosmopolitanism'. In the western Zones, as in Britain, France, and America, Zhdanovist ideas about music had very little attraction, and even the most left-wing composers and musicians found themselves defending the indefensible when they tried to interpret them.[54] Most striking in the transmission of the 'historic decree' into the Soviet Zone, and its later development in the GDR, is the way its original language was moderated.

Zhdanov himself set the tone, telling a 'Convocation of Activists of Soviet Music' that 'a whole series of works by contemporary composers are infiltrated and overloaded to such a degree by naturalistic sounds that one is reminded – forgive the inelegant

---

53   The non-Russian reader should consult Alexander Werth, *Musical uproar in Moscow* (London: Turnstile Press, 1949), and Elizabeth Wilson, *Shostakovich: A Life Remembered* (London: Faber and Faber, 1994). Both contain long verbatim translations of contemporary documents, and eyewitness accounts of developments in the Soviet Union.

54   A striking exception was the English composer Rutland Boughton, who wrote to Alan Bush: 'The Russian Communist Party criticism of modern music is as you can imagine, a great satisfaction to me.' British Library, Alan Bush Papers, Boughton to Bush, 18 February 1948. See also Rutland Boughton, 'Russian and British Censorship', *The Musical Times*, 89 (May 1948), pp. 153–4.

expression – of a piercing road drill, or a musical gas-chamber'.[55] Khrennikov, the new Chairman of the Composers' Union in the Soviet Union, followed, describing Messiaen, Jolivet, Hindemith, Berg, Menotti and Britten as 'modernist, decadent, pathological, erotic, cacophanous, religious or sexually perverted monsters'. The path taken by Prokofiev and Stravinsky, he said, had 'all ended in Monte Carlo, where the Diaghilev Ballet found its right mission at last – to cater to an audience of gamblers, profiteers, and prostitutes'.[56] Soviet cultural officers had the difficult task of importing this kind of rhetoric into Germany, where until this point they had encouraged the *Kulturbund*'s performances of precisely these composers. Although the Soviet officer first to enter the lists, Gorodinski, caught something of the authentic flavour of Zhdanovism by attacking the 'pathetic clownery' of Stravinsky, and the 'pathological sexuality' and 'sick obsessions' of Britten,[57] his colleagues quickly toned down their criticisms. The music officer Captain Barski, writing in February in the main Soviet-licensed newspaper, warned more cautiously of 'the quest for a false originality'.[58]

His colleague Peresvetov, who had encouraged Karl Laux to present new music in Dresden, tried in March to reverse the tide of suspicion, arguing in more restrained terms in the *Tägliche Rundschau* that the threat to cultural freedom came from the West. He again singled out French composers, naming Messiaen and Honegger, but his strongest criticism was only the veiled comment that they 'do not find any meaningful tasks in the present'.[59] In another Soviet commentary, Honegger, Stravinsky, Messiaen, and Hindemith were criticised, not for sexual aberration, but for mysticism, and Berg and Schoenberg for extreme individualism.[60] This was a far cry from the rhetoric being used in the Soviet Union itself at the time.

Musicians working for the *Kulturbund* were understandably alarmed by the sudden reversal of Soviet policy. Laux wrote to Barski for guidance, and received in April a revealing reply. Barski again toned down the overheated criticism being thrown at Shostakovich and his colleagues in the Soviet Union. He did not refer to sexual deviance, or use any of the more abusive and less musical terms being

---

55   Cited in Levitin Y, 'The Year 1948', Wilson, *Shostakovich*, pp. 208–15, p. 209. Zhdanov apparently used the Russian term for a mobile gas van, as used in the early stages of the 'Final Solution'.

56   Cited in Werth, *Musical Uproar*, pp. 93–4.

57   Gorodinski, 'Jenseits des Schönen. Die Musik der dekadenten Bourgeoisie', *Tägliche Rundschau*, 17 January 1948, cited in Pike, *Politics of Culture*, p. 466.

58   Sergei Barski, 'Für eine volksverbundene Kunst', *Tägliche Rundschau*, 13 February 1948. Maren Köster suggests that Barski and other Soviet cultural officers were subsequently removed from their posts in Germany because of their insufficient commitment to Zhdanovism. See her *Musik-Zeit-Geschehen*, pp. 54–67.

59   Roman Pereswetow, 'Von wo kommt die Gefahr?', *Tägliche Rundschau*, 24 March 1948.

60   Sergejev B, 'Das Recht des Volkes auf Kunstkritik', *Weltbühne*, 3:15, cited in Hans-Heinz-Stuckenschmidt, 'Was ist bürgerliche Musik?', *Stimmen*, 1947/8, pp. 209–13, p. 211.

used there. He also attempted, unconvincingly, to distance himself from the idea that the 'historic decree' implied a new censorship. Laux had apparently asked him, bluntly 'Does it follow from the decree that so-called atonal music is undesirable (*unerwünscht*) and therefore forbidden (*verboten*)?' In the Soviet Union, Barski replied, such 'fascistic' terms as '*unerwünscht*' and '*verboten*' were not used.[61] Laux might have been convinced by Barski's sophistry, but Stuckenschmidt in Berlin was not. In July 1948, he weighed in with a crushing analysis of the 'historic decree': 'If we reduce all these objections to their essence, we find the struggle directed against two things, which are stressed in modern bourgeois music: lack of melody and dissonance.' He then placed Zhdanovism in the German context:

> For us German avant-gardists these publications have had the effect of a cold shower. They concur not only factually but in the individual details of their formulation with the artistic maxims of the National Socialists, from whose intellectual terror we have only recently been freed for three years. They defame also the same great leaders of contemporary music, who were banned in Hitler's Reich, and for as long as they lived in Germany, were forced into internal emigration. 'Decay', 'alienation from the people', 'subjectivism', 'atonal discords', these were the charges used to ban the performance of works by Paul Hindemith and Alban Berg, and to declare a war of extermination against all those who championed them. ... One asks oneself why the struggle for modern art has been fought, why an elite of German artists and intellectuals took upon itself and survived the sufferings of persecution, of banning, and of emigration, if today almost exactly the same arguments ... are set against them. Was Hitler right then, who named as 'degenerate' those who today are rejected as representatives of western-bourgeois decadence?[62]

The Soviets had no sufficiently qualified German musician in the Soviet Zone to refute Stuckenschmidt's critique. Where the British had taken up Schmidt-Isserstedt in Hamburg, the French Strobel in Baden-Baden, and the Americans Hartmann and Rosbaud in Munich, the Soviets had no German composer, conductor, or critic with similar credentials who was also a committed Communist. Through the spring and summer of 1948, as the 'historic decree' was debated in blockaded Berlin, the *Kulturbund* there was still relying on Stuckenschmidt, and its concerts continued to reflect the full spectrum of music that Stalinist cultural policy represented as degenerate, mystical, individualistic, and sexually aberrant. Stuckenschmidt was particularly pleased to bring back to Berlin the émigré pianist Eberhard Rebling

---

61   Barski's letter is printed in Karl Laux, *Die Musik in Rußland und in der Sowjetunion* (Berlin: Henschelverlag, 1958), pp. 412–15. It is revealing that Laux's autobiography, *Nachklang* (1977), although full of details about the reconstruction of musical life in post-war Germany, and in the Soviet Zone, does not mention the 'historic decree', or this correspondence with Barski, suggesting that by the 1970s, Laux, like others in the GDR, was embarrassed by the whole episode.

62   Stuckenschmidt, 'Was ist bürgerliche Musik?', p. 211. The full text of the 'historic decree' was later published in German in A. Shdanow, *Über Kunst und Wissenschaft* (Berlin: Dietz, 1951).

to perform a programme of contemporary Dutch music in April.[63] The *Kulturbund* leadership might well discuss with the Soviets appropriate themes for a public meeting on 'The danger of Americanisation',[64] but they had no one able to explain what this meant in musical terms without risking public ridicule.

Stuckenschmidt's involvement with the *Kulturbund* was coming to an end as summer approached. The Music Commission heard in June that he would no longer be able to introduce the monthly concerts, which were (in consequence?) not attracting so many listeners.[65] In July, Tiessen stressed how important it was that the non-party nature of the *Kulturbund* be announced at its concerts. Stuckenschmidt, he argued, was best placed to do this.[66] Stuckenschmidt was no longer attending the Commission's meetings, and the others there became suspicious. In September, Berner, evidently speaking for several of his colleagues, questioned whether the *Kulturbund* really was 'above party'.[67] Tiessen made a courageous final call for unity in public. At the concert in October, he gave a speech praising the *Kulturbund* for its support of new music, and paid tribute to Stuckenschmidt. He spoke of peace, goodwill, and international understanding. Schoenberg was again on the programme that night.[68] Tiessen's valiant efforts were to no avail, though. Harth and Graf both resigned that month, because of what they saw as the politicisation of the Commission's work.[69] Höffer died unexpectedly in 1949, leaving Tiessen further isolated. Stuckenschmidt did not return to the Commission. He had had enough of Berlin, and was angling for a job in the French Zone.[70] Nothing came of this though, and as late as November 1948, he travelled to Leipzig to introduce a Schoenberg concert. In February 1949 he left for the USA, as part of a 'Cultural Exchange Project'.[71] Stuckenschmidt's choice of sides in 1948 would not be forgotten.

'Our New Language'

It was not for a want of trying that the SED had no Communist musicians. In December 1946, Johannes Becher had written to Hanns Eisler out in California:

63   SAPMO-BArch DY 27/215. Ironically, Rebling was an ardent Communist, and later settled in the GDR.

64   SAPMO-BArch DY 27/213, Besprechung bei der SMA am 11 July 1948.

65   SAPMO-BArch DY 27/433, Protokoll der Sitzung der Kommission Musik am 25. Juni 1948.

66   SAPMO-BArch DY 27/433, Protokoll der Sitzung der Kommission Musik am 21. Juli 1948.

67   SAPMO-BArch DY 27/433, Protokoll der Sitzung der Kommission Musik am 3. September 1948.

68   SAPMO-BArch DY 27/215, Vortrag, 29 October 1948.

69   SAPMO DY 27/433, Graf to Kulturbund, 9 October 1948; SAPMO-BArch DY 27/249, Harth to Kulturbund, 27 October 1948.

70   AOFC/AC 505/3, Stuckenschmidt to Stachel, 10 August 1948.

71   SAAdK Hans-Heinz-Stuckenschmidt-Archiv, Korrespondenz, 2618, Travel Orders, 18 February 1949. See also Stuckenschmidt, *Zum Hören Geboren*, p. 186, and p. 192.

'Let's hear from you soon, and above all come soon, we need every individual.'[72] In fact, Eisler was probably more use to the SED in America, where his persecution provided a concrete example of musical censorship to charge the capitalists with.[73] In his absence, the SED leaders even desperately tried to cast Tiessen as one of their own. Pieck and Grotewohl urged him to participate in the SED's 'German People's Congress for Unity, Righteousness, and Peace' in December 1947, asking him to send a 'statement of his position' if he was unable to attend.[74] Showing a similarly misplaced optimism, Becher, Gysi, and Abusch constantly urged Stuckenschmidt actually to join the *Kulturbund*.[75] In March 1948, Eisler did leave America, but he returned first to Prague and then to Vienna, after briefly meeting with Ernst Hermann Meyer and Alan Bush en route at Heathrow.[76] Through the summer, the SED badgered him to come and work in Berlin.[77] He finally arrived in Berlin for the 'Peace Demonstration' in the State Opera on 24 October 1948. His appearance there, along with other returned exiles like Dessau, Brecht, Zweig, and Fürnberg, was celebrated in the SED press,[78] and over the next few months Eisler made several other public appearances in Berlin. He was always something of a disappointment to the Party, even though it felt constrained publicly to venerate him. He kept his Austrian passport, and did not commit himself entirely to the Soviet Zone. He did not take up SED membership.

In a press conference on his arrival, Eisler revealed a number of the ambivalent positions that were to dog his subsequent career in the GDR. Asked about the Zhdanov decree, he did not take the opportunity to criticise any fellow composers, of whatever nationality, but rather sidestepped the question by welcoming the passion and intensity of the debate that the decree had provoked. Asked directly whether it would cause him any problems as a composer, he answered: 'In no way.' He was happier talking about music in America though. This, he said, was entirely in the grip of big business; the Americans themselves lived behind a 'newspaper curtain'. Nonetheless, there were progressive composers there, like Copland, Harris, Bernstein

---

72   SAAdK Hanns-Eisler-Archiv, Korrespondenz, 413, Becher to Eisler, 2 December 1946.

73   Peresvetov, for example, highlighted Eisler's persecution in the U.S.A. in 'Von wo kommt die Gefahr?', *Tägliche Rundschau*, 24 March 1948. There is a considerable literature on Eisler, much of which is reluctant to explore his ambiguous relationship with the SED. For an exception that provides an overview of his career, see Maren Köster (ed.), *Hanns Eisler: 's müßt dem Himmel Höllenangst werden* (Hofheim: Wolke Verlag, 1998).

74   SAAdK Heinz-Tiessen-Archiv, Korrespondenz, Wilhelm Pieck, Pieck and Grotewohl to Tiessen, 2 December 1947.

75   Stuckenschmidt, *Zum Hören Geboren*, p. 185.

76   Jürgen Schebera, *Hanns Eisler: Eine Biographie in Texten, Bildern, und Dokumenten* (Mainz: Schott, 1998), p. 210.

77   SAAdK Hanns-Eisler-Archiv, Korrespondenz, 801, 814, 823, and 416, Deutsche Verwaltung für Volksbildung, Abt. Kunst und Literatur to Eisler, 24 May 1948; Meyer to Eisler, 3 June 1948; Abusch to Eisler, 25 June 1948; Becher to Eisler, 11 October 1948.

78   See *Neues Deutschland*, 23 October 1948 and 24 October 1948.

and Piston. Digressing on 'Negro music', Eisler displayed the contradictory attitudes that undermined all SED efforts to get to grips with jazz. He said first 'the really great American composer will be a Negro', but describing the ubiquitous presence of jazz in America he added: 'I say yes, this is filth (*Schmutz*), but however, in this filth the Negroes show real talent and originality'.[79] Eisler was never prepared mindlessly to parrot the Party line, always mixing his own views with the current orthodoxy. He furthermore had no stomach for the endless meetings and committee work demanded of an SED activist, and never took more than a peripheral part in the various Party organisations that sought to influence music.

Salvation arrived from an unlikely direction. Ernst Hermann Meyer had been very ill in a Swiss sanatorium during much of 1946 and 1947, but following his recovery, he had returned to London to resume his work with the BBC. Meyer, as we know, had given a great deal of thought to the reconstruction of German music. As an academic historian, musicologist and composer, he was uniquely well placed to theorise about music and society. His dedication to the SED was absolute, and he had a huge capacity for work, which he placed entirely at the Party's service. He wrote enthusiastically to Eisler in June 1948 that he had been appointed to the new chair of Music Sociology at the Humboldt University, then a discipline barely recognised in the English-speaking world. Meyer was clear that he and Eisler had been given great responsibilities by the Party, speaking of 'brighter prospects of success for our common goal which is so great and wonderful'.[80] Meyer had, in fact, been negotiating for some time with the SED about his return to Germany. The German Administration for People's Education (*Deutsche Verwaltung für Volksbildung*, or DVV), led by Paul Wandel, had, in October 1947, assessed him as 'an exceedingly valuable comrade, who could play a leading role in the musical life of a new democratic Germany'.[81]

Meyer's background is difficult to reconcile with his development as a composer and theoretician in the GDR, where he was at the heart of all critical decisions on music. From a middle-class Jewish Berlin family, Meyer had studied musicology under Blume and Besseler, and composition with Eisler, Hindemith and Butting. As a young man, he had worked with the KPD in the final years of the Weimar Republic, contributing articles on music to the journal *Die Rote Fahne*. He escaped to England in 1934. There, after experiencing many difficulties, he had, like so many other German refugee musicians, gradually built a new life. Meyer always defined himself

---

79   SAAdK Hanns-Eisler-Archiv, 2152, Tonband 02, Interview with Eisler, 25 October 1948.

80   SAAdK Hanns-Eisler-Archiv, Korrespondenz, 814, Meyer to Eisler, 3 June 1948.

81   SAPMO-BArch DY 30/IV 2/11/v.5404, Betr.: Dr. Ernst Meyer, 1 October 1947. Paul Wandel, although not a musician, was to play a unique role as a cultural adviser to the SED regime. One of the 'Ulbricht Group' brought into Berlin in May 1945, Wandel was put in charge of the Administration for People's Education in Berlin, which later developed into the GDR's Education Ministry. Wandel was subsequently involved in a number of the central musical projects of the early GDR. He fell from favour in the late 1950s, and was sent as ambassador to the People's Republic of China.

as first and foremost a composer, and in Britain he made his name writing film music, in particular for some forty wartime documentaries like *A Few Ounces a Day*, and *Mobilise your Scrap*. His scores were noticeable for their use of naturalistic sounds, and while theoreticians in the Soviet Zone talked about 'realism' and 'nearness to the people', Meyer was putting these ideas into practice. Before writing the score for Cavalcanti's film *North Sea*, he spent several days on a working trawler, listening to the sounds of the crew, the sea, and the wind in the rigging. He spent much time on academic work, eventually publishing *English Chamber Music: The History of a Great Art from the Middle Ages to Purcell* in 1946, described in *Grove* as a 'seminal influence on English musicology'.[82]

Meyer was always a practical musician. He recovered many old manuscripts from libraries in England and on the Continent, editing and arranging works for performance by groups like the Boyd Neel Orchestra. His early efforts to introduce the public to these unknown treasures through the BBC gradually won him audiences and the confidence of programmers. His reputation as a broadcaster grew, and in December 1944 he was congratulated by the BBC on 'a magnificent programme'; 'from all quarters', it had 'heard nothing but appreciation for the excellent music'.[83] In July 1947, the newly established Third Programme commissioned a ten-part series by Meyer, called *Music of the Sixteenth and Seventeenth Centuries.* The house orchestra formed to broadcast the music he prepared later became the English Chamber Orchestra.[84] Meyer did not confine himself solely to these highbrow activities, though. Most of his active music-making was with the Workers' Music Association, founded in 1936. Meyer also directed the Battersea and Clapham Singers, and he chaired the émigré Free German League of Culture, which gave many concerts, often featuring British musicians as well as German exiles.[85]

Responding to the 'historic decree', Meyer was notably more restrained than Khrennikov or Zhdanov. In the debate amongst British communist composers, Meyer evidently counselled moderation. While still in England, he wrote: 'Let us

---

82 Percy Young, 'Meyer, Ernst Hermann', Stanley Sadie (ed.), *The New Grove Dictionary of Music and Musicians*, (2nd edition, Oxford: Grove, 2001), **16**, pp. 560–61, quote on p. 560.

83 BBC/WAC, RCONT 1, Ernst Hermann Meyer, Artists File 1, 1931–1962, Drewry to Meyer, 15 December 1944.

84 Carpenter, *Envy of the World*, pp. 55–6.

85 There is no written study of Meyer that captures the multi-faceted nature of his life's work, and above all the tension between his development in the liberal climate of wartime London and his subsequent adherence to Party orthodoxy in the GDR. Many official GDR publications detail his work there (e.g. Konrad Niemann, *Ernst Hermann Meyer – für Sie porträtiert* (Leipzig: Deutscher Verlag für Musik, 1989)), and Jutta Raab Hansen, *NS-verfolgte Musiker in England – Spuren deutscher und österreichischer Flüchtlinge in der britischen Musikkultur* (Hamburg: von Bockel, 1996), pp. 361–79, gives some detail about his time in England. Fortunately for the historian, Meyer left many documents in different archives. I am particularly indebted to Meyer's daughter Sylvia Armit, and to his late brother Klaus Meyer, for their help with my research.

not bar progress and experiment. We must go forward, not back.'[86] By September 1948, Meyer was finally able to leave Britain, and on his arrival in Berlin, he was interviewed by the SED press. Like Eisler, he went out of his way to praise composers from the land of his exile. Highlighting a whole group of contemporary composers, including Bush, Bliss, Rawsthorne, Frankel, Britten, Tippett and Stevens, he said: 'England is a long way away from being the "Land ohne Musik".'[87] Meyer's internationalism was deep, and it would ensure that the subsequent musical culture of the GDR, even at its most intolerant, was never as inward-looking as the Soviets would have wished.

Under Meyer's leadership, the SED musicians in Berlin were at last able to form a distinctive cohort, and to embark defiantly upon the construction of a musical culture in clear opposition to the one coalescing around Baden-Baden, Munich, and Hamburg. Meyer's colleagues, as well as the somewhat wayward Eisler and Dessau, included the pianist Nathan Notowicz, who had spent the war years with the Dutch resistance. Since 1946, Notowicz had worked with the KPD in Düsseldorf. In 1947, he had been arrested and held by the British in Aachen for four weeks. He subsequently went back to Amsterdam, but in July 1948, Wandel sanctioned his return to Berlin.[88] Notowicz had two of the qualities most needed for success in the SED: unqualified loyalty to the Party line, and a willingness to spend many hours in committee. Karl Laux, who had gained the Party's trust in Dresden, was invited, in November, to work in Berlin as the music critic for the *Tägliche Rundschau*, and to serve on the Music Commission.[89] Max Butting was the one existing member of the Music Commission who now found his moment, becoming a completely committed member of Meyer's inner circle.

This group was charged collectively with defining a Marxist-Leninist theory of music in society. This demanded a revision of musical history, based not, as in bourgeois musicology, on exclusively technical analysis, but rather on the relationships between music and its societal context. Only on this basis could a new musical culture be built in the Soviet Zone – one in which the grandeur and nobility of German music, above all, could be brought to the hitherto alienated proletariat. Capitalist distinctions between producer and consumer, as exemplified in the polar opposition of the isolated artist and a passive but increasingly distant audience, had to be erased to bring music into the lives of workers and peasants, engaging them as creative musicians. All aspects of musical activity had to be reassessed. If music was to be a positive force in what would later be called the 'building of socialism', and not a decorative dead weight, a pervasive activist culture of appropriation had

---

86   SAAdK Ernst-Hermann-Meyer-Archiv 631, Untitled paper, 1948.

87   SAAdK Ernst-Hermann-Meyer-Archiv 205, Conversation between Meyer and Notowicz, 1948.

88   SAPMO-BArch DY/30 IV/2 11/v.710, Ergänzungen zum Fragebogen, 14 December 1962; Aktennotiz, 22 July 1948.

89   SAPMO-BArch DY 27/249, Willman to Singer, 20 October 1948; and SAPMO-BArch DY 27/433, Kulturbund to Laux, 11 November 1948.

to be developed. It would have to be present in every town and village, in the top professional orchestras as in village choirs, in the schools, churches, universities, and in the branches of the economy concerned with the mechanical reproduction of music (publishing, recording, film, radio, and later television). The SED's musicians found a finely tuned instrument for their purposes: probably nowhere in the world was there a greater physical concentration of musical history and practice. The Soviet Zone contained a dense superstructure of musical institutions, rooted in traditions of German history, which gave them a unique resonance worldwide. This was a society suffused in music, in which every workplace, village, and school had its own choir. Even the practical difficulties that dogged the Western Allies were less apparent in the Soviet Zone. Leipzig was the centre of German music publishing, and the Soviets had more paper than the Western Allies to allocate for printing music. Well before the recording industry resumed production in the West, the Soviets had licensed the singer Ernst Busch to produce records under the label *Lied der Zeit* (*Song of the Time*) at Babelsberg and Ehrenfriedersdorf.[90]

Meyer and his colleagues had the full support of the Party. They were mightily relieved to have someone of his calibre to implement the commitment to music embodied in its 'Basic Principles' of January 1948, which declared that 'the SED is not only a fighting political party, but also a progressive cultural movement, in which alongside Marx and Engels, Goethe and Schiller also are at home'.[91] It would now not be long before Bach and Beethoven would be similarly co-opted. *Neues Deutschland* gave renewed approval to the *Kulturbund*'s ambitious programming in November 1948.[92] After the years of unpoliticised work, the Music Commission was transformed. Meyer, Notowicz, and Laux attended its meeting on 16 November 1948, and took it over. The tone of proceedings was radically altered, as the new members outlined the larger tasks awaiting the Commission. Notowicz, who had recently attended the Party conference on 'Artists and the Two-Year Plan', spoke first, and reported the conclusions of that conference. Concerts were now to represent the relationship between composers and society. A new orchestra financed by the DVV was to be formed; and the lack of contemporary vocal music had to be remedied. He continued:

> In the conference the demand was further made that music should be understandable, without however being banal. Fundamentally, to support contemporary music, it was necessary (1) to put together the right programmes; (2) to get closer to composers by discussing their compositions; and (3) to support active artistic work (the formation of workers' choirs).

---

90   Alexander Gulyga, 'Ernst Busch 1945', *Sinn und Form*, 1968/4, pp. 1370–83.

91   Leitsätze der Abteilung Parteischulung, Kultur und Erziehung beim Zentralsekretariat der SED, Januar 1948, reprinted in Gerd Dietrich, *Politik und Kultur in der Sowjetischen Besatzungszone Deutschlands (SBZ) 1945–49: mit einem Dokumentenanhang* (Bern: Peter Lang, 1993), pp. 294–6.

92   'Neue Musik im Kulturbund', *Neues Deutschland*, 3 November 1948.

Meyer's contribution was, typically, both practical and theoretical. He noted the lack of printed music in the Zone, and stressed the need for more lending libraries. Deferring to the sensibilities of the liberals still present, he explained that no rigid control of music was envisaged, 'that naturally, not a production plan in the musical sphere, but rather the raising of cultural standards was intended'. He also spoke of the need for a greater centralisation of control over music in the Zone.[93]

The *Kulturbund*, though, was not an appropriate vehicle for the wholesale transformation of a musical culture. In December 1948, the SED musicians held a separate meeting at the SED's main office, the 'Party House' in Wallstrasse, to discuss such a transformation. According to the surviving record:

> Comrade Heymann opened the meeting with the observation that painters and writers had already on several occasions been invited to conferences in order to secure, and programmatically to establish guidelines for the progressive cultural shaping of art. It was all the more desirable to do the same for party comrades who were musicians and composers. Professor Doctor Ernst Meyer spoke on the present musical situation and our tasks.

Curiously, the report then moves into the first person, and we seem to hear Meyer himself:

> Social realism must find expression in the art and also in the musical composition of the present. Our music must be understandable to the people. Without being unoriginal, we must be simple in our new musical creativity. Our new language must be marked by content, not by strivings for originality. The overestimation of dissonance which is demanded by a certain school is recognised even in the Soviet Union. We must represent not the pessimism of a dying bourgeoisie, but the new social realism of our present, and adhere to the tradition of our classicists. A new music, which embodies the tasks of the present, with fighting songs for young people, for the activist movement, and concerts in the workplace, can support the Two Year Plan and bring it positive strength. This new music must have a positive influence, without basing its effect solely on drums and trumpets.

Rather contradicting Meyer's recent assurances to the *Kulturbund*, Notowicz demanded 'a Marxist-based planning for our musical creativity'. The composer Ottmar Gerster, for long blacklisted by the Americans, made his first significant appearance in East Berlin, calling for 'the publication of a music journal for the Zone'.[94] It would be some years before all these demands were realised, but here, in outline, with its emphasis on 'collective work' and 'central regulation', was the blueprint for subsequent music in the GDR.

---

93   SAPMO-BArch DY 27/433, Protokoll der Sitzung der Kommission Musik am 16. November 1948.

94   SAPMO DY 30/IV 2/9.06/284, Bericht über die Konferenz der parteigenössischen Musiker und Komponisten am Mittwoch, dem 15. Dez. 1948, im Parteihaus Wallstr. 76–9.

As for the *Kulturbund*'s chamber concerts, the SED typically demanded not their abolition, but their appropriation. The 'Evenings of Contemporary Music' continued, notably with a repertoire that had been explicitly criticised by Zhdanov and his various mouthpieces in the Soviet Zone. Hindemith's *Marienleben* was chosen for performance in May 1949.[95] There were also conscious gestures towards the composers and performers gathering in Berlin. February's concert was devoted to Eisler. Eberhard Rebling, who would in 1951 settle in the GDR and become one of Meyer's staunchest allies in the crusade for '*Parteilichkeit*', or Party loyalty, was invited back to give June's concert, which was celebrated in the Soviet-licensed press.[96] In September 1949, only weeks before the founding of the GDR, the Commission was planning a 'Schoenberg Festival Hour' to honour the composer's 75th birthday.[97]   *Die Aussprache*, an internal *Kulturbund* newsletter, showed a similarly tolerant attitude, praising a youth concert that had featured Distler, Weismann, Scriabin, Pepping and Hindemith.[98] A review of the Commission's July concert (presumably written by Laux) celebrated the new orientation: 'A political declaration therefore – how far is chamber music here removed from its point of departure in aristocratic chapels or rooms.'[99]

1949: Facing the Future

In both the East and West of occupied Germany, 1949 was dominated by preparations for their respective new constitutional arrangements. The British, French and Americans prepared to turn control of culture over to German authorities, which would be integrated into the new political structures of the Federal Republic. The Basic Law, adopted in May 1949, stipulated that cultural affairs should be the preserve of regional, and not federal, government. There would be no central Ministry of Culture; music would be supervised and sponsored at *Land* and municipal level. 'High Commissions' would replace 'Military Governments' in Germany. In cultural affairs, the former occupiers would play an indirect role, largely through their network of information centres, and through a continued supervision of broadcasting. They had to accept that West German musical culture and its educational infrastructure were largely unreconstructed, particularly in terms of personnel. After the ending of denazification in 1948, even the most flagrant examples of former Nazis returning to perform, or to resume musical instruction in schools, colleges, and churches, went unchallenged.

---

95   SAPMO-BArch DY 27/433, Protokoll der Sitzung der Kommission Musik am 19.Mai 1949, p. 1.

96   See *Vorwärts*, 15 June 1949, *Nacht-Express*, 15 June 1949, *Sonntag*, 26 June 1949, and *Berliner Palette*, 1 July 1949.

97   SAPMO-BArch DY 27/433, Protokoll der Sitzung der Kommission Musik am 29. Juni 1949, p. 1.

98   'Jugend spielt zeitgenössische Musik', *Die Aussprache*, 1949, 6/7, p. 13.

99   *Tägliche Rundschau*, 16 July 1949.

What Michael Kater has recently characterised as 'retrenchment' was painfully obvious at the time.[100] Hindemith, visiting Germany at the invitation of OMGUS in 1949, caused controversy in both East and West by stating publicly that as yet he saw no signs of anything really new in the German music scene. Hindemith gave lectures and concerts in Munich, Nuremberg, Frankfurt, Wiesbaden, and Berlin,[101] and his subsequent report in *The New York Times* gave further offence. The Music Commission in Berlin was particularly upset by his declaration: 'I'm an American, and don't want to go back and stay in Germany. I will go back if the American Military Government wants me', but presumed that he was acting under political pressure.[102] Boris Blacher was one of several Berlin composers who were genuinely torn in their sense of loyalty in 1949. He committed himself to the West, but wrote (in English) to a friend at the BBC: 'The musical life is now quite normal with Furtwängler playing Brahms and Bruckner in the same way as nothing happened in the past. All the hopes that something has changed since 45 are gone.'[103]

Symbolic of the Western integration of 'Trizonia' was the freedom granted to its musicians to visit Britain, America, and France, and the reappearance in the musical press there of articles about music in Germany. The Berlin Philharmonic toured Britain in November 1948,[104] and appeared at the Edinburgh Festival in 1949.[105] The Cultural Relations Branch sponsored the visit of four German musicians to the Bryanston Summer School in 1949.[106] General Koenig intervened personally with the *Sûreté* to ensure that the SWF Orchestra could appear at the Aix-en-Provence Festival in July 1949.[107] There was a commercial dimension to this traffic. German musicians such as Karajan and Schwarzkopf had been signed up for the Gramophone Company by Walter Legge in Austria while they waited for denazification clearances, and were rapidly becoming established as market leaders in Britain and the USA. Nor were these exchanges entirely trouble free. In America, particularly, the appearance of formerly blacklisted German musicians generated protest. Furtwängler received anonymous threats before a planned performance in Chicago in 1948.[108] The pianist Walter Gieseking, who had been blacklisted by all four Allies after 1945, likewise found himself at the centre of a storm. In April 1948, rumours that he was planning

---

100   Kater, *Composers*, pp. 264–84.

101   John Evarts, 'Hindemith Gives Germans New Outlook on Music', *Information Bulletin*, 22 March 1949, pp. 11ff.

102   SAPMO-BArch DY 27/213, Protokoll der Sitzung der Kommission Musik am 19. Mai 1949, p. 2; also Tiessen, 10 May 1949.

103   Blacher to Glock, 1949, cited in Heribert, *Blacher Boris*, p. 89. Glock, a champion of contemporary music, was later Controller of Radio 3. In 1947 he was sent on a fact-finding mission in Germany by the BBC. See Carpenter, *Envy of the World*, pp. 57–8.

104   *Monthly Report*, 3:11 (November 1948), p. 25.

105   *Monthly Report*, 4:7 (July 1949), p. 26.

106   *Monthly Report*, 4:9 (September 1949), p. 49.

107   AOFC/AC 600/4, Koenig to Diréction Générale de la Sûreté, June 1949.

108   See Fred Prieberg, *Trial of Strength: Wilhelm Furtwängler in the Third Reich* (trans. Dolan, Boston: Northeastern University Press, 1994), pp. 6–8.

to return to New York provoked protests from the American Veterans Committee, and further investigation from Public Safety Branch.[109] In February 1949, Gieseking actually made it to Carnegie Hall, but was seized there by immigration officials, who took him away for questioning. Held for several hours, and threatened with deportation proceedings, Gieseking decided to leave.[110]

Broadcasting was the one area that the 'High Commissions' still controlled. By 1949, the Allied radio stations in Hamburg, Cologne, Berlin, Baden-Baden, Frankfurt, Stuttgart and Munich were all being operated by German personnel.[111] The model presented by the British in Hamburg was widely followed throughout the (former) western Zones. The NWDR was governed by an advisory Council representing political parties, trade unions, the churches, *Land* Governments, the theatres, and the Music Academy in Cologne.[112] The fortnightly reports from Broadcasting Liaison Branch in 1948, which had the responsibility for supervision of programming, were, though, concerned almost exclusively with non-musical programming.[113] In fact, the radio stations in West Germany were already functioning well as instruments for musical propaganda, combining a commitment to classical music with strong support for new music, and some jazz. This highbrow diet was leavened with plenty of dance music. Opera and operetta were also strongly supported. Each station ran its own orchestras, choirs, and dance bands, and sought to develop its own distinctive musical profile.

By 1948, the SWF in Baden-Baden had laid a solid foundation for its later position as the most progressive station musically. Strobel, the musical director, had gathered there a particularly strong team, including Joachim Berendt to run the jazz programming. In July 1948, the French lured Hans Rosbaud from Munich to direct the SWF orchestra. They gave him a particularly lucrative contract, on the grounds of his importance 'for the prestige of French cultural propaganda in the Zone'.[114] In 1950, the SWF restarted the Donaueschingen festivals as an extension of the station's activities. By the same token, the NWDR had an extensive portfolio. Schmidt-Isserstedt, who led its Symphony Orchestra, was considered by the BBC as 'a very effective channel through which English music might become better

---

109   *The New York Times*, 20 April 1948; IfZ/OMGUS AG48/139/2, Public Safety Branch CAD to O/SS, 22 April 1948.

110   BHA/OMGB 10/48-1/3, OMGB, Education and Cultural Relations Branch, Monthly Summaries for Period from 1 Feb 1949 through 28 Feb 1949, pp. 6–7.

111   See Bausch, *Rundfunk, Band 3*, on the transfer of radio stations in the western Zones from Allied to German control, and their legal status.

112   TNA/PRO/FO 1056/151, Military Government – Germany, British Zone of Control, Ordinance No. 118.

113   See the reports in TNA/PRO/FO 1013/1903.

114   AOFC/AC 600/5, Administrateur Délégué pour le G.M. du District de Baden-Baden to L'Administrateur Chef du Service Général du C.C.F.A., 23 September 1948; also Conditions posées par M. Rosbaud, 11 May 1948.

known in Germany',[115] but was best known there as a Mozart specialist. In Cologne, the NWDR had already established the 'night studio' format that later became indelibly associated with the German avant-garde of the 1950s. Its *Musical Evening Programme* titles from 1949 could not be accused of dumbing down, including as it it did such offerings as: *Stravinsky's confrontation with Bach, Thomas Mann: Doctor Faustus, Societal critique and politics in the opera, Goethe and new music* and *Paul Hindemith: Hérodiade.*

Like the *Kulturbund*, the NWDR celebrated Schoenberg's birthday, with the pianist Peter Stadlen speaking on him. Other presenters included Herbert Eimert and Heinrich Strobel.[116] Later, through Eimert and Stockhausen, and its pioneering work with electronic music, *NWDR-Köln* would assume its own distinctive profile.[117] In Berlin itself, with Stuckenschmidt's help, the Americans had developed RIAS as a musical organisation of distinction. RIAS could occasionally use the Berlin Philharmonic, but it had its own Symphony Orchestra, led by Ferenc Fricsay. By this time, the British were also encouraged by the continued success of the BBC German Service, and by the popularity of the Third Programme in Germany.[118] As for live performances, the western Zones quickly overcame the crisis brought on by currency reform. The French, in 1948, were planning to re-establish the Baden-Baden International Festival, with appearances by Furtwängler, Karajan, Koussevitsky, Munch, Walter, Gieseking, Lipatti, Menuhin, Rosbaud and Ginette Neveu.[119] The Americans, in July 1949, reviewed their 'Theater and Music project', and suggested that it should be scaled down. In the musical field, its principal remaining task would be 'screening German cultural organizations for financial support', in other words, funding German performance of new music. This, it was felt, 'may well prevent the Germans from sinking back into the cultural isolation that obtained until 1945. ... At the same time it should serve as a rebuttal to critical feeling regarding the U.S.'[120]

In the Soviet Zone, the criticisms of modern music abated in 1949, as the SED turned its attention to the material base of the socialist culture under construction. SMAD Order No. 234 introduced further benefits for intellectuals and artists, ranging from the provision of a hot meal at midday to extra housing, coal allowances and

---

115   BBC/WAC R46/503, European Music Supervisor, Visit to Hamburg, February 12–22, 1948, p. 2.

116   WDR, *Zwanzig Jahre Musik*, p. 9.

117   The station in Cologne was developed first as the *NWDR-Köln*, but separated in 1956 to become the *WDR* (West German Radio).

118   BBC/WAC E1/739, Rowntree, Further Education Programme, to Controller, *Third Programme*, 21 November 1949. Ironically, the *Third Programme* could often be received more clearly in parts of Germany than in Britain. Its programme schedules were printed in the NWDR magazine *Hör Zu!*

119   AOFC/AC 28/2, Chef de la Division de l'Information to Monsieur le Général Commandement en Chef, 7 August 1948.

120   IfZ/OMGUS 5/364–2/38, Theater and Music Functions of E&CR Division, 13 July 1949, p. 3.

rest homes.[121] The direct beneficiaries included the members of sixteen orchestras, hundreds of musicians working for radio stations in Berlin, Leipzig and Dresden, the State Opera and the Comic Opera in Berlin, and the *Thomanerchor* and *Kreuzchor*.[122] The SED was determined to carry through its commitment to freeing artists from the yoke of material need – in the face of hostility from other workers not similarly privileged, if need be.

An absolute priority was a new national anthem. This was discussed by the *Politbüro* on 13 September 1949,[123] and the subsequent story of its creation by Becher and Eisler, and its first playing on Chopin's piano in Warsaw, quickly became part of the GDR's self-created mythology.[124] The front page of the October issue of *Die Aussprache* was given over to a reproduction of Eisler's manuscript, and the *Politbüro* called for a plan to popularise the new anthem.[125] The oft-rehearsed story of how the new anthem was chosen, winning the competition against a rival offering from Ottmar Gerster, omits to mention one reason why Gerster's could never have been chosen: his past. Gerster, like Eisler, had been a socialist composer in the 1920s, but had stayed after 1933. His operas were particularly well received in Nazi Germany, and he was one of the most popular living composers there by 1944. He enjoyed some favour with the Party. At the 1939 Reich Music Festival in Düsseldorf, an unmistakably Nazi ceremony, his *Festliche Musik* (Festive Music) was played. What was Gerster celebrating here?[126] In 1941, Gerster won Düsseldorf's Robert Schumann Prize, an event closely supervised by the Reich Music Chamber and the local Nazi Party.[127] Inevitably, he was blacklisted by the Americans.

Gerster lived after 1945 in Essen, in great hardship, but was offered a job at the recently reopened Weimar Music Academy in 1947. There, he joined the SED, and became one of the Party's most dedicated composers. His *Lied der Holzfäller* (*Song of the Woodcutter*), written for the Goethe festivities in 1949,[128] has a ring not unlike the title *Mit der Hacke, mit dem Spaten* (*With the pickaxe, with the spade*), which is credited to him on an American blacklist of Nazi songs.[129] In the competition between Gerster and Eisler, both composers were invited to perform their compositions, in

121   'Förderung der Kultur', *Die Aussprache*, 1949, 4/5, pp. 3–6.

122   Beschluß des kleinen Sekretariats des Politbüros der SED, 6 May 1949, cited in Dietrich, *Politik und Kultur*, pp. 382–5.

123   SAPMO-BArch DY 30/IV 2/2/44, Protokoll Nr. 44 der Sitzung des Politbüros am 13. September 1949.

124   See Wiens E, 'Wie unsere Hymne entstand', in Abusch and Gemkow, ... *einer neuen Zeit Beginn*, pp. 565–70.

125   SAPMO-BArch DY 30/IV 2/2/55, Protokoll Nr. 55 der Sitzung des Politbüros am 8. November 1949, p. 5.

126   SAAdK Heinz-Tiessen-Archiv, Db1450-Kasten, *Reichsmusiktage, Düsseldorf 1939, 14. bis 21. Mai.*

127   See the documents on the 1941 competition in Stadtarchiv, Düsseldorf, IV 1763.

128   SAAdK Hans-Pischner-Archiv 1116, Autobiographical notes.

129   GLAK/OMGWB 12/91–2/10, Blacklist of Songs.

turn, with a choir, before an audience of Party activists, who then 'chose' a winner. We must ask, as the Party activists listened to the rival choirs sing the proposed new anthems, each accompanied by the composer at the piano, whether they could really afford to saddle the Party and country with the unlimited liability of one written by Gerster.

All eyes were now on the future, and on both sides of a divided Germany musical attention was focused on the coming year, which would provide a unique, if coincidental, opportunity for cultural re-definition: the 200th anniversary of Bach's death. This was picked up in possibly the last document produced by the Music Commission, which reviewed its work of the past few years, confessing, in the new spirit of self-criticism, to early 'difficulties and mistakes'. Things had improved since 1948, with the formation of 'work groups' and the institution of 'workplace concerts'. It declared that the main task awaiting the *Kulturbund*'s musicians in 1950 was clear: to bring Bach closer to the people.[130] Meanwhile, in August 1949, a press conference in Göttingen heard that a Bach Festival would be held there in 1950, with the support of the International Bach Society in Switzerland, and of the *Neue Bach Gesellschaft*. Why in Göttingen, a town which had no direct connection with Bach?

> In the present situation, the West German *Länder* also have the duty of commemorating Johann Sebastian Bach, one of the greatest German masters, in a worthy manner, in at least one part of western Germany.

There was nothing here about bringing Bach to the people. The press was told, rather, that

> The connection of Johann Sebastian Bach's music with the church and with religion must be particularly clearly affirmed by the performance of his works.[131]

---

130   SAPMO-BArch DY 27/249, untitled and undated report.
131   SG Sammlung 5, Bach-Fest 1950, 19 August 1949.

PART 2
New Musical Cultures, 1949–1955

Chapter Five

1950: Bach 'Shenanigans'[1]

The Bach year in 1950 provides us today with a lens through which to view many interlinked aspects of the two new states created in 1949, as both tried to define what it meant to be German after the catastrophe of the 'Third Reich'. As we have seen, planning on both sides for the Bach year began before the Federal Republic and the GDR were formally created, and developed therefore alongside new political structures. What ultimately came down to a contest for ownership of Bach, and by extension, the whole classical tradition of German culture, though, ultimately involved far more than music. In political terms, the Bach year was an opportunity to define the relationship between new governmental structures and the arts, and to rewrite German cultural history as both states tried to reconstruct a Bach with contemporary resonance. The question of whether Bach was to be perceived as a secular or religious composer brought religion into the centre of the debate. Unlike Beethoven, Bruckner, or Wagner, Bach had withstood various half-baked efforts by the Nazis to appropriate him as a symbol of their new culture, and was thus largely untainted by their memory.[2]

The Bach year also allowed Germans to define their cultural politics after the years of occupation. On both sides of the Iron Curtain, the former Allies stood back, and allowed their protégés to take the lead, giving tactful but distant support. Both the Federal Republic and the GDR were intensely conscious that the eyes of the world were upon them, and that if they did not take the initiative in honouring Bach, others would. Both consciously appealed to Germans, on either side of the Iron Curtain, as well as to a wider international audience. The contest was played out in the ritual setting of concert halls and churches, in the newspapers, in cinemas and over the radio. Leading politicians, musicians, and theologians were drawn into the whirlpool as old fault lines were papered over and new ones appeared. An unwanted ghost, in the form of the Nazi past, was present at both feasts. And strangely, although

---

1   Alfred Dürr summarises the SED's Bach celebrations, 'In Göttingen', *Musica*, 9 (1950), pp. 340–44, quote from p. 340.

2   The crudest Nazi efforts to appropriate Bach, like that of Gerhard Stiebler in 1940, tended to see his music as a model for a new 'heroic festival music'; this was 'the music of the Third Reich, grown from the original source of strength of music, from J. S. Bach'. Cited in Otto Riemer, 'Der entchristianisierte Bach', *Melos*, 6 (1948), pp. 295–300, quote from p. 299. See also Ingeborg Allihn, '"Verwurzelung in Deutscher Stammesart". Das Reichs-Bach-Fest 1935', Bach-Archiv-Leipzig (ed.), *Leipziger Beiträge zur Bach-Forschung* (Hildesheim: Olms, 1995), pp. 199–209.

on the surface, the Bach year seemed to be about the definition of difference, when analysed in detail, the two sides end up looking remarkably similar.

'A Political Demonstration'

The West German *Länder* jealously guarded their control of culture in the early 1950s, and the frequent calls for centralisation always provoked heated debate. From the perspective of central government, it was actually very helpful to have the arts, including music, financially supported by the *Länder* and individual towns, and the provisions of the Basic Law gave it a justification for avoiding responsibilities it had no desire to assume.[3] Equally, music was not altogether outside the control of central government in the early Federal Republic: there were in fact several central bodies that concerned themselves with music. The Standing Conference of *Land* Culture Ministers provided the *Länder* with a strong mouthpiece. The *Bundestag* and the *Bundesrat* had cultural committees, which included officials from the Federal Interior Ministry and the Ministry for all-German Affairs, as well as elected party politicians. These ministries both had cultural departments, and cooperated on the political questions arising from the many musical connections with what West German politicians called the 'Soviet Occupied Zone'. In addition, the Foreign Ministry was responsible for promoting German culture abroad, and did not underestimate the role of music in the rehabilitation of the Federal Republic. Last but not least, Adenauer himself made great use of a personal Chancellery, which often concerned itself with musical matters. These bodies all had access to money, and lavished considerable sums on favoured projects like the Bayreuth Festival and the Bamberg Symphony Orchestra. The Ministry for all-German Affairs alone had an annual fund of 3 million DM 'for subsidies and research institutes, for cultural and folk-political questions, and for general cultural purposes'.[4]

The two main financial providers for music were the towns, which supported orchestras, operas and music schools, and the radio stations. The institutional link between towns, *Länder*, and *Bund* was the *Deutscher Städtetag* (German Council of Towns). This originated in the British Zone in 1946, and by 1949 also represented towns in the former American and French Zones. The *Städtetag* had close links with the Conference of Culture Ministers, and with central government as well. Minutes of its meetings, and its publications, were sent directly to Adenauer's Chancellery. It had a Cultural Committee, but of greater importance for music was the Working Group for Concert Affairs (*Arbeitsgemeinschaft für Konzertwesen*). This was formed in April 1948, initially representing the *Städtetag*, the *Länder*, and the

---

3   This argument was, for example, used to refuse a request from Furtwängler for 250,000 DM to support the Berlin Philharmonic. BAK B136/5815, Thedieck to Furtwängler, 16 May 1951.

4   BAK B106/1072, Ständige Konferenz der Kulturminister to Mitglieder der SKdK, 20 January 1950.

professional associations.[5] At a meeting of the Working Group in June 1949, West German politicians decided to take the initiative on Bach. They faced three major difficulties. The first was geographical. With the exception of three years spent at school in Lüneburg, Bach had had only fleeting connections with towns outside the Soviet Zone. The second was political. Music had been reconstructed as an art form standing outside and above politics, and it was undesirable that central government should manipulate or finance a Bach festival. It might act in a ceremonial capacity, but must not be seen to exert influence on the event. The third problem was religious, but if skilfully handled, it could be turned to great advantage. Bach was a Lutheran, but to present him as such in 1950 would have been unhelpful. Given the way in which regionalism had been fostered in the western Zones by the over-centralisation of the former Reich and the devolutionary politics of the occupiers, there was a real possibility that local rivalries and confessional differences would prevent any cooperation in a 'national' Bach festival. On the other hand, this was the West's strongest suit. If Bach had to be celebrated in absentia, almost as a prisoner in captivity, he could at least be presented, ecumenically, as a religious composer, with the churches drawn into full support.

Having considered these factors, the Working Group decided on Göttingen as the best place for a festival. Early press releases were defensive, arguing that as so many music lovers from the 'western zones' would be unable to travel to Leipzig in 1950, it was necessary to hold some kind of 'worthy' parallel celebration in the western *Länder*.[6] Göttingen had no direct connection with Bach, but it was centrally located, in a region populated by both Protestants and Catholics. Moreover, the town had been left virtually undamaged by the war, and had been at the heart of the movement for authentic Bach performance in the pre-war period. Its University was a centre for Bach research. A strong musical argument was put forward, but again, a virtue was made of necessity. Göttingen did not actually have one of Germany's more famous choirs, or an orchestra of particular repute. It was, though, the site of the Mahrenholz-Furtwängler organ, built in the *Marienkirche* in 1926 by the 'Organ Movement', which sought to return to Baroque musical principles. The *Johanniskirche* provided another suitable building for the performance of Bach's liturgical works. To coordinate the musical performances, the Working Group engaged Fritz Lehmann, who had run the *Händel Festspiele* in Göttingen before the war. The Frankfurt organist Helmut Walcha, and rising stars like the baritone Dietrich Fischer-Dieskau, would support him. Choirs from Göttingen, Frankfurt, and Wuppertal would take part.

Over the next few weeks, a small committee worked to put the flesh on the bones of this plan. This group was chaired by Bernhard Sprenger, an official from Hanover, and included Christhard Mahrenholz, chairman of the *Neue Bach Gesellschaft* (NBG), and a leading figure in the world of Protestant church music. One of its first

---

5   Nordrhein-Westfälisches Hauptstaatsarchiv, Düsseldorf (hereafter NWHA), NW 60/861, Arbeitsgemeinschaft für Konzertwesen, 21 April 1948.

6   *Hannoversche Neueste Nachrichten*, 23 June 1949, p. 3. See also *Mitteilungen des deutschen Städtetags*, Nr. 223–57, 15 July 1949, p. 63.

documents reveals a clear political purpose: 'If at the same time a Bach Festival in Leipzig is celebrated as a political demonstration, then the West German *Länder*'s Bach Festival should present to the world a weighty and genuine articulation of the German will to peace.'[7]

The role of the NBG is complicated. There was real uncertainty about the society's legal status in 1949, and this allowed both the Federal Republic and the GDR to manipulate it to their apparent advantage. Before 1939, the NBG's president was the elderly *Thomaskantor*[8] Karl Straube, and the society was based in Leipzig. The NBG's records had though been destroyed in an air raid in 1943, and by 1949 Straube himself was very ill. In the West, it was accepted that Mahrenholz was his successor. In the East, the SED believed that Straube had passed on his office to his successor as *Thomaskantor*, Günther Ramin, and that he now represented the NBG. Ramin and Mahrenholz had a long shared history in the Organ Movement in the 1920s and 1930s. Ramin, though, had tenuously resisted offers to resettle the *Thomanerchor* in the West after 1945. He was already working closely with the SED, and had apparently agreed to the incorporation of the NBG into the *Kulturbund*.[9] Equally ambivalent was the role of academic musicology. The Society for Music Research (*Gesellschaft für Musikforschung* or GfM) had been formed in Göttingen in 1947, and embodied a commitment to German unity. Its president, Friedrich Blume, was based in Kiel, and its vice-president, Walther Vetter, worked at the Humboldt University in East Berlin. Coincidentally, both were Bach specialists. The GfM had been planning to hold its annual conference in 1950 in Lüneburg over the Bach anniversary, but Blume readily agreed to hold the conference a few days earlier to avoid conflict with the Göttingen Festival.

In August 1949, a press conference was held to publicise the successful conclusion of these preliminary arrangements. The public was informed that the Göttingen Festival had the support of the International Bach Society, based in Switzerland, the NBG, and the GfM. A *Kuratorium*, representing *Land* culture ministers, the NWDR, the universities, and including artists and musicians, would be formed to direct the Festival.[10] Thus the stage was set for a celebration of Bach, which would be 'representative', but apolitical. It would combine the best of contemporary Bach performance and academic research, and Bach's faith would be honoured by some of West Germany's most prominent clerics.

After the elections in September and the formation of the Adenauer government, work started on one of the strongest aspects of the Göttingen Festival: an exhibition of manuscripts and documents supporting the historical vision of Bach, the church composer. The Federal Republic had an advantage here, being in possession of

7   NWRA/NW 60/891, Abschrift, Bach-Fest 1950, 26 July 1949.

8   This is the title given to the Director of the *Thomanerchor*. As Bach himself had been an earlier *Thomaskantor*, it was a title which carried great prestige in Germany.

9   SAPMO-BArch DY 27/1530, untitled paper with notes of a conversation between Ramin, Biebrich, Gelbe-Haussen, and Gysi.

10   SG Sammlung 5, Bach-Fest 1950, 19 August 1949.

material from former Prussian collections in Berlin. The story of these documents, which included many Bach manuscripts of great importance, is a remarkable one. In May 1945, the Americans had found a huge mass of stored material in a salt mine at Heimboldshausen. Some 100,000 theatrical costumes were stored there, hung neatly on rails. Music and books from the Prussian State Opera, the State Library, and elsewhere, were simply piled up in huge heaps. To add to the confusion, before the Americans could act to secure the mine and its contents, it had been plundered by liberated slave labourers. Local inhabitants apparently described with wonder the exotic clothing subsequently displayed by foreign workers and former prisoners of war.[11] Fortunately, the huge heaps of music were not so attractive, and were largely left alone. The Americans soon sealed off the mine, and employed German POWs to sort out the music.[12] Eventually, despite assertions that the material would be returned to the Soviet Zone, much of it was dispersed to theatres and libraries in the American Zone, particularly in Marburg, which by 1949 had 170,000 items from former Prussian collections.[13] The Bach manuscripts, including the *B minor Mass*, and parts of the *St John Passion* and the *St Matthew Passion*, were lodged with universities in Marburg and Tübingen. In October 1949, Göttingen University librarian Wilhelm Martin Luther took on the responsibility for presenting an exhibition based upon them in the town's museum.[14]

In the GDR, all artistic activity was political, and there were no reservations about state involvement in a musical celebration. Bach, in 1950, would be used to cement the identification of the SED with German culture, and to showcase its determination to bring this culture to the working population. The performance of Bach's music would be accompanied by a reworking of his role in musical history, which would then also serve as the model for the broader construction of a new sociology of music. When it came to Bach, the GDR had overwhelming natural advantages. Bach was born in Eisenach, and had spent almost all his life in towns now in the GDR, above all in Leipzig. Here, too, was the *Thomanerchor*, and its director Günther Ramin. He is little known now outside Germany, but in 1950 his reputation as a virtuoso organist, choral director, and Bach interpreter was unparalleled. Highly successful tours in Europe and America had brought him international renown. No German musician questioned that Ramin and the *Thomanerchor* should head the musical celebrations of the Bach year.[15]

---

11   GLAK/OMGWB 12/91–1/7, Weekly Report of the Film, Theater and Music Control Section, 6871st DISCC, 21 July 1945, p. 4.

12   American lists of manuscripts from the *Preussische Staatsbibliothek* are in IfZ/ OMGUS POLAD 757/19. Apparently a number of books in the mine were burnt. See the photograph at http://www.ushmm.org.

13   *Mitteilungen des deutschen Städtetags*, Nr. 258–94, 15 August 1949, p. 74.

14   Wilhelm Martin Luther, *Johann Sebastian Bach: Documenta* (Kassel: Bärenreiter, 1950)

15   Ramin's relationship with Nazism is hard to judge. See the references to him in Kater, *The Twisted Muse.*

There was, though, a macabre prelude to the serious planning, involving Bach's body. What were thought to be Bach's remains had been exhumed in Leipzig in 1894, and a sarcophagus had been constructed in the *Johanneskirche*. For years, there had been calls to have the body moved to the *Thomaskirche*, and to build a larger memorial there, but the *Johanneskirche* had refused to release the body. During the war, the *Johanneskirche* had been destroyed, leaving the Bach tomb effectively standing out in the open. After 1945, the SED politicians running Leipzig decided to build a new civic mausoleum containing his body, and, in 1949, ordered that the body should be moved. According to Charlotte Ramin, the wife of the *Thomaskantor*, a master mason and a group of workmen from the church took the matter into their own hands. They removed the zinc inner coffin with Bach's remains from the ruins of the *Johanneskirche*, and brought them into the sacristy of the *Thomaskirche*. Confronted with this, the SED accepted the construction of a new sarcophagus in the *Thomaskirche*.[16] Consequently, in 1950, if they wanted to lay wreaths at Bach's tomb, they would have to conduct the ritual in a church.

A committee of experts was constituted by the SED in October 1949 – only weeks after the founding of the GDR. It included men from the Central Committee, the *Kulturbund*, and a group of musicians, Meyer, Notowicz, Laux and Pischner.[17] This group discussed the planned Göttingen Festival, and agreed that an 'all-German' Bach Festival in Leipzig in 1950 was 'of extraordinary political importance'.[18] Paul Wandel, now Education Minister, wrote to Walter Ulbricht, the *de facto* leader of the SED: 'Music, as an art form which is not tied to words, appears as a cultural instrument of the highest worth, because it serves as an internationally understood language. This is a further reason not to underestimate the political importance of a Bach Year in the GDR.'[19]

The SED knew that a successful celebration in Leipzig depended on Ramin and his choir. Nor did it have any illusions about his politics. A preparatory document for the Central Committee noted only by his name: 'Exercises a strong influence on the St Thomas school in Leipzig, in a reactionary manner.'[20] The Party was determined to make the Leipzig Festival a central part of its campaign for the 'National Front', and to involve as many organisations and individuals from the West as possible, using a so-called German Bach Committee (*Deutscher Bach-Ausschuss* or DBA).[21] Given the obvious likelihood of such tactics after the Goethe anniversary in 1949, it seems

---

16   Ramin, *Ramin*, pp. 122–4.

17   Hans Pischner was a harpsichordist who had returned to work in Weimar after being trained at the 'Antifa' school in Taliza.

18   SAPMO-BArch DY 27/1567, Protokoll der Sitzung des Arbeitsausschusses für die Feier des 200. Todestages von Joh. Seb. Bach im Jahre 1950 am 27 Oktober 1949.

19   SAPMO-BArch DY 30/J IV 2/3/70, Wandel to Ulbricht, 24 November 1949.

20   SAPMO-BArch DY 30/IV 2/9.06/70, Charakteristiken der Mitglieder des Bach-Ausschusses, undated.

21   The National Front was a body run by the SED to campaign, ostensibly, for a united, democratic, free Germany. It was also active in West Germany, particularly before the Communist Party there was banned in 1956.

incredible today that the SED had any success with this. In the event, their strategy, which was to give Ramin the Presidency of the DBA, was the key move. Once Ramin had accepted, it could leave the musical side of the Festival in his capable hands, and use him to lure in others. The SED could also rely on the Soviet Union to provide some first-class musicians. Shostakovich and Rostropovich quickly agreed to appear at the Festival in an all-Soviet concert.[22]

The Central Committee discussed the whole plan in December 1949, and allocated the huge sum of 1.1 million Marks for the Festival.[23] Invitations to join a German Bach Committee, signed by Paul Wandel, were sent out from the Ministry for People's Education to musicians and churchmen all over Germany.[24] As a result, thirty-two men and two women met in Berlin on 29 December 1949. Four can be clearly identified as living in the Federal Republic, the composers Hartmann, Pepping, and David, and the conductor Keilberth. Several, like the musicologists Besseler and Vetter, the conductor, Konwitschny, and Ramin himself, could be regarded as being compromised by their conduct between 1933 and 1945, and were GDR citizens more by force of circumstance than because of any Communist convictions. The rest were SED members, bureaucrats like Irmgard Schöningh, Fred Oelßner and Stefan Heymann, and Saxon politicians like Helmut Holtzhauer and Leipzig mayor Max Opitz. Meyer and his inner circle of musicians, thus Notowicz, Eisler, Butting and Laux, were also present. Ramin was called to the presidency. There was immediate agreement that the Göttingen planners had to be called to order.

> The committee considered further the Bach Festival planned in Göttingen, and was unanimous that for worthy Bach festivals only the towns of Leipzig or Eisenach came into question. In the interests of the spiritual unity of Germany, it mandated Herr Harry Goldschmidt therefore to make contact with the Göttingen Generalmusikdirektor Lehman [sic] to bring about a postponement and coordination of the Göttingen Bach Festival with the Leipzig German Bach Festival.

The DBA was also concerned about the GfM's planned conference in Lüneburg, and it was determined that Blume would be asked to hold this instead in Leipzig. Vetter was appointed to head a sub-committee to organise this conference, and mandated to travel to Kiel to negotiate with Blume. Preparations were also put in hand for an exhibition in Leipzig to rival Luther's in Göttingen.[25]

---

22   SAPMO-BArch DY 27/1567, ZK des SED, Abt. Kultur to Tetzner, Kulturbund, 26 November 1949.

23   SAPMO-BArch DY 30/J IV 2/3/70, Anlage Nr. 5 zum Protokoll Nr. 70 vom 5. Dezember 1949.

24   See the example in SAAdK, Heinz-Tiessen-Archiv, Korrespondenz, Deutscher Bachausschuss.

25   SAPMO-BArch DY 30/IV 2/9.06/70, Beschlussprotokoll der konstituierenden Sitzung des Deutschen Bach-Ausschusses 1950 am 29.12.1949. Goldschmidt was another émigré, recently returned from Switzerland. There seems no reason to doubt that Ramin was motivated primarily by his commitment to church music. See Ramin, *Ramin*, pp. 131–3.

One of the most significant figures of the Bach year was a long way from Germany at this time, but posed a particular problem for the SED. Its response to this challenge was supremely ironic, and brought about one of the most improbable partnerships of the twentieth century, between Paul Wandel and the saintly figure of Albert Schweitzer. Schweitzer, correctly identified by the SED as 'Author of the most important Bach biography',[26] had done more than any other individual to create the popular image of Bach. His portrait of the composer, first published in 1905, had been translated into many languages by 1950, and was still being reprinted.[27] Schweitzer's reputation, particularly in the West, was at its height: *Life* magazine in October 1947 had run an article on him headed 'The Greatest Man in the World', and reported that 'a poll in Europe had classed him alongside Goethe and Leonardo da Vinci'.[28] To present Bach more or less as a card-carrying member of the SED, Schweitzer's Bach had to be dismantled. Who better to preside over the demolition than Schweitzer himself? It was decided to offer him, jointly with Paul Wandel, the Honorary Presidency of the Leipzig Festival. In a deft piece of manipulation, the SED used Ramin, now representing the DBA, as its messenger. Whether Schweitzer would have responded positively to an invitation from the SED is something we will never know. He was certainly touched by the request from Ramin to serve as President, and replied from Equatorial Africa in February 1950 that although he could not attend the Festival, he was prepared to help. In March, he confirmed to Ramin that he would undertake the Honorary Presidency jointly with the 'Culture Minister' (by whom he presumably meant Paul Wandel).[29]

The SED's other schemes met with mixed fortunes. The plan to use the *Neue Bach Gesellschaft* and the *Gesellschaft für Musikforschung* to give the Festival an 'all-German legitimacy' was eventually successful, although Mahrenholz did not quite play the part intended. The role of the GfM was particularly odd. Blume, having successfully maintained his position as the doyen of German musicology through the Nazi years and after, was no stranger to political intrigue. Unlike many in positions of influence in the Federal Republic, though, Blume was not prepared to abandon his colleagues in the GDR. Through 1950, as plans to celebrate Bach developed in an increasingly confrontational atmosphere, Blume carefully kept a foot in both camps. He agreed to transfer the GfM's conference to Leipzig, and

---

26   SAPMO-BArch DY 30/IV 2/9.06/70, Charakteristiken der Mitglieder des Bach-Ausschusses, undated.

27   His *J. S. Bach, le musicien-poète* (Leipzig, 1905) was followed by an enlarged German version, entitled *J. S. Bach*, in 1908. Newman's English translation was first published in 1911.

28   See James Brabazon, *Albert Schweitzer* (London: Gollancz, 1976), pp. 371–91.

29   SAPMO-BArch DY 27/1568, Schweitzer to Ramin, 7 February 1950, and 27 March 1950; see also SAPMO-BArch DY 30/IV 2/9.06/70, Beschlussprotokoll der zweiten Sitzung des Deutschen Bach-Ausschusses 1950 vom 21.1.1950, p. 6. I have seen no reference in literature on Schweitzer to the SED's Bach Festival in 1950.

authorised Vetter to organise this in the society's name.[30] Until a late stage in the proceedings, the SED believed that Blume would deliver the opening speech at the conference.[31] He was firmly committed to the Göttingen Festival though, and was on its *Kuratorium*. In July 1950. he chose to stay there.

The plan to get the Göttingen Festival called off did not work. Goldschmidt's request to Lehmann was rejected, and the DBA followed this up by appealing directly to Mahrenholz in Hanover. A distinctly new note now appeared in the dialogue. The Göttingen planners were accused of using Bach 'for divisive machinations'.[32] *Radio-DDR* broadcast a vicious attack on the Göttingen Festival, which, it alleged, was being staged by 'politicians of division', agents of American imperialism. Mahrenholz, in a letter to Ramin, threatened to resign from the NBG because of this.[33] He, like Blume, was committed to a religious festival in Göttingen, but determined finally to travel to Leipzig to challenge the SED there.

Visions of Bach

The stage was set. In both Göttingen and Leipzig, Festivals would be held over the anniversary of Bach's death in July 1950. Both would present international guests with a programme of concerts, with academic seminars, and with scholarly collections of documents. There would be commemorative speeches, church services, and the laying of wreaths. The hostility between the two young German states meant that each would present a different Bach, and claim that theirs alone was the true, historical, German, Bach. The Federal Republic had the easier task here, as it could draw on existing images of Bach – most obviously as a church composer. Even if Schweitzer's central musicological idea was discredited, four aspects of his vision had penetrated deeply into the popular consciousness of Bach, and were unacceptable to the SED. First and foremost, he had presented Bach as a composer inspired by religion: 'The S.D.G. (*Soli Deo Gloria,* "to God alone be praise") and the J.J. (*Jesu juva,* "Help me, Jesus!") with which he garnishes his scores are for him no formulas, but the Credo that runs through all his work. Music is an act of worship with Bach.'[34] Second, Schweitzer had also emphasised the mystical element in Bach's faith, expressed in a wish to turn away from the world, and to embrace death. Third, and on a purely musical level, he had described Bach as 'a terminal point', taking existing

---

30   SAPMO-BArch DY 30/IV 2/9.06/70, Beschlussprotokoll der zweiten Sitzung des Deutschen Bach-Ausschusses 1950 vom 21.1.1950, p. 4.

31   See SAPMO-BArch DY 30/IV 2/2/73, Vorschlag für die internationale Bach-Tagung, which the *Politbüro* considered in February 1950.

32   SAPMO-BArch DY 30/IV 2/9.06/70, Beschlussprotokoll der zweiten Sitzung des Deutschen Bachausschusses 1950 vom 21.1.1950, p. 5.

33   Klingberg, *Politisch fest*, p. 84.

34   Albert Schweitzer, *J. S. Bach* (trans. Newman, Boston: Bruce Humphries, 1962), **I**, pp. 166–7.

forms to their full expressive potential, and leaving them exhausted.[35] Finally, he had argued that Bach's art was 'objective', and had no relationship with everyday reality: 'Bach's works would have been the same even if his existence had run quite another course. Did we know more of his life than is now the case ... we should still be no better informed as to the inward sources of his work than we are now.'[36] Although he wrote before the term 'Socialist Realism' was first used, Schweitzer could hardly have written a better description of its antithesis.

The SED entrusted the intellectual preparation of its Festival to Ernst Hermann Meyer, and it was he, more than any other individual, who had to confront the sheer improbability of the whole scheme. The GDR was a secular, materialistic, state, and to celebrate Bach as one of their own, the SED had to cast him as a worldly, progressive – even 'realistic' – composer. Meyer was told to determine 'what aspects of Bach might be renovated',[37] and to ensure that a consistent image of the composer was presented in the GDR in 1950. In speeches, newspapers, journals, and schoolbooks, on film, radio, and in travelling exhibitions, Bach was to appear, not crudely as a socialist, but as a progressive humanist, a man of his time and place who had written music which derived from the people and reflected their world. Despite the GDR's emphasis on nationality and unity, Bach was also to be presented as an international figure, and his would be an international festival. Here, the link with Leipzig was central. Meyer in 1950 presented Bach as an artist who had emerged from provincial obscurity in a divided feudal Germany, and in the unique setting of 18th-century Leipzig, had come into contact with international culture. Here, he had learnt to unite the qualities of German folk music with a wider international musical language, thus creating the works that were so loved worldwide, and giving a 'progressive' impetus to musical development. Here, Bach combined eclecticism with local traditions of craftwork and musical instrument manufacture. More improbably, Meyer portrayed Bach as an unfortunate slave of the church, constantly at odds with the petty limitations imposed by religious dogma, but finding intellectual sustenance in the advanced, secular milieu of Leipzig's coffee houses. That so much of his music was liturgical was something enforced on Bach by his socio-economic circumstances, and reflected no more than the prevailing relations of production.

It is no coincidence that Meyer's vision of Bach's Leipzig recalls the London of Defoe and Swift. Meyer was no opportunist hack, and to be fair to him, we should not imagine that his vision of Bach was dreamed up in 1949 or 1950 to suit the SED's requirements. It was, in fact, developed in London during the war years, as Meyer wrestled with the application of Marxist theory to musical history. He wrote in 1944, in English:

> In his work there lives a new humanism. ... But Bach worked in Weimar and Leipzig, cities which were socially, economically and intellectually among the most advanced in

---

35   *Ibid.*, **I**, p. 3.
36   *Ibid.*, **I**, p. 1.
37   SAPMO-BArch DY 27/1567, Protokoll der Sitzung des Arbeitsausschusses für die Feier des 200. Todestages von Joh. Seb. Bach im Jahre 1950, 27 October 1949, p. 14.

Germany, cities which at the same time were absorbing most readily the teachings of humanitarianism which came from abroad to Central Europe. ... In such an atmosphere Bach's genius could develop comparatively freely – even though we will recognise certain traces of Pietist devoutness and introversion in some of his liturgic compositions.[38]

The Bach year gave him the chance to expand on and propagate these ideas more widely. In dozens of speeches and articles, in academic treatises, in thousands of pamphlets, and in teaching materials for schools, Meyer's Bach was spread to every corner of the GDR. The SED's identification with this vision was confirmed in March 1950 by the *Politbüro*'s acceptance of a 'position statement' prepared by Meyer. This document combined historical analysis with an embattled view of the contemporary situation:

> The whole exchange of these decisive arguments between the defenders of cosmopolitanism, this reactionary, imperialistic ideology in West Germany, which is intended to undermine any national self-sufficiency of our people, and the progressive bearers of a new German culture, is revealed in the position statement on the Bach Year, 1950, which is celebrated on the occasion of the 200th anniversary of this great German composer's death.

Bach, through contact with currents from abroad, had led the way to a new stage in German cultural development. He was a progressive secular artist, who spoke with the idioms of the people. The German bourgeoisie had, though, failed to understand him:

> The liberal bourgeoisie saw Bach exclusively as the church musician, and every connection with the people was deliberately overlooked or covered up. In the period of imperialism the bourgeoisie falsified Bach as a formalist or an advocate of a cold, content-less splendour.

Only the defeat of fascism by the armies of the Soviet Union had cleared the way for an objective appreciation of Bach, but this was now threatened by the emergence of a clerical-fascist puppet regime in West Germany. The document ended with a call to arms:

> In the Bach Year, 1950, we will defend our national culture against all destructive and divisive efforts of American imperialism. Through dogged and indefatigable struggle against all efforts to falsify Bach, and to present him, in the fashion of cosmopolitan propaganda, as a "supra-national" church musician or formalist, we will show the national importance of Bach to the whole German people.[39]

---

38   SAAdK Ernst-Hermann-Meyer-Archiv, 385, Germany and Music, 1944. Only weeks before starting work on the Bach year, Meyer was briefly back in London to work with the BBC Third Programme on a *History in Sound of European Music*. BBC WAC RCONT 1, Ernst Hermann Meyer, Artists, File 1: 1931–62, Music Booking Manager to Meyer, 8 July 1949, and 1 September 1949; also JR to Music Booking Manager, 24 August 1949.

39   SAPMO-BArch DY 30/IV 2/2/76, Stellungnahme des Parteivorstandes der Sozialistischen Einheitspartei Deutschlands zum Bachjahr, Anlage Nr. 4 zum Protokoll Nr. 76

Many in the Federal Republic felt, equally strongly, that the secular Bach being celebrated in the GDR was a travesty, and were determined to make the Göttingen festival a worthy surrogate. At *Land* and *Bund* level, there were debates on how best to stage what the Conference of Culture Ministers called 'a united, representative, German Bach Festival', and the consensus on Göttingen was maintained.[40] The government of Lower Saxony played a coordinating role, negotiating between different individuals and groups. In an important symbolic gesture, the first President of the Federal Republic, Theodor Heuss, took on the patronage of the Festival.[41] We must assume that Heuss did exercise some discretion here. Neither he nor Adenauer were willing, in 1951, to accept a similar role for the re-opened Bayreuth Festival.[42] After some haggling, the money needed for the Festival was found, with the burden, not surprisingly, weighted towards institutions from northern Germany. A number of towns like Ansbach and Würzburg felt, with some justification, that they were home to a stronger Bach tradition than Göttingen, and were not entirely content to take second place. The *Länder* agreed in January 1950 to contribute 40,000 DM.[43] Christine Teusch, the Culture Minister in North Rhine-Westphalia, was advised that the Göttingen plan should be supported because 'a Festival which does justice to the matter can not be held in the Bach towns of the Russian Zone'.[44] The NWDR provided 30,000 DM. At *Bund* level, it was agreed to issue a set of Bach postage stamps, and eventually 40,000 DM from the sale of these was diverted to the Festival in Göttingen. Adenauer's Chancellery provided 11,000 DM, specifically for Luther's exhibition.[45]

As the SED's attacks became more vicious, new members were appointed to the Festival *Kuratorium*. Under Heuss's patronage, this grew to represent a broad coalition, including several senior *Land* politicians, West Berlin mayor Ernst Reuter, and the NWDR's director, Adolf Grimme. Mahrenholz and Bishop Hanns Lilje represented the Protestant church. Blume was a member, as were the Bach scholar Wilibald Gurlitt and Göttingen musicologist Rudolph Gerber. Just as in the East, other famous musicians and artists were enrolled to gain wider credibility. Where the SED had roped in Hanns Eisler, Bert Brecht and Arnold Zweig, the Göttingen planners secured Paul Hindemith, and notably the Nobel Prize winner Hermann Hesse.[46] His

vom 13. März 1950.

40   NWRA/NW 60/891, Voigt, der Niedersächsische Kultusminister, to Teusch, 30 December 1949. See also Wende, Bundesministerium des Innern, to Kultusministerium des Landes Nordrhein-Westfalen, 3 February 1950.

41   *Göttinger Tageblatt*, 24 March 1950.

42   BAK B136/5815, Seebohm, Bundesminister für Verkehr, to Adenauer, 8 March 1951, and Mai, persönlicher Referent des Bundeskanzlers, to Seebohm, 29 March 1951.

43   NWRA/NW 60/891, Vormerk: Betr.: Bachfest, 24 January 1950.

44   NWRA/NW 60/891, Abteilungsleiter III K3 to Teusch, undated.

45   SG Sammlung 5, Protokoll der Sitzung des Kuratoriums des westdeutschen Bach-Festes am 28. Juli 1950, p. 2.

46   The festival programme, *Bach Fest 1950. Göttingen 23–30 Juli* (Kassel: Bärenreiter, 1950) lists the *Kuratorium* in full.

recent novel *Das Glasperlenspiel* (*The Glass Bead Game*) had presented a vision of Bach's music that, in its spirituality and abstraction, perfectly complemented the apolitical orientation of music in the Federal Republic.[47] The town council in Göttingen was delighted at the opportunity to raise its status as a cultural centre, and hoteliers and caterers there naturally looked forward to the profits to be made from an anticipated two thousand guests.[48]

Both sides suffered setbacks as they fought for the cultural high ground. The manipulation of Bach involved compromises that were uncomfortable, and in some cases impossible, to sustain. In Göttingen, a municipal official, Dr Pfauter, hit on the idea of making a Bach film. In the western Zones, the film industry had been fragmented by the Americans, British and French, and Göttingen now had its own studio. Perhaps unwisely, Pfauter suggested a naturalistic drama rather than a documentary, and ran into difficulties. While concerned that the film should present 'the real, human, Bach', Pfauter was aware that it could not be shot in Leipzig, and suggested using Göttingen instead. After all, he argued, 'The musical world, and musical circles in England and America will direct their attention to Göttingen in the coming year.'[49] With what appears now as remarkable insensitivity, the famous actor Werner Krauss, who had appeared in the notorious film *Jud Süss* (1940), was earmarked to 'play' Bach. Hans Besch, a Hamburg priest, was asked to write the script, but progress was very slow. A further blow came when Pfauter heard that Krauss was also taking the role of Hitler in an Austrian production, *The last days in the Reich Chancellery*.[50] The plan was scrapped in April 1950.[51] In the GDR, the state film company DEFA was ordered to prepare a 40-minute documentary, to reflect the themes of the Festival, and bring the new Bach to a wider audience. DEFA drew heavily on the services of Meyer, and an old comrade from England, Georg

---

47   Bach was indeed at the very heart of the vision of the future presented by Hesse. He wrote: '[W]e consider the cantatas, passions, and preludes of Bach as the ultimate quintessence of Christian culture.' Hermann Hesse, *The Glass Bead Game* (Harmondsworth: Penguin, 1977), p. 30. We should note also Hesse's view of the relative unimportance of the details, such as were known, of Bach's life and mental outlook: 'Thus ... we have no idea whether Johann Sebastian Bach or Wolfgang Amadeus Mozart actually lived in a cheerful or despondent manner. Mozart moves us with that peculiarly touching and endearing grace of early blossoming and fading; Bach stands for the edifying and comforting submission to God's paternal plan of which suffering and dying form a part. But we do not really read these qualities from their biographies and from such facts about their private lives as have come down to us; we read them solely from their works, from their music.'(pp. 47–8)

48   SG Sammlung 5, Stadt Göttingen, Finanzabteilung, to Stadtkämmerei, 21 January 1950.

49   SG Kulturamt Nr. 189, Vorschlag zu einem Film über Johann Sebastian Bach, undated.

50   SG Kulturamt Nr. 189, Pfauter, Kulturdezernat, Rathaus Göttingen, to Besch, 14 October 1949.

51   SG Kulturamt Nr. 189, Abich, Filmaufbau GmbH Göttingen, to Besch, 18 April 1950.

Knepler, who had been working for the Austrian Communist Party, to write the script of the film.[52] The film itself mixed images of singing trade unionists and earnest FDJ members playing Bach's music with a heroic narrative of the composer's life. Setting a pattern for subsequent GDR film biographies of composers, it displayed many historical documents.[53]

The all-German gloss of the SED's preparations was rather dulled, though, by the desertion of a key official. Eberhard Gelbe-Haussen, one of the DBA's two Leipzig-based secretaries, fled to Stuttgart in March 1950 with many documents that revealed clearly the manipulations of the SED. The West German press made much of this, as they had with the earlier controversy over Bach's body. Now, syndicated articles with titles like 'Misuse of Bach', and 'Let's get Bach into the National Front', appeared in regional and national newspapers.[54] Gelbe-Haussen's revelations only confirmed what had been previously suspected, and deepened the cynicism felt in the West about the Leipzig Festival. Luckily (and crucially) for the SED, there were no further desertions. The NBG and the GfM maintained their support; Ramin and the key performers held fast. Whether the spreading ripples of the controversy reached Schweitzer in Lambaréné is not known.

There was collusion over the one area where both sides risked equal embarrassment, namely the compromised Nazi background of so many participants. The new governments of the Federal Republic and the GDR wanted the services of Germany's top musicians, and (like the Nazis) they needed the academic window dressing that could be provided by senior German musicologists. They could not afford to be too choosy. In both Göttingen and Leipzig in 1950, numerous musicians and academics who had taken part in appalling earlier cultural-political events were involved. Several of the musicologists had previously met at the Reich Music Festival in Düsseldorf in May 1938, accompanied by the notorious exhibition on 'Degenerate Music'. Many of the musicians and churchmen, like Mahrenholz, Ramin, Söhngen, Gurlitt, Mauersberger, and Blume, had signed the famous declaration of May 1933 about a new German church music, and taken part in the Berlin Festival of church music in 1937, where one item displayed had been a massive chiselled sculpture of the head of a 'Nordic–Germanic' Bach. Mahrenholz, who showed courage in 1950 in going to Leipzig to defy the SED, had, on this earlier occasion celebrated the 'healthy, worldly, organ music' that the Organ Movement had promoted alongside a renewed

---

52   See SAAdK Ernst-Hermann-Meyer-Archiv, Korrespondenz bis 1950, D, Chefdramaturg, DEFA to Meyer, 11 October 1949; Dahle to Meyer, 24 March 1950; and Meyer to Dahle, 5 April 1950. Knepler had left Austria in 1934, and met Meyer in England. He also worked with the BBC, where he pioneered broadcast opera in the 1930s, and with the Free German Cultural League.

53   The screenplay of the film is in SAPMO-BArch DY 30/IV 2/9.06/70

54   SAPMO-BArch DY 30/IV 2/9.06/70, Tetzner to Heymann, 24 March 1950, and 24 April 1950.

church music.[55] He had held high office in the Reich Music Chamber.[56] Perhaps the worst was Rudolph Gerber, a former employee of Rosenberg's *Sonderstab Musik* and *Hohe Schule* who, in 1950, gave an address at the Göttingen Festival on 'Bach's art in the development of the spirit of the Christian West'.[57] During the Third Reich, he had written about the threat posed to German music by 'international Judaism', as represented by 'the Czech ghetto-Jew Gustav Mahler'.[58] There was at least some discussion of these problems in the GDR. Enquiring whether a certain Dr Matzke should be excluded from the Leipzig conference because he had been a Nazi, Notowicz was realistic: 'I am of the opinion, that one can only exclude him from the conference if he is genuinely – also compared with the mass of the other participants – extraordinarily compromised.'[59]

It is appropriate to comment here on one other dissenting voice that was raised, belatedly, in the West, to 'defend Bach against his devotees'. Theodor Adorno, another returned émigré, repelled by the way that Bach had been turned into a 'neutralized cultural monument', in an article first published in 1951, criticised several of the ways in which Bach was represented in his anniversary year. Adorno had rejected Stalinist orthodoxy, and his rather opaque critique made no direct reference to the manipulations of the SED. It must be read, rather, as an attack on the West German celebrations. 'Reaction', wrote Adorno, 'deprived of its political heroes, takes complete possession of the composer whom it had long claimed as one of its own by giving him the ignominious name of the "Thomas Cantor"... They have made him into a composer for organ festivals in well-preserved Baroque towns, into ideology.' Adorno criticised the representation of Bach as 'the consummation of the Middle Ages', and ridiculed the developing passion for a historically authentic performance praxis. He called for a 'social deciphering' of Bach, in opposition to an 'impotent nostalgia' which 'degraded' Bach as a 'church composer'. In this he appears at one with the SED, and like the Party's theorists, Adorno stressed Bach's development of equal temperament. Through this, Bach had reconciled 'the aesthetic domination of nature' with the 'voice of humanity', at the very dawn of the bourgeois era.[60] Adorno

---

55   Cited in Kaufmann, *Orgel und Nationalsozialismus*, p. 73. He cites the 1933 declaration on pp. 61–3; see Anhang A, Abbildung 3, for a picture of the Bach sculpture. See also Kater, *Twisted Muse*, pp. 159–76.

56   Mahrenholz was leader of the *Fachschaft evangelischer Kirchen- und Posaunenchöre* in the *Reichsmusikkammer, Abteilung III*. One of his stated responsibilities, 'the accreditation of choirs for planned Festivals', suggests that he was no stranger to ideological manipulation. See Hans Hinkel (ed.), *Handbuch der Reichskulturkammer* (Berlin: Deutscher Verlag für Politik und Wirtschaft, 1937), pp. 101–2.

57   *Bach-Fest 1950*, p. 11. See the references to Gerber in de Vries, *Sonderstab Musik*.

58   Cited in Potter, *Most German of the Arts*, pp. 229–30. See also her many references to Blume, Vetter, Besseler, and others involved in 1950.

59   SAPMO-BArch DY 27/1568, Notowicz to Schöningh, 12 May 1950.

60   Theodor Adorno, 'Bach defended against his Devotees', *Prisms* (trans. Weber and Weber, Letchworth: Garden City Press, 1967), pp. 135–46. This essay was first published as

was no supporter of the SED, for all his criticisms of the way in which culture was developing in the Federal Republic.[61] Perhaps the most striking feature of his 1951 essay on Bach is its avoidance of any engagement with the SED's ideas. In this, as we shall see, Adorno's studied indifference was of a piece with broader reactions in the West.

'Ideological Exaggerations'

In both Göttingen and Leipzig, there were flurries of activity as the anniversary approached. Both towns wanted to put their best foot forward, and to make their guests feel welcome. In Göttingen, a commemorative medallion was planned. Festival brochures and travel guides were prepared, in English and Italian as well as in German versions. Invitations were sent to Canada, Sweden, Belgium, Turkey, Holland, and Switzerland. Naturally, an American Control Officer, Dr Biel, was on the guest list.[62] There was disappointment that Heuss could not attend the Festival as planned, and the government of Lower Saxony took great care with the preparation of a speech for his replacement, Vice-Chancellor Franz Blücher. The speech conceded that 'If the Iron Curtain did not divide Germany into two opposed parts, the representative German Bach Festival could only be celebrated this year in Leipzig.' In these circumstances, the Göttingen Festival deserved recognition because of its high artistic merit. There should be no confusion: 'The Federal Government refuses to make a political demonstration on the occasion of the Bach Festival. It is obeying, rather, a cultural duty.'[63]

There were more difficulties in Leipzig, where local activists were overwhelmed at the last moment as they tried to coordinate gifts and free tickets for the lists of foreign guests and SED officials.[64] 12,000 Festival brochures and 85,000 posters in different sizes were produced. There was no time to vet all the speeches made, which also led to some embarrassments.[65] For the many hundreds of Party workers involved,

---

'Bach gegen seine Liebhaber verteidigt' in the journal *Merkur* in 1951. It is striking, and says much about the way some of Adorno's work on music has been decontextualised, that this essay has not been connected directly with the Bach Year. This may also partly be because the essay became better known after it was published in *Prismen* in 1955, and did not appear in English translation until 1967.

61   Adorno's sharpest critique of the Soviet-inspired musical culture of the Eastern bloc countries was first published in 1956. See 'Die gegängelte Musik', *Gesammelte Schriften, Band 14, Dissonanzen; Einleitung in die Musiksoziologie* (Frankfurt-am-Main: Suhrkamp, 1990), pp. 51–66.

62   SG Sammlung 5, Abschrift, Der Niedersächsische Ministerpräsident, Staatskanzlei, 3 July 1950.

63   SG Sammlung 5, Thema-Vorschlag für Eröffnungs-Rede, Niedersächsische Staatskanzlei to Blücher, undated.

64   SAPMO-BArch DY 27/1567, Richtlinien für die Ausgabe von Geschenken an Ehrengäste, undated.

65   SAPMO-BArch DY 27/1567, Bericht, undated, p. 6.

the GDR produced an example of the self-mythologising kitsch that became one of its distinguishing characteristics: a Bach 'memorial brooch'. Members of the DBA were invited to a private screening of DEFA's *Johann Sebastian Bach 1950* at the end of June in Berlin.[66]

After the months of preparation, the actual Festivals were quickly over and done with. In both Göttingen and Leipzig, thousands of visitors turned up to hear the speeches, attend the concerts, services, and seminars, and to consume celebratory dinners. All over Germany, many more tuned in to the broadcasts. In Göttingen, Blücher gave the opening speech, and read out a telegram of good wishes from Heuss. Nobody appears to have remarked after Gerber's speech how he had changed his tune since 1945.[67] Luther's exhibition at the town Museum was widely praised. The 1748 Haussmann portrait of Bach, which had been brought over from England and was now publicly displayed in Germany for the first time, attracted particular attention.[68] Lehmann's musicians performed well, especially Walcha and Fischer-Dieskau.[69] The concerts were sold out, and there was apparently a lively black market for tickets. In Leipzig, the brittle truce between SED activists and visiting churchmen was not easily maintained, and both sides made thinly veiled attacks on one another. The musicological conference was held in a tense atmosphere of superficial courtesy and underlying hostility, as Meyer tried to manipulate proceedings. Many, including some of his colleagues, must have squirmed in their seats when he explicitly referred to Nazism:

> The efforts of a few of today's theoreticians, to portray Bach as an otherworldly cosmopolitan, and at the same time totally to deny his societal role, are every bit as hostile to culture and as reactionary as were the attempts to proclaim this great artist as a racially blessed personality.[70]

A number of churchmen, from East and West, challenged his materialist interpretation of Bach. Wilibald Gurlitt, one of several who divided their time that week between Göttingen and Leipzig, spoke for many: 'For Johann Sebastian Bach, the meaning

---

66   SAAdK Ernst-Hermann-Meyer-Archiv, Korrespondenz bis 1950, D, Brandes, DEFA to Meyer, 26 June 1950.

67   Even Stuckenschmidt reported to the American public only that Gerber had given a 'brilliant talk'. 'Radio Stations Take On Added Musical Responsibility', *Musical America*, 71 (February 1951), pp. 122ff., quote on p. 122.

68   The portrait, owned by Walter Jenke, had been brought to England from Silesia before the war. The better-known 1746 portrait was still in Leipzig. See Stanley Godman, 'A Newly Discovered Bach Portrait', *Musical Times*, 91 (July 1950), p. 263.

69   See Dürr, 'In Göttingen'.

70   Walther Vetter and Ernst Meyer (eds), *Bericht über die wissenschaftliche Bachtagung der Gesellschaft für Musikforschung, Leipzig, 23. bis 26. Juli 1950* (Leipzig, 1951), pp. 45–6.

and mission of all music, not only church music, but all spiritual and secular vocal and instrumental music, is based on God, not on man, on the Creator, not the created.'[71]

Meyer was supported by speakers from the Soviet Union and the 'peoples' democracies', by other GDR musicologists, and by his fellow émigrés. Georg Knepler highlighted Bach's use of equal temperament, casting him as a musical progressive who had laid the foundation for a new expressive language.[72] The most crudely ideological paper was given by Eberhard Rebling, styled at the conference as a Dutch representative.[73] Abandoning the traditional language of musical analysis, Rebling used a Marxist-Leninist vocabulary to link Bach, through Beethoven, with contemporary Soviet 'realist' composers. In passing, he dealt mercilessly with the 'formalist' presentation of Bach as an 'aimless' numerical symbolist. His paper prompted a baffled response from Annelise Liebe, who politely asked what the word 'progressive' (repeatedly used by the SED delegates as a complimentary term) actually meant in musicological terms. She was brutally told by a Czechoslovak delegate that this was obvious to an ordinary citizen, and did not merit scholarly discussion.[74]

As we have seen, a central tenet of Schweitzer's vision of Bach was his willing embrace of death. In similar vein, Herman Hesse had recently written of 'the tranquil, composed readiness for death in Bach',[75] and this was another point of dispute during the conference. The SED wanted to portray Bach as a believer in progress in this world, as a man with a deep faith in, and commitment to living humanity, and could therefore not accept this theological view of the composer, which suggested rather a deep disillusionment and world weariness. Oskar Söhngen, a leading figure in West German Protestant church music, strongly defended the mystical view of Bach, referring to his Cantata No. 161 *Komm, du süße Todesstunde*, as one work in which 'Bach indeed ecstatically longs for death'.[76] He might of course have referred to the text of several others.

The arguments came to a head on Friday 28 July, the anniversary of Bach's death. Wilhelm Pieck delivered an extraordinary speech at the Congress Hall, in which he bitterly attacked the reduction of Bach's music to the level of 'a formalistic plaything' in the West. Only the 'democratic development in our Republic' had allowed the people a true understanding of their national cultural heritage. Pieck praised Bach's 'humanistic genius', which reflected 'the earthiness and thoughtfulness of handworkers and the contemplativeness of the peasants'. It was no geographical coincidence that the GDR's Festival had the character of a national celebration.

---

71   Wilibald Gurlitt, 'Bach in seiner Zeit und heute', Vetter and Meyer, *Bericht*, pp. 51–80, p. 72.

72   Georg Knepler, 'Bemerkungen zum Wandel des Bachbildes', Vetter and Meyer, *Bericht*, pp. 308–17.

73   Eberhard Rebling, 'Der Rationalismus, eine Grundlage des Bachschen Realismus', Vetter and Meyer, *Bericht*, pp. 420–28.

74   Vetter and Meyer, *Bericht*, pp. 429–30.

75   Hesse, *The Glass Bead Game*, p. 44.

76   Vetter and Meyer, *Bericht*, p. 186.

Even if Eisenach and Leipzig had been in West Germany, Pieck alleged, 'national celebrations' could not have taken place there. Overcome by 'American cultural barbarism', West Germany was ruled by trust directors and Wall Street bankers. German culture there had been replaced by 'erotic magazines, cops and robbers novels, and films in which the mentally ill and gangsters appeared as heroes'. If composers there did not write 'boogie woogie rhythms or abrasive neo-fascistic marches', they had to vegetate in poverty.[77]

He was robustly answered by Mahrenholz, who had spoken earlier in the week in Göttingen. In the *Thomaskirche*, before wreaths were laid at Bach's tomb, Mahrenholz declared: 'Music not dedicated to the glory of God ... is according to Bach himself, not real music, but a devilish blaring and droning.' Alluding to the earlier controversy over Bach's remains, he argued that the church was the only fit place for them.[78] After this, Party activists could no longer maintain the veneer of courtesy, and wreaths representing the *Thomanerchor*, the NBG, and Bishop Lilje of Hanover were unceremoniously shoved to one side so that an SED wreath could take pride of place at the sarcophagus. In a private act of defiance, Christian Weichert, a journalist reporting for the *Düsseldorfer Nachrichten*, came back later that night and returned the NBG's wreath to its former position.[79] By common consent, though, the music was hugely successful. This was Ramin's finest hour, and the culminating performance of the *B minor Mass*, in which he led the combined forces of the *Thomanerchor*, the *Kreuzchor*, and the Gewandhaus Orchestra, was widely praised. The Soviet performers shone, the young pianist Tatyana Nikolayeva winning the prize competition. Shostakovich gave a dutiful speech at a final ceremony.[80] An added bonus was a strong French presence, including the Loewenguth Quartet.[81]

The guests departed, and the musicians, politicians and academics dispersed. Over the next few months, there was a continued outpouring of material about Bach. In the West, the organisers of the Göttingen Festival were praised for distancing Bach 'from all ideological exaggerations'.[82] Luther's exhibition, which had attracted international attention, was soon taken to other West European countries.[83] In the GDR, Pieck's speech was endlessly reprinted, and the open debate at the musicological

---

77   Wilhelm Pieck, 'Ehren wir Bach, indem wir seinem friedlichen Werk den Frieden erhalten!', Vetter and Meyer, *Bericht*, pp. 19–27.

78   Christhard Mahrenholz, 'Gedenkrede', *Bach-Jahrbuch, 39. Jahrgang, 1951–52*, pp. 5–15.

79   SAPMO-BArch DY 27/1567, Weichert to Landesleitung des Kulturbundes, Berlin, 15 August 1950.

80   Shostakovich's speech, which was presumably written for him, is reprinted in Vetter and Meyer, *Bericht*, pp. 457–61. It is unfortunate that the ever-growing literature on Shostakovich's relationship with Communism does not consider his role as a propagandist at the Leipzig Festival.

81   See Hans Mayer, *Gelebte Musik. Erinnerungen* (Frankfurt am Main: Suhrkamp, 1999), pp. 211–18.

82   Dürr, 'In Göttingen', p. 340.

83   Godman, 'The Bach Exhibition at Göttingen', p. 485.

conference was praised.[84] Notowicz denounced the Americans for keeping the Bach manuscripts in the West, and the Federal Republic for trying to prevent its citizens from travelling to Leipzig.[85] The *National Zeitung* criticised the Federal Republic for the lack of publicity it gave to events in Göttingen, and reported that Bach was now typically played by jazz bands to a samba rhythm in the West. There was, it said, a hit song going around there with a rhyming refrain about how people would rather play *Krach*, or make a racket, than Bach.[86]

Unity and Division

Fifty years on, it is worth asking whether the events of 1950 in Göttingen and Leipzig had any wider and lasting significance. Adopting for a moment the methods of symbolic anthropology, it is striking how similarly the two states behaved. With their committees of artists and politicians, their speeches, films, and exhibitions, grey suits, wreaths and flowers, there seems little to distinguish between them. Both issued commemorative postage stamps. The surviving documents even share a similar vocabulary, arguing that there was only one 'worthy', 'true', 'representative', 'German' Bach festival. In the music chosen for performance, there was considerable overlap, both Festivals using the *B minor Mass* as a focal point. Behind public façades, in both states coalitions of politicians from central, regional and municipal levels supervised and financed the presentation of a Bach that was consonant with their political beliefs. These similarities raise further questions. Why did the SED make this uncomfortable compromise with the church? After all, it could have opted for a purely secular commemoration. Turning the question on its head, why did so many priests and musicians travel from the West to suffer in person the hostility of the SED in Leipzig? Here again, there was unity, because in fact all involved did want, in some way, to pay homage to Bach. It would be idle to pretend now, as both states did then, that one was more sincere in its veneration of Bach than the other. For the SED, it was unthinkable to jettison Bach's sacred music, and celebrate only that which could be clearly identified as secular. Equally, for the churchmen and women from the West, Bach's spiritual home was in Leipzig, in the *Thomaskirche*, and however good the organ was in Göttingen's *Marienkirche*, no building there was an adequate substitute. The undignified squabbling over the wreaths at Bach's tomb can be read as a summary of the compromises both sides had made over the previous twelve months.

In retrospect, the Festivals were significant in three ways. First, on the level of Bach scholarship, they gave impetus to the establishment of two parallel institutes,

---

84   See for example Karl Laux, 'Das Fazit von Leipzig', *Tägliche Rundschau*, 2 August 1950.

85   Nathan Notowicz, 'Deutsche Bachfeier Leipzig 1950', *Die Aussprache*, 1950/7-8, pp. 17–19.

86   Uwe Fischer, 'Nationale Bedeutung der deutschen Bachfeier', *National Zeitung*, 4 August 1950.

both dedicated to research and conservation. Through the 1950s, in both Leipzig and Göttingen, teams of scholars and technicians worked on Bach manuscripts and documents, and laid the basis for a revised understanding of the chronology of his compositions. The research in both towns has informed significant changes in performance practice. Second, in personal terms, the Festivals gave impetus to the careers of many of the actual musicians, like Fischer-Dieskau, Nikolayeva and Rostropovich. Ramin was awarded the GDR's 'National Prize' in November 1950,[87] and until his death in 1955, allowed to travel widely with the *Thomanerchor*. Luther was later appointed to head the Bach Institute in Göttingen. In the GDR, a striking number of activists who had acquitted themselves well went on to more prominent careers. Leipzig's mayor, Max Opitz, was appointed as personal secretary to Wilhelm Pieck. Helmut Holzhauer, the Saxon Minister for Education, was called in 1951 to head the State Commission for Artistic Affairs, and Rudolf Hartig, a Leipzig official who had been active behind the scenes, was appointed to run its Music Department. Above all the reliability of Meyer's group was confirmed, and they were entrusted with the further development of the GDR's musical culture. Meyer himself was subsequently rewarded with the editorship of the journal *Musik und Gesellschaft* and a leading role in the Association of German Composers and Musicologists (*Verband deutscher Komponisten und Wissenschaftler*, or VDK), both established in 1951. In December of that year, he was chosen to lead the delegation to a cultural congress in the Federal Republic,[88] a decision which at that particular time, given Meyer's Jewish background and British connections, reflects an extraordinary degree of trust from the SED leadership. Hans Pischner was put in charge of music at Radio Berlin in 1950, and later became Deputy Minister for Culture. Rebling, who settled in the GDR after his appearance in Leipzig, became an important figure in Meyer's inner circle. Knepler, confirmed as Director of the Music Academy in Berlin, also went on to play a leading role in the GDR. Third, in terms of wider cultural politics, the Bach year established patterns that prevailed through the Cold War, and revealed profound differences in how the two Germanys saw the role of music in their respective societies. In the GDR, music was to be a servant of the Party; artists would represent the people, and work for them. Creativity would be valued in so far as it related to the working population and could be understood by them. Where it strayed from its 'national' cultural inheritance, and departed from 'realism', it would be condemned. The demand for adherence to the classics was strengthened, and new composition was pressed into a distinctly archaic mould.[89] The example of the Leipzig Festival was constantly held up before the GDR's musicians as a guiding light, and the cult of

---

87   *Die Aussprache*, 1950/11, pp. 8–9.

88   SAPMO-BArch DY 27/38, Beschlußprotokoll der Sekretariatsitzung von 10.12.1951, p. 1.

89   None of the pieces written in the style of Bach in the GDR after the Leipzig Festival is at all well known. Shostakovich, greatly impressed by Tatyana Nikolayeva's interpretation of Bach in Leipzig, was inspired to write his own Twenty-Four Preludes and Fugues. See Wilson, *Shostakovich*, pp. 247–58.

Bach was further developed. He remained a pre-eminent symbol of artistic greatness in the GDR. The theoretical positions put forward by Meyer were adopted as the foundations for further historical revision, and similar ideas were applied to other composers: Beethoven in 1952, Schubert in 1953, Mozart in 1956, and above all the *Händel Festspiele*, started in Halle in 1952. These all followed the Leipzig pattern, with academic outpourings, films, broadcasts, and commemorative concerts. None, though, was carried through on such a large scale.

In the Federal Republic, the Göttingen Festival announced that music was unconnected with politics. This was the prelude to the 'golden years', celebrated in so much of the literature on music there. In public, music was supported by consumers who paid to attend concerts and buy records, by radio license fees, and by generous grants from regional and municipal authorities. This pluralism should, according to Allied calculation, have guaranteed artistic freedom and an absence of censorship. Behind the scenes though, the institutional coalition that had supported the Göttingen Festival was kept in operation, allowing the *Bund* to intervene discreetly in musical matters where and when it felt appropriate. The Göttingen *Kuratorium* seems to have developed a taste for intrigue. It met on the day of the anniversary, and decided to build on the success of the Festival by starting a new Bach edition. It was particularly keen to support this historically, and laid plans to photocopy the Bach manuscripts kept in East Berlin. As for the newly discovered Haussmann portrait: 'Herr Luther advised that it was particularly important to get the picture for Germany, as it was in much better condition than the Leipzig portrait. ... Nothing about these plans should be publicised.'[90]

A detailed report on the Festival was drawn up, and copies were sent to the committee appointed to oversee the new Bach edition, which included Lehmann and Walcha, the musicologists Blume and Albrecht, and Erich Wende, head of the Department of Culture at the Federal Interior Ministry.[91] The surplus revenue from the Festival was used to help finance the new edition. The Conference of Culture Ministers and the *Städtetag* also maintained their involvement with this project, and the whole coalition was represented at the festive presentation of the first volume in Cologne in September 1954. This time Heuss was present.[92]

In the way that the Federal Republic reacted to the Leipzig Festival, the Bach year also set a precedent. The musical performances of the East were reported on and discussed, but their political and academic accretions were simply ignored. Meyer and his colleagues' scholarly reworking of Bach was, like the GDR's new music in the 1950s, scarcely referred to in the West. Even today, in the thousands of articles and books on Bach churned out

---

90   SG Sammlung 5, Protokoll der Sitzung des Kuratoriums des westdeutschen Bach-Festes am 28.Juli 1950, p. 5.

91   NWRA/NW 60/891, Arbeitsgemeinschaft für Konzertwesen to Voigt, und die übrigen Herren Mitglieder des vom Kuratorium des Deutschen Bach-Festes eingesetzten Unterausschusses, 12 September 1950.

92   NWRA/NW 60/891, Auszug aus der Niederschrift über die Sitzung des Kunstausschusses der Ständigen Konferenz der Kultusminister, 12/13 October 1951; also Rundschreiben Nr. 12 an die Herren Mitglieder des Kuratoriums des J.S.Bach-Instituts, 8 April 1952. On the new edition, see Chapter Eight.

by scholars all over the globe, there is a deafening silence on the academic conference at Leipzig in 1950.[93] Nor can the West's ostentatious neglect of Bach scholarship in the GDR be attributed to secrecy there. Journalists, scholars, and musicians from the West were welcomed to Leipzig in 1950. The proceedings of the conference were published in 1951, as was much of the work of the Bach Archive in Leipzig in the 1950s. This censorship of ideas and music from the GDR in the Federal Republic did not need to be coordinated or enforced. It existed as an unspoken law, and was ultimately far more effective than any intellectual effort at engagement or refutation.[94]

What of the societies that were involved with both festivals? Both the NBG and the GfM carried on a double life after 1950, or an elaborate charade, or a mixture of the two.[95] The case of the GfM is particularly interesting. Vetter continued as vice-president, and the GDR worked carefully to maintain editorial influence on the society's journal, *Die Musikforschung*. At the founding conference of the VDK in April 1951, Vetter stressed the unity of German musicology, and read to the assembled delegates a telegram explaining that Blume was unable to join them because he was ill. Similar excuses were presented for Albrecht.[96] Clearly neither was prepared actually to break with the GDR. Blume and Albrecht were, as we know, in close touch with the Federal Interior Ministry in the early 1950s. The only explanation for the continued cooperation between the GDR and organisations like the GfM and NBG, is that both sides saw in them equal potential as Trojan horses.

Above all, the Bach year made it plain that music would play a unique role in relations between the two new German states. The GDR, particularly, was reinforced in its determination to use music as a weapon in the struggle for German unity. Over the next few years, great efforts were made to maintain and strengthen links between musicians there and in the Federal Republic. Commitment to the classics, and to high standards of performance, would be used in the Cold War as a propaganda tool to win hearts and minds in the West; institutions with a particular place in the German public imagination, like the *Thomanerchor*, would play a leading role. And just as the celebration of Bach had done, this propaganda offensive would evoke a confused response from the Federal Republic. Was it entirely wrong of the GDR to honour the great German composers, and to celebrate them by performing their music? Was it a bad thing to try to bring this music

93   Malcolm Boyd (ed.), *Composer Companion to J. S . Bach* (New York and Oxford: Oxford University Press, 1999), a large lexicon with contributions from many international Bach specialists, is a recent example. The NBG's 1994 colloquium on 'Bach under the dictatorships', Bach-Archiv-Leipzig (ed.), *Leipziger Beiträge zur Bach-Forschung* (Hildesheim: Olms, 1995), is an exception, but is still dismissive.

94   One exception was Alfred Dürr. In '25 Jahre Johann-Sebastian-Bach-Institut', *Musica*, 1976/3, pp. 231–2, he paid tribute to the work of the Leipzig Bach Archive.

95   The SED finally banned cooperation with 'all-German' societies in 1967. See Klingberg, *Politisch fest*, p. 91; also Lars Klingberg, 'Neue Bach Gesellschaft und DDR', Bach-Archiv-Leipzig, *Leipziger Beiträge zur Bach-Forschung*, pp. 141–67.

96   Walther Vetter, 'Einheit der deutschen Musik', *Musik und Gesellschaft*, 1951/2, pp. 44–46.

to ordinary working people? Could music be separated from politics, or must it inevitably be contaminated by the machinations of the SED?

Chapter Six

Music and State in Germany: 1950–1955

The early 1950s were perhaps the most anxious and intense years of the Cold War. The Soviet Union successfully tested its first nuclear weapon in 1949, and followed this with a hydrogen bomb in 1953; the conflict in Korea seemed to many a preamble to a larger conflict. After the execution of the Rosenbergs, McCarthyism reached a peak in 1953, when America House libraries in West Germany were purged of suspect books and music.[1] In Germany, this Cold War tension was particularly felt, and was manifested in the hostility between the two new states, neither of which was prepared to recognise the other. In the eyes of the Federal Republic, the GDR was a Soviet creation, and the SED a Stalinist tool. Its politicisation of music was yet another proof of its wickedness. To the GDR, the Federal Republic was a staging post for the American army. Music was systematically used there by the Americans and their agents in the Adenauer government to undermine the German people, and to destroy Germany's cultural inheritance.

'No So-called Unpolitical Art'[2]

In discussions of music in the early GDR, the threat of war was ever present; editorials, speeches, and internal reports were almost invariably introduced with reference to 'atomic war', 'the death of millions', 'war-hatred', and so forth. This perception of menace was undoubtedly genuine, and it lent an embattled, almost frenzied quality to debates about all aspects of music. This was further heightened by Soviet demands for greater vigilance and censorship, echoed in March 1951 by Hans Lauter, who called for a complete politicisation of all artistic expression.[3] The 'building of socialism' was announced at the Second Party Congress of the SED

---

1   *Neues Deutschland* on 19 June 1953, anxious to divert attention from events closer to home, reported that the music of Copland, Bernstein, Sessions, Harris, Gershwin, Randall Thompson, and Virgil Thomson had been banned from America House libraries in West Germany.

2   The *Kulturbund* welcomes the founding of the GDR on the front page of *Die Aussprache*, 1949, 8/9.

3   Hans Lauter, *Der Kampf gegen den Formalismus in Kunst und Literatur, für eine fortschrittliche Deutsche Kultur: Referat von Hans Lauter, Diskussion und Entschließung von der 5. Tagung des Zentralkomitees der SED vom 15.–17. März 1951* (Berlin: Dietz, 1951)

in 1952, demanding renewed commitment and engagement from artists.[4] It was in this climate that the musical culture of the GDR developed. As the regime's leading musicians sought to mobilise all aspects of music-making, they found themselves torn between affirmation and repression, their outlook oscillating wildly between optimism and paranoia. It is hardly surprising that this was a culture characterised by contradiction and paradox.

Since 1948, the SED had, in discussion with the Soviets, been selecting potential candidates for an Academy. A select group of 21 was chosen, and a German Academy of the Arts was founded in March 1950 to act as the arbiter of taste, the exemplar of standards, and to demonstrate the SED's commitment to high culture. Four composers were initially selected: Eisler, Meyer, Gerster and Butting. Although membership did bring its privileges, the Academy was not an ivory tower. Meyer later described how its members went out into the workplace to experience life at first hand: 'There we got to know production in all of its ramifications, its specifics, and its harshness.'[5] Nor was the Academy a haven for bourgeois individualists. The academicians were formed into 'sections' to coordinate their politicised activities. Meyer's energetic leadership of the Music Section was soon noted; an SED report in October 1950 singled him out for praise, noting that he was both politically and artistically qualified. Of the sections, the musicians were 'the most positive and clear in their goals'.[6] Eisler taught a composition master class; Butting taught radio composition, and the Academy supported many concerts. An archive of workers' songs and folk music was established, and musical broadcasting was supervised in conjunction with Hans Pischner at Berlin Radio. Through the 1950s, the Academy acted as a separate agency, investigating particular artistic problems, convening conferences, and running its own journal, *Sinn und Form*. Butting, who took over the leadership of the Music Section in 1952, was particularly active. He intervened frequently to influence radio programming, tirelessly promoted contemporary music, and led an enquiry into the problem of dance music in 1952. He campaigned for a new concert hall in East Berlin, and in 1957 exposed the calamitous situation of the GDR's record industry. He worked hard to maintain links with composers in the Federal Republic, and immersed himself in practical issues of musical copyright.[7]

---

4   Sozialistische Einheitspartei Deutschlands (ed.), *Protokoll der Verhandlungen der 2. Parteikonferenz der Sozialistischen Einheitspartei Deutschlands, 9. bis 12. Juli 1952 in der Werner-Seebinder-Halle zu Berlin* (Berlin: Dietz, 1952); see pp. 440–49 for Becher and Ulbricht's comments on culture.

5   This is from SAAdK Ernst-Hermann-Meyer-Archiv, 308, Kulturpolitisches Ereignis von Rang, written in 1984/5, by which time Meyer and the dancer Gret Palucca were the only two surviving founder members of the Academy.

6   Cited in Stiftung Archiv der Akademie der Künste (eds), *Zwischen Diskussion und Disziplin: Dokumente zur Geschichte der Akademie der Künste (Ost) 1945/1954 bis 1993* (Berlin: Henschel, 1997), p. 36; see also p. 32.

7   Butting is unknown as a composer now. For a biographical sketch see Dietrich Brennecke, 'Max Butting – Die Musik und die Menschen', *Sinn und Form*, 1968/4, pp. 1345–68.

The Academy, by its nature, was restricted to elite work. The SED's Central Committee had noted 'the lack of any direction of public musical life by the Party',[8] and in January 1951 decided to form an Association of German Composers and Musicologists (*Verband Deutscher Komponisten und Musikwissenschaftler*, or VDK).[9] Great care was taken with the VDK's founding conference, which was used to display the SED's identification with music, and to establish the parameters of musical debate in the GDR. Meyer was entrusted with a key role, which included editing the VDK's journal, *Musik und Gesellschaft* (*Music and Society*). The first issue was published in March 1951, and was prefaced with a manifesto. In answer to the question 'What does this journal want?' Meyer wrote:

> It wants to help spread the knowledge that music is part of societal life of humans, and is indissolubly bound up with this. …
>
> It wants to support artistic realism in German music life and music creation; it wants to take up this fight for artistic realism on behalf of this Party.

In developing these ideas, Meyer combined idealism and intolerance in equal measure:

> It wants to support folk and amateur music in Germany with all powers; it wants to help to bridge the gap which exists in ever more ways between art and people; to bring art to the people and the people to art; and to encourage the working masses to active music-making in the spirit of the new building of our societal life …
>
> It wants to combat all manifestations of degeneration in contemporary music life as strongly as possible.[10]

The VDK's founding conference in April was a striking demonstration of the link between music and the state. The leaders of Party and state, Pieck, Dieckmann, Grotewohl, Ulbricht and Wandel, were there in person, together with a Soviet delegation. Eberhard Rebling was welcomed, and telegrams of goodwill from sympathisers like Alan Bush in England were read out. Ottmar Gerster was appointed to the largely decorative role of Chairman, and Nathan Notowicz to the more influential position of First Secretary.[11] Meyer gave the opening and closing speeches, presenting a view of the international situation that appears now to verge on paranoia:

---

8   SAPMO-BArch DY 30/IV 2/9.06/284, Betrift: Einberufung einer Musikkonferenz, undated.

9   SAPMO-BArch DY 30/J IV 2/3A/152, Protokoll Nr. 42 der Sitzung des Sekretariats des ZK am 25. Januar 1951.

10   Ernst Meyer, 'Geleitwort: Was will diese Zeitschrift?', *Musik und Gesellschaft* (hereafter *MuG*), 1951/1, p. 1.

11   *MuG*, 1951/3, p. 86–7.

American monopoly capitalism, rotten and destructive through and through, strives for world domination and has already begun a bloody war of aggression against free peoples of the world. ... The west of our homeland is to become a deployment area, the German economy an arsenal for the American war party. In this manner German youth will be made into 'American listeners' (*amerikahörig*), corrupted in mind and soul, each one robbed of individual agency.

Meyer then identified two musical enemies. The first was 'American entertainment music', which he described as 'poison', 'repulsive and dangerous kitsch', 'imperialistic decadence', 'spiritual unproductivity', and 'cheap, revolting, perfumed mass production'. The second was twelve-tone music, which he characterised as a 'pseudo-revolutionary' product of the 1920s:

> [Twelve-tone music] appeared, as did other modern developments at that time, subjectively as an anarchistic, avant-gardist revolt against capitalist-corrupted mass taste, but going beyond that, it was, objectively, above all a revolt against folk music, and at the same time a negation of all the positive values of content, which the classics from Bach to Brahms had.

Meyer refuted the claim that twelve-tone music was progressive, a description the GDR reserved for its own culture:

> If since then twelve-tone music has become ever more refined, complicated, dissonant, abstract, and mathematical, it has not thereby become more progressive. ... "Above all, the idea of progress is not to be constituted in general abstraction," says Marx in connection with artistic production. An art is always only progressive in relation to the progressive forces in society.

Schoenberg, Berg and Webern had sought a way out the crisis of capitalism, but had fallen into 'hopeless decadence'. Their contemporary imitators were the puppets of monopoly capital. 'Today, objectively, however, the formalists writing in the sense of American imperialism disseminate the barbarity of nihilism.'[12]

Although attitudes to these two 'manifestations of degeneration' would alter subtly over the years, the GDR never abandoned its hostility to twelve-tone music, and Americanised dance music. New developments in both were invariably condemned as subtle attempts to poison the German population, East and West. Meyer's words at the VDK's conference were delivered only weeks after the cancellation of the Brecht/Dessau opera *Das Verhör des Lukullus*, and there could be no mistaking that behind them lay the will to censor any music that might be played in public in the GDR. There has been much comment on the decision to censor *Lukullus*, including the suggestion that the SED publicly emphasised criticisms of Dessau's music partly

---

12　　Ernst Meyer, 'Realismus – die Lebensfrage der deutschen Musik', *MuG*, 1951/2, pp. 38–40.

to avoid any direct criticism of the better-known Brecht.[13] Be that as it may, Dessau's score for *Lukullus*, after much discussion between the leading politicians of the SED and its musical theorists, was condemned for its use of percussion and natural sounds, and for its lack of melody. In a critical letter written on 12 March 1951, Meyer judged that parts of Dessau's score displayed 'all elements of formalism … a prevalence of destructive, corrosive dissonances, and mechanical percussion sounds'. Where Dessau had used triadic tonalities, Meyer alleged that this was largely for parody. Further, and this links the critique of *Lukullus* with his comments at the VDK's conference, Meyer condemned Dessau for using the tonal language of the avant-garde bourgeoisie of twenty-five years previously.[14]

In fact, the SED overestimated the influence and popularity of avant-garde music in West Germany. Most of the music written by Boulez, Stockhausen, Cage, and other avant-gardists in the early 1950s was incomprehensible to German music lovers. There was virtually no public interest in, or demand for, this music in the GDR; the very few individuals who were interested could listen to late night broadcasts from West German radio stations, and students could even travel to the Darmstadt Summer Schools. Dance music was another matter. In this case, the SED's ideological hostility was compounded by academic disdain. The SED was conscious, also, that dance music was almost universally beloved in Germany. The hostility to American jazz, and German 'hit music' brought the Party into direct confrontation with its own population, and will be analysed more fully in the next chapter.

The VDK, which quickly established branches across the GDR, had two conflicting roles – one supportive, and one repressive. It represented composers, supported them financially, and sponsored new works. The VDK was, first and foremost, a Party organisation, and SED members on its committee acted as a conduit between the Party leadership and the musical profession. *Musik und Gesellschaft*, which was presented as an apolitical academic journal, was similarly used. The VDK used two further mechanisms to control the composition of new music. The idea of 'professional discussion' was adopted from the Soviet Union: composers had to meet for long discussion of any new work, carried out in the spirit of 'criticism and self-criticism'. This meant that any traces of abstraction or modernity, 'objective' distortions that might have crept in despite the 'subjective' intentions of the composer, could be removed. Secondly, the VDK organised commissions, typically headed by placemen, to investigate particular areas of music. During the 1950s, as many as twenty separate commissions dealt with subjects as diverse as 'Film music', 'Children's songs', 'Wind music', 'Musicology', 'Youth and school music',

---

13   See Joy Haslam Calico, '"Für eine neue deutsche Nationaloper": Opera in the Discourses of Unification and Legitimation in the German Democratic Republic', Applegate and Potter, *Music and German National Identity*, pp. 190–204, particularly pp. 195–197.

14   SAAdK Ernst-Hermann-Meyer-Archiv, 565, Ueber 'Das Verhör des Lukullus', 12 March 1951. See also Ulrich Dibelius and Frank Schneider (eds), *Neue Musik im geteilten Deutschland: Dokumente aus den fünfziger Jahren* (Berlin: Henschel, 1993), pp. 176–181; also Stiftung Archiv der Akademie der Künste, *Zwischen Diskussion und Disziplin*, pp. 105–11.

and 'Opera'. Under the watchful eyes of Meyer, Notowicz, Knepler and Rebling, the VDK was largely a compliant body, and such dissent as was occasionally voiced from within its ranks was easily contained.

The curious match of the SED's Marxism-Leninism and traditional German musical culture resulted, particularly, in the encouragement of vocal music. Singing embodied a sense of collectivity, of equality, and of shared participation. It was not, like looking at a painting, or watching a film, a passive act of absorption and reflection, but an active form of recreation. Texts could carry programmatic meanings in a way that instrumental music could not. Everybody could sing. The SED's commitment to high culture meant that it was keen on cantatas that could be performed by a professional orchestra and lay chorus, bringing ordinary people into active collaboration with artists. This was the best way for composers in the early GDR to demonstrate their political commitment. Meyer set an example with his *Mansfelder Oratorium* (*The Mansfeld Oratorio*), followed by *Die Partei* (*The Party*), *Der Flug der Taube* (*The Flight of the Dove*), and *Des Sieges Gewißheit* (*The Certainty of Victory*). Eisler wrote *Mitte des Jahrhunderts* (*The Middle of the Century*) for the Party Conference in 1950. Gerster wrote *Eisenhüttenkombinat Ost* (named after a huge new integrated steel plant built near Berlin) in 1952 in response to Ulbricht's demands at the 1952 Conference. Finke wrote *Freiheit und Friede* (*Freedom and Peace*) in the same year.

At their worst, these cantatas and oratorios celebrating industry, the party, and its politics, veered towards the banal, expressing sentiments that appear ridiculous today, and sit uneasily with any definition of realism. Heinz Kleeman and Fritz Gregor co-wrote the *The Erzgebirge Oratorio* in 1952. The text combined obsequious and exaggerated adulation of the Red Army, Marx, Engels, Stalin, and the USSR with slogans of peace and unity, along with thanks to the SED, and sentimental lyrics about the beautiful land of the Erzgebirge. This at a time when the area was being ruthlessly despoiled by the Soviets, using forced labour on a huge scale to extract uranium, with a total disregard for any long-term health and environmental consequences.[15] It appears that many of these works, and others like them, were given one performance, typically at a Party ceremony of some kind, and never played again. An exception was Meyer's *Mansfelder Oratorium*. After its premiere in 1950, this work, celebrating 750 years of copper mining in Mansfeld, was performed frequently in different towns of the GDR. It was also performed in other Eastern bloc countries, and recordings of the work were even played to select audiences in West Germany, England, and France. Meyer's correspondence includes letters of congratulation on the work not only from the leaders of the Party and various high-ranking officials, who might be conforming to what they perceived as an obligatory viewpoint, but also what appear to be genuine letters of appreciation from ordinary citizens and music lovers.[16]

---

15   The libretto is in SAPMO-BArch DY 30/IV 2/9.06/284.
16   See the many examples in SAAdK, Ernst-Hermann-Meyer-Archiv.

Instrumental music was not entirely neglected. Meyer wrote string quartets and a chamber symphony, and a number of other GDR composers used traditional forms such as the symphony and the concerto. In the suspicious climate of the early 1950s, though, it was difficult to write instrumental music that was not judged as 'formalist'. Butting and Wagner-Régeny were cited as being particularly backward in their symphonic work in 1952. Eisler was criticised in the same report for spending too long at his desk, and not getting close enough to the people.[17] He had already been the subject of a complaint to the Central Committee because of the emphasis on instrumental composition in his Academy master class.[18] One instrumental work wholeheartedly celebrated by the SED was Günther Kochan's Violin Concerto, a tuneful and pleasant work, which was likened to the Brahms Concerto. Another was Cilensek's First Symphony. One reviewer wrote, as a favourable comment on this, that it was easily understood at first hearing. One wonders if the reviewer knew that in the Soviet Union, a joke amongst musicians was that any piece which could not be understood at first hearing was 'formalist'.[19]

Stakuko

However successful the VDK was in overseeing new composition, it was not a vehicle for the complete control of music: it was, for instance, not equipped to monitor concert programmes. Its members were composers and academics; they could hardly be expected to spend their working lives as bureaucrats. The *Politbüro* decided in July 1951, shortly after the VDK was founded, to centralise the control of the arts. The State Commission for Artistic Affairs (*Staatliche Kommission für Kunstangelegenheiten* – soon known internally as *Stakuko*), was modelled on the similarly named committee formed in the Soviet Union in 1936, and was led by Helmut Holzhauer.[20] In one crucial respect, however, *Stakuko* differed from previous SED organisations set up to influence the arts: its key personnel were not artists, but party functionaries. Notably, its Main Department for the Visual Arts and Music (*Hauptabteilung Darstellende Künste und Musik*) was headed not by one of the

---

17   SAPMO-BArch DR 1/7, Einschätzung des Kongresses der Deutschen Komponisten und Wissenschaftler und der Festtage zeitgenössischer Musik, Abt. Musik, Stakuko, 11 September 1952. Adorno, in a searing critique of Eastern bloc musical politics written in 1955, reduced the preference for vocal music to a simple formula: 'Human voices = human = social; instruments = inhuman = formalistic.' See 'Die gegängelte Musik', p. 62.

18   SAPMO-BArch DY 30/IV 2/9.06/284, Asriel to Rentzsch, 24 November 1952.

19   Ilse Schött, 'Immer noch am Anfang', *Berliner Zeitung am Abend*, 5 November 1954.

20   See 'Verordnung über die Aufgaben der Staatlichen Kommission für Kunstangelegenheiten vom 12.7.1951', *Gesetzblatt der DDR*, 1951, pp. 684–5; also Toby Thacker, '"Anleitung und Kontrolle": Stakuko and the Censorship of Music in the GDR, 1951–1953', in Beate Müller (ed.), *Censorship and Cultural Regulation in the Modern Age* (Amsterdam and New York: Rodopi, 2004), pp. 87–110.

émigrés, but by Rudolf Hartig, an old KPD fighter, originally a schoolteacher, who had been imprisoned by the Nazis after 1933. Hartig had distinguished himself in the reconstruction of culture in Leipzig since 1945, and in organising the Bach Festival there.[21] *Stakuko* was given responsibility for professional orchestras, choirs, and opera houses. It was to control their concert programmes, and supervise their personnel. It was to oversee higher education institutions for music, the state publishing house VEB *Lied der Zeit*, and the German Concert Agency, the GDR body that engaged touring musicians. Musical broadcasting came within its remit, as did musical criticism, the production of records, and musical relations with the Federal Republic. *Stakuko* was responsible for national commemorations, such as the celebrations of Beethoven in 1952 and of Schubert in 1953, which were accompanied by huge programmes to take performances into even small villages. It was also expected to disseminate ideas about music with books and films. All this work had to be theoretically grounded, and was approached with great ideological rigour. Between 1951 and the end of 1953, Hartig's office meddled with every conceivable aspect of music in the GDR.

And here lay the roots of *Stakuko*'s failure. How on earth was Hartig, with a handful of full-time officials, to exercise this total control? To compound the problem, the SED demanded commitment to 'collective work'. What this entailed is suggested by the party jargon used in the introduction to the *Stakuko* files in the German Federal Archive: 'After the 2nd Party Conference in July 1952 the principles of collective work (service and work conversations, conferences, brigade work), of planning in work, of responsibility, of scientific approach, of watchfulness, as well as of criticism and self criticism, were even more stressed.'[22] All sections of *Stakuko* had to produce regular plans. Yearly and quarterly plans were not sufficient; Hartig required his senior colleagues to produce them weekly. They then had to write further reports on the implementation of the plans.

Examination of the resulting paperwork yields many insights. It shows repeatedly how great the chasm was between ambitious pretensions and limited achievements, and how poorly *Stakuko*'s work was coordinated with the Academy and the VDK. Above all, the surviving files convey an extraordinary sense of paradox. Stalinist organisations like *Stakuko* are typically conceptualised almost exclusively in terms of censorship and repression, and the accompanying idealism is neglected. Hartig's work was, though, primarily concerned with supporting music – above all with bringing the classical inheritance to the people, and with raising standards of performance. The nature of repression in the early GDR is also frequently misunderstood. *Stakuko* did not imprison musicians or intimidate them physically. It exercised a paternalistic didacticism, in which words like 'education' and 'guidance' were used as often as 'control'. Hartig was constantly looking over his shoulder at an imagined situation in West Germany, and could not afford to provoke musicians to flee from the GDR

---

21 SAAdK Hans-Pischner-Archiv, 740, Rede zur Trauerfeier für den Genossen Rudolf Hartig am 29.11.1962.

22 Johanna Marschall-Reiser, *Findbuch zu Beständen des Bundesarchives. Band 70* (Koblenz: Bundesarchiv, 1999), xix.

to the West. Relationships between *Stakuko* and practising musicians were therefore characterised by a strange mixture of hectoring and whingeing. Criticism was obligatory, but so was optimism, and when failings were detected, there was always hope that they might be remedied, typically by more 'political understanding' and 'collective work'. An ever-present sense of imminent war gave Hartig's work a final feverish twist.

Stakuko relied heavily on the cooperation of local officials. Since 1945, the *Länder* of the Soviet Zone had developed considerable powers over their own cultural affairs. This situation persisted when they were reorganised as *Bezirke* in 1952, and one of Hartig's main tasks was to try to exercise central regulation. Confronted with pessimistic reactions to his demands for a thorough monitoring of all concert programmes, Hartig argued that this was neither impossible nor over-bureaucratic: 'Local areas <u>must</u> observe performances; they must give direction and orientation. They must know what is going on and exercise influence.'[23] Music officials from the thirteen *Bezirke* were required to report regularly to Hartig, summarising developments locally. These reports provide many insights into local musical culture. Often they reveal that the rosy pictures of socialist cultural life painted in the press and at Party ceremonies were misleading. A report from Frankfurt an der Oder in 1952 provides an interesting commentary on the programme to bring music into the workplace. Analysing the situation at the GDR's huge new integrated iron and steel complex, the *Eisenhüttenkombinat Ost*, ironically the subject of Gerster's cantata, it notes that the workers were not keen to hear the choral music so beloved of the regime: 'It has to be said that all concerts staged in the *Eisenhüttenkombinat Ost* which are not orchestral, are catastrophic in terms of the number of guests.'[24] The report described a similar lack of enthusiasm for concerts in factories and workplaces in Potsdam.

Frequently, Hartig had to intervene to keep local officials in line. In April 1953, he instructed *Bezirk* Dresden not to include West German 'formalist' works in their concert programmes.[25] Rostock was a particular problem. Hartig had heard that there was 'cultural chaos' there,[26] and in July 1953 had to write at some length to the local authorities about the lack of political leadership, and in particular a neglect of preparations for that year's Schubert celebrations.[27] There were hopeful signs, though. From Mecklenburg, Hartig heard: 'There is singing or playing in almost

---

23   SAPMO-BArch DR 1/335, Zum Konzertmeldebogen, 29 December 1952, underlined in the original.

24   SAPMO-BArch DR 1/335, Frankfurt/Oder [1952], p. 6.

25   SAPMO-BArch DR 1/335, Hartig to Rat des Bezirkes Dresden, Abt. Kunst u. Kulturelle Massenarbeit, Ref. Musik, 10 April 1953.

26   SAPMO-BArch DR 1/335, Bericht über die Arbeit des Referates Musik der Abteilung Kunst und kulturelle Massenarbeit beim Rat des Bezirks Rostock [1953], p. 4.

27   SAPMO-BArch DR 1/335, Hartig to Rat des Bezirks Rostock, Abt. Kunst u. Kulturelle Massenarbeit, Referat Musik, 25 July 1953.

every house.'[28] Hartig was particularly taken by the 1953 report from Karl-Marx-Stadt (as Chemnitz had been re-named). He wrote back to Weissenfels, its author, commending him especially, and asking him to send copies of the report to all other *Bezirke*. What undoubtedly impressed Hartig was that Weissenfels' report was couched in the language that he himself used, with a lengthy introduction on the dangers of American imperialism, and the need for music to play a conscious and aggressive role in society as a weapon for peace and unity.[29]

One of *Stakuko*'s main strategies was to convene meetings of local musicians or officials, and to use these to communicate the line from the centre. The agendas and outcomes were prearranged, with previously prepared 'unanimous' declarations for press release, and Hartig appears to have been very unwilling to listen to viewpoints coming in from the provinces. In 1952, a programme of conferences for local music officials (*Musikreferente*) was held; others were run for dance band leaders and orchestral conductors. Max Butting, the Academy's specialist on dance music, directed the conferences for bandleaders; Meyer and Rebling led those for the conductors.[30] These conferences were particularly important for influencing programming. One of Hartig's first steps in 1951 had been to establish performance quotas. Orchestras were to devote 50 per cent of their programmes to the classics, 25 per cent to contemporary music from the GDR, and 25 per cent to music from the Soviet Union and the 'peoples' democracies'. They were to avoid playing 'formalist' music altogether.[31] Orchestras had to submit detailed statistical breakdowns of their programming. It is clear from surviving returns that the quotas were rarely adhered to. In particular it proved impossible to get orchestras to perform so much contemporary music by GDR composers – presumably because the public responded poorly to it, for after all, the orchestras and conductors had every other incentive to do this.

A national conference for orchestral conductors in November 1952 was used to survey their responsibilities in 'the building of socialism'. Hartig's colleague Schott highlighted the continuing relevance of Zhdanov's pronunciations in 1948, and named Henze, Liebermann and Schoenberg as examples of decadence and formalism, which should not be found in the GDR's programming. He noted that Liebermann's *Sinfonia* had been taken out of the 1952/53 programme of the Dresden State Orchestra because he was 'an out and out "twelve-toner"', and added: 'We are opposed to performances of Bruckner's symphonies, and are rather of the opinion, that the work of Bruckner, with its particular mystical underlying tendency, is no longer suited to contribute much to the support of concert life in the building of socialism.'[32] Curiously, although this hostility can be found in other *Stakuko*

---

28   SAPMO-BArch DR 1/335, Bericht über die Situation auf dem Gebiet der Musik im Lande Mecklenburg [1952].

29   See SAPMO-BArch DR 1/335, Die Entwicklung 1953 auf dem Gebiete der Musik in Karl-Marx-Stadt, and Hartig to Weissenfels, 12 March 1954.

30   SAPMO-BArch DR 1/141, Bericht über die Erfüllung des Arbeitplanes III/52.

31   SAPMO-BArch DR 1/141, Zum Arbeitsplan IV./51, 21 September 1951.

32   SAPMO-BArch DY 30/IV 2/9.06/279, Referat zur Orchesterleiter-Tagung am 26.11.52: Kritische Beleuchtung der Konzertprogramme der DDR.

documents, there seems to have been no serious attempt to censor Bruckner, and his symphonies were frequently performed.

Schott portrayed the Thuringia *Land* Symphony Orchestra as an example of good programming. Copies of the orchestra's 1952/53 programme were evidently distributed as exemplary material, providing us with an exact insight into what *Stakuko* saw as good practice. This orchestra is particularly interesting because it was not one of the five deemed 'important to the Republic', and expected to tour in other countries. Its primary responsibility was to play at the highest standard for local people: in concert halls, in the workplace, at Party ceremonies and at sporting events. In return for state support, the orchestra agreed to present 'a progressive concert programme, in which the works of the national, progressive classical inheritance, the works of the Soviet Union and the peoples' democracies, as well as contemporary German works have a deserved place'.[33] It planned 80 concerts, in cities like Gotha, Erfurt, Weimar, Jena and Mühlhausen, and in specified industrial plants, like the *Mercedeswerke Zella-Mehlis* and the *Simonswerke Suhl*. It planned a Beethoven cycle, a Schubert/Brahms cycle, two 'special concerts' dedicated to the rebuilding of Berlin, four concerts for local VDK members, 'five contemporary music days' in Gotha, five school and youth concerts, six 'folk concerts' and five chamber concerts. At the head of the programme stood ten symphonic concerts with soloists. Serving the public in border areas was deemed, in military terms, a 'strongpoint task' (*Schwerpunktaufgabe*). Nor was the proposed repertoire as provincial as we might imagine from an orchestra that embellished its programmes with quotes from Zhdanov. It was planning to play Britten's *Concerto for Left Hand* in February 1953 and Bartok's Third Piano Concerto in May. The soloist on that occasion was to be Helmut Roloff, a noted West German pianist who taught at the Darmstadt Summer Schools. Heinz Stanske from Baden-Baden played the solo part in the Sibelius Violin Concerto in September 1952.[34]

No discussion of the musical culture of the early GDR would be complete without reference to the promotion of Baroque music. The cult of Bach in the GDR has already been mentioned, and the celebrations of 1950 were followed by a similar veneration of his contemporary Handel, also born coincidentally in what was now an industrial city of the GDR, Halle. Although the the cult of Handel in the GDR was fully developed only after the anniversary year of 1958, as early as 1951 he was being represented in the GDR as a 'progressive', 'humanist' fighter. His *Israel in Egypt*, *Judas Maccabeus* and *Belshazzar*, styled as 'freedom oratorios', were performed and broadcast in 1951 by the Berlin Radio Choir directed by Helmut Koch. Celebrating this in *Musik und Gesellschaft*, Koch wrote that this was no mere act of piety, but 'above all today an act of national self-consciousness', which developed 'our strength in the fight for the unity of our Fatherland and the

---

33　　SAPMO-BArch DY 30/IV 2/9.06/284, Vereinbarung über gegenseitige Verpflichtungen [1952], p. 2.

34　　SAPMO-BArch DY 30/IV 2/9.06/284, Konzertplan 1952/53 des Landessinfonieorchesters Thüringen.

peace of the world'. Handel's oratorios should not be seen as biblical, but rather as 'worldly' compositions whose grand choral settings articulated the strivings of the people. According to Koch, who had mastered the militarised jargon of the SED, the soloists in Handel's oratorios also 'suffer with the people in slavery, they fight with the people for freedom, and they celebrate with the people after the victory has been gained.'[35] These themes were subsequently developed in musicological and biographical studies; Handel, Bach, and other seventeenth and eighteenth-century composers featured prominently on live and broadcast GDR programmes through the 1950s and after.

Inevitably there was some tension between Hartig's office and other musical bureaucracies, not least because *Stakuko* felt that its job included supervision of the Academy and the VDK.[36] Equally, these organisations were anxious to preserve and extend their spheres of influence. Thus, the VDK, in April 1953, demanded representation on the *Stakuko* committee overseeing all music critics.[37] There was, though, more cooperation than conflict. Paradoxically, given the initial conception of *Stakuko* as a controlling body, it appears to have lacked final authority in musical matters great and small; in doubt it would refer to the Central Committee's Department of Culture, which was always liable to turn for final judgement to the VDK or the Academy. So, even trivial problems went on an almost circular route. The result was frequently chaotic, and even the most dedicated Party supporters were treated with incompetence and indifference.

Consider the case of the now unknown composer Hans Schusser, who wrote hopefully to the Central Committee in November 1952. He had written an orchestral piece, *Stalin, der Friedensfreund, sei uns gegrüßt* (*Stalin, Friend of Peace, We Greet You*), and requested that it be considered for use in the celebrations of Stalin's birthday on 21 December of that same year. He referred the Central Committee to a recording of the piece by the Leipzig Radio Orchestra. One might imagine that Schusser would be courteously treated, even commended for his enthusiasm. But not until eight weeks later, *after* Stalin's birthday, did he get a brusque reply stating that unfortunately the radio archive had no trace of the recording, and that therefore no judgement could be made on his request.[38] A more determined colleague, Rudolf Schweitzer, was similarly treated. Schweitzer wrote to the VDK and the Central Committee in February 1953, demanding more planning and guidance in the fight for social realism in music. He called specifically for 'particular methods to direct our creative work'. Evidently Schweitzer had been making a nuisance of himself within the VDK's Berlin branch with his over-zealous behaviour, and finding no support, had turned to higher authorities. Ten days later, he wrote again, enclosing a

---

35   Helmut Koch, 'Gedanken zur neuen Händel-Pflege', *MuG*, 1951/9, pp. 21–2.

36   SAPMO-BArch DR 1/141, Arbeitsplan III/52 Musik, 5 June 1952, p. 4.

37   SAPMO-BArch DR 1/141, Protokoll über die Sitzung des geschäftsführenden Vorstandes am 23.4.1953, p. 1.

38   SAPMO-BArch DY 30/IV 2/9.06/284, Schusser to ZK, Abteilung Kultur, 4 November 1952, and ZK, Abteilung Kultur, to Schusser, 30 December 1952.

twelve page document, 'Basic principles for a system for the realistic composition of songs'. This worthy effort met with complete silence, and nearly three months later Schweitzer felt compelled to try again. Not given to understatement, he reminded the Central Committee of the 'decisive importance of my work', and rather pathetically asked if they could at least return his document.[39]

Alois Förster, a worker at the Ploißengrund textile works who tried his hand at composition, was treated with more courtesy, but could be forgiven if he felt equally discouraged after his enquiry. In 1953, Förster sent the Central Committee an *Activists' Song* he had written for workers' choir. The song was sent to the VDK for assessment. After a delay of months, the VDK wrote to Förster. Unfortunately it could not recommend or publish his song, on 'musical grounds'. The text was also flawed, on 'literary grounds'. The Association clearly hoped that Förster would not lose heart, and provided him with the address of the Writers' Association, which could comment further on the text. To further his musical education they suggested that he contact the 'Central Office for Amateur Art' in Leipzig.[40]

The best chance for music in the GDR to break its bonds came in 1953. Stalin's death in March was followed by clear signs of a more liberal approach to the arts, marked in music by composition of Shostakovich's Tenth Symphony, and its performance in Moscow in December. The uprising of 17 June 1953 gave Party members and organisations in the GDR a rare chance to indulge in genuine criticism. The dissolution of *Stakuko* in December was an opportunity to change both personnel and political priorities. What is clear now is that the SED managed skilfully to create an impression of debate and change in 1953, which was largely illusory.

Meyer was aware in early 1953 of the increasingly tense situation in the Soviet Union and the GDR. His article on 'The lessons of Stalin's new work for music' in February, which reaffirmed the importance of the Zhdanov decree, must be seen as an effort to keep the ship steady on course.[41] The uprising in June came as a terrible shock to the SED; inevitably musicians were caught up in the turmoil. The Dresden Philharmonic was coincidentally in Berlin on 17 June, and its planned concert that night in Potsdam was cancelled. The orchestra's conductor, SED stalwart Heinz Bongartz, was due to make a guest appearance with the Berlin State Orchestra, but was roughly treated when he tried to get on with business as usual. One member of the orchestra told him: 'We are not in Moscow here, we're in Berlin.' Another was sarcastic, saying: 'I would like to be wearing your blinkers.'[42] Members of the Academy met that same evening to formulate a response to the uprising, and quickly came up with the line which dominated the cultural reaction to the uprising: it was

---

39   SAPMO-BArch DY 30/IV 2/9.06/284, Schweitzer to VDK, 2 February 1953; Schweitzer to VDK, 12 February 1953; and Schweitzer to ZK, 22 April 53.

40   The correspondence between Förster, the ZK, and the VDK is in SAPMO-BArch DY 30/IV 2/9.06/284.

41   Ernst Meyer, 'Lehren aus dem XIX. Parteitag der KPdSU', *MuG*, 1953/2, pp. 48–9.

42   SAPMO-BArch DR 1/7, SED-Betriebs-Parteiorganisation der Dresdner Philharmonie an die SED, 19 June 1953.

all *Stakuko*'s fault. The bureaucrats from *Stakuko* did not understand artists or their creative work, and their heavy-handed interference had generated great discontent. The academicians did not criticise the principles that lay behind *Stakuko*'s attempts at control and regulation, but rather the way that Holzhauer and his colleagues had gone about the task. Having condemned *Stakuko* for its over-bureaucratic approach, the academicians set up a committee to review the whole problem. Bertholt Brecht, *Stakuko*'s most vocal critic, was unhappy that Meyer should serve on this committee; presumably he knew that Meyer's loyalty to the Party would be unswerving, even if tactical moves were necessary in the short term.[43]

Meyer was one of the first artists to publish a statement of absolute loyalty, in *Neues Deutschland* on 19 June 1953. He articulated here the line subsequently adopted by the *Politbüro*. The disturbances were the work of 'fascist bandits'; the SED and the Red Army were to be praised for their reaction to the 'provocations'. As for the bandits, they should be ruthlessly pursued and 'exterminated'. A statement from Rebling was printed alongside Meyer's; he spoke of 'fascist hordes' and 'provocation'. Both musicians referred cryptically to 'serious mistakes'. On 21 June, the SED's Central Committee expanded on these themes. Although there had been legitimate protests by workers in response to failings on the part of the leadership, the rioting had been orchestrated by the Western media, the secret services, and by gangs of 'war criminals', 'militarists', and 'bandits' from West Berlin.[44]

As the SED shored up its position over the next few months, *Stakuko* was actually very useful, acting as the whipping boy for frustrated artists and intellectuals, and deflecting criticism from more serious issues. The Academy set the tone and led the vendetta. The *Kulturbund* leadership followed at a meeting on 30 June. Even the VDK joined in: 'The working methods which have prevailed until now do not contribute to raising the joy of artists in their work, but rather have had a damaging effect on the reputation of state offices, which then in the final analysis leads to the events of a 17 June.'[45]

Over the next few months, criticism of *Stakuko* continued, and preparations were set in motion to replace it with a Ministry for Culture. Instead of *Stakuko*'s bureaucratic muddling, artists would now regulate their own affairs. As a token of this intent, Johannes Becher was appointed to head the new Ministry in January 1954, and Hans Pischner was installed as his Deputy. The academicians were bought off, presumably by the hope that they would be restored to supremacy in cultural affairs. A 'Declaration of the Ministry for Culture's Programme' was published in the Academy journal, *Sinn und Form*, and preceded by statements of support.

---

43   'Aus dem Protokoll der improvisierten erweiterten Präsidiumsitzung 17. Juni 1953', cited in Stiftung Archiv der Akademie der Künste, *Zwischen Diskussion und Disziplin*, pp. 78–9.

44   See Arnulf Baring, *Uprising in East Germany: June 17, 1953* (New York and London, 1972), pp. 160–73.

45   SAPMO-BArch DR 1/41, Protokoll über die Sitzung des Zentralvorstandes am 10.7.1953, p. 2.

Speaking for the musicians, Butting included the obligatory criticism of *Stakuko* before welcoming the 'extensive influence' that artists themselves would exercise in the new Ministry.[46] Reading the 'Declaration', it is easy to see how firmly grounded the old attitudes were. Becher first rehearsed all the old accusations against the West. American imperialism, and its West German puppets, were preparing for war, using culture to propagate their race hatred and to prise the German people from their cultural inheritance. Turning specifically to music, Becher declared:

> In fact, our opinion that the leading circles of society, crisis-ridden, oriented towards anaesthesia and sensation, with an existential angst brought on by fear of war, by the European Union Treaty and a 'European Army', have in consequence a music of fear, of noise, of war, of emptiness, of purposelessness and lack of direction, is confirmed.[47]

No composer or musician could have imagined that this heralded a new freedom or tolerance.

Behind the façade, the continuity is even more apparent. Pischner, charged with organising the new Ministry's Main Department of Music, effectively took over the whole department from *Stakuko*. Hartig effectively remained in his post, now in the new ministry, and brought his key subordinates, Uszkoreit and Schott, with him; their work continued without interruption. They were still using *Stakuko*'s letterhead well into 1954. More significantly, they brought their working methods and attitudes. A comparison between Hartig's departmental plans from 1953 and 1954 reveals no significant differences. If anything, at the MfK, his mania for 'guidance' and 'control' became greater, and the drive for more efficiency led to an extension of state regulation. The MfK soon became involved with the development of new musical instruments, and other previously unregulated areas came under Hartig's gaze. In July 1954, he was writing about the need for 'control of private music education and the musical trade'.[48] Even the rhetoric of the 'new course' was not new to Hartig. He had had to master this vocabulary in his final months with *Stakuko*; his last quarterly plan there had been full of comments on over-centralisation, poor communication with musicians, and a lack of artistic involvement.[49]

There were some changes. The SED leadership had considered replacing Hartig in November 1953, and finally in November 1954 he was moved to chair the committee supervising the introduction of the *Jugendweihe*, the GDR's rite of initiation for teenagers.[50] Hans-Georg Uszkoreit, appointed in his place, was a product of the SED's own training system, and not a great innovator. Pischner undoubtedly had

---

46   'Die Deutsche Akademie der Künste zur Gründung des Ministeriums für Kultur', *Sinn und Form*, 1954/1, pp. 142–5, quote on p. 142.

47   Johannes Becher, 'Programmerklärung des Ministeriums für Kultur', *Sinn und Form*, 1954/2, pp. 279–321.

48   SAPMO-BArch DR 1/20, Betr: Überarbeitung der Struktur der Stadtkreise, 17 July 1954.

49   See SAPMO-BArch DR 1/7, Abteilung Musik Quartalsarbeitsplan IV/53.

50   SAAdK Hans-Pischner-Archiv, 1118 , 'Meine Jahre im MfK', pp. 50–54.

much greater influence within the Ministry, and we can detect his influence behind the very cautious liberal steps that were now permitted. In 1955, Berg's *Wozzeck* was performed at the State Opera, and Eisler's 1951 Academy lecture on Schoenberg was finally published.[51] We must place these moves in the context of broader musical developments. *Wozzeck* had, after all, first been performed thirty years previously, and Schoenberg was of an earlier generation still. Music had moved on, and even in the GDR these were hardly particularly daring steps. Nor should we interpret them as conveying a seal of approval for expressionism or atonality. The attacks on Schoenberg and Berg continued well after 1955, and the SED never abandoned its hostility to the avant-garde, which now conveniently presented new enemies like Henze and Stockhausen. Pischner, who much later represented himself as a critic of the most intense manifestations of Stalinism, led the offensive in 1955, denouncing that old enemy, Stuckenschmidt, as 'the apostle of un-humanity, of the esoteric, of nihilism'.[52]

'Rather a Snob Than a Peoples' Comrade!'

If the supremacy of live performance was recognised in both German states in the early 1950s, politicians and musicians were equally aware that music on the radio actually reached far more people. Listeners in Germany were presented with a wide choice of stations, although the vagaries of medium wave reception make it difficult to generalise about who could listen to which particular ones. It is safe to say that most could pick up several. The NWDR's magazine *Hör Zu* (*Listen Up!*), in the early 1950s, published daily programmes for around twenty-five, including the six major stations established by the Allies in the Federal Republic, the three Soviet-licensed stations in the GDR, three BBC stations, and RIAS, which was operated by the Americans. Programmes from Vienna, Prague, Beromünster, Hörby, Paris, Copenhagen, Florence, Luxembourg, Rome, Hilversum and Brussels were also listed.

It was broadly accepted that the spoken word was the main means of influencing people through broadcasting. Music was consciously used as a 'hook', to get people to tune in to a particular station, thus exposing them to its spoken content. All radio stations monitored listener reactions closely, and altered their programmes to appeal to different audiences. In the GDR, musical programming conformed to a strangely bourgeois ideal of respectability, avoiding modernity, and was manipulated in several ways to appeal to listeners. Pischner was responsible for musical programming, initially from 1950 as *Musikreferent* at Berlin Radio, and after 1952 from within the State Radio Committee. His background as a harpsichordist, allied with Meyer's

---

51   Hanns Eisler, 'Arnold Schönberg', *Sinn und Form*, 1955/1, pp. 5–15. See also David Blake, 'The Reception of Schoenberg in the German Democratic Republic', *Perspectives of New Music*, 21 (1982–83), pp. 114–37.

52   SAAdK Hans-Pischner-Archiv, 874, 'Zur Krise des musikalischen Avantgardismus', p. 18.

specialisation in early music, ensured that the idea of 'the classical inheritance' in the GDR extended well beyond the eighteenth and nineteenth centuries.

In his memoirs, Pischner mentions how listener letters from the Federal Republic confirmed the SED's view that this music appealed to a wide audience, and was highly respected. GDR stations also broadcast a great deal of church music, including a regular Sunday Bach cantata from Leipzig. The SED overcame its objections to Christmas to the extent of allowing Pischner to broadcast the series *German bells ring in Christmas*, which had huge emotional appeal to exiles in the Federal Republic.[53] Pischner's programming was also consciously internationalist, but in a highly selective way. Music from the Soviet Union and the 'people's democracies' was favoured, but the GDR also broadcast African, South American, and black American folk music. 'Progressive' composers and artists from the capitalist countries, like Alan Bush and Paul Robeson, were occasionally broadcast. For its audience's more relaxed moments, GDR radio played plenty of operetta and dance music. The flavour of its programming can be judged by Pischner's pride in the series *Heitere Klassik (Cheerful Classics)*, which he hoped would educate his audience away from 'hit music'.[54]

Radio in the Federal Republic was decentralised, but the stations broadcasting for home audiences from Hamburg, Cologne, Munich, Stuttgart, Frankfurt, Baden-Baden and Bremen had strikingly similar musical profiles. Although each had particular strengths, they all broadcast a wide range of music, and used it consciously as a way of integrating with Western Europe and America. The 1950s have been celebrated as the 'golden years' of broadcast music in the Federal Republic, and the radio stations derived much of their identity from their role as musical patrons. All six commissioned works, and sponsored concerts and festivals. They gave particular support to the classics, and to what was still called 'new music', paying highly for specialist musicians who could perform the increasingly difficult scores produced by composers like Stockhausen and Boulez. These high salaries were a constant preoccupation of municipal and *Land* politicians, who feared that they would lose their best professional musicians to radio stations.

The NWDR, based in Hamburg, and with subsidiary studios in Cologne, Berlin, and Hanover, had the largest audience, and it is clear from the proceedings of its Committee of Directors between 1950 and 1955 that musical programming was not controversial. The Committee itself was a typical example of the coalition that controlled culture in the Federal Republic, including several senior *Land* politicians, senior clerics, and the President of the Supreme *Land* Court. Otto Braunfels, whom

---

53   The SED was not content to leave the emotional power of Christmas music entirely to the Christians. Louis Fürnberg wrote an *Old-New Christmas Song* at this time in the style of a Christmas carol, in which Joseph and Mary are greeted by a children's choir, which directs them and their new baby to the earthly paradise of the GDR. A recording was made, on Aurora 40657 Ag 732/5/64 3-3.

54   See SAAdK Hans-Pischner-Archiv, 1117, 'Meine Jahre im Rundfunk'.

the British had reinstated as Director of the Music Academy in Cologne in 1946,[55] represented the musical community. He displayed a Riethian commitment in 1951 when audience demands for more light music were debated, arguing that 'the wishes of listeners should influence programming less than the pedagogic duty of the radio'.[56]

In 1953, the NWDR considered a complaint from composers in the Federal Republic that too little German music was being broadcast. Apparently, two recent contemporary music series had overwhelmingly played music by foreign composers. The music director, Schnabel, reassured the Committee that 'German music is given particular value and effect through concentration in programming.'[57] Rudolf Hartig would surely have approved of these sentiments. There was, though, a significant difference between the position of 'contemporary music' on the radio in the Federal Republic and the GDR. The promotion of avant-garde music by West German radio stations in the 1950s has taken on iconic status in historical representations. Experimental music has become a metaphor for a Germany seeking to remake itself. The post-war consensus, which saw 'new music' as a symbol of anti-fascism, was indeed maintained in the Federal Republic, particularly by the radio stations, but it is easy to overestimate how much was actually played. A glance at programme schedules in the 1950s reveals that every day, there were many hours of classical music, operetta, and dance music being played. There was plenty of twentieth-century music broadcast, but overwhelmingly by neo-classical composers. Very little music that can be identified as experimental, electronic, aleatory or serialist was broadcast, and then only late at night. Public opinion surveys confirm that these were unpopular;[58] the programmers knew this, but felt a duty to support new music. A very public demonstration of this ideological orientation came in May 1953, when the NWDR, in cooperation with the *Centre de Documentation de Musique Internationale*, a foundation in Paris, staged an international festival in Cologne. During the festival, it opened an electronic music studio, the first of several in Germany. The NWDR's Director, Adolf Grimme, wrote in the programme that the whole event was conceived in an internationalist spirit. Music, he argued, was a supra-national force; it provided a sense of community which connected people culturally, and was 'therefore also of political importance'.[59]

In this spirit, Jack Bornoff, former music controller of the NWDR, now executive secretary of UNESCO's International Music Council, was invited to the opening

---

55   TNA/PRO/FO 1050/1375, Controller-General, Education Branch, to H.Q. Military Government N. Rhine Region, 16 April 1946.

56   WDR/HAC 10070, Protokoll der 15. Sitzung des Hauptausschüsses des NWDR am 10. März 1951 in Hamburg, p. 11.

57   WDR/HAC 10070, Niederschrift über die 27. Sitzung des Hauptausschüsses des NWDR am 5. Dezember 1953 in Hamburg, p. 8.

58   See Karl-Georg Stackelberg (ed.), *Jugend zwischen 15 und 24: Untersuchungen zur Situation der deutschen Jugend im Bundesgebiet. Zweite Untersuchung* (Hamburg: Jugendwerk der Deutschen Shell, 1955), p. 99.

59   WDR/HAC D919, *neues musikfest 1953, 25. bis 28. mai. funkhaus köln*.

of the electronic studio.[60] It appears that there was concern about the exclusive nature of the festival, and some discussion of how this could be overcome. The resulting correspondence between the gurus of West German modernism reveals their scepticism about the whole idea. Stuckenschmidt was inevitably involved in the planning, and he wrote to Herbert Eimert about the accessibility of 'new music' in November 1952. German efforts to overcome this, he noted sceptically, 'mostly end with the workers demanding Beethoven's Fifth Symphony'. Eimert, employed by NWDR Cologne since 1945, was the director of the electronic studio, and one of the first in Germany to compose electronic music. He agreed with Stuckenschmidt, and declared himself 'Rather a snob than a peoples' comrade!'[61]

RIAS was an exception amongst West German stations in that it was directly run by the Americans, and projected aggressively into the GDR, 'for the maximum effectiveness in furthering United States aims and policies in Germany'.[62] It had, though, a similar musical programme. The Americans had developed the outlines of their radio propaganda in Germany before 1945, but it was fine-tuned during the Cold War. The secret was to achieve a 'balance of news, commentary, and music to obtain [the] maximum listener audience for propaganda messages'.[63] According to this formula, musical programming should be ambitious, with plenty of modern music and first performances.[64] This approach helped West German radio stations to act as symbols of cultural freedom, but caused problems for RIAS, which had to try to coax listeners away from the GDR stations. As we have seen, GDR musical broadcasting was safely embedded in a conservative and German national groove, but RIAS was constrained by both its American identity and its position in West Berlin. The former demanded jazz, the latter a commitment to contemporary music. Listener letters made it clear that both were unpopular.[65] The Adenauer government also analysed the effect of RIAS broadcasting very closely. A report to the Ministry for all-German Affairs in 1952 echoed listeners' criticisms. The public in 'the Zone', it argued, would rather hear familiar harmonies from broadcasters there 'than the unusual sounds of RIAS'.[66] American public opinion surveys confirmed that GDR

---

60   WDR/HAC 10929, Ehrenkarten für 26. "Elektr. Musik".

61   WDR/HAC 10929, Stuckenschmidt to Eimert, 4 November 1952; Eimert to Stuckenschmidt, 8 November 1952.

62   BAK/OMGUS 5/245-1/25, Supervision and Control of RIAS, 15 July 1949.

63   BAK/OMGUS 5/261–3/22, Outline and Notes of Suggested Study of P W Techniques Developed during European Campaign by the Western Allies, p. 3.

64   BAK/OMGUS 5/260–2/4, Consolidated Semi-Monthly Report of U.S. controlled Radio Stations Covering Period 16–31 October 1947.

65   BAK/OMGUS 5/245–1/25, Kurze Zusammenfassung von Hörerzuschriften für die Zeit vom 15.–21.2.1949.

66   BAK B136/2305, Die Propaganda des RIAS und ihre Wirkung in der SBZD [1952].

listeners valued the news output of RIAS more than its music, and felt conversely about their own radio stations.[67]

The BBC German Service played a particular role in the propaganda war. For an impoverished post-war Britain conscious of its declining influence in world affairs, broadcasting was a cheap and sensible option. The German Service built on the large audiences it had gained in Germany before 1945, and as far as music was concerned, played it fairly safe. A classical diet was leavened by twentieth-century British music, little of it particularly challenging, and judicious servings of jazz. Until 1953, there was no systematic jamming of Western broadcasts in the GDR, and stations like RIAS, the BBC German Service, and *NWDR-Berlin* could be easily heard there. American surveys in 1953, though, reported that GDR listeners were switching to NWDR because of interference with RIAS transmissions.[68] In the summer of 1954, there were discussions between the BBC and the Ministry for all-German Affairs about this. Apparently the BBC German Service was 'the only Western programme that is and can be consistently heard' in the GDR.[69] By October 1954, this was also being jammed, and the BBC noted: 'Mail from the East Zone fell last month to 72, almost the lowest figure for any month in 1954.'[70] By the end of the year, 'extensive discussions' were taking place between the BBC, RIAS, and the NWDR on 'jamming and the means of combating it'.[71]

'Free from World-views and Political Influences'

In contrast with the GDR, music in the Federal Republic was supposedly not a matter for state interference. A myth has been created of an entirely free-floating musical culture, but this cannot be sustained. In practice, there was an almost total political and societal consensus on music, and the Federal Government only had to keep one eye on the workings of *Land* politicians, municipal officials, and the radio stations. The one musical issue that was transparently a matter of national concern – the adoption of a national anthem – was handled very oddly. The Federal Republic proved unable to break cleanly with the past like the GDR, and became rather bogged down in trying to adapt the *Deutschlandlied*. This led to uncertainties and confusion, which persist to this day. Debates over which words should accompany Haydn's

---

67   See Anna Merritt and Richard Merritt (eds), *Public Opinion in semisovereign Germany: The HICOG Surveys 1949–1955* (Urbana, Chicago, and London: University of Illinois Press, 1980), pp. 126, 133, 142, and 216.

68   *Ibid.*, p. 222.

69   BBC/WAC E1/753/4, Fraser to Thomson, 5 June 1954.

70   BBC/WAC E1/753/4, Assistant Head of German Service to Chief European Service, 8 December 1954.

71   BBC/WAC E1/753/4, Extract from a report of a Visit to Germany by H.G.S., 11–21.12.1954.

melody, and how the anthem should be taught in schools have continued for decades, generating a considerable analytical literature.[72]

Adenauer himself was determined to retain the *Deutschlandlied*, aware of its emotional appeal, and its symbolic power in representing a whole, united Germany. By omitting the first two stanzas of Fallersleben's text, he hoped to keep the old anthem in an internationally acceptable form. His gesture in asking an audience in West Berlin in April 1950 to join him in singing the third verse was obviously prepared beforehand, and Adenauer robustly defended this when taken to task by the Allied High Commissioners.[73] Heuss favoured a new anthem altogether. Both took a close and prolonged interest in the whole question, spurred on by reports of problems caused by the lack of a national anthem in 1949 and 1950. At one level, this manifested itself in a bizarre spectacle at a political meeting in Munich, when the audience spontaneously broke into a rendering of the *Deutschlandlied* at the end of proceedings. Vice-Chancellor Franz Blücher, Justice Minister Thomas Dehler, and others on the platform remained ostentatiously silent until the third stanza, at which point they heartily joined in.[74] More alarming were reports that the hit song *We are the inhabitants of Trizonia* was being used unofficially as a new anthem.[75] This was an intolerable humiliation, and prompted nationwide debate. In an outpouring of patriotic sentiment, many citizens wrote new texts and melodies, addressed directly to Heuss or Adenauer.

Those which survive in Adenauer's Chancellery files are revealing. Typically, the authors recognised that the greatest problem lay with the opening line of the *Deutschlandlied*, '*Deutschland, Deutschland, über alles*', and sought to replace this with something more innocuous, like 'Deutschland, Deutschland, du mein Alles, du mein Alles in der Welt' (Germany, Germany, you my all, you my everything in the world), 'Frieden, Freiheit, über alles' (Peace and Freedom above all), or 'Deutschland, lieb ich, über alles' (Germany, I love above all).[76] Other suggested first lines were openly nostalgic, like 'Deutschland, Deutschland, immer bleibe, was Du warst für uns bis heut' (Germany, Germany, remain always what you were for us until today).[77] One was strikingly insensitive to the nature of the problem: 'Mit der alten Fahnentreue, grüssen wir das Vaterland' (With the old loyalty to the flag, we greet the Fatherland).[78] Several suggested keeping the first line, apparently unaware that

---

72   See Jost Hermand, 'On the History of the "Deutschlandlied"', Applegate and Potter, *Music and German National Identity*, pp. 251–68.

73   See the conversation between Adenauer, François-Poncet, and Robertson reprinted in Werner Bührer (ed.), *Die Adenauer-Ära. Die Bundesrepublik Deutschland 1949–1963* (Munich: Piper, 1993), pp. 104–6.

74   BAK B136/479, Zwei Nationalhymnen?

75   See NWHA/NW 60/339, Causemann to Kultusminister des Landes Nordrhein-Westfälen, 12 July 1949.

76   BAK B136/479, Spurrer to Adenauer, 5 April 1951; Auszug aus der Fuldaer Volkszeitung vom 26.1.1951; Egar to Bundespräsident, 7 November 1951.

77   BAK B136/479, Heinrichs to Adenauer, 25 April 1951.

78   BAK B136/479, Merkle to Bundeskanzler, 29 October 1951.

it was completely unacceptable in the countries Germany had occupied after 1939. A number grappled with the geographical problems, and suggested substitutions for the landmarks in Fallersleben's text. Ewald Hiller made an ingenious suggestion. Germany could be a moveable feast, with 'Memel' replaced by either 'Elbe', 'Oder' or 'Weichsel' as appropriate.[79]

Virtually all the texts suggested were structured around the repetition of words like *Deutschland, Vaterland*, and *Heimat*. Many dwelt on German hills, mountains, oaks, woods, poets, and thinkers. Many mentioned German youth and the future; fewer German women and girls. There was an overwhelming demand to keep Haydn's melody, although many substitutes were put forward. Most of the composers seemed unaware of potential militaristic overtones, and chose march times – something Eisler had carefully avoided with his new anthem for the GDR. Heuss was aware of these difficulties, and commissioned a new text and melody by Rudolf Schröder and Hermann Reutter, which he presented to the public on New Year's Eve, 1950. It never caught on though, and at the Winter Olympics in 1952, the German national team used the *Freude, schöne Götterfunken* theme from Beethoven's Ninth Symphony as an anthem. Adenauer never lost sight of his intention to adopt the third verse of the *Deutschlandlied*, and in April 1952, he persuaded Heuss to accept this. Strangely, this was not done by law but was proclaimed in the Federal Government's *Press and Information Office Bulletin*, which wrote under the heading 'The *Deutschlandlied* is the National Anthem' in 1952: 'On state occasions the third verse will be sung.'[80] As a result, for many years it was not entirely clear what the Federal Republic's national anthem was, and both the first and third verses of the *Deutschlandlied* were used. In 1954, when the German football team won the World Cup in Berne, German supporters sang the first verse, at which point Radio Switzerland immediately broke off its live broadcast of the event.[81]

The Federal Government's support for musicology was disguised. As we have seen, the Bach Festival in Göttingen had brought Blume, president of the GfM, into collaboration with Erich Wende, head of the Federal Interior Ministry's Department of Culture. Blume was concerned to rebuild German musicology, and hankered after the state support that had been so helpful to the discipline between 1933 and 1945. In 1952, he published an analysis of the state of German musicology, arguing that it was the vital foundation of all German musical life. Noting the terrible losses from libraries and archives during the war, and a collapse in educational standards, Blume called for support from all levels of government, and from the churches in the Federal Republic, above all to restore something like the former Reich Institute for

---

79   BAK B136/479, Hiller to Adenauer, 18 January 1951.

80   Cited in Benjamin Ortmeyer, *Argumente gegen das Deutschlandlied. Geschichte und Gegenwart eines Lobliedes auf die deutsche Nation* (Cologne: Bund-Verlag, 1991), pp. 82–5. See also Eberhard Pikart (ed.), *Theodor Heuss. Der Mann, das Werk, die Zeit. Eine Ausstellung* (Tübingen: Wunderlich, 1967), pp. 321–6.

81   Heike Amos, *Auferstanden aus Ruinen ... Die Nationalhymne der DDR 1949 bis 1990* (Berlin: Dietz, 1997), p. 127, fn. 341.

German Music Research (which he called the State Institute, presumably to avoid the Nazi overtones), and to bring to fruition the projects started there.[82]

Blume, who like many in the Federal Republic, often referred to the 'catastrophe of 1945', rather than that of 1933, glossed over the complicity between German musicology and Nazism. He undoubtedly knew that many of his colleagues in the Federal Republic and the GDR were gravely compromised by their publications and by their actions between 1933 and 1945. In the early 1950s, this was not an issue many wanted to explore, and in 1953 the Federal Ministry of the Interior agreed to support the establishment of a 'Music History Commission'. It was to be headed by Blume, and to pick up the work of the former Reich Institute, specifically the publication of *Das Erbe deutscher Musik*, and *Musikalischen Denkmäler*, both large series celebrating the tradition of German music.[83] In 1954, Blume's commission opened the German Music Archive in Kassel. Announcing this in *Die Musikforschung*, Blume did not mention that this was supported by the Ministry of the Interior, but did make clear that 'the archive takes over ... a great part of the duties which were fulfilled by the one time State Institute for Music Research in Berlin.'[84]

German musicology has been castigated for concealing its Nazi history. I will briefly explore here one example that displays this, but also proves that not all German musicologists were content with the embarrassing silences. One of many institutions which wrote to the Federal Government to ask for money after 1949 was an International Archive of Musicians' Letters in Berlin, run by Erich Müller von Asow. He was a prolific writer who had published several editions of composers' letters. In 1953, his Archive was admitted to membership of the *Centre de Documentation de Musique Internationale*, which, as we have seen, was supporting the most avant-garde music of the period together with the NWDR. Between 1949 and 1953, von Asow wrote repeatedly to different government agencies to ask for funds, arguing that his archive was making a vital contribution to international scholarship. The Ministry of the Interior was at this time being pestered by many cultural organisations looking for grants, and naturally made enquiries about von Asow to various academics, including Blume, Gerber and Hans-Joachim Moser.

Reactions were divided. Blume was cautiously supportive, but Gerber was highly critical of von Asow's academic credentials. One response, addressed directly to the Interior Minister, went further. Hans Mersmann, Director of the Music Academy in Cologne, wrote that in 1934, von Asow, under the name Erich Müller, had written the section on Jews in music in the *Handbuch der Judenfrage* (*Handbook of the Jewish Question*). Müller's contribution to this book, the most widely read of its type, named many individual musicians as Jews, and accused them of corrupting German music. In this way it was a forerunner of later publications like the *Lexicon*

---

82   Friedrich Blume, 'Zur Lage der deutschen Musikforschung', *Die Musikforschung*, 5, 1952, pp. 97–109.

83   BAK B106/299, Musikgeschichtliche Kommission E.V., Denkschrift betr. Deutsches Musikgeschichtliches Archiv in Kassel, October 1958.

84   *Die Musikforschung*, 7 (1954), p. 510.

of Jews in Music (1940), and we should pause to consider quite how terrible the consequences could be for an individual named in one of these books. Mersmann also notified the Minister that von Asow had unscrupulously denounced individuals in the *Handbook of the Jewish Question* who were not Jews because they were his personal enemies, and that he had taken him to court about this in 1934.[85]

In the end, the Ministry refused von Asow's requests for money. More significant, though, is that in a résumé of the whole affair, prepared in the Ministry in 1953, no reference was made to von Asow's contribution to the *Handbook of the Jewish Question*, or to Mersmann's other allegations.[86] Several recent historians have researched the Erich Müller who wrote for the *Handbook of the Jewish Question* in 1934, but have not connected him with the post-war archivist Müller von Asow. Even the 2001 edition of *Grove*, which has had entries on musicologists like Blume, Gerber and Boetticher rewritten to take account of their collaboration with Nazism, contains an article on von Asow which similarly omits to mention the *Handbook*.[87] Müller had in fact altered his name to 'Müller von Asow', for reasons which are unclear, between 1939 and 1943.

The Federal Government did take on other musical responsibilities. One was the Bayreuth Festival, which reopened in studiously apolitical guise in 1951. Although Heuss and Adenauer both refused to link themselves with this in a ceremonial capacity,[88] their government was willing to give Bayreuth substantial material help, partly because of the tourist revenues it generated. In 1952, the Interior Ministry paid 230,000 DM for new lighting in the Festival House, and the Ministry for the Marshall Plan paid off debts of 300,000 DM from the previous year. In 1953, the Finance Ministry provided 170,000 DM. By 1954, the Bayreuth Festival was expected to cost the Federal Government 1 million DM.[89] A second project was the Bamberg Symphony Orchestra, formed in 1945 on American prompting, from

---

85   The correspondence is in BAK B106/299. See in particular Mersmann to Bundesminister des Innern, 9 October 1950. Müller in fact wrote the chapter on 'The Jews in Music' in the 1932 edition of the *Handbuch*, and revised this in 1934 to celebrate the changes in German musical life instigated by Hitler. See Erich Müller, 'Das Judentum in der Musik', Theodor Fritsch (ed.), *Handbuch der Judenfrage. Die wichtigsten Tatsachen zur Beurteilung des jüdischen Volkes*, (31st edition, Leipzig: Hammer Verlag, 1932), pp. 323–33, and 'Das Judentum in der Musik', Theodor Fritsch (ed.), *Handbuch der Judenfrage. Die wichtigsten Tatsachen zur Beurteilung des jüdischen Volkes*, (36th edition, Leipzig: Hammer Verlag, 1934), pp. 324–34. On the evolution of books naming Jews in music in Nazi Germany, see de Vries, *Sonderstab Musik*, pp. 64ff. Müller's contribution to the *Handbuch der Judenfrage* was replaced in 1935 by one written by Hans Költzsch.

86   BAK B106/299, DBMdI 3546 – 1037IV/53, Bonn, 12 August 1953.

87   Following representations from this author, the online edition of *Grove* has been revised to include reference to Müller's contribution to the *Handbuch der Judenfrage*.

88   BAK B136/5815, Seebohm, Bundesminister für Verkehr, to Adenauer, 8 March 1951, and Mai, persönlicher Referent des Bundeskanzlers, to Seebohm, 29 March 1951.

89   BAK B136/5815, Bundesminister des Innern to Staatssekretär im Bundeskanzleramt, 4 February 1954.

German musicians exiled from Prague and Breslau. The orchestra, which rapidly established itself as one of Germany's best, was considered 'an expression of idealism',[90] and was supported by the Bavarian Government, and subsequently the Federal Government.

The town of Bamberg itself was not large enough to finance a symphony orchestra of the first rank, but the particular membership of the orchestra guaranteed it a place in public imagination of the Federal Republic. After 1949, it was groomed for work overseas. The Bavarian government wrote in 1951 to the Federal Interior Ministry that the orchestra was important for 'cultural propaganda abroad'.[91] By this time it was costing 349,000 DM annually in public subsidies, a figure that rose to 523,000 DM in 1953.[92] Appropriately, the orchestra was led by Joseph Keilberth, who had conducted in Prague during the war. In 1954, the orchestra began a series of intensive foreign tours. In March it played in Mexico City, and in April in Havana and New York. In 1955, it played in Brussels, Lisbon, Paris and the Hague. Keilberth's concert programmes were overwhelmingly conservative, and were a huge success with audiences. The ambassador in Belgrade reported in 1955 on the extraordinary success of the Bamberg Symphony 'at a difficult time', with 'a purely German programme, in which also the *Meistersinger* Overture was not missing.'[93] Further support was given to musical and theatrical groups in border regions by the Ministry for Border Lands. In 1953, it was paying 120,000 DM yearly to the State Theatre in Trier, and 110,000 DM to the Nordmark Symphony Orchestra in Schleswig.[94]

Professional music was primarily supported at *Land* and municipal level, and here conservative German nationalism was mixed with a commitment to the international avant-garde. The continued star-status in the Federal Republic of famous conductors from the Nazi period, like Furtwängler, Karajan, Keilberth, Jochum and Schmidt-Isserstedt, has been invoked to exemplify this conservatism. Certainly there was enough continuity with the music scene before 1945 to justify some use of the term 'restoration'. Despite the best efforts of the French, the German classical composers who had been appropriated by the Nazis were quickly rehabilitated. We should not, though, underestimate the public commitment to new music. Just as in broadcasting, there was a consensus that this was, like an unpleasant medicine, a good thing.

The *Städtetag*, in 1949, concerned about music in smaller towns, took up recommendations from its Working Group on Concert Affairs on how civic officials and responsible citizens could form local concert societies. This was not considered an optional luxury: 'Each town is requested to check whether within its walls good concerts are regularly held, which correspond to the needs and the taste of music-

---

90   BAK B106/119, Die Erschaffung des Orchesters der Bamberger Symphoniker.

91   BAK B106/119, Bayerisches Staatsministerium für Unterricht und Kultus to BMI, 19 October 1951.

92   BAK B106/119, Zusammenstellung der Rechnungsergebnisse der Bamberger Symphoniker, e.V., in Bamberg, für die Rechnungsjahre 1951 bis 1953.

93   BAK B106/119, Botschaft der Bundesrepublik Deutschland, Belgrad, to Gussone, Bundesministerium des Innern, 10 February 1955.

94   BAK B136/5815, - 5 - K - 1182/54, Bonn, 8 March 1954.

loving and musically aware people, and to the level which is worthy of our great musical tradition.' Equally important was 'the unpolitical direction of the society, which must exercise an influence free from world-views and political influences.'

The *Städtetag* also recommended a quota for contemporary music, strikingly similar to that adopted by *Stakuko* in the GDR: 'In every concert, or indeed at the least in every second concert … a contemporary work by a known or unknown composer should be performed.'[95] Concert programmes issued by different West German towns in the early 1950s show that this commitment, if not followed to the letter, was widely and publicly accepted. In Bielefeld in 1952/53, the Municipal Orchestra, as well as recognising a particular obligation to its native son, Henze, was proudly performing Bartok, Roussel, Scriabin, Khachachurian, Honegger and Hindemith.[96] The programme issued in Bochum pledged 'to make ever-closer the connection between the concert-goer and contemporary music'.[97] Often, civic authorities recognised that this was unpopular, but stoically maintained their purpose. In Karlsruhe, the town council in 1952 reported on how it was working to enlarge its small circle of devotees, 'although Karlsruhe is not particularly thankful ground for contemporary music'.[98]

The former occupiers provided a further layer of support for new music. The French maintained their cultural offensive, even when they ran into the same conservatism that worried German officials. The report on a festival of new French music and film in Mainz in May 1952 explained why many of the concerts were poorly attended: 'The quality of the music offered surpasses the Mainz public's capacity for absorption.'[99] The musical programme of 'The Bridge' – the British Centre – in Göttingen, opened in May 1950, gives a representative example of the British effort. Although the centre could not host many live performances, it did hold a fortnightly 'records evening', and interspersed these with lectures. British music was very much to the fore, with an emphasis on contemporary composers like Britten, Moeran, Ferguson, Bliss, Bush and Finzi. Evenings were devoted to other modernists, like Schoenberg, Berg and Bartok. A special occasion was the collaboration with the America House in nearby Hanover in October 1953 to stage Menotti's *The Old Maid and the Thief.* Ironically, given his previously mentioned connections with looting and plundering during the war, the British engaged Göttingen University musicologist Wolfgang Boetticher as one of a number of speakers highly qualified to present talks on English music.[100]

---

95   BAK B105/192, Betr.: Lage der Kulturinstitute nach der Geldneuordnung IX, 9 May 1949.

96   WDR/HAC 07362, *Städtisches Orchester Bielefeld, Abonnementskonzerte 1952/1953.*

97   WDR/HAC 07362, *Das Orchester der Stadt Bochum, Spielzeit 1952/1953.*

98   GLAK 481/398, Karlsruher Kulturbericht für 1951/1952, Stadtverwaltung Karlsruhe an den Regierungspräsidenten von Nordbaden, 8 September 1952, p. 8.

99   AOFC/AC 28/2, Gouverneur Commissaire du Land de Rhénanie-Palatinat to l'Ambassadeur, Haut Commissaire de la République Française en Allemagne, 23 May 1952.

100   See the programmes for *Die Brücke*, Göttingen, in SG III B 146.

The American effort, like the British, was at its strongest in the early 1950s. The Speakers and Artists Bureau at the High Commission in Frankfurt supervised performances by visiting American musicians at the 27 America Houses. Everett Helm, reporting in 1952, presented this programme as anti-Nazi rather than anti-Communist. He denied that there was any manipulation of the artists involved, arguing, implausibly, that 'there is no regulation or requirement'. When an artist learnt 'the nature and purpose of the America House program', he usually chose a modernist programme 'by his own volition'.[101] In 1952, the Boston Symphony Orchestra played in Germany as part of its European tour, which was financed by the CIA.[102] More specific to Germany was the US Seventh Army Symphony Orchestra, which 'originated strictly as an army project'[103] and was then further developed as a useful propaganda tool. This orchestra, made up of service personnel stationed in Germany, was used to project a microcosm of the new American society. The *Military Government Information Bulletin* went out of its way to note the varied backgrounds of the musicians: 'a captain, a few sergeants, a young woman dependent [*sic*], one airman, but mostly soldiers'. It described German audiences, which 'seemed strongly impressed at seeing soldiers and non-commissioned officers of different races and the others – all in uniform – playing together'. Listeners at Bad Hersfeld were apparently 'greatly impressed at seeing men of various races work together'.[104] The Seventh Army Symphony first toured in 1952, when it appeared at the 'European Weeks' festival in Passau; its tours became a regular annual feature in the Federal Republic.

There has been speculation on whether the USA funded the Darmstadt Summer Schools in the early 1950s. Obviously, the courses could not have started without American approval and support. This has been well documented, as has the payment from 1949 to 1951 of about 20 per cent of the total costs by the American High Commission.[105] In 1950, the State Department paid for Edgard Varèse to lecture on electronic music at Darmstadt, and to give other talks in West Germany. These were the crisis years, in which the Summer School might have collapsed, but in fact it was mainly financed by German politicians at *Land* and municipal level. Just as they had financed the Göttingen Bach Festival in 1950, the *Länder*, by paying students' fees, supported new music at Darmstadt and elsewhere.[106] By this time, Darmstadt particularly was recognised as a Cold War symbol of 'artistic freedom'. The Mayor of Darmstadt thanked Christine Teusch, Culture Minister in North Rhine-Westphalia,

---

101   Everett Helm, 'America Houses in Germany: Good-Will and Understanding', *Musical America*, 72 (February 1952), pp. 12ff.

102   Saunders, *Who Paid the Piper?*, pp. 124–5.

103   Everett Helm, 'West Sector Roundup', *Musical America*, 74 (February 1954), pp. 150ff.

104   'Cultural Envoys in Uniform', *Military Government Information Bulletin*, November 1952, pp. 7ff.

105   Beal, 'Negotiating Cultural Allies', p. 116.

106   NWHA/NW 60/849, Auszug aus dem Kurzprotokoll über die Tagung des Kunstausschusses der Ständigen Konferenz der Kultusminister am 10./11. Januar 1951.

for supporting the Summer School in 1950, adding: 'the cultural-political aspect of this arrangement is particularly welcome'. The courses were 'a decisive contribution to the intellectual renewal ... which should not be overlooked as an important factor in the new political order.'[107] Through the early 1950s, the Institute for New Music and Music Education in Bayreuth was similarly supported.[108] In 1953, *Land* Culture Ministers agreed that 'serious contemporary musical composition is both as an ideal, and materially, to be supported in every way.'[109]

Music and Politics

The GDR proudly declared that music was a political affair, and tried to regulate every aspect of musical life within its borders. It supported a network of orchestras and choirs, and financed composers by commissioning new works. Music was taken into factories and workplaces, and lay participation was encouraged. The highest standards of performance and scholarship were demanded, and leading ensembles were encouraged to tour abroad, where they were typically very well received. There was censorship of avant-garde music from Western Europe and America, and musical education, in schools and academies, was conservative. Broadcast music was closely supervised. Musicians in Party organisations like the VDK played a central role in state regulation.

In the Federal Republic, any open link between music and politics was denounced.[110] Like the GDR, the Federal Republic supported a complex musical infrastructure, dedicated equally to high standards, and to the preservation of Germany's musical heritage. It financed selected musical projects for cultural prestige abroad. Behind the scenes, the Ministry of the Interior kept a close eye on musical developments, and sponsored academic work on German music.

In both Germanys, bureaucratic networks of politicians, musicians, and administrators supervised music. The Federal Republic was, though, publicly committed to Western liberal ideals, expressed nowhere more strongly than in the centres of 'new music', Darmstadt, Cologne and Donaueschingen, all of which were supported by taxpayers and license payers. To make amends for the shameful isolation and xenophobia of the Hitler years, the Federal Republic made a virtue of internationalism and an ideal of freedom – belied by its outright censorship of only one kind of music, that of the GDR.

---

107   NWHA/NW 60/849, Bürgermeister, Darmstadt, to Kultusminister von Nordrhein-Westfalen, 30 October 1950.

108   See the correspondence between Land Nordrhein-Westfalen and the Institut in NWHA/NW 60/885.

109   BAK B106/1073, Beschluß der Kultusministerkonferenz vom 17. April 1953 in Bonn.

110   See for example 'Eine unselige Verquickung. Musik und Politik', *Musikleben*, 8, 1955, pp. 83–4.

Chapter Seven

Dance Music: The Enemy Within?

If avant-garde, or 'new music' was the least popular of the various musical offerings served up in post-war Germany, there is no doubting which was the most beloved. Radio schedules in the early 1950s were full of programmes with titles like *Entertainment Concert, Dancing Notes, Immortal Waltzes, Tango Serenades, Come Dancing* or simply *Dance Music*, to take one day in May 1951 as a random example.[1] Analysis of this music is complicated. Where the English language struggles with a number of imprecise categories like 'popular music', 'light music', 'jazz', and 'swing', German presents a brusque, value-laden distinction between 'serious music' (*ernste Musik*) and 'entertainment music' (*Unterhaltungsmusik*). The latter covers a host of musical forms, ranging in the post-war period from light-hearted dance music to the most improvisational jazz emerging from America. Jazz in Germany has attracted a great deal of attention. Its particular position, which after 1945 challenged existing, and newly emerging ideas of race, gender, and class, has been carefully analysed. Dance music, which has had fewer publicists to advance it as an art form worthy of historical or musicological analysis, has been neglected. This is doubly unfortunate as it was far more popular than any kind of real jazz in post-war Germany. It was enjoyed by almost all, young and old, urban and rural, male and female.

There is, of course, no absolute or clear dividing line between 'dance music' and 'jazz', as we can see if we return to our sample day, 17 May 1951. Alongside many programmes broadcast that day, like those already named, which are clearly at one end of the scale, there were only a handful which might have appealed to a serious jazz fan. Further, these were all late at night, like Stuttgart's *Jazz on the Radio*, and *Jazz Season 1950/51* starting on RIAS just after midnight. At 22.35 NWDR's *Dr Jazz* presented *Music Box*, bringing other worlds of music into a still impoverished Germany. He was playing numbers like *High Tide* (Basie), *Calling Dr Gillespie* (Krupa), *Blue Rhythm Fantasy* (Hill), *I'm sorry I made you cry* (Capitol Jazzmen), *Stomp it off* (Dorsey), *Tulip or turnip* (Ellington), *Old man Blues* (Bechet), *Boomsie* (Jackson) and *Blue rhythm swing* (Blue Rhythm Band). At 0.30 NWDR was broadcasting *Sounds from London*, with Robert Farnon and his Orchestra playing songs like *Paper Orchid, Daisy Bell, Limehouse Blues*, and Gershwin's *Love walked in*.[2]

---

1   All from schedules for 17 May 1951, in *Hör Zu!*, 1951 (20), pp. 22–3.
2   *Ibid.*

To muddy the waters further, there were other programmes the same day broadcasting a mix of dance music and jazz. The best example is Radio Frankfurt's *Dance Music* at 22.45. This featured the big names of the German dance scene – interestingly from both sides of the Iron Curtain – the Orchestras of Kurt Edelhagen and Kurt Henkel. This description alerts us to a further complication. Linguistic images of jazz in English frequently refer to a counter-cultural scene, associated with bars, liquor, sex, and drugs. The musicians are 'gone'. Here, Jack Kerouac describes the English pianist George Shearing at Birdland 'in his great 1949 days, before he became cool and commercial':

> The drummer, Denzil Best, sat motionless except for his wrists snapping the brushes. And Shearing began to rock; a smile broke over his ecstatic face; he began to rock in the piano seat, back and forth, slowly at first, then the beat went up, and he began rocking fast, his left foot jumped up with every beat, his neck began to rock crookedly, he brought his face down to the keys, he pushed his hair back, his combed hair dissolved, he began to sweat. The music picked up. The bass-player hunched over and socked it in, faster and faster, that's all. Shearing began to play his chords; they rolled out of the piano in great rich showers, you'd think the man wouldn't have time to line them up. They rolled and rolled like the sea. Folks yelled for him to 'Go!'[3]

In Germany at this time, dance bands were orchestras, and referred to themselves as such. They played in dinner jackets and bow ties, sitting respectably on a platform and reading music from stands. Typically, they were led by a conductor with a baton. The musicians were classically trained, and did not use electric instruments. Audiences danced tangos, foxtrots, and waltzes, occasionally livened up by a samba or a mamba. German bands played a synthesis of international musical styles, and it was this that prompted such anxiety in the post-war period. It led to public disorder and generational conflict, and was at the heart of the cultural Cold War. In the GDR, particularly, dance music played a uniquely corrosive and disruptive role. An analysis of reactions to dance music in post-war Germany must be conscious of this complex and changing mix of German and international styles, and bear in mind that traditional forms were overwhelmingly most popular. Only a tiny minority of the population, largely urban, young, and male, was fanatical about jazz.

No part of Germany, geographical or social, was immune, though, to the characteristic lure of the 'hit' or *Schlager*. The titles of the first post-war hits summarise the themes a population took to its heart: *Capri Fisher*; *Seagull, you are flying home*; *In the harbour at Adano* and *Maria from Bahia*. Over the next few years, thousands of songs rehearsed these dreamy, sentimental themes of the Mediterranean, the Pacific, sailors going away, and young men called Toni and Enrico falling in love with young women with similarly Italian names like Viola. Songs from Italy and France were often as popular as those from America and Britain. The 'hit industry', overwhelmingly concentrated in West Germany, adapted songs from overseas by translating their lyrics into German, republishing sheet music for them,

---

3   Jack Kerouac, *On the Road* (Harmondsworth: Penguin, 1972 [1957]), p. 122.

and distributing copies all over Germany, often sending them free to bandleaders by post. The bands then played cover versions of the hits the public was listening to on the radio. By the mid 1950s, this process was taking only a few weeks, so the latest hits could be brought into Germany very quickly. In the last few years before television changed social habits, the dance halls were crowded, and there was good money to be made.[4]

The Fifth Column[5]

The official history of music in the GDR has only a short entry under the heading 'Dance and Entertainment Music' (*Tanz- und Unterhaltungsmusik*). It describes the development of an alternative to the products of the 'bourgeois-capitalist entertainment industry', giving examples of the new kinds of text, of music, and of dances that were developed during the 1950s. The authors stress the collective work of the SED, the Ministry for Culture, the VDK, and the State Radio Committee, and praise the 'high artistic level' that the best of their efforts reached. Virtually nothing is said about the early part of the decade, and *Stakuko* is not mentioned.[6] The reader might infer from the brevity of the article – only a few pages in a multi-volume history – that dance music was a matter of minor importance in the cultural life of a state committed to elevating the artistic taste of the masses, but this would be mistaken. The SED and its musical elite recognised the enormous influence of dance music, and in the first years of the GDR's existence, an unrelenting struggle was waged against its westernised forms. Sustained theoretical analysis was matched with a range of practical initiatives; repression and censorship were accompanied by a studious cultivation of new songs and dances. And, however the GDR's own historians tried to cover this up, it failed completely. In contrast to a historiography that has focused on oppositional youth cultures that developed around jazz and rock in the later GDR, this chapter will analyse the struggle for a 'socialist dance culture' in the early 1950s, and argue that in fact the battle against Western popular music had been fought and lost already back then.

In fact, the damage had been done before the founding of the GDR. Jazz and dance music enjoyed a resurgence of popularity in the cities of eastern Germany after they were occupied by the Red Army. The *Stars and Stripes*, noting in June 1945 how quickly the Soviets had got Radio Berlin working, observed that it was broadcasting

---

4   See Siegfried Schmidt-Joos, *Geschäfte mit Schlagern* (Bremen: Carl Schünemann, 1960).

5   Some of the material in this chapter has appeared in Toby Thacker, 'The fifth column: dance music in the early GDR', in Patrick Major and Jonathan Osmond (eds), *The Workers' and Peasants' State: Communism and Society in East Germany under Ulbricht 1945–71* (Manchester: Manchester University Press, 2002), pp. 227–43. This essay extends its analysis up to the building of the Berlin Wall in 1961.

6   Autorenkollektiv, *Sammelbände zur Musikgeschichte der Deutschen Demokratischen Republik, Band V: Musikgeschichte der DDR 1945–1976* (Berlin, 1979), pp. 189–92.

'plenty of jazz and swing'.[7] In the relative cultural pluralism of the Soviet Zone, the enthusiasm for these forms of music spread. Kurt Henkel's orchestra was engaged in 1947 to play for Radio Leipzig, a city that quickly developed its own jazz scene around the *Hot Geyer* club opened by Kurt Michaelis. In 1948 and 1949, a number of musicians, including Michaelis, left the Soviet Zone for the West as the Soviet repression of jazz in eastern Europe after the 'historic decree' took effect.[8] Many more dance musicians – like Henkel – stayed though, and it is clear that a deep-rooted fascination with jazz and dance music had taken hold, particularly in the industrial cities of Thuringia and Saxony. The new state found itself in conflict with its own population. What had been considered an ephemeral but harmless entertainment was declared the decadent expression of late bourgeois society that was being cynically used as an imperialist tool to destroy the taste and culture of the masses.

This attitude was expressed most clearly at the VDK's founding conference in April 1951. Addressing an audience that included the leaders of party and state, Meyer devoted a considerable part of his opening speech to what he called 'American entertainment kitsch':

> Today's boogie-woogie is a channel through which the poison of Americanism penetrates and threatens to anaesthetise the minds of the workers. This threat is just as dangerous as a military attack with poison gases – who would not wish to protect themselves from a Lewisite attack? Here American industry kills several flies with one blow. It conquers the music markets of countries and helps at the same time to undermine their cultural independence through boogie-woogie cosmopolitanism. It propagates the degenerate ideology of American monopoly capitalism with its lack of culture, its criminal and psychopathic films, its prostitution rackets, its empty sensationalism, and above all its mania for war and destruction. …
>
> In West Germany American hit kitsch is propagated on a huge scale. Through radio, film, and records a veritable tidal wave of boogie-woogie is released upon the German people, by which our German Democratic Republic is certainly not unaffected. Particular West German publishers and record companies, as direct agents of American monopoly capitalism, play here a role which is extremely hostile to the people. Few factors contribute so strongly to the Americanisation of people as Hollywood hits and sensational kitsch. One must speak plainly here of a fifth column of Americanism. It would be mistaken to deny the dangerous role of American hit kitsch in the preparation for war.[9]

This perception resulted in a systematic effort to stop this kind of music from being played in the GDR and to replace it with 'socialist realism'. Although the Central Committee's Department of Culture, the VDK, and the Academy played a part, it

---

7   *Stars and Stripes Magazine – Weekly Supplement*, 1:4, 23 June 1945.

8   See Rudolf Käs, 'Hot and Sweet. Jazz im befreiten Land', Glaser et al., *So viel Anfang*, pp. 250–55. On the Soviet Union and Eastern Europe see Starr, *Red and Hot*, pp. 204–34.

9   Ernst Meyer, 'Realismus – die Lebensfrage der deutschen Musik', *MuG*, 1951/2, pp. 38–43, p. 41. Given that Meyer's mother and one of his brothers had been murdered in Auschwitz, his use of such language is particularly striking.

was Rudolf Hartig at *Stakuko* who was given the primary responsibility for dealing with dance music between 1951 and 1953, a task he subsequently continued in the MfK until November 1954.[10]

Stakuko pursued two approaches. The first was repressive, and consisted of a series of measures, administrative and practical, to prevent any music deemed as unacceptable from being played. The second was creative, and involved a range of efforts to promote new dance music. Both were underpinned by close theoretical analysis, and carried out in the style of 'collective work'. As far as can be judged from surviving files, this resulted in terrible confusion, and its officials soon found themselves in a crossfire, caught between the demands of the Central Committee on the one hand, and complaints from other ministries, local officials, the party press and the public on the other. Frequently, the reality of 'collective' and 'planned' work was the very opposite of what was intended.

As a first step, Hartig met in October 1951 with representatives from government ministries, the trade unions and the People's Police (*Volkspolizei*), to discuss the control of dance music.[11] After this, he was ordered by Holzhauer, *Stakuko*'s Chairman, to produce directives that would ensure uniform control over the employment of all performing musicians in the GDR. Before acting, Hartig decided to take stock of the situation. A series of letters from Saxony clearly impressed him. The regional government there had a concise regulation for licensing dance musicians and controlling their programmes. This stressed the importance of education in developing good taste, and highlighted the responsibility of all Party organisations, including the SED's 'Free German Youth' movement (the FDJ), *Stakuko*, the radio, composers and the police, to work actively in the struggle against Americanised dance music.

The regulation stipulated that dance bands should be prevented from playing if they did not support these goals, and that the proprietors of dance halls should be made aware 'that they are also responsible for the purity (*Sauberkeit*) of their dance orchestras'.[12] A conference had already been held in Halle for bandleaders.[13] Hartig expressed full agreement with this approach, and sent copies of the regulation to all other *Länder*, asking them to report on what they were doing in comparison.[14] The responses from around the country were dismaying. Clearly there was no

---

10   On 'realism' in dance music, see Max Butting, 'Zur Situation der Tanzmusik', *MuG*, 1951/3, pp. 77–9, Hanns Eisler, 'Brief nach Westdeutschland , *Sinn und Form*, 1951/6, pp.14–24, Reginald Rudorf, 'Für eine frohe, ausdrucksvolle Tanzmusik', *MuG*, 1952/8, pp. 247–252, and 'Prof. Hans Pischner über Unterhaltungs- und Tanzmusik', *MuG*, 1952/11, pp. 367–370.

11   SAPMO DR 1/6137, Protokoll über die Besprechung am 10.10.1951 wegen der Vermittlung von Musikern.

12   SAPMO-BArch DR 1/6133, Resolution über Verbesserung der öffentlichen Tanzmusik, 16 August 1951.

13   SAPMO-BArch DR 1/6133, Siegmund-Schultze, Landesregierung Sachsen, Verwaltung für Kunstangelegenheiten, to Hartig, 27 November 1951.

14   SAPMO-BArch DR 1/6133, Hartig to all Länderregierungen, 21 February 1952.

uniformity of either theory or practice. Even where there were harsh rules on paper, implementation of licensing and control of performance were inconsistent.[15] Reporting to the Central Committee, Hartig wrote: 'In all *Länder* of the GDR an apparent chaos prevails with respect to the employment of musicians.'[16]

Two administrative measures were central to *Stakuko*'s plans. The first – a crudely worded prohibition of the performance of jazz – was published in December 1951:

> It is now time also to create order in the area of the 'light muse', that is to find an appropriate form of dance music for our changed societal development. On these grounds the performance of all jazz music is immediately to cease. In all public dance events there should only be music played which is essentially stressed by melody and not rhythm. The arrangements must accordingly be written in a folksy manner, which does not offend the ear of our working people. Syncopations and dissonances are the characteristics of a rapidly accelerating capitalistic collapse.[17]

Implementing the ban was more difficult. Hartig's plan was simple in conception, but proved unworkable in practice. He intended, by determining *who* was allowed to play, to control *what* was played. Since 1948, there had been complaints from professional musicians in the Soviet Zone about unregulated competition from amateur dance bands, particularly from FDJ bands. Hartig added to this trade unionist concern the SED's didactic belief that better trained musicians would naturally confine themselves to more respectable music. By January 1952, he had a draft 'Order' ready, according to which all musicians would have to get a permit from a local licensing commission. First they would have to pass an examination with a practical, a music theory, and a general educational component. The employment of musicians without a permit was to be punished by a fine of up to DM 500, or by arrest. Any private engagement of musicians was to be forbidden. Hartig's draft included blank specimen permits, to be signed by a number of local Party offices.[18]

This fantastically complicated scheme was obviously impractical, and over the next few months Hartig received suggestions for amendments. At the same time, complaints about the situation in the provinces poured in. As Hartig produced revision after revision, his patience began to wear thin. He wrote a long letter to

---

15   In Mecklenburg, for example, there were supposedly commissions to oversee dance programmes and prevent the performance of 'western "hot" music'. SAPMO-BArch DR 1/6137, Richtlinien für die Kreis-Prüfungs-Kommission für Tanz- und Unterhaltungsmusiker des Landes Mecklenburg, 1 August 1950.

16   SAPMO-BArch DR 1/6137, Hartig to Seidel, Sekretariat der ZK der SED, 27 February 1952.

17   Cited in Käs, 'Hot and Sweet', p. 255.

18   Violinists for instance, would be expected to play scales and arpeggios of three octaves, a study at the level of one by Mazas or Kreuzer, and one of the 'easier' concertos. The resemblance to Associated Board Grade 8 in Britain is striking. SAPMO-BArch DR 1/6137, Entwurf einer Verordnung zur Sicherung der Qualität der künst. Veranstaltungen und der Mitwirkung der künst. Kräfte; and Entwurf einer einheitlichen Prüfungsordnung für Musiker.

Holzhauer in June, complaining about the time it was taking to get this sorted out. He was now working on an eighth draft of the Order, and the prestige of *Stakuko* was at stake.[19] In July, an abbreviated version was sent to various ministries and to the Central Committee.[20] This only brought a storm of criticism down on Hartig. Roman Chwalek, Minister for Labour, wrote to the office of the President, Wilhelm Pieck, demanding a ruling on whether or not the GDR's trade union organisation, the FDGB, should be involved in the issuing of permits for musicians.[21] A month later he wrote angrily to *Stakuko*, complaining that the 'thus far un-clarified situation of professional musicians has become unacceptable'.[22] The Ministry for Justice and various *Länder* governments quite sensibly pointed out that *Stakuko*'s proposed regulations would, for instance, prevent somebody playing music informally at a wedding party. A Berlin trade union leader wrote to Hartig, telling him that local efforts to deal with the situation had made him a laughing stock.[23] There was open criticism of *Stakuko* in the GDR press. And still, further revisions of the order passed from one office to another. By October, Hartig was at work on a fourteenth draft. By December he was on the sixteenth. Finally, an 'Order' was published in April 1953.[24]

The matter was far from settled though. The central provision of the new regulation – that only professional musicians should be allowed to perform dance music in public – was immediately thrown into question by an article titled 'An Order which creates Disorder' in the FDJ newspaper *Junge Welt*. How could young musicians play, even at relatively informal events, or at Party events, when they were not sufficiently competent to qualify as professional musicians? By early June, Hartig had already had to ask twice for alterations to the decree to be published.[25] Officials at *Stakuko* had constantly to redraft, and ever-changing versions of the decree were shuffled from one ministry to another. Hartig was still negotiating with the Office for Youth Questions when *Stakuko* was disbanded in November 1953.

It is interesting to compare this bureaucratic activity with the reports coming in from around the GDR. Party officials at local and national level were inundated with complaints about the kind of music being played, and the effect it was having. A selection taken from 1952 and 1953, after *Stakuko*'s prohibition of jazz, is revealing.

19　SAPMO-BArch DR 1/6137, Ordnung im Musikberuf, Hartig to Holzhauer, 11 June 1952.

20　SAPMO-BArch DR 1/6137, Verordnung zur Ausübung von Unterhaltungs- und Tanzmusik, 10 July 1952.

21　SAPMO-BArch DR 1/6137, Chwalek to Staatssekretär beim Präsidenten der DDR, 17 July 1952.

22　SAPMO-BArch DR 1/6137, Chwalek to Stakuko, 15 August 1952.

23　SAPMO-BArch DR 1/6137, Kolinski, Kreisvorsitzender der Gew. Kunst, Kreisvorstand Teltow to Stakuko, 9 August 1952.

24　Anordnung über die Befugnis von Ausübung von Unterhaltungs- und Tanzmusik vom 27.3.1953, *Zentralblatt der DDR*, (11), 4 April 1953.

25　SAPMO-BArch DR/1 6192, Hartig to Regierungskanzlei, 2 May 1953, and 3 June 1953. A revised 'Order' was published on 27 May 1953, and a 'Supplement' on 4 June 1953.

Town councillor Federbusch wrote from Jena in October 1952 to complain about the *Melodia-Rhythmiker Halle*, led by Horst Hartmann. He had seen this group playing, and noted with dismay that towards the end of their first set they had played 'particularly American hot music'. He had complained to Hartmann about this, only to be told that bands had to make concessions to the public and 'that in other towns, it was passed over with a smile'. Hartmann had then gone on to direct the band's second set, which according to Federbusch, descended into 'the shrillest atonality', and became 'a primitive, sanctimonious prating'. Slipping easily into Nazi terminology, Federbusch demanded that 'such degeneracies' (*Entartungen*) should not be tolerated.[26]

A lively correspondence between *Stakuko* and municipal authorities in Cottbus and Liebenwerda suggests that this casual disregard for Party authority was widespread. The local council, on 8 September 1952, had banned the Hans-Georg During Dance Orchestra from playing in Liebenwerda. During then nevertheless announced, in the local newspaper, that the orchestra would play on 18 September in the Liebenwerda *Kurhaus*, and he was as good as his word. An official from the Education Department went along with a police officer to observe the performance. Their shocked description was mailed to *Stakuko* two days later. The band had apparently started the evening with a RIAS-style medley of American hits, sung in German. They had then stopped playing, and a member of the band had read out to the audience the local Party's ban, which was greeted by a chorus of whistles. He had then read two letters of praise for the band from other Party organisations. Worse followed. The audience was told that the band could play 'respectable music'; the band demonstrated this by playing a medley of waltzes, again greeted with ear-splitting whistles and jeers. After this display of sarcasm, the band went back to playing 'wild' American music to great applause and acclaim.[27] Nor was this kind of display confined to the cities. An official of the State Radio Committee was shocked by what he saw and heard in the village of Regis Breitingen in Saxony, where he had stayed the night. In a report he described 'torrents' and 'wild cascades of sound at high volume', which provoked many to 'wild bodily dislocations'.[28]

Other reports confirm that dance evenings were often accompanied by violence and rioting. At regional conferences in Gera and Chemnitz, Max Butting, the Academy's expert on dance music, heard from bandleaders of the 'wildest dancing, amidst smashing beer glasses', and was told that 'chairs were frequently smashed up'. Apparently, bands were unwilling to play too 'hot', in case they were unable to escape the ensuing chaos with their instruments intact. One bandleader told of how a

---

26   SAPMO-BArch DR 1/6133, Federbusch, Der Rat der Universitätsstadt Jena, Dezernat Volksbildung – Abt. Kunst u. kulturelle Massenarbeit, to Stakuko, 25 October 1952.

27   The whole correspondence is in SAPMO-BArch DR 1/6133. These officials were evidently familiar with RIAS broadcasting.

28   SAPMO-BArch DR 1/6137, Unkultur in Regis Breitingen, Abteilung Funkkorrespondenten, 19 September 1952.

policeman had danced so shamelessly in front of the audience that he had not wanted to go on playing.[29] From Leipzig, a succession of letters reported terrible scenes in the *Felsenkeller*, where before 1914 Rosa Luxemburg and Karl Liebknecht had spoken to earnest audiences. FDJ evenings there had ended with 'bloodied heads and smashed up cloakrooms'. Apparently, the young men involved in this were typically 'activists' (workers achieving high production targets) with money to spare who had been drinking too much beer. *Stakuko*'s correspondent also felt that the *tempi* bands played were a causative factor. He suggested that bands should be ordered to make every second dance a tango, and every fourth a waltz.[30] Fortunately, nobody at *Stakuko* appears to have taken up this idea.

While the plans for regulation ran into difficulties, *Stakuko* was also trying to generate alternatives to the Americanised kitsch currently on offer. This involved an offensive on several fronts. The State Radio Committee had a role to play in supervising radio programming, where the wrong kind of music was apt to creep in through the back door. Meyer, ever vigilant, intervened in 1953. He demanded at a meeting of the VDK's Council 'that in sports broadcasts American hot music is not used for continuity', suggesting instead: 'Our new mass songs and youth songs could be used here.'[31] Composers and songwriters had to be encouraged to write 'progressive', 'realistic', new music reflecting everyday life, to help the workforce to relax and unwind after its daily exertions. The state music publisher VEB *Lied der Zeit* and the state record company VEB *Schallplatten*, had to react quickly, and get sheet music and records to the public. A series of articles in the Party press, and a pamphlet entitled *Dance Music – like this* would take the message about this new music to the people.[32]

As an immediate measure, *Stakuko* and the VDK announced a competition in May 1952 for composers and writers, with prize money of up to 1000 DM for the best entries in several categories. The dismal results of this exercise gave an early warning of how difficult it would be to realise the aims of *Stakuko*'s campaign slogan, 'Against a cosmopolitan – for a national dance music and dance culture'. The competition results were announced in November 1952. Apparently the entries received had not, in the understanding of the prize jury, really contributed to 'a new German dance music', and only consolation prizes could be awarded. The GDR was at 'an apparent low point', and in the opinion of the prize jury, most of the dance

---

29   SAPMO-BArch DR 1/6133, Butting to Pischner, Staatliches Rundfunkkomitee, 14 November 1952.

30   See SAPMO-BArch DR 1/6133, Expose über Tanzveranstaltungen, 4 January 1953, Tanzveranstaltungen, 19 March 1953, Und wieder Tanzmusik, 10 May 1953, Expose über Tanzveranstaltungen, 20 September 1953, and Roll to Stakuko, 18 September 1953.

31   Protokoll über die Sitzung des geschäftsführenden Vorstandes am 26.3.1953, p. 3. SAPMO-BArch DR 1/41

32   SAPMO-BArch DR 1/6133, Perspektivplan für eine neue deutsche Tanzmusik, 1 September 1952.

music on offer to the public in the GDR could be described as a 'dream factory'.[33] *Stakuko* published its own verdict on the competition entries: 'Virtually all the compositions entered showed melodic, harmonic, and rhythmic poverty, and kitschy-sweet sentimentality in their texts.' The seeming inability to get songs written in the GDR printed and published quickly was isolated as a cardinal problem.[34]

Another response was to create further bureaucratic structures, in this case a 'Dance Music Commission' within the VDK, which could deal with all ramifications of the problem. It would include representatives from *Stakuko*, the State Radio Committee, the Writers' Association, and the Academy. The organisation of the opening conference in December 1952 was typically chaotic, but reports were sent to *Stakuko* and the Central Committee, and a 105-page protocol was written up for the files.[35] Excerpts were published in February 1953, together with a unanimous resolution, which strayed from its immediate purpose and linked the creation of 'melodically healthy and rhythmically expressive dance music' with the wider political situation, and ended up rambling about the 'war politics of the Adenauer clique'.[36]

By this time, the failure of *Stakuko*'s efforts at regulation was obvious, and was discussed in the highest echelons of the Party. Stung by criticism, and armed with lengthy analyses from Butting at the Academy, and from the Dance Music Commission, Hans Lauter of the Central Committee summed up the situation: 'Most difficult at the moment is the development of new dance movements, and we must concentrate our main attention on the solution of this question.' His concern extended to details of instrumentation and arrangement: 'There is a whole group of good dance musicians, who lay down basically good rhythms. But many orchestras hot-up this music and also the rhythm, and thus turn what is acceptable dance music into a terrible racket.'[37]

This intervention was followed by a conscious effort to produce new dance steps. The VDK's Berlin branch had already suggested to *Stakuko* that local composers should work with a dance-partnership, the Kornills, to develop new dances, accompanied by a booklet containing various sheet music arrangements, and a card with details of the new dance steps. Foreshadowing later initiatives of this kind, they suggested that the new dances could be popularised on radio, television, and with

---

33   'Ergebnis des Preisausschreibens für Tanz- und Unterhaltungsmusik', *MuG* 1952/11, pp. 384–5.

34   'Um eine neue Tanzmusik', *MuG*, 1953/2, pp. 69–70.

35   SAPMO-BArch DR 1/240, Protokoll der erste Tagung der Kommission "Tanzmusik" am 17.12.1952.

36   'Arbeitstagung der Kommission "Tanzmusik" des Verbandes Deutscher Komponisten und Musikwissenschaftler', *MuG,* 1953/2, pp. 70–72.

37   SAPMO-BArch DY 30/IV 2/9.06/284, Lauter to Schlieder and Niesky, 24 February 1953.

records.[38] A similar initiative was undertaken in Dresden, but neither appears to have produced anything worthy of note.

Attention also turned to the thorny question of new texts. None of the escapist themes of the typical post-war German hit were in any sense helpful in positively reflecting existing conditions in the new socialist state. *Stakuko* had already written to the Writers' Association to seek its involvement in the creation of new texts in October 1952.[39] Meeting in March 1953, the Dance Music Commission reviewed some, and their suggestion for improvement to one was minuted: 'The harbour of Lübeck should be used instead of the harbour of Hawaii'.[40] The next sitting in April reviewed 19 texts, but could only recommend a few of these without alteration. Many were beyond redemption. Hans-Joachim Fleischer had written a song called *Rosalinde*, which prompted this reaction:

> Why texts, which stand in relationship to nothing? ... For a progressive text, for instance with relevance to a tractor driver, a foxtrot is out of the question. The tractor driver must have music which is full of life and zest. A foxtrot, a left-over from the time of the bourgeoisie, simply won't do for someone who stands firmly in our new world.

The commission proposed to hold further discussions with Comrade Fleischer. It was more enthusiastic about a song called *Coffee Beans*, but even with this excellent text there were potential difficulties: 'In the interests of quick popularity we advise rapid publication – as long as the import of coffee beans holds out.'[41] The commission met again twelve days later, and at last found a text that could be unreservedly recommended, *We are dancing only for joy*. Others were still missing the point: one titled *In the little pavilion by the sea* was scornfully rejected.[42] In this climate, it was, unsurprisingly, very difficult to get writers to submit texts, and harder still to find any that were acceptable for publication.

Stakuko and the Central Committee had also long been aware that sheet music for GDR-produced songs was virtually unobtainable, and this had been highlighted by complaints from the regions as well as in every analysis of dance music produced so far.[43] Although West German hits were publicly characterised in the GDR as the weapons of monopoly capitalism, internal reports contradicted this. There were, in

---

38   SAPMO-BArch DY 30/IV 2/9.06/284, VDK, Bezirksverband Berlin, to Stakuko, 17 January 1953.

39   SAPMO-BArch DR 1/6133, Hartig to DSV, 14 October 1952.

40   SAPMO-BArch DR 1/240, Protokoll der 2. Sitzung der Kommission "Tanzmusik" des Verbandes Deutscher Komponisten und Musikwissenschaftler, 17 March 1953, p. 31. The Commission's suggestion was particularly odd given that Lübeck, although closer than Hawaii, was also outside the GDR.

41   SAPMO-BArch DR 1/240, Protokoll über die Sitzung der Kommission "Tanzmusik" am 8.4.1953, pp. 2–3.

42   SAPMO-BArch DR 1/240, Protokoll über die Sitzung der Kommission "Tanzmusik" am 16.4.1953.

43   See for example SAPMO-BArch DR 1/6133, Der Rat des Bezirkes Halle, Abt. Kunst u. kulturelle Massenarbeit to Stakuko, 30 March 1953.

the 1950s, over a thousand small West German publishers pouring out songs. Their release, on record and on radio, was frequently accompanied by free distribution of sheet music arrangements to orchestras, in the GDR as well as in the Federal Republic. The songs were only popular for a short period of time, and this again worked against the GDR publishing house VEB *Lied der Zeit*, which, despite the claim to contemporaneity in its title, took months at least to publish the music for any new song. Music finally published by *Lied der Zeit* was usually arranged for a large ensemble, perhaps a 16-piece orchestra. Most bands playing in the GDR were much smaller, though, typically consisting of five or six musicians. There were simply no home-grown arrangements available for them. In the circumstances, they played what the public wanted, and what they could get free from the West.

In November 1953, *Stakuko* was disbanded. In the specific field of dance music, *Stakuko* had been criticised before 17 June for its failure to deal with 'boogie-woogie',[44] and certainly its record of achievement here was one of utter futility. In the MfK, the struggle for a new dance culture was initially carried on by more or less the same people. Rudolf Hartig was put in charge of the Main Department of Music, and the Dance Music Commission continued its work. Although there was now a commitment on paper to some kind of devolution to artists, muddled attempts at centralised regulation continued. Later in the decade, there was much complaint within the GDR that the situation had worsened dramatically after June 1953. An impression was created that a loosening of control then permitted Western music to gain a foothold that it never subsequently lost. In fact, for all the rhetoric of the 'New Course', SED hostility was unabated.

Hartig's difficulties after 17 June are exemplified by the case of the Karl Walter Dance Orchestra from Chemnitz, or, Karl-Marx-Stadt as it was renamed in 1953. Walter's band had a considerable following, and was first reported to *Stakuko* in 1952 by Paul Roll in Leipzig, who suggested that Walter should be prevented from making records. In 1953, Walter was banned several times from performing by local officials, but like During and Hartmann, he was not intimidated. According to the Party press, this 'champion of American un-culture' encouraged his audiences to drink beer from buckets, and even appeared on the podium with rolled-up shirtsleeves. Claiming that it was reacting to widespread local protest, 'above all from our youth', the council of Karl-Marx-Stadt took the radical step, in March 1954, of banning Walter permanently, and forbidding his musicians from appearing together in any other group.[45]

Other local officials objected, but before the issue was resolved, Walter and his colleagues simply fled to West Germany, where their *Republikflucht* was much celebrated. Hartig, who made an immediate journey to Karl-Marx-Stadt to investigate, was furious with the insensitivity of the local officials. His fury derived from the international propaganda dimension, which he thought was far more damaging than

---

44   See 'Wir wollen gute Tanzmusik haben', *Junge Welt*, 29 April 1953.

45   'Runter vom Podium, Karl Walter', *Volksstimme*, 30 March 1954, and 'Massenprotest verhindert Wiederauftreten K. Walters', *Volksstimme*, 31 March 1954.

the actual performance of the band.[46] How much more frustrated would he have been had he known that Walter's fans were writing to the BBC in London to contradict the official line being given out by the SED, and to ask for regular broadcasts of his music. Intriguingly, these anonymous fans mentioned that they received the BBC 'pretty much without interruptions', and much preferred it to the 'Russian station in Leipzig'.[47] Within only days of Walter's arrival in West Germany, the BBC was in fact considering making recordings of his band for broadcast 'back to the Zone in the "Jazz with Joe" programme'. AFN and RIAS apparently already had recordings ready for use.[48]

There was a shift in the debate in 1954, as embattled optimism gave way to a jaded acceptance. A report to the new Minister for Culture, Johannes Becher, was frank, stating: 'The discussion on dance music, in expert circles as well as in public, has thus far brought no noteworthy outcome.' Becher was told that it still took between 12 and 18 months to produce sheet music for songs written in the GDR after they first appeared on records and on the radio. The reason given for this incredible slowness was, ironically, 'paper shortages'. Hinting at a more liberal approach, this report called for courses for the saxophone to be introduced in higher education, but also demanded that the police and the FDJ should get more involved with the whole problem.[49] The Ministry's response was complacent, and typically bureaucratic. Yet another committee was formed to look into the printing problem. This body lost its focus, and highlighted musical and textual problems instead. Its recommendations tell us more about the mentality of the SED than many better-known documents:

> Composition: preference for a German intonation; and for a good and logical, typically melody-led approach.
> Text: themes for a dance song are, amongst others: seasons of the year, the joy of creation, affirmation of our life, sport, travel, holidays, conviviality, the beauty of *Heimat*, the beauty of foreign lands (if this also communicates a subjective reality of their pleasures), and dreams (if a generally possible and recognisably attainable fulfilment is connected with them).
> Lecherousness, pornography, obscenity, filth and trash do not belong in a dance song.[50]

By the end of the year, the luckless Hartig had been taken off the case. He has not been given the dubious honour of an entry in two recently published lexicons of

---

46   SAPMO-BArch DR 1/7, Bericht zur Sache Tanzkapelle Karl Walter, 12 April 1954.

47   BBC WAC E1/753/4, A B C D 225 10 28 to Londoner Rundfunk, 18 April 1954.

48   BBC WAC E1/753/4, BBC German Representative, Berlin, to O'Rorke, 23 April 1954.

49   SAPMO-BArch DR 1/240, VDK and Gewerkschaft Kunst to Becher, 10 May 1954.

50   SAPMO-BArch DR 1/240, Anlage zur Protokoll 29.6.1954 – Richtlinien für die Auftragserteilung für Tanzmusik.

GDR functionaries.[51] The poisoned chalice was passed to Hans-Georg Uszkoreit, who tried to combat the increasing sense of resignation. A plan for the first quarter of 1955 declared that the 'urgent question' of dance music 'must be clarified' in discussions with the VDK and the Academy. Uszkoreit's wording suggests that the 'New Course' had not changed anything: 'With regard to programming and quality of performance, entertainment music and dance music in culture houses and in clubs is particularly to be guided and controlled.'[52]

Before 1956, the principal concern of the SED was not with the performance of real American jazz, but with West German kitsch. Jazz was, by the middle of the decade, achieving a degree of academic and artistic respectability in the Federal Republic, just as in the USA and in Britain. This was reflected in the GDR, where a more discriminating approach was being taken, both in public as well as in internal Party discussions. Unfortunately there is not scope here for a full discussion of the unique case of Reginald Rudorf – that unusual animal – an SED activist who was also a genuine jazz lover. Rudorf, after graduating from the University of Leipzig in 1952, was accepted by the SED as an expert on jazz, and allowed to speak and write about it. Over the next few years, Rudorf became increasingly disillusioned with the SED's hostility to jazz, and engaged in an increasingly acrimonious correspondence with Uszkoreit, Notowicz and Pischner, arguing that jazz had become the legitimate voice of the international proletariat. After meetings with experts, including Meyer and Knepler, Rudorf was warned not to pursue this line, but he continued to lecture throughout the GDR, giving radio programmes and speaking at jazz concerts. He also appeared in West Germany, and became involved in the production of a DEFA jazz film. Uszkoreit reported him to the *Stasi* in 1955. Undeterred, Rudorf even spoke at a jazz performance in a church in Halle. Finally, after giving a lecture in Leipzig, he was denounced by FDJ zealots, and arrested in April 1957. He was charged under the notorious 'boycott-hate' law of 1951, and sentenced to two years' imprisonment. Paradoxically, during the Rudorf debate, the Party had been gradually softening its line on jazz.[53]

By 1955, the SED's campaign for a 'socialist dance culture' had completely failed. Dance music remained adrift in escapist sentimentality, and contaminated by foreign influences. By this time, English was replacing German as the preferred

---

51   Andreas Herbst, Winfried Ranke, and Jürgen Winkler (eds), *So funktionierte die DDR. Band 3, Lexikon der Funktionäre* (Hamburg: Rowhlt, 1994), and Jochen Cerny (ed.), *Wer war wer, DDR: ein biographisches Lexikon* (Berlin: Ch. Links, 1992). Hartig died in 1962.

52   SAPMO-BArch DY 30/IV 2/9.06/284, Arbeitsplan der Hauptabteilung Musik für das I. Quartal 1955, 10 January 1955, p. 2.

53   Many documents on Rudorf are in SAPMO-BArch DR 1/243; see also SAPMO-BArch DR 1/236. He subsequently left the GDR, and wrote *Jazz in der Zone* (Cologne: Kiepenheuer and Witsch, 1964). On Rudorf, and changing attitudes to jazz in East and West Germany, see Poiger, *Jazz, Rock, and Rebels*, pp. 137–67. On the DEFA jazz film, see Thomas Heimann, 'Vom Lebensweg des Jazz. Notizen zu einem umstrittenen Dokumentarfilm der DEFA', *Das Jahrbuch der DEFA-Stiftung*, 2000, pp. 229–40.

language for song titles, and even whole texts. Efforts on the ground to regulate performance had been completely unsuccessful. In September 1954, *Musik und Gesellschaft* published a description of 'American hot music' as 'out of hand' and 'not controllable'.[54]

Jazz: A 'Cultural Product'?

Given the enormous problems caused by jazz and dance music in the early GDR, we must ask whether, and how, they were used by the Federal Republic and its NATO allies as propaganda weapons. Curiously, it appears that before 1955, they were not consciously used in this way. To understand why, we must go back to the immediate post-war situation, when jazz was universally recognised as a language of anti-fascism. For the British, despite their commitment to modernism, 'no direct propaganda [was] admissible in Light Music'.[55] It was left to the British Forces Network, which was particularly esteemed by German jazz fans, to propagate jazz informally. Information Control did research German attitudes in the British Zone in 1946, and made the radical suggestion that 'the "liberal" influence of jazz is a good medicine. It may prove to be one of the most effective elements in debunking the Siegfried psychology, and democracy may yet be borne to the Germans on the wings of boogie woogie.' An accompanying analysis found, though, that 60 per cent of German listeners wanted less jazz on the radio; only 3 per cent wanted more.[56]

As far as broadcasting was concerned, the British left 'light music' to the German staff of NWDR in Hamburg. The existing radio dance orchestra was used, but that this played 'light music', rather than 'proper jazz'. It was not British policy to introduce jazz.[57] Similarly, the NWDR studio in Cologne engaged the Hans Bund Orchestra in April 1946, and later developed its own 35-piece Dance and Entertainment Orchestra, directed by Adalbert Luczkowski.[58] Bund had complete control over what was played during his programmes.[59] The station also engaged other dance musicians, such as Kurt Edelhagen and the prolific writer Kurt Feltz. Feltz had written many pre-war hits, with titles like *Malaga*, *Star of Rio*, *If Toni with Vroni*, and *I dream of the first kiss*, which suggest a distinct continuity with post-war escapism. With musicians like Luczkowski and Feltz in charge, jazz was confined

---

54 'Tanzmusik in Theorie und Praxis', *MuG*, 1954/9, pp. 335–6.

55 BBC/WAC E1/758/2, Post War Music Programmes for Germany, 12 January 1945, p. 5.

56 TNA/PRO/FO 371/55798, ISCB, Summary for period ending 1.6.1946, pp. 25–6, and Appendix A.

57 Jack Bornoff, interview with the author, 7 December 2000.

58 WDR/HAC D756, Aufstellung des Kölner Rundfunk-Tanzorchesters, Stand vom 17.9.1947.

59 WDR/HAC 04069, Abschrift. Eidesstattliche Erklärung zur Vorlage bei Gericht, 8 December 1949.

to the margins. Its unpopularity was a frequent theme of listener letters in *Hör Zu* in 1947 and 1948.[60]

Jazz was particularly difficult for the Americans. It was the one kind of music universally recognised as 'American', but was also typically used in Germany to deny that America had any real culture. Reinhard Fark notes how a Radio Bremen series, broadcast from 1946 to 1954, was called *American Dance Music*. Apparently the Station Chief, Mr Harriman, was anxious to avoid using the word 'jazz' in the title.[61] The American *Information Bulletin*, in 1947, displayed a similar insecurity, quoting a 'Letter to America' that had appeared in an Ulm newspaper complaining about the 'jazz that pours on us out of the radio'.[62] Music officers were particularly sensitive to conservative and nationalistic prejudices, and made only sporadic and local efforts to promote jazz as a legitimate musical form. One notable effort was at the Stuttgart Festival in June 1947, where a potted history of jazz was presented by Gene Hammers and his orchestra.[63] By this time, the Americans were also a running a 'Hot Club of Heidelberg', but restricted membership to some forty 'young people seriously interested in jazz'.[64]

This was the kernel of the problem. It was obviously not politic to denigrate jazz in a post-Hitler Germany as 'negro music', and it was equally inappropriate in 1946 or 1947 to use a Nazi vocabulary to label it as 'degenerate' or 'unhealthy'. Nonetheless, there was an overlap in the perception of many music lovers, Allied and German, that jazz was not 'culture' in the same way that Bach or Beethoven was. This allowed the early propagation of ideas later used to denigrate jazz in both the Federal Republic and the GDR, even as jazz clubs were springing up all over Germany. Paul Höffer, a composer who had continued working in Nazi Germany, but then cooperated with Heinz Tiessen in the *Kulturbund* between 1945 and 1948, provides an example of the confusion that could ensue when conservative musicians attempted to master the new language of anti-fascism. Writing in 1946, Höffer categorically refuted the racial critique of jazz: 'To call it Negro music is a superficial and tendentious manner of speaking.' Nonetheless, the burden of his article was clear:

Art music holds a number of spiritual gifts ready for us, it takes us to the edges of life, as if by a miracle it presents us with a view of the ultimate. Jazz music can only do one thing: it

---

60   See 'Die Jazzsendungen im Hörfunk der Federal Republic' in Fark, *Die mißachtete Botschaft*, pp. 168ff.

61   Fark, *Die mißachtete Botschaft*, p. 178.

62   'US Cultural Products', *Military Government Information Bulletin*, 17 March 1947, p. 21.

63   GLAK/OMGWB 12/91–2/10, Program for Musical Show, Stuttgart Festival 19–20 June, 1947. See also GLAK/OMGWB 3/407–3/3, Quarterly History of Theater and Music Control Branch, period 1 April to 1 July 1947, pp. 1–2.

64   GLAK/OMGWB 12/91–1/9, Heidelberg Detachment, Theater and Music Control Branch, Activities Report for 3.3.1947 to 9.3.1947, 7 March 1947.

sets our bodies rhythmically swinging by its suggestive rhythmic force. It arouses pleasant bodily feelings, but it is completely un-spiritual. [65]

He might have added that it was fully un-German. By 1948, as the influence of Allied music officers waned, and was replaced by that of German producers and concert managers, there was a pronounced reaction against jazz, which remained on the margins of acceptability in the early Federal Republic. Rudolf Käs cites the case of a club in West Berlin, which was denied a license in 1952 on these grounds:

> According to the view of the overwhelming majority of German people jazz is not recognised as a cultural product ... Jazz is a kind of music which is alien to German cultural sensitivity and is rejected by the greatest part of the German people.[66]

The response of jazz lovers was to argue that jazz was an art form. The most influential advocate of this cause in the early Federal Republic was Joachim Berendt, who from his base with SWF in Baden-Baden worked tirelessly to organise jazz festivals and to educate a largely hostile public. In 1953 his best-seller *das jazzbuch* was published. The frontispiece of the first edition consciously used words like 'cultural-historical' and 'musicological' to introduce the book.[67] Berendt was helped by other developments in the early 1950s. Jazz was more sophisticated musically than rock 'n' roll, or rhythm 'n' blues. By the mid 1950s it was freeing itself from the counter-cultural associations Kerouac had depicted, and the American-style mass media in the Federal Republic started to take a more favourable approach. In September 1953, *Der Spiegel* profiled Stan Kenton, and his search for a 'classless music of the future'.[68] Kurt Edelhagen was featured on the magazine's front cover in October 1953, and inside, his orchestra was pictured over the caption 'Living from dance music, to play jazz'.[69] Jazz programmes on the radio reflect this shift. Fark notes how titles like *Among friends of Jazz*, and *Saturday after midnight – Jazz friends' rendezvous*, which suggested exclusivity and intimacy, were replaced by ones which stressed cultural respectability, like *The Jazz Workshop – One aspect of contemporary Music*.[70] By the late 1950s, jazz concerts in the Federal Republic were becoming rather studious affairs, where groups of earnest students sat down to listen thoughtfully to expert musicians. The CIA-funded journal *Der Monat* reviewed the Modern Jazz Quartet's appearance at Donaueschingen in 1957, observing that 'Over

---

65   Paul Höffer, 'Jazz-Musik', *Aufbau*, 1946/5, pp. 541–3.

66   Cited in Käs, 'Hot and Sweet', pp. 254–5.

67   Joachim Berendt, *das jazzbuch* (Frankfurt-am-Main: Fischer, 1953)

68   'Klang der Gläsernen Stadt', *Der Spiegel*, 7:43 (16 September 1953), pp. 24–7. The GDR was slower to accept that jazz was 'ernste Musik'. Meyer, in 1952, described Stan Kenton's *Jazz Fantasy* as 'an incoherent, evil, barbaric raving'. 'Selbstmord heißt ihr neuester Tanz', *Nacht-Express*, 19 April 1952.

69   'Eisgekühlter Hot', *Der Spiegel*, 6:43 (22 October 1953), p. 279.

70   Fark, *Die mißachtete Botschaft*, p. 175.

the masterly playing of the four ... is a yearning for the instruments they are not playing, the harpsichord, gamba, and viola d'amore.'[71]

Dance music, however, could not so easily cross the boundary between 'serious music' and 'entertainment music'. As West German songwriters stepped up their output after currency reform, it became ever clearer that they were driven above all by profit. In the early 1950s, a stream of technological innovations caught the mood of the times, and increasing proportions of disposable income went into the pockets of publishers and record companies. These were the years when jukeboxes first came to West Germany, when LPs replaced 78s, record players became household items, and transistor radios were first built into cars. Naturally, West German businessmen were content to derive ever-larger royalties from consumers in both Germanys, but politicians were less comfortable with this. There was huge concern about young people in the early Federal Republic. In the eyes of conservative politicians, priests and educators, there was a connection between the music they listened to and their behaviour.

At the same time, the very commentators who bemoaned the influence of 'boogie-woogie' were stung by the SED's criticisms of West Germany, and were not content to abandon the cultural high ground. There was no deliberate use of dance music as a propaganda weapon. One could argue, cynically, that there was no need for politicians to get involved with this, as the business community was making a perfectly good job of it in any case. In fact, there is evidence that both American officials and West German politicians were uncomfortable with the projection of jazz and dance music into 'the Zone'. The Chief of Radio Control, OMGUS, reported in 1949: 'The quality of RIAS music has been a problem since the establishment of the station. ... The music program contains too much jazz and not the best kind of it.' He suggested using 'dollar funds' to improve the station's stock of music and records, and playing more German folk music.[72] A selection of comments from listeners from 1949 paints a depressing picture of the audience RIAS was trying to win over:

'Female listener ... criticises the music programming and rejects Hottentot music.'
'Male listener objects strenuously to the music programming, particularly to jazz.'
'There is too much dance and hit music.'
'Female listener criticises the jazzing-up of old hits.'[73]

The Adenauer government was sensitive to the SED's accusation that its musical sensitivity was Americanised, and was not happy to be identified with jazz broadcast by RIAS. A lengthy analysis of the effect of RIAS broadcasting in the GDR, compiled for the Ministry for all-German Affairs in 1952, described the station as the strongest propaganda instrument available to the West, but complained that 'its

---

71   Cited in Rieple, *Musik in Donaueschingen*, p. 113.
72   BAK/OMGUS 5/245–1/25, Meyer, Chief Radio Control, to Lewis, 28 February 49, pp. 2–3.
73   BAK/OMGUS 5/245–1/25, Kurze Zusammenfassung von Hörerzuschriften für die Zeit vom 15.–21.2.1949.

dance music is overwhelmingly made up of jazz'. The report reflected conflicting pressures and the need to avoid appearing too reactionary. Conversely, it also noted the potential for appealing to GDR listeners, above all young adults uninterested in the 'progressive entertainment music' and 'fighting songs' broadcast there. It could not, though, identify a clear strategy to attract them.[74] In the final analysis, West German politicians did not want to appeal to fellow Germans in 'the Zone' by corrupting their musical taste.

Even the dreamiest dance music alarmed policy-makers concerned with aesthetic and cultural standards. The Protestant magazine *Church and Radio* summed up this vein of criticism in 1955, criticising the 'increasing frivolity and arrogance in the hit business'.[75] The NWDR's Board of Directors wrestled with the problem in 1951. Speaking of the need 'to raise the general level of entertainment music', Dr Pleister outlined a plan, which might equally have been conceived in the Third Reich or in the GDR, to replace some of the dance music with 'the programme "A mother sings with her children", to support folksong'.[76] By 1954, the NWDR was more ambitious, and had developed the series *Music knows no borders*. This involved linked transmissions with over twenty stations overseas, mostly West European, but including one from Yugoslavia, and promised to bring listeners the best contemporary dance music from around the world. Its rationale was clearly didactic, 'to offer light music which is not superficial and banal, but is uncomplicated and of a high standard, which ... makes its listeners joyful and speaks to their real feelings'.[77] The SED's charge that the Federal Republic had abandoned Bach and turned instead to *Krach* (noise) had stuck.

Living with the Enemy

Both Germanys struggled after 1949 to come to terms with the massive popularity of jazz and dance music. Jazz appeared to threaten expectations of class, gender, and race, and dance music challenged accepted standards of aesthetic taste. In the East, both conflicted with the demand for 'realism'. It is clear now that the Federal Republic, for all the agonies it went through, proved more successful at integrating these musical forms, and at making money from them. The Adenauer government slowly learnt to live with greater cultural diversity, coming to accept that its ability to manipulate musical tastes was in practice very limited. After 1956, the mania for rock 'n' roll would make the platitudinous sentimentality of dance music and the increasingly earnest complexities of jazz appear less menacing.

74   BAK B136/2305, Die Propaganda des RIAS und ihre Wirkung in der SBZD [1953].

75   Cited in the *Bonner Rundschau*, 17 January 1955.

76   WDR/HAC 10070, Protokoll der 15. Sitzung des Hauptausschusses des NWDR am 10. März 1951, p. 11.

77   WDR HAC 04129, Musikalische Unterhaltung to Hartmann, Fischer, and Hemmer, 9 March 1954.

This leaves the larger question of why the GDR's campaign for a 'realistic' dance culture was such a dismal failure. Commonly, it is assumed that as the GDR could not seal itself off from the capitalist world, it was thus fatally handicapped from the start. It is clear, though, that the authorities in the early GDR were far more concerned with the live performance of American jazz and West German hits, and with their own broadcasts, than with those reaching them from outside. This argument also assumes that Western popular music had some intrinsic attraction that made it irresistible, regardless of geography or social context, and this is demonstrably untrue. Certainly, the inept leadership of the campaign and the constant bungling of officials involved did not help. The application of the principles of 'collective' and 'planned' work resulted in the haphazard and inconsistent application of censorship. It ended in the creation of music by committee, which could not match the casual style and easy spontaneity of Western offerings.

The GDR's creative effort was earnest and thoughtful, and this may have been quite inappropriate in working with musical forms that were typically light-hearted and vacuous. This gulf was also reflected in the musical interests of the officials and musicians involved. Typically, they were serious composers and musicologists, whose conceptions of dance music started with Johann Strauss and Offenbach; they were increasingly out of touch with changing public tastes. In a debate dominated by words like 'education' and 'guidance', nothing reflects better the misguided didacticism of the SED than Hartig's belief that giving performance licences only to academically qualified musicians would deal with the problems of jazz and dance music.

The root causes for the failure of the GDR's campaign are to be found in the thinking behind its creative effort, and particularly in the two main demands it made of songwriters. These were that songs should be 'realistic', and should draw on the people's own musical heritage. We have seen some of the absurd themes that were used, and they are indeed easy targets for satire, but what were songwriters expected to write about? Should they have tried to portray the conditions in a uranium mine in the Erzgebirge? Or rows of elderly men in drab suits sitting in interminable meetings before giving unanimous assent to previously drafted resolutions? How could they 'positively reflect' the physical or psychological reality of life in cities that had been reduced to rubble by British bombers, and seen many of their women raped by Red Army soldiers in 1945? Even a focus on the enforced jollity of a Party rally, or on the constructive pleasure of comradely work in building a new society was apt to produce a song that was wooden and tedious.[78] The very essence of dance music was escapism. Whether the music conjured up images of affluence and glamour in the

---

78   GDR composers found it easier to use 'realistic' themes in 'mass songs' and 'fighting songs'. By the mid-1960s the VDK had published no fewer than 225,000 of these. Verband Deutscher Komponisten und Musikwissenschaftler, Musik Informationszentrum (ed.), *Komponisten und Musikwissenschaftler der Deutschen Demokratischen Republik* (Berlin: Verlag Neue Musik, 1965), p. 10.

USA, or warm sunshine and easy living under southern skies, its lack of contact with any kind of reality was its greatest attraction in post-war Germany.

The demand for an organic connection with the rhythms and melodies of the people was less damaging. After all, as GDR analysts pointed out, jazz was originally the genuine folk expression of oppressed black slaves in the American South, and West German hits drew constantly on folk rhythms and tunes. Musically, though, this demand prevented the GDR's songwriters from using the new instruments and arrangements that characterised the music from the West. It led to a preference for strings and accordions rather than drums, saxophones, trumpets and trombones, and made it quite unthinkable that musicians in the GDR should exploit the electric guitar. The GDR's dance music was condemned to archaism in a world embracing modernity.

Even in its censorship and repression, the GDR was ineffective. We have seen how the Nazi vocabulary of denigration was used there, and it may be that some of those who railed against jazz in the 1950s had said much the same thing in the 1930s and 1940s in another context. It is important to discriminate, though – particularly in the larger context of the debate about Germany's two twentieth-century dictatorships. The SED's musical elite, and senior officials like Hartig, made a distinction between 'original jazz', the legitimate expression of an exploited sub-proletariat, and the subsequent commodified product of the American entertainment industry. Less thoughtful local officials, often not musically trained, frequently allowed a racist undertone to slip into their denunciations of jazz and 'boogie-woogie' with the use of adjectives like 'primitive' and 'wild'. Only later in the 1950s was the term 'ape music' widely used. Uta Poiger has argued that the characterisation of Western dance music as 'cosmopolitan' carried clear anti-Semitic overtones, but this again should be qualified. There was a strong Jewish element amongst the SED's elite core of musicians, and the GDR's musical discourse was strikingly free from anti-Semitism. Meyer, Knepler, Rebling and other émigrés in fact regarded much West German dance music as a Nazi hangover, accusing songs like *There were three comrades*, *The Legionary* and *Comrade, where are you?* of pandering to SS veterans' nostalgia, and others like *Without a home* and *Back Home* of revanchism.

There was, furthermore, nothing in the GDR in the early 1950s to compare with the physical brutality of Nazi repression. Musicians were not beaten up, imprisoned, or killed. Performance licences could be withdrawn, and thus a musician's ability to earn a living was easily threatened, but even this punishment was used sparingly. The fines levied were relatively small.[79] Typically performance bans applied only to a given town, and for a short period, usually three months, leaving bands free to play elsewhere. They were thus in the nature of a warning, allowing the musicians to fine-tune their programme to find acceptability. It is abundantly clear from the

---

79   In Dresden for example, five fines between 30 and 200 DM were levied in 1953. SAPMO-BArch DR 1/335, Bericht des Referates Musik über die Erfüllung der Arbeitspläne 1.4. Quartal 1953, 26 January 1954, p. 2.

truculent behaviour of musicians like Hartmann, During and Walter that they were not intimidated.

In one respect though, the GDR's leaders and theorists were absolutely right. Dance music was a 'Trojan Horse', a 'Fifth Column'. Its whole culture, and the behaviour and attitudes associated with it, were profoundly antithetical to the values of the GDR. The continued performance and popularity of this music constituted a victory of escapism and individualism over 'realism' and 'collective work' and remained a significant aspect of most peoples' lives that the SED could never reach. This recognition, and the accompanying frustration, were reflected in the continued hostility of the Party towards western popular music after 1955. Although various forms of censorship and repression continued until the GDR's collapse, there was never again the conviction of the early 1950s that this enemy within could be defeated.

Chapter Eight

Collaboration, Confrontation, and Infiltration

In August 1950, a citizen from Berlin wrote to Chancellor Adenauer to ask why GDR musicians and ensembles were allowed to visit the Federal Republic. He referred to the recent appearance of Franz Konwitschny at the Hamburg State Opera, and above all to the 'propaganda tours' of the Dresden Philharmonic.[1] The letter evidently touched a raw nerve. It was circulated to other ministries, and it quickly became clear that there were completely divided opinions about this. The Ministry for all-German Affairs reported that these visits had not been seen as political matters, but noted the reservations of the City Council in Berlin about giving them any official support.[2] Gustav Heinemann, the Federal Minister of the Interior, contacted the government of North Rhine-Westphalia, where the Dresden Philharmonic was actually touring, to seek its opinion. The Culture Minister there, Christine Teusch, reported that the tour was an entirely private matter. She did not see how the concerts could be prevented, except on political grounds. The Interior Minister, on the other hand, reported that the tour was purely a propaganda exercise, probably organised by the National Front. Noting the great success of the orchestra's concert in Düsseldorf, he argued that these tours should not be allowed.[3] Here, thrown into sharp relief, were several questions for West German politicians.

Were tours by GDR orchestras and choirs purely private matters, or should they be politically controlled, either at *Land* or *Bund* level? Were these tours purely cultural, or were they propaganda exercises? If the latter, was there a way of diluting their propaganda function while allowing the cultural purpose to carry on uninterrupted? If cultural exchanges had to be prevented, how could this be done without playing into the hands of the SED? One might imagine that with the experience of the Bach Year, West German politicians would have been fully prepared for the SED's use of music as a propaganda tool, but they were evidently not. Through the early 1950s, they were torn between fear of the SED's manipulations and their own desire to maintain links with 'the Zone'. By 1956, when the Communist Party was formally

---

1   BAK B106/21462, Breuer to Adenauer, 2 August 1950.
2   BAK B106/21462, Bundesminister für gesamtdeutsche Fragen to Bundesminister des Innern, 14 November 1950.
3   BAK B106/21462, Kultusminister des Landes Nordrhein-Westfalen to Bundesminister des Innern, 25 September 1950; Innenminister des Landes Nordrhein-Westfalen to Bundesminister des Innern, 25 September 1950.

banned in the Federal Republic, politicians had found themselves interfering time and again in musical affairs, for all their self-proclaimed commitment to cultural freedom.

From the perspective of the GDR, music was a weapon in the fight for German unity. Recent research has shown how much effort the SED devoted to its ultimately unsuccessful *Westpolitik* in the 1950s,[4] but the role of music in this offensive has not been explored. Music was in fact one of the most powerful weapons in a rather under-stocked arsenal, capable of working at several levels. Firstly, by exhibiting high standards of performance, and performing the German classics, the GDR could demonstrate its respect for high culture. Well-established ensembles, like the Dresden Philharmonic, had great emotional appeal to citizens of the Federal Republic, who had watched and listened to them before 1945. This was above all true of the *Thomanerchor* and *Kreuzchor*, which held a unique place in the German imagination. Secondly, the SED hoped to undermine the affiliation of individual musicians in the Federal Republic by offering them engagements, commissions, and prizes in the GDR. By working with organisations like the *Neue Bach Gesellschaft* and the Society for Music Research (GfM), the SED offered a practical demonstration of its commitment to unity, while also hoping to influence them from within. Finally, music offered an unparalleled opportunity for mass agitation in the Federal Republic. When, in 1953, the SED developed friendly links with the General League of German Singers, the Adenauer government was painfully aware that this organisation claimed nearly a million members in the Federal Republic, mostly from the working class. When citizens in a divided Germany thought of one another as 'Brother singer' or 'Sister singer', where might these friendships lead?[5]

'All-German Work': Music and Manipulation

Responsibility for what the SED called 'all-German work' in music was vested in 1951 with *Stakuko*, and featured prominently in its earliest plans. By 1952, *Stakuko* was running a whole programme of activities in the Federal Republic, including tours by high profile ensembles like the Dresden Philharmonic, the Leipzig Radio Symphony Orchestra, and the Leipzig Opera Ballet. It was placing articles about GDR musical life in West German musical journals, and supporting GDR participation in events like the conference on musical education held at Darmstadt in June 1952.[6]

---

4   See Heike Amos, *Die Westpolitik der SED 1948/49–1961. 'Arbeit nach Westdeutschland' durch die Nationale Front, das Ministerium für Auswärtige Angelegenheiten und das Ministerium für Staatssicherheit* (Berlin: Akademie Verlag, 1999).

5   The old custom in Germany for singers in different choirs to use the term *Sangesbrüder* or *Sangesschwester* when greeting one another was ostentatiously re-asserted in the 1950s, particularly by singers from either side of the 'Iron Curtain'.

6   SAPMO-BArch DR 1/141, Bericht über die Arbeit II/1952, 8 July 1952, listed 23 such articles placed in *Musica*, 11 in *Die Musikwoche*, and 8 in *Musik und Kirche*. See also Abteilung Musik, Gesamtdeutsches Arbeitsprogramm II/52, 17 March 1952.

All this activity was manipulated for maximum propaganda effect. Thus, GDR ensembles touring in the Federal Republic always performed very conservative programmes. The Dresden Philharmonic, which stirred up such controversy in 1950, performed 'with great success' in 20 West German towns in September 1952,[7] playing Bruckner, Beethoven, Brahms, Mozart, Schubert and Weber, with some Tchaikovsky, Smetana and Dvorak for good measure.[8] The *Thomanerchor* and *Kreuzchor* always performed religious music on tour. The SED was well aware that the West regarded the GDR's contemporary music with great suspicion, and not until December 1953 did Hartig consider a scheme to promote compositions by Finke, Wagner-Régeny and Dessau in the Federal Republic. If this proved successful, it was proposed to move on to more obviously Communist composers like Gerster, Asriel and Butting.[9] This was, of course, only a pipe dream. There was no possibility that music that openly celebrated the values or achievements of the GDR would be performed in the Federal Republic in the 1950s.

An important part of *Stakuko*'s programme was the engagement of West German musicians to play in the GDR. Hartig encouraged this in 1952 and 1953, and the founding of the Ministry for Culture in January 1954 was used to give all forms of 'all-German work' new impetus. At a party rally in April 1954, the SED renewed its determination to 'annihilate the Iron Curtain', allegedly erected by 'imperialists' to 'destroy the unity of German culture'.[10] Hartig's frequent exhortations to GDR ensembles to engage West German conductors and soloists bore fruit in terms of quantity but not quality. In 1952 some 20 West German musicians performed in the GDR;[11] by 1954, this figure had doubled, but included few leading lights of the West German musical scene.[12] Indeed, in many cases the West German musicians performing in the GDR were those who for one reason or another found it difficult to get the recognition they sought in the West. The pianist Elly Ney, one of the few musicians whose Nazi sympathies had been so pronounced as to hinder her post-war career, was allowed to play in the GDR in 1952, although Hartig stipulated that her appearance must not be accompanied by any political propaganda.[13]

There was a similar situation in relation to guest conductors. Those engaged in the GDR in the early 1950s have largely disappeared now from the pages of musical history.[14] There was one exception, and it appeared briefly in early 1955 that the GDR had pulled off a musical coup that would attract attention worldwide.

---

7 SAPMO-BArch DR 1/141, Arbeitsbericht III/52, 13 October 1952, p. 2.

8 SAPMO-BArch DR 1/141Die nächsten Aufgaben auf dem Gebiete der Musik, 10 August 1952, p. 11.

9 SAPMO-BArch DR 1/41, Protokoll, 24 November 1953, p. 3.

10 SAPMO-BArch DR 1/141, Zum Arbeitsplan 1954, 10 May 1954.

11 SAPMO-BArch DR 1/141, Kontrollbericht IV/52, 20 January 1953, p. 1.

12 SAPMO-BArch DR 1/154, HA Musik, 28 June 1954.

13 SAPMO-BArch DR 1/286, Hartig to Bongartz, Dresdner Philharmonie, 29 April 1952.

14 For a representative sample, see SAPMO-BArch DR 1/141, Jahres-Arbeitsplan 1954, Abt. II, p. 4.

For years, the SED had negotiated with Erich Kleiber, hoping to secure him as the resident conductor at the reconstructed State Opera in Berlin. Amongst the great German conductors of the early twentieth century, Kleiber had a unique reputation. He had conducted the first performance of Berg's *Wozzeck* in Berlin in 1925, and in a unique act of cultural defiance had conducted the orchestral suite from Berg's opera *Lulu* in Berlin in 1934. Kleiber made no secret of his wish to return to the State Opera after 1945, and in the early 1950s, as the building on Unter den Linden was restored, he made several guest appearances in the GDR with the State Opera and with the Dresden State Orchestra. In June 1954, he spelt out to the SED his terms for accepting the post at the State Opera permanently, demanding 'that in musical matters I have the first and the last word'.[15] As the ceremonial re-opening of the State Opera neared in January 1955, it appeared that Kleiber and the SED had reached an agreement. A number of key singers from Hamburg, Vienna, and the Municipal Opera in West Berlin were persuaded to sign lucrative contracts with the State Opera to work with Kleiber. This was accompanied by loud complaints from the West German press,[16] and the private dismay of the British High Commission, which had carefully promoted the Municipal Opera.[17] Within only weeks though, the SED's hopes were dashed. Kleiber resigned from the State Opera in March 1955, ostensibly because the inscription *Fridericus Rex Apollini et Musis* was removed from the building. Evidently, he had belatedly realised that his hopes of working at the State Opera without political interference were misplaced. The SED put the best possible gloss on this disaster. In an open letter to Kleiber, the *Intendant* of the State Opera, Max Burghardt, regretted the damage that had been done to 'all-German cultural ties'. Years later, in his account of the affair, Burghardt portrayed Kleiber as misguided, an emigrant cut off from his national roots by Hitler's racial hatred. His forced exile in South America had left him unable to appreciate where, as an artist, his true loyalties should lie.[18]

The SED's sponsorship of West German composers fell into a similar pattern. *Stakuko*, and after 1954 the Ministry for Culture, encouraged the performance in the GDR of selected West German composers, and even gave out commissions. In 1952, *Stakuko* paid Gottfried Madjera 600 DM for *Peace Fanfares*, Heinrich Schliepe 600 DM for an overture, *New Life*, and made an initial payment of 300 DM to Alfons Hansch for an overture entitled *Berlin 1952*.[19] This sponsorship naturally reflected the larger twists and turns of GDR cultural policy, resulting in certain ironies. In 1950, the GDR awarded its National Prize to Carl Orff, whose *Antigone* was performed with great success in Dresden. In March 1951, the same work was

---

15　　SAPMO-BArch DR 1/34, Kleiber to Rentmeister, 25 June 1954.

16　　See for example 'Der Berliner Sängerkrieg', *Musica* (9), 8 March 55, pp. 56–8.

17　　TNA/PRO/FO 1056/354, Turner to Information Services Division, U.K. High Commission, 3 January 1955.

18　　Burghardt, *Erinnerungen*, pp. 346–366; he quotes from his open letter to Kleiber on p. 365.

19　　SAPMO-BArch DR 1/141, Forschungsaufträge, 13 August 1952, pp. 2–3.

being highlighted as an example of formalism, 'unmelodic, even repulsive, and full of noise'.[20] After this, the SED's hostility to avant-gardism lead it to criticise those composers in the Federal Republic, like Hartmann and Henze, who were most likely to sympathise politically with the ideals of the GDR, and to favour instead neo-classicists like Pepping and Driessler. A review of new West German compositions by Eberhard Rebling in *Musik und Gesellschaft* in February 1953 illustrates this well. Rebling identified two currents in West German musical life: one dominated by the 'cosmopolitan cultural politics' of the radio stations, *Melos*, and Schotts,[21] and the other dedicated to 'the expression of genuine human thoughts and feelings'.[22]

Rebling's article also points to a broader problem for the SED, namely the sources of its information about music in the Federal Republic. Obviously, the SED's leading musicians had access to the West German musical press, and radio broadcasts, but they drew also on some bizarre personal contacts, which helped to shape their extraordinarily charged view of music in the Federal Republic. One major source was the Cologne composer and musicologist Kurt Driesch, who sent regular analyses of West German musical life, along with press photographs and cuttings, and programme notes to Hartig at *Stakuko*, and after 1954 to Pischner at the MfK. Reading Driesch's reports today, it is difficult not to feel sorry for him, isolated in one of the citadels of the Western avant-garde, neglected by the currents of artistic and intellectual history. Driesch was even separated from the shared sense of embattled commitment that sustained the SED's musicians. In April 1955, he complained to Pischner: 'Here in the distance, I have unfairly a more difficult situation than my colleagues in the GDR.'[23]

Driesch was keen to please, and in his monthly reports, which went into detail about individual performers, performances, and compositions, he attempted to mimic the language of the SED. Thus, describing how Franz Marsalek at the NWDR was trying to bring serious music to the masses, Driesch praised him for his 'goal-conscious, constructive Pioneer activities'.[24] In 1954, he reported on alarming new developments at an NWDR concert in Cologne: the performance of music for prepared piano by John Cage and David Tudor, and of electronic music by Eimert, Stockhausen, Goeyvaert, and Pousseur. He asked: 'Where, in "music" like this, is the spiritual experience behind the combination of tones, raised to an art, as was recognised, and even in part desired by Bartok, Stravinsky, and Hindemith?'[25]

---

20   Aus der Rede Hans Lauters auf der 5. Tagung des ZK der SED vom 15.–17.3.1951, cited in Dibelius and Schneider, *Neue Musik*, p. 111.

21   *Melos* was a prominent avant-garde journal, and Schotts the well known modernist publisher.

22   Eberhard Rebling, 'Zwei neue Opern in Westdeutschland', *MuG*, 1953/2, pp. 52–4.

23   SAPMO-BArch DR 1/288, Driesch to Pischner, 8 April 1955.

24   SAPMO-BArch DR 1/288, Juli-Bericht 1954, Driesch to Pischner, 23 August 1954.

25   SAPMO-BArch DR 1/288, Oktober-Bericht 1954, Driesch to Pischner, 12 November 1954.

At the MfK in Berlin, this must have seemed like a realisation of their worst nightmares: a clique of American, British, French, and West German composers pushing music into a meaningless world of abstract sound. Driesch's reports were sent on to Rebling, who after 1952 edited *Musik und Gesellschaft*. They undoubtedly served to influence the SED's perception of music in the Federal Republic. Hartig, particularly, seems to have believed the worst exaggerations of SED propaganda they mimicked and contained. In one of the last meetings he attended as Head of Department with *Stakuko*, in December 1953, Hartig met Driesch, amongst others, at a musicological congress in Berlin. He anxiously asked how far 12-tone and atonal music was catching on with the public in West Germany. He appears to have had no realistic sense of how restricted the appeal of the avant-garde was. Driesch reassured him to some extent, stating that most of the public still preferred to listen to the German classics being broadcast from Leipzig, Berlin, and Dresden.[26]

Ironically, the impressions supplied by Driesch were often confirmed by contact with some of the most conservative figures of West German musical life. At times, the SED's hostility to modernism was peculiarly comforting to reactionaries in much the way that Nazi hatred for *entartete Musik* had been. Walther Siegmund-Schultze is a musicologist best known today for his work on Handel. In the early 1950s, he was a dedicated SED activist, working with the government in Saxony, and later serving as the key SED representative with the Handel Society in Halle.[27] Siegmund-Schultze was named an ex-Nazi in a West German publication in 1965,[28] and this is certainly the impression one might derive from some of his utterances in the GDR. It was Siegmund-Schultze who in 1951 wrote the 'Resolution' on dance music for Saxony, which demanded 'purity' (*Sauberkeit*) from dance bands.[29] In his work with the Handel Society, Siegmund-Schultze was allowed to travel widely, and he always took care to record his impressions of musical life in other countries for the SED. In June 1954, he sent the VDK a report on his meeting with Walter Abendroth, the West German composer and critic for *Die Zeit* (which Siegmund-Schultze described as the organ of the British occupying Power). Abendroth has been described by Kater as 'a former Nazi and pronounced anti-Semite',[30] and the two men seem to have got on rather well. Abendroth complained that he could not get his own compositions performed, as only 12-tone music, electronic music, and 'other crazy monstrosities' were fashionable in the Federal Republic.

On the same journey, Siegmund-Schultze met with Hans Albrecht, now the director of Göttingen Bach Institute. Albrecht also expressed his 'full agreement

---

26   SAPMO-BArch DR 1/41, Protokoll, 24 November 1953.

27   SAPMO-BArch DY 30/IV 2/9.06/294, Pischner to Mückenberger, ZK der SED, Kulturabteilung, 8 October 1954.

28   Untersuchungsausschuß Freiheitlicher Juristen (ed.), *Ehemalige Nationalsozialisten in Pankows Diensten* (Berlin: no publisher given, 1965), p. 88.

29   SAPMO-BArch DR 1/6133, Resolution über Verbesserung der öffentlichen Tanzmusik, 16 August 1951.

30   Kater, *Composers*, p. 277.

with the rejection of the decadent musical currents of the West'.[31] It is not difficult to imagine why these men got along: after all they had shared much the same views about music before 1945. It is more difficult to understand how SED officials, who had most reason to hate Nazism and all it stood for, and who had been persecuted or had to flee from persecution, were so insensitive to the kind of company they were keeping, and to the origin of the viewpoints they sometimes gratefully endorsed.[32] Pischner, in December 1954, suggested to Rebling that *Musik und Gesellschaft* should publicise a book recently published in Munich by Alois Melichar, *The Overcoming of Modernism*, writing: 'Here, important oppositional currents in West Germany are revealed which we must join in with.'[33] Melichar, who published several books in the 1950s attacking Schoenberg, has also been identified by Kater an anti-Semite.[34] In 1959, Melichar himself wrote to Uszkoreit at the MfK to canvass support for his new book *Music in the Straitjacket*, which, he said, was the subject of a 'ban of silence' in the Federal Republic. Uszkoreit responded by publishing a supportive article in the *Kulturbund* weekly *Sonntag*, in which amongst other things, he accused Carl Orff of having turned German youth into 'hottentots'. On this occasion, Uszkoreit went too far, and at least one *Sonntag* reader wrote to accuse him, in no uncertain terms, of 'brown cultural barbarism'. Evidently there was some public debate about this comparison between Nazi and GDR cultural politics, and Uszkoreit was forced into a tactical retreat. He attempted in a second *Sonntag* article to refute the comparison with Nazism, and to deny the worst excesses of the Stalinist musical policy that prevailed in the GDR in the earlier years of the decade.[35] There was no public debate of this kind in the GDR before 1955.

One musical project of this period differs from all others, in that it was a genuine cooperation between the GDR and Federal Republic, with government support on both sides. This was the plan that emerged from the contested celebrations of the Bach Year, to publish a complete new Bach edition. Once embarked upon, this project was of great cultural and economic significance to both states, if only to ensure that they provided most of the printed music by Bach for a global market. Only a pooling of resources, though, would allow common access to all the important manuscript material needed for a complete new edition. The situation confronting both sides in 1950 was that roughly two thirds of Bach's manuscripts were in West Germany, one third in the GDR, and a handful in what was now the People's Republic of Poland. As we know, on the 200th anniversary of Bach's death in 1950, a coalition of politicians, academics, and musicians met in Göttingen to consider how to get

---

31   SAPMO-BArch DR 1/291, Siegmund-Schultze to Zentralleitung des VDK, 3 June 1954.

32   See Chapter 7, p. 183, for Hartig's enthusiastic endorsement of Siegmund-Schultze's ideas about dance music.

33   SAPMO-BArch DR 1/291, Pischner to Rebling, Musik und Gesellschaft (Redaktion), 29 December 1954.

34   See the references to Melichar in Kater, *Composers*, pp. 264ff.

35   See copies of these articles, and the correspondence between Melichar and Uszkoreit in SAPMO-BArch DR 1/323.

access to the Bach manuscripts in the East.[36] The answer was through cooperation. In the GDR, the project was similarly driven by necessity. Although it could offer access to the manuscripts in Poland besides its own, it was still in the weaker position. In October 1951, *Stakuko* agreed to a joint Bach edition, and authorised two leading GDR musicologists, Walther Vetter and Heinrich Besseler, to travel to the West to strike a deal there. It is no coincidence that Vetter and Besseler were chosen. They were, in effect, old colleagues of Blume and Albrecht in the Federal Republic, well known to one another from the Nazi years. Vetter and Besseler were closely supervised by Holzhauer, and behind him Ernst Hermann Meyer.[37]

On 6 October 1951, Blume, Albrecht, Besseler and Vetter met in Kassel and agreed on the broad outline of the new Bach edition.[38] All negotiations would be conducted through *Stakuko* in the East, and through the Göttingen Bach Institute, directed by Albrecht, in the West. Holzhauer was clearly told by Besseler that the Bonn government had been involved with the project from its inception.[39] Over the next two years, the scholarly work in Göttingen and Leipzig went smoothly, and in 1952 both states agreed to work similarly on a new Handel edition. All manuscripts were pooled, and there was close cooperation on purely musical problems. The greatest difficulties were with the actual printing. The last Bach edition had been published by Breitkopf and Härtel in Leipzig, but this firm had relocated after 1945 in Wiesbaden. The Göttingen coalition[40] decided to give the contract to Bärenreiter in Kassel, and overruled all subsequent objections from Breitkopf and Härtel.

In the GDR, key musical publishers had been lost to the West, and there was a further ideological complication: it was not appropriate for the workers' and peasants' state to leave a project of this importance in private hands. The contract was initially given to the *Mitteldeutscher Verlag* in Halle, but in 1953 Stakuko created the *VEB Deutscher Verlag für Musik*, in Leipzig, to print the new edition. Both sides were ready to sign a contract in October 1953. The same editions would be printed, in the West by Bärenreiter, and in the East by *VEB Deutscher Verlag*. The costs would be split equally; the *Deutscher Verlag* would have sole rights over sales and distribution to the Soviet Union, China, and all Communist states; Bärenreiter retained sole rights in the rest of the world.[41] In 1954, the Göttingen coalition started planning a festive ceremony for the publication of the first volume. Predictably, in the GDR, printing

---

36   See Chapter Five, p.148.

37   SAPMO-BArch DR 1/383, Protokoll über die Besprechung der Gesamtausgabe Bachs, 1 October 1951.

38   SAPMO-BArch DR 1/383, Vetter to Stakuko, 26 October 1951.

39   SAPMO-BArch DR 1/383, Besseler to Holzhauer, 9 October 1951.

40   In representational terms, this group involved the *Bundespräsident*, the *Kultusministerkonferenz*, and the *Städtetag*; in practical terms, its key members were the musicologists at the Bach Institute in Göttingen and Erich Wende, head of the *Kulturabteilung* at the BMI. See NRWA/NW 60/891, Auszug aus der Niederschrift über die Sitzung des Kunstausschusses der Ständigen Konferenz der Kultusminister, 12/13.10.1951.

41   SAPMO-BArch DR 1/383, Vertrag über die "Neue Bach-Ausgabe", 9 October 1953; Ergänzungsvertrag über die "Neue Bach-Ausgabe", 9 October 1953.

was held up by paper shortages, and it soon became clear that the first volume would appear there later.

This left the Federal Republic free to present the new edition on its own territory, and to play down its collaboration with the GDR. A festive presentation was planned for September 1954 at the newly opened House of Radio in Cologne. The NWDR, which offered to host the occasion, would provide its own specialist early music group, the *Cappella Coloniensis*, to demonstrate the authentic performance style made possible by the new edition. Theodor Heuss would attend to accept formally the presentation of the new edition. *Land* culture ministers, the *Städtetag*, and many prominent musicians would also take part. This news was received in August 1954 with dismay in the GDR, where the MfK realised that this made a mockery of the whole 'all-German' idea.[42] Pischner and Uszkoreit travelled at once for discussions with Albrecht at his home in Bad Wildungen. He blandly played down the scale of the planned ceremony, reassuring Pischner, 'that this was not an event of central importance'.[43] This was patently untrue. The ceremony, and the involvement of politicians, from Heuss on down, had been planned months previously.[44] On this occasion, the GDR was outmanoeuvred. The festive presentation was held in Cologne in September 1954. Heuss was present, as were many other politicians. The programme for the evening did not mention the GDR's participation in the New Bach Edition; nor was this something the West German press chose to publicise.[45]

Cooperation and Repression

As we have seen from the muddled reaction to the tour of the Dresden Philharmonic in September 1950, there was great uncertainty in the Federal Republic about how to react to the SED's musical infiltration. Through the early 1950s, the Adenauer government was torn between a desire to intervene and regulate from the centre, and a recognition that if it did so, it was trespassing on regional cultural autonomy, and on accepted liberal views of cultural freedom. Similarly, it knew perfectly well that the SED was using music as a propaganda weapon, but was unable in practice to define how this was being done without falling into the trap of appearing hostile to culture in general, and to German music in particular. West German politicians also realised that cultural exchanges could be used to advertise their own society,

---

42 See SAPMO-BArch DR 1/161, Jahnke, Abt. Kulturelle Einheit, to HA Musik, 6 August 1954, and Beschlußvorlage für das Kollegium im Ministerium für Kultur, 3 August 1954.

43 SAPMO-BArch DR 1/383, HA Musik, Bericht über die Reise der Kollegen Prof. Pischner und Uszkoreit zu Herrn Prof. Dr. Albrecht, 25 August 1954, p. 3.

44 See NRWA/NW 60/891, Rundschreiben Nr.12 an die Herren Mitglieder des Kuratoriums des J.S. Bach-Instituts, 8 April 1954.

45 *Festakt aus Anlass des Erscheinens der neuen Bach-Ausgabe, 18.9.1954*; see also Fred Hamel, 'Schwingt freudig euch empor', *Musica*, 8 (1954), pp. 448–9.

and were unwilling to renounce them because of what they perceived as the SED's unbridled cynicism. The result was confusion and paralysis.

The uncertainty was also reflected amongst the various institutions that supported music in the Federal Republic, in the press, and amongst the public at large. Frequently individual *Länder*, and musical associations like the Society for Music Research and the General League of German Singers argued that they should be left to make their own arrangements with musicians and ensembles from the GDR; at other points appeals were made for guidance from the centre. Politicians, musicians and journalists veered between pessimistic acceptance that every musical contact with the GDR had a propaganda dimension, and naive hope that somewhere, there was space for a purely artistic commitment to the greatness of German music, and for developing relationships uncontaminated by Cold War politics. The SED, with its straightforward belief that all art was political, was clearly at an advantage here, and it gleefully exploited the inconsistencies and hesitancies of the Federal Republic.

In September 1950, the Emergency Community for German Art (*Notgemeinschaft der Deutschen Kunst*), an organisation set up to help support artists of all kinds, wrote to the Federal Minister for all-German Affairs to ask for guidance on cultural exchanges with the GDR.[46] As we know, at this point, the Ministry was struggling to formulate a response to the tour of the Dresden Philharmonic, and its response was unhelpful and ambivalent. The Emergency Community was advised to treat each case individually, and always to refer to the Ministry for advice. The *Thomanerchor*, the Ministry argued, had not yet been used for propaganda (an extraordinary statement to make only weeks after the Bach Festival in Leipzig!), but it was not so sure about the Dresden Philharmonic.[47] In April 1951, the Ministry sent out similar guidance to municipal authorities.[48] With each new enquiry, though, the situation became more complicated. What about musicians and ensembles from the West who went to 'the Zone', and found themselves performing in halls decorated with SED banners, or sharing a platform with speakers praising the work of Pieck and Grotewohl in the fight for peace and German unity? Clearly a framework of guidance was needed.

Ironically then, at exactly the same time as Hartig and Holzhauer at *Stakuko* embarked on their fruitless campaign to regulate dance music in the GDR, ministers and officials at the Federal Ministry of the Interior, and at the Ministry for all-German Affairs in Bonn commenced an equally long and unsuccessful effort to regulate cultural exchanges with GDR. Jakob Kaiser, appointed Minister for all-German Affairs in October 1950, had the primary responsibility for this, and presented his

---

46   BAK B106/1079, Notgemeinschaft der Deutschen Kunst to Bundesminister für gesamtdeutsche Angelegenheiten, 7 September 1950.

47   BAK B106/1079, Bundesminister für gesamtdeutsche Fragen to Notgemeinschaft der Deutschen Kunst , 6 October 1950.

48   BAK B106/1079, Bundesminister für gesamtdeutsche Fragen to Deutschen Städtetag, Präsidium des Deutschen Städtebundes, and Deutschen Landkreistag, 5 April 1951.

first plan to the *Land* Culture Ministers in December 1951. He proposed to make a distinction between individual musicians who were known to have supported, by word or deed, what he called the 'Soviet system of cultural unfreedom', and those who were prepared to make it clear that they were 'politically neutral'.[49] This was no great help, and Kaiser's plan was rejected by the *Länder*. The SED knew that crude Communist propaganda would not be allowed in the Federal Republic, and was prepared to use church choirs, led by reactionaries like Ramin and Mauersberger, to demonstrate its respect for the classics. Strangely, Kaiser seems to have been equally aware of this. Approached by the German Singers' League (*Deutscher Sängerbund*) about a proposed tour by the Leipzig Male Voice Choir only a few weeks later, he urged great caution, because 'in the final analysis, this was a political action'.[50]

Aware that he was making no progress, Kaiser called a meeting in Bonn in March 1952. *Land* Culture Ministers, and representatives from the press, radio, film, the *Städtetag*, the Interior Ministry and the President's office attended. Also present was one of the SED's greatest opponents, Joachim Tiburtius, who was in charge of cultural affairs in West Berlin. It was agreed that new, more positive guidelines for cultural exchanges were needed, and that the Federal Republic must not be seen to be on the defensive.[51] Over the next year, as the SED stepped up its offensive, Kaiser struggled to come up with a formula that would please all parties.

In the meantime, the initiative passed to the East. In May 1952, the SED hosted a 'German Expert Conference for People's and Amateur Art' in Berlin, which was attended by over 100 West Germans. These representatives voiced a series of complaints about musical life in the Federal Republic that might well have been prepared by *Stakuko*. Apparently, composers in the West had a hard life, and amateur choirs were not supported. Schotts, it was alleged, exercised a monopoly over publishing, and were able to insist that at least one of their pieces be performed at every concert in the Federal Republic.[52]

Only days later, Kaiser wrote to the German Association of Mixed Voice Choirs (*Verband gemischter Chöre Deutschlands*) that if any of its choirs visited 'the Zone', they must not sing in halls decorated with pictures of Lenin and Stalin, or participate in peace appeals and declarations of thanks to the SED.[53] The Federal Minister of the Interior, Robert Lehr, was evidently frustrated by the lack of progress on the new guidelines, and repeatedly harassed Kaiser about this during the summer of 1952. When he heard in October that they were still not ready, he expressed himself in

---

49   BAK B106/1079, Bundesminister für gesamtdeutsche Fragen to Ständige Konferenz der Kultusminister, 13 December 1951.

50   BAK B106/1079, Bundesminister für gesamtdeutsche Fragen to Bundesminister des Innern, 8 January 1952.

51   BAK B106/1079, Vermerk: über die Besprechung am 13 March 1952 im Bundesministerium für gesamtdeutsche Fragen.

52   BAK B106/1079, Bericht, sent by Bundesminister für gesamtdeutsche Fragen to Ständige Konferenz der Kultusminister, 9 May 1952.

53   BAK B106/1079, Bundesminister für gesamtdeutsche Fragen to Verband gemischter Chöre Deutschlands, 14 May 1952.

words reminiscent of Hartig at *Stakuko*, demanding 'a more active approach in the area of culture'.[54]

As late as early 1953, nothing had been done, and Lehr's mood will not have been improved by reports from Berlin, where Hans Lauter had spoken at another cultural conference, confirming that for the SED, 'art serves only as material for agitation'.[55] Enquiries to the Ministry for all-German Affairs about cultural exchanges still elicited the unhelpful responses of previous years. Wolfgang Wagner wrote from Bayreuth in February 1953 to ask about engaging singers from 'the Zone' for the Festival. Should he get in touch with *Stakuko*, as he had been instructed? Kaiser's office could only tell Wagner that if he wanted the singers, he had no choice but to negotiate with *Stakuko*.[56] As the government prevaricated, its ambivalent position was reflected in the West German press. An article in the *Deutsche Zeitung*, 'Should the Thomanerchor no longer sing here?' summed up the difficulties the Federal Republic was facing.[57] In May 1953, new guidelines were finally presented to the *Land* Culture Ministers, but they were rejected. Bavaria objected to the imposition of binding guidelines from the centre, and a number of other *Länder* could not agree or disagree because they did not attend the meeting.[58]

Kaiser issued another set of guidelines in August 1953, in an attempt to find 'a middle way', but these still left regional authorities effectively trying to judge each cultural exchange on its merits.[59] In the end this was a compromise that did not work, because these exchanges appeared in a different light when viewed from different perspectives. Individual West German citizens and musical ensembles tended to see first the opportunities cultural exchanges presented for travel, for making friends and renewing old contacts, for music-making, or simply to see a first-class orchestra or choir. From the perspective of political authorities, the propaganda dimension loomed far larger.

As a result, through the early 1950s, there was no consistency in the way that the Federal Republic handled musical exchanges with 'the Zone'. Typically, there was great enthusiasm amongst private musicians and music lovers, which contrasted notably with varying degrees of hostility expressed by *Land* and *Bund* politicians. Unsurprisingly, the most suspicious here were the conservative Bavarians, and what *Neues Deutschland* called the 'front city politicians' in West Berlin. It appears, from

---

54   BAK B106/1079, Bundesministerium des Innern, 17 October 1952.

55   BAK B106/1079, Auszugsweise Abschrift, Vertreter des BMI, Berlin, 11 February 1953.

56   BAK B106/1079, Wagner, Leitung der Bayreuther Festspiele, to Bundesminister für gesamtdeutsche Fragen, 11 February 1953; Bundesminister für gesamtdeutsche Fragen to Wagner, 27 February 1953.

57   'Soll der Thomaner-Chor hier nicht mehr singen?', *Deutsche Zeitung*, 28 February 1953.

58   BAK B106/1079, Aktenvermerk aus der Kultusministerkonferenz vom 17. April 1953.

59   BAK B106/1079, Bundesminister für gesamtdeutsche Fragen to Länderregierungen der Bundesrepublik, 17 August 1953.

a range of different sources, that the GDR's elite ensembles became increasingly popular in the Federal Republic during this period. The concert agency in Kassel, which arranged the tours of the *Thomanerchor* in the Federal Republic, wrote to Holzhauer, the Chairman of *Stakuko*, in March 1953, that every town in the Federal Republic wanted the choir to visit and perform.[60] In fact the *Thomanerchor* and *Kreuzchor* were touring so much in the early 1950s, all over Europe, Scandinavia, and South America, that the parents of the boys complained that they were missing their schooling. Holzhauer, noting that both choirs were 'so extraordinarily important', came up with an ingenious plan for intensive work in the brief periods the boys had between tours to make up this deficit.[61]

In October 1953, Günther Ramin passed on to *Stakuko* a request from the Westminster Recording Company in New York to record the *Thomanerchor* in Vienna.[62] Hartig was obviously pleased that a GDR ensemble had in this way scaled the enemy heights, but was frustrated that the GDR's recording industry was not considered good enough to make the actual recordings. Rather petulantly, he wrote to *Lied der Zeit* to ask if they could not do this.[63] The *Thomanerchor* and *Kreuzchor* were by no means the only GDR choirs successful in the West. The newly formed Thuringian Boys Choir, which also performed church music, was very well received, particularly in Darmstadt. The Institute for New Music and Music Education there invited the Thuringian Boys Choir to its annual congress in 1955. It could think of no higher flattery than to say that it would be an honour to have such a marvellous choir from the GDR amongst them.[64]

The Leipzig University Choir, which toured northwest Germany in December 1954 with a programme of 'old German Christmas songs and motets', was also very successful.[65] Interestingly, the SED was not content to see the supremacy of the church choirs go unchallenged. Ulbricht, Wandel and Holzhauer in 1952 briefly considered a plan to create a new choir, to be called the 'Beethoven Choir' or 'Beethoven School', specifically to rival the church choirs, and to specialise in contemporary works like Meyer's *Mansfelder Oratorium* and Gerster's *Eisenhüttenkombinat Ost*.[66]

---

60   SAPMO-BArch DR 1/230, Schmidtke, Kasseler Konzertbüro, to Holtzhauer [sic], 6 March 1953.

61   SAPMO-BArch DR 1/230, H[olzhauer] to Laabs, Staatssekretär, Ministerium für Volksbildung, 4 November 1953; see also Laabs to Holzhauer, 9 October 1953.

62   SAPMO-BArch DR 1/230, Grayson, Westminster Recording Co. Inc., to Ramin, 14 October 1953.

63   SAPMO-BArch DR 1/230, Hartig to Lied der Zeit, 14 December 1953.

64   SAPMO-BArch DR 1/232a, Institut für Neue Musik und Musikerziehung, Darmstadt, to Leiter der Thüringer Sängerknaben, 2 November 1954; Institut für Neue Musik und Musikerziehung, Darmstadt, to die Regierung der DDR, 13 September 1954.

65   SAPMO-BArch DR 1/232, Bericht über die Arbeit des Leipziger Universitätschores im Studienjahr 1954/55.

66   See SAPMO-BArch DR 1/232, Hartung an den Präsidenten der DDR, 30 March 1952; also Akademie der Künste, Sektion Musik, to Stakuko, 14 June 1952.

It is difficult to imagine that these works would have been as popular in the Federal Republic as traditional Christmas songs, and nothing came of this plan.

The Federal Republic's failure to form a consistent response to Communist musical propaganda was embarrassingly highlighted in 1954. On 18 February, the celebrated Soviet violinist David Oistrach was due to appear at the *Sportpalast* in West Berlin with the Dresden State Orchestra, at the conclusion of a European tour. The first performance in Germany of Shostakovich's Tenth Symphony, by the Leipzig Gewandhaus Orchestra led by Konwitschny, had been scheduled for 19 February at the *Titania-Palast*. The authorities in West Berlin knew that the concerts would be used to trumpet the supposed musical superiority of Communism; at the last moment both were cancelled, providing SED propagandists with a field day. *Neues Deutschland* led the way, with series of articles. Why it asked, was Oistrach allowed to play all over the world, even in Paris, in Hamburg, but not in West Berlin?[67] Oistrach himself asked: 'What is so bad about it, if I play works by Beethoven and Tchaikovsky in West Berlin?'[68] *Neues Deutschland* named Tiburtius as the villain of the piece, contrasting this censorship with the tolerance he showed in West Berlin for gangster films 'like those by Harlan', for 'noisy hot orchestras of half-grown adolescents', and for it what it bizarrely called 'catch-as-catch-can wars'.[69]

Musik und Gesellschaft concentrated its fire on the cancelled Shostakovich concert. Its headline, 'Shostakovich "unwanted" in West Berlin', deliberately recalled Nazi censorship. The journal described how Konwitschny had been to Moscow to study the score of the symphony with the composer for this first German performance, and noted that instead of the Shostakovich concert, the *Titania-Palast* was rented out that day for the presentation of a 'magic-musical revue'.[70] On the Oistrach concert, the journal quoted Ernst Hermann Meyer. This was, he said, 'the face of fascism'. The journal also printed open letters of protest from the VDK, the Academy of the Arts, and the *Kulturbund*.[71] The performance of the Shostakovich Symphony was quickly rearranged in Leipzig.

If the Federal Republic was embarrassed at the elite level, its amateur musicians and singers were easy prey for the SED, which played on the deeply rooted German affection for choral singing. In December 1953, a meeting took place in Frankfurt-am-Main in the Federal Republic between representatives of the GDR's Choral

---

67   'Empörendes Verhalten westberliner Frontstadtpolitiker zum Oistrach-Konzert', *Neues Deutschland*, 18 February 1954.

68   'Der Empfang in Hamburg hat uns erfreut', *Neues Deutschland*, 20 February 1954.

69   'Tiburtius bläht sich auf', *Neues Deutschland*, 20 February 1954. Veit Harlan had directed notorious films like *Jud Süss* (1940) in the 'Third Reich'.

70   'Shostakovitch in Westberlin "unerwünscht"', *MuG*, 1954/3, p. 83. It is notable that none of the SED documentation on the cancellation of the Shostakovich concert reflects any concern that his Tenth Symphony may have carried anti-Stalinist or oppositional meanings.

71   'Der Triumph David Oistrachs und die Schande des Herrn Tiburtius', *MuG*, 1954/3, pp. 82–3. Meyer had a long association with Oistrach, who gave the first performance of Meyer's own Violin Concerto at the State Opera in Berlin in 1965.

Committee, and the West German General League of German Singers (*Deutscher Allgemeiner Sängerbund* or DAS). The DAS claimed to be the re-incarnation of the German Workers' Singing League (*Deutscher Arbeiter Sängerbund*) of the 1920s, and had been founded with a specifically anti-Nazi programme in January 1947 in Hanover.[72] Many of its leading members were old friends with leading GDR choral singers; Hermann Kutzschke, the Chairman of the DAS, had been at school with that great hero of the GDR, the martyred KPD leader Ernst Thälmann.

The two organisations agreed to cooperate more closely, to promote further amateur choral exchanges, and to use the DAS journal *Der Chor* to publicise choral matters in both Germanys.[73] Above all, they agreed to build on the success of the Wartburg Singers' Meeting of October 1953, when amateur choirs from East and West had met in Eisenach for a festival of singing, which concluded with joint ceremonies at the Wartburg. In Bonn, the Ministry for all-German Affairs was immediately concerned about the dangers of SED infiltration of the Federal Republic's amateur choral associations. The bourgeois rival of the DAS, the German Singers' League (*Deutscher Sängerbund*), which boasted 800,000 members, was similarly concerned, and its chairman, Pesch, agreed to come to Bonn to meet the Minister for talks.[74] Kutzschke of the DAS was less helpful though, and was not deterred by warnings from his cooperative work with the GDR.[75] His first priority was the forthcoming Federal Singers' Festival in Hanover, and he was determined to use this to showcase the new cooperation.

These big choral festivals were a particularly German phenomenon. Lasting several days, they provided an opportunity for literally hundreds of choirs of all kinds, amateur and professional, to meet and sing. The participants, staying with host families, divided their time between concerts, many in the open air, meetings, discussions and celebratory meals. International visitors might add extra spice, but these were primarily German affairs, which celebrated German music. The Festival in Hanover in August 1954 attracted 50,000 singers, of whom 2000 came from the GDR; the Wartburg Singers' Meeting in September 1954 brought together 20,000, including some 6,000 from the Federal Republic. There could hardly have been a better vehicle for the SED's *Westpolitik* in the early 1950s. Through these festivals, it could reach potentially hundreds of thousands of singers in the Federal Republic; it could demonstrate its commitment not only to the German classical tradition, but also to German folksong, and to the whole tradition of amateur singing.

Both governments sought and received reports on the Festivals from participants, and each used these to gauge the state of affairs in the other. The Federal Republic

---

72   BHA/MK 51335, Deutscher Allgemeiner Sängerbund to Bayerisches Staatsministerium für Unterricht und Kultur, 9 March 1947.

73   BAK B137/1850, Abschrift aus "Der Chor", Nr. XII, 1953.

74   BAK B137/1850, Min. Rat Hütten, Ministerium für gesamtdeutsche Fragen, to Pesch, 15 January 1954; Pesch to Bundesminister für gesamtdeutsche Fragen, 20 January 1954.

75   See for example BAK B137/1850, Bundesminister für gesamtdeutsche Fragen to DAS, 14 April 1954.

was reluctant to publicise the Festivals, but the SED enthusiastically endorsed them as evidence of popular support for its campaigns for peace and unity. In August 1954, *Musik und Gesellschaft* proudly reported that the Swiss conductor Hermann Scherchen had reworked a little known work of Beethoven's as a *Peace Cantata,* which was jointly sung by choirs from the GDR and Federal Republic at the Festival in Hanover. It quoted West German participants who were impressed by the GDR's support for choirs, and their approval of the presence of many young people in the GDR's choirs. Rather smugly, the journal noted that most West German singers were over fifty years old.[76] Privately, the SED was secure in its conviction that it was maintaining higher standards. A worker who had travelled to the Festival was thanked for his report on the Hanover Boys Choir; the Party agreed with him that 'the Hanover choir in its performance does not match the top ensembles of the GDR'.[77]

The Wartburg Singers' Meeting in September 1954 was elaborately arranged to make the best possible impression on West German visitors. The town of Eisenach was stripped of obviously propagandistic posters or notices, and carefully provisioned with food and drink. Visitors were treated with particular courtesy at every stage of their journey, given free accommodation, and even 8 DM daily for pocket money. The Adenauer government had decided that it could not prevent West German choirs participating in the Festival, but its irritation grew when it was asked to pay for them. A request from the Hanover Oratorio Choir for 1800 DM to travel to Eisenach was pointedly refused, and the choir was told that these meetings were used for the Zone's propaganda.[78] The government received very different accounts of the actual Festival. One, which came through the Lower Saxon Ministry of the Interior, was effusive in its praise for the organisers, and for life in the GDR as it appeared to many participants. Many complimentary passages were underlined in Bonn, although whether in admiration, astonishment, or irritation is not clear. The presence of '<u>food of all kinds</u>' in Eisenach's shops was emphasised, as was the appearance of a 120 strong GDR orchestra, '<u>all in dinner jackets</u>'.[79] The Federal Office for the Protection of the Constitution conceded that the Meeting was 'artistically ... for the most part good', and warned that it would be even larger in 1955.[80] All reports agreed that the visitors had been very well treated, and that the GDR had staged an impressive spectacle. There was general embarrassment in the Federal Republic that

76   Hau P, 'Es gibt keine Grenze zwischen den Menschen in Ost und West unseres Vaterlandes', *MuG*, 1954/10, pp. 350–52.

77   SAPMO-BArch DR 1/154, Grösch, Deutsche Konzert- und Gastspieldirektion –Zentrale, to Rollberg, VEB Chemische Werke Buna, 17 August 1954.

78   BAK B137/1850, Geschäftsführer, Hannoverscher Oratorienchor to von Zahn, Bundesministerium für gesamtdeutsche Fragen, 3 July 1954 and 31 July 1954; von Zahn to Geschäftsführer, Hannoverscher Oratorienchor, 13 August 1954.

79   BAK B137/1850, Abschrift, II Wartburg-Treffen Deutscher Sänger vom 24.– 26.9.1954 in Eisenach, sent from Niedersächsischer Minister des Innern to Bundesminister für gesamtdeutsche Fragen, 16 October 1954.

80   BAK B137/1850, Bundesamt für Verfassungsschutz to Bundesminister für gesamtdeutsche Fragen and Bundesminister des Innern. 5 November 1954.

amateur choirs were clearly better supported in the GDR, and that state support for music appeared so much stronger there.[81]

The SED pulled out its big guns for the occasion. Helmut Koch and the Berlin Radio Choir were the star performers. Ernst Hermann Meyer and Johannes Becher spoke at public meetings. In the months after the Wartburg Meeting, bourgeois choral associations and officials in Bonn earnestly debated how they could deal with the problem. In October, a number of choral leaders and *Land* officials met at the Ministry for all-German Affairs to try to find a way forward.[82] The League of German Singers was concerned by the advantage the DAS had gained through its cooperation with the GDR, and agreed that it could not afford to be seen as 'backward looking and reactionary'.[83] The Chairman of the Association of German Mixed Voice Choirs had also been to Eisenach, and demanded that Western participation be prevented in the future. He was more alert to SED propaganda during the Festival than other reporters, and spelt out for Kaiser how it had been manipulated for maximum effect. He noted that a Soviet General was present at the final ceremony at the Wartburg, that many GDR choirs sang in Russian, and that a choir from the People's Republic of China had sung a song of praise for Pieck and Grotewohl.[84]

Through the early months of 1955, ministers and officials in Bonn debated whether to accept this advice and prohibit further choral exchanges. The more they investigated the problem, the more it appeared that the DAS was in league with the GDR politically as well as musically. The Interior Ministry had noted that its own magazine, *The Choir*, had come under the influence of the SED, and in January 1955 the DAS was formally warned of the 'consequences' of this.[85] Kutzschke was evidently unimpressed, and went ahead with the preparations for the next Wartburg Meeting. By now, the Bonn government was realising the extent to which it had lost control. The Ministry for all-German Affairs, describing amateur choirs as 'extraordinarily effective tools of political struggle', declared that further visits from the GDR should not be tolerated.[86] In March, *Land* Culture Ministers met again with the Minister of the Interior to discuss 'the question of East-West cultural exchanges, including the attempts at infiltration from the East'.[87]

Opinion was still divided though. Some *Länder* evidently wished to pursue the exchanges; Tiburtius from West Berlin was more concerned to strengthen

---

81   See also BAK B137/1850, Oberborbeck to Bundesministerium für gesamtdeutsche Fragen, 12 October 1954.

82   BAK B137/1850, Choraustausch mit der sowjetischen Besatzungszone, 6 October 1954.

83   BAK B137/1850, Vermerk, Berlin, 5 October 1954.

84   BAK B137/1850, Drifte to Bundesminister für gesamtdeutsche Fragen, 29 November 1954.

85   BAK B137/1850, Bundesminister des Innern to Bundesminister für gesamtdeutsche Fragen, 2 October 1954; Vermerk, 3 January 1955.

86   BAK B137/1850, Vermerk, 5 January 1955.

87   BAK B106/1079, Frey, Generalsekretär, Ständige Konferenz der Kultusminister, to Bundesminister des Innern, 16 February 1955.

the Federal Republic's cultural activities, and particularly to get young people to concerts.[88] In April 1955, the *Städtetag* reaffirmed its belief in the importance of choral exchanges.[89] Further salt was rubbed in the wound by a joint choral conference in Berlin, where Kutzschke appeared alongside Helmut Koch from the GDR to announce plans for the 1955 Wartburg Meeting. Koch cleverly used the SED vocabulary to embrace the wider German choral community, describing the exchanges as 'weapons of the people', and folk song an expression of the 'oppressed class'.[90] Koch's pronouncements were accompanied by similar remarks in a speech given by Walter Ulbricht in Leipzig and in a 'declaration' by the GDR *Volkskammer* in March.[91]

This was the final straw in Bonn, where Kaiser declared that the participation of West German singers at the forthcoming Wartburg Meeting was 'highly undesirable'.[92] It appeared that Kutzschke and the other leaders of the DAS were not merely being manipulated by the SED, but that they were actively working together. The Adenauer government's studious non-recognition of the GDR was being undermined by the SED's infiltration of a genuine mass movement in the Federal Republic. In the summer of 1955, individual amateur choirs from the GDR were prevented from visiting the Federal Republic. In early July, a railway workers' choir from Magdeburg was prevented from appearing in North Rhine-Westphalia.[93] Since March, there had been a complete ban on choral visits from the GDR arranged by the DAS in Bavaria.[94]

If these prohibitions were not actually prompted by the Adenauer government, they were certainly not out of step with its attitude at that point. The West German authorities, though, were not prepared ultimately to place a blanket prohibition on their own choirs and singers travelling to the GDR, or on GDR choirs visiting the Federal Republic. These would have been hugely unpopular, and obviously illiberal. Presumably, Kaiser and his advisers knew that the SED would exploit any such decision for maximum effect. They were warned that it would, in any case, be impossible to enforce a ban, that DAS choirs would still try to attend the Wartburg Meeting, and that the 'bourgeois' choirs of the German Singers' League and the Association of German Mixed Voice Choirs were well aware of the risks they took by attending. The Meeting was held in August 1955, with some 6–7,000 West German

---

88   BAK B106/1079, Tiburtius, Gedanken für das Referat über die Kommunistische Partei in der Ost-West Spannung, p. 2.

89   BAK B106/1079, Deutscher Städtetag, Betr.: Kulturaustausch zwischen der Bundesrepublik und der sowjetischen Besatzungszone, 7 April 1955.

90   'Volkslied ist Politikum', *Neue Rhein-Zeitung*, 29 March 1955.

91   SAPMO-BArch DR 1/291, Studien- und Arbeitsgemeinschaft zur Förderung der Deutschen Volks- und Laienkunst to Pischner, Ministerium für Kultur, 10 March 1955.

92   BAK B137/1850, Bundesminister für gesamtdeutsche Fragen to Bundesminister des Innern, 28 April 1955.

93   *Unser Tag*, 10 July 1955.

94   SAPMO-BArch DR 1/291, Studien- und Arbeitsgemeinschaft zur Förderung der Deutschen Volks- und Laienkunst to Pischner, 10 March 1955.

visitors. They were joined by choirs from France, Austria, Finland, Czechoslovakia, and the Mongolian Peoples' Republic. *Musik und Gesellschaft* approvingly quoted Kutzschke, who declared: 'We want no more zonal boundaries.' The Beethoven *Peace Cantata* had by now become an anthem for the choral movement, and was sung again. Koch and the Berlin Radio Choir performed Meyer's *The Certainty of Victory*. According to the SED, 25,000 West German singers wanted to come to Eisenach, but many had been prevented by their own government.[95] Kaiser was particularly concerned by press photographs showing what appeared to be an official delegation from Brunswick at the Festival, and anxiously demanded an explanation from the Lower Saxon Ministry of the Interior.[96]

This was a low point for the Adenauer government. Evidently, it feared that those of its citizens who were involved in these exchanges would be convinced that things were better in the East, and perhaps that they would spread this idea amongst friends and acquaintances at home. It need not have been so fearful. The SED's hopes of reaching the masses in the Federal Republic were not realised. It does appear that most visitors were impressed by the quality and quantity of choral singing in the GDR. Although the amateur singers from the Federal Republic appear, on the whole, to have thoroughly enjoyed visiting Eisenach, and to have had many propagandistic images of life in the GDR challenged by the friendly reception they received there, there were only isolated individual converts to the broader cause of the SED. Hans Herwig, the conductor of the Westphalia Symphony Orchestra, was one. He wrote to Pischner to ask for a post in the GDR in March 1956. He wanted to settle there because

> In the Federal Republic an atmosphere of decadent corruption prevails, a deep laziness and hypocrisy ... which is simply unbearable. On the other hand, I had the opportunity last summer to get to know the sympathetic and pure air of the GDR, when I took part in the Wartburg German Singers' Meeting with the Solingen Children's Choir, which I direct.[97]

Herwig, who unwisely named the ex-Nazi Elly Ney as a character referee, was an isolated example.

There was a definite hardening of feeling about what was construed as Communist activity in the Federal Republic during 1955, which resulted in the banning of organisations like the Society for German-Soviet Friendship, and indeed the Communist Party itself, in 1956. West German politicians had long considered

---

95   Kunze W, 'Das III Wartburgtreffen Deutscher Sänger', *MuG*, 1955/10, pp. 336–7.

96   BAK B137/1850, Betr.: 3. Wartburgtreffen deutscher Sänger, 16 September 1955; Bundesminister für gesamtdeutsche Fragen to Niedersächsischen Minister des Innern, 21 September 1955. See also Niedersächsischer Minister des Innern to Bundesminister für gesamtdeutsche Fragen, 22 November 1955, in which the officials from Brunswick argued that they had been at the Festival in a purely private capacity. Given that they were photographed in the front row of the audience, wearing chains of office, this appears questionable.

97   SAPMO-BArch DR 1/219, Herwig to Pischner, 18 March 1956.

the National Front and the *Kulturbund* as 'camouflaged Communist organisations', but now many other cultural and educational bodies, like the Chopin Society, were added to the registers kept by *Land* Governments and by the central government in Bonn.[98] In 1955, the Bavarian Interior Ministry added the German Society for Cultural and Economic Exchanges with Poland, which was organising the prestigious international Chopin competition, to its list.[99] *Länder* governments were warned not to allow music academies to take part in the 1955 competition.[100] Individual musicians in the Federal Republic were persecuted if they could be identified as communists. Two long-serving members of the Lüneburg Symphony Orchestra were dismissed in November 1955 because of their work for the National Front.[101] In 1956, Hermann Kutzschke, that thorn in the flesh of the Adenauer government, was ousted from his position as Chairman of the DAS, and replaced by Robert Seiler from Nuremberg. Jakob Kaiser must have been relieved to receive reports confirming that Seiler and other newly appointed committee members were politically more reliable.[102]

Representation and Reality

The most significant conclusion to be drawn from this brief survey of German musical transactions concerns the distance between representation and reality. Between 1949 and 1955, both German states were desperately concerned with establishing some kind of identity, above all a claim to represent the 'real' Germany. Both believed that the division of Germany was only temporary, and therefore each extended its claim to include the other. This feeling was particularly strong in the GDR, which claimed to be the first genuinely anti-fascist German State, and the sole guardian and guarantor of Germany's humanistic past. It regarded the Federal Republic as a disastrous consequence of late monopoly capitalism – a hybrid entity run by Western imperialists, the Americans, British, and French and a clique of West German capitalists who had previously supported Hitler. Its only purpose was to serve international capital, which meant ultimately the destruction of the GDR

---

98   BAK B137/2305, Kommunistische oder von Kommunisten beeinflußte Organisationen, Gruppen und Aktionen, undated.

99   NWHA/NW 60/851, Bayerisches Staatsministerium des Innern to Bundesminister des Innern, 7 February 1955.

100   NWHA/NW 60/851, Bundesminister für gesamtdeutsche Fragen to Kultusminister des Landes Nordrhein-Westfalen, 2 September 1954.

101   See SAPMO-BArch DR 1/213, Vissering, Vorsitzender des Lüneburger Sinfonieorchesters to Rothämel, 18 November 1955. There are other letters in SED files from this period from musicians claiming to have been victimised by employers in the Federal Republic because of their political views.

102   BAK B137/1850, Bayerisches Staatsministerium des Innern to Bundesminister für gesamtdeutsche Fragen, 17 August 1956; Hessische Minister des Innern to Bundesminister für gesamtdeutsche Fragen, 22 August 1956.

and its guardian, the Soviet Union. The SED's cultural politics therefore had to be extended to the oppressed and captive German population of the Federal Republic.

The Federal Republic had cast its lot with the NATO powers, and was completely dedicated to a course of Western integration. It regarded the GDR as the 'occupied Soviet Zone', and refused utterly to recognise its national claims. Although politicians and musicians in the Federal Republic accepted a vestigial sense of obligation to the 16 million or so Germans left in 'the Zone' after 1949, they were less dedicated than their SED counterparts to working with them and for them. In the final analysis, if integration with the West demanded that they turn their backs on 'the Zone', they were prepared to do this.

When it came to music, the demands of national representation and the creation of new ideologies led to confusion and misunderstanding. The bizarre combination of cynicism and idealism that characterises most of the musical transactions described here can only be understood within this context. SED musicians genuinely believed that monopoly capital would destroy national cultural forms, and that therefore German music, that most hallowed inheritance, was threatened. They regarded the Western idea that music could exist as an entirely free art form, and develop in ways which had nothing to do with society, economics, or politics, as either an example of false consciousness, or more cynically, as a deliberate obfuscation. New musical forms emerging in the West after 1945 were not, in their eyes, purely aesthetic or stylistic developments, which one could take or leave, according to personal taste. They were intended to corrupt and destroy the taste and culture of the masses, to leave them uprooted and helpless in the face of exploitation.

There was, *prima facie*, plenty of evidence to support the SED's view. They knew perfectly well that the Adenauer government worked with the *Länder* and the towns to support music in the Federal Republic. They knew of the leading role played by the radio stations, which had been set up by the Americans, British and French, under whose direct control they still remained in the early 1950s. It was thus entirely predictable that the radio stations would support jazz and avant-gardism. The idea of what the SED called the '*Melos* clique' was not far-fetched. There were institutional, personal and financial links between the radio stations, the Occupying Powers, West German politicians and commercial interests. The idea that, for instance, the SWF's patronage of jazz and new music, or the NWDR's support for electronic music was a purely accidental stylistic development appeared quite ludicrous to the SED. The domination of music in the Federal Republic by composers, performers, teachers, critics and academics who had thrived under Nazism was no more surprising. These people were as ready, in the eyes of the SED, to serve international monopoly capital as they had been to support Fascism.

These genuine convictions made it very difficult though for the SED to understand the support given in the Federal Republic to the German classics. The SED representation of music in the Federal Republic is dominated by images of rampant avant-gardism, hostility to composers working in traditional modes, and of popular German music overcome by a 'tidal wave' of commercialised dance music. Conversely, much Western musical literature, and some of the most sophisticated contemporary historical analyses, portray the opposite, a hidebound musical establishment, nationalistic and conservative, prone to anti-Semitism, Nazism, and hostile to foreign influences. According to this latter view, the most important and representative images of music in the early Federal Republic are of Furtwängler, Karajan and Böhm, endlessly conducting Beethoven and Wagner cycles before a public still hostile to Mahler and Schoenberg. The ideological convictions of the SED left it genuinely unable to understand that the Federal Republic was equally committed to the classics, to Bach and Beethoven, to German folk music, and to universal ideals of musical education.

When politicians and musicians in the Federal Republic looked into 'the Zone', they were equally confused. Steeped in anti-Bolshevism, they regarded Soviet Communism as profoundly hostile to high culture. The egalitarian demands of Communism could only, in their eyes, lead to a degradation of the arts. Just as the SED found evidence for its views in the West, conservatives in the Federal Republic found confirmation of what they suspected in the GDR. Above all, they despised the ideological music of the Party, its oratorios and mass songs. These, with their straightforward melodies, their uncomplicated harmonies and rhythms, and above all with their banal texts extolling the heroic achievements of the workers and peasants, appeared as the worst possible degradation of classical forms. The censorship of avant-garde music and jazz in the GDR, and the state regulation of all musical activity, served as further proof of the evils of Communism.

Indeed, for many West German musicians, the threat that Communism posed to the very existence of an art form like music was one of the most compelling reasons for rejecting it completely. This perception, though, left many completely baffled by aspects of the GDR's musical culture – above all its promotion of the classics. How on earth were they to understand the SED's support for elite church choirs, or for a composer like Bach? What did they make of visiting orchestras that played Beethoven symphonies, or of amateur choirs that sang traditional German folk songs, typically in ways that elicited unbounded admiration? At the official level, concerned with regime legitimation, this had to be portrayed as a sophisticated deception, the final proof of Communist wickedness. Could there be anything more sacrilegious than the SED's manipulation of German folk song and children's choirs, of Bach and Beethoven? It was not possible, in the context of the larger representation of the GDR by the Adenauer government, to concede that the SED's commitment to bring German classical music to the people was genuine.

This left both German states unable to understand – or indeed recognise – those areas of their musical culture that were in fact so strikingly similar. These were, firstly, a conviction that music was important, that it was an art form the Germans excelled in particularly. Secondly, they shared an unbridled veneration for the German classical tradition, whether expressed through the Protestant church music of Schütz and Bach, the secular music of Beethoven and Schubert, or Wagnerian music-drama. Thirdly, they had a common belief in music as a force for social improvement, and an accompanying recognition of the duty of public authorities to support music. The similarities extend to fears about music. Both German states were, in the early

1950s, exposed to rapid and far reaching social and economic changes. Both had to confront similar problems, the huge extension of the mechanical reproduction of music, changes in mass culture, and increasingly strident generational conflicts.

Musicians and administrators had, for the most part, grown up in the German-speaking musical culture of the first half of the twentieth century, and thus inherited many similar cultural preconceptions – most notably a rather muddled social Darwinism. This had developed both on the political right and left, and is one reason why those whose personal allegiances changed between 1918 and 1955 often found themselves articulating the same ideas from different political standpoints. This simplistic Darwinism, applied to music, resulted in an evolutionary view of music as an organism, which was not only influenced by people, but in turn influenced them. This was expressed above all in the language of cultural pessimism, which took on a nationalistic fervour in Germany in the 1920s. Absorbed into the ideology of National Socialism, this Darwinism appeared in its most strident form in the tirades directed against 'cultural bolshevism' and 'degenerate music', and in the frequent use of words like 'Judaification', 'niggerising', and 'jazzification'.

After 1945, the most obviously anti-Semitic and racist elements of this vocabulary were suppressed, but its underlying ideas remained the common currency of musical analysis in both German states. Whether it was Meyer speaking of 'manifestations of decay' and 'perfumed mass commodities' in the East, or societies in the Federal Republic warning of 'alarming symptoms of the decay of our musical life', and the danger of 'mass entertainments', the language, and the ideas behind the words, are recognisably the same.[103] These two examples are drawn from published documents, but the shared German vocabulary of decadence, health, and hygiene is even more striking in private correspondence and in bureaucratic documents about music which were not intended for public consumption.

Empirical analysis confirms how far the representations of the two German states, so assiduously constructed for public consumption in the early Cold War, were divorced from reality. Music in the Federal Republic was not a free-floating artistic activity, but was closely supported, shaped, and policed by coalitions of political, institutional, and financial interests. When necessary, these coalitions, or various constituent parts of them, were quite prepared to censor musical expression. On the other hand, music in the GDR, for all the SED's efforts, was by no means fully regulated. Nor was it purely inward-looking. The musical culture of the GDR was strikingly international, and cultivated links not just with other Communist states. Above all, it is a mistake to imagine at this point in history the existence of two entirely separate German musical cultures. It is abundantly clear that music and musicians in the Federal Republic and the GDR were intimately connected, and that the musical traffic between the two states was very considerable.

---

103   Meyer, 'Realismus', pp. 39 and 41; Arbeitsgemeinschaft für Musikerziehung und Musikpflege (ed.), *Zur Notlage der Musikerziehung und Musikpflege* (Kassel, 1953), p. 4. This was a pamphlet sent to the President, the central government, national and regional political bodies, and to radio stations in the Federal Republic.

Even in the case of genuine collaborative work, such as that over the new Bach and Handel editions, the Federal Republic and the GDR were each unable to acknowledge the positive cultural achievements of the other. Indeed, each state depended for its own legitimacy on the projection of the other as a polar opposite. To this extent, the SED's clumsy bureaucratic machinations were a necessary part of the Federal Republic's self-projection as a land of cultural freedom. Equally, the increasingly abstract experimentalism in Darmstadt and Cologne was actually helpful to the SED as a confirmation of its cultural critique of the West. The last thing either state could afford in this contest was openly to recognise or celebrate those aspects of musical culture in the Federal Republic and the GDR that appear so similar today. Only at the private, the amateur, or the individual levels was this possible, and this was precisely why the Adenauer government was so concerned by the thought of its citizens going to the Wartburg Meeting, or listening to the *Thomanerchor* singing Bach.

Conclusion

When Music Mattered

In May 1955, the Federal Republic was restored to full nominal sovereignty when the Occupation Statute lapsed. At the same time it became a member of NATO. In March 1954, the GDR was granted the rights of an 'equal peoples' democratic state' by the Soviet Union. In 1956, the GDR formed its 'National People's Army', and joined the Warsaw Pact. Both German states were tied to their respective superpower alliances by a network of other agreements. The presence of large contingents of American, British, French and Soviet troops on German soil was a reminder of this for many years to come. In this conclusion, I ask how the respective Allies viewed the success or failure of their efforts to reconstruct German musical culture, ten years after the defeat of the 'Third Reich', and briefly examine how this culture is being reassessed now, in the post-Cold War period.

The question of how the wartime Allies might have viewed German music in 1955 is complicated, and it should be said, largely hypothetical. By this time, each of the former occupying Powers, whatever its diplomatic, commercial, and military ties at the time, was to an extent pursuing a separate national agenda; all had much larger concerns than the state of music in Germany. It is important also to bear in mind that 'an American viewpoint' or 'a British perspective' is no more than a historical construct. There were, in reality, many differing viewpoints in each country, as of course there were in each of the two Germanys. This applies above all to the issue of denazification. It would be possible to generalise, and to say for instance that in Britain in 1955, there was little general knowledge of – or interest in – the connections between music and Nazism. Any such statement would, though, need to be qualified. There were individuals – by then in many different walks of life – who had intimate knowledge of particular cases. They may well have been totally dismayed to see individual musicians or musicologists they had investigated before 1948 masquerading in Germany as anti-Nazis, or as apolitical artists and academics. The same applies to France, the USA and the Soviet Union.

In the West, the successes of the re-education programme far outweighed the expectations the planners in London, Washington and Paris had in 1945. The reconstructed musical culture of the Federal Republic was, in many ways, all they could have hoped for. There had been no resurrection of anything resembling Goebbels' Propaganda Ministry or the Reich Music Chamber. Control of music had been devolved to *Land* and *Stadt* level, and appeared free of sinister political influences. Financial support for municipal orchestras, operas, and for musical education at school and university levels was very generous. The result was a flourishing, devolved musical life, pluralistic and competitive, nourished by local pride and tradition. Musical broadcasting was similarly pluralistic, and the radio stations established by the western Allies after 1945 had become centres of musical excellence and diversity.

The goal of internationalising German music was also hugely successful. At the professional level, German performers and ensembles were once again an important part of the concert scene in the capitalist West. A network of amateur exchanges was also developing, particularly between the Federal Republic, France and Great Britain. In these countries, music was to become a central part of the town-twinning arrangements inaugurated before 1949 by the partnerships between Bristol and Hanover, and Reading and Düsseldorf. The French could certainly point to the Franco-German cooperation of the early 1950s, and the success of embryonic bodies like the European Coal and Steel Community as a vindication of their policy of 'peaceful penetration' of Germany after 1945. The signing of the Treaty of Rome in 1957, and the strengthening of ties between France and the Federal Republic after De Gaulle's return to power in 1958, helped to build the Franco-German axis that dominated the European Community into the 1990s. Turning specifically to music, the continued success of the SWF was one proof of the success of their ambitious, modernist programme. The potentially controversial appointment of Strobel to direct the musical output of the SWF had been a triumph; the ties he had cultivated with the French avant-garde were displayed by Pierre Boulez's decision in 1958 to move to Baden-Baden.

On the cultural front, the Federal Republic had been accepted as a member of UNESCO in 1951; in 1953 it sent a delegate to the secretariat in Paris, and in December it was granted membership of UNESCO's Executive Council. A German Committee for Work with UNESCO was formed in August 1951, which although representing the Federal Republic, clearly saw its role as also symbolising and keeping alive the memory of a larger Germany. There were considerable difficulties in finding a suitable West German musician to represent the Federal Republic in the councils of UNESCO. Carl Orff was offered the place reserved for a musician on the German Committee in 1951, but turned it down; it was then offered to Werner Egk, who only a few years previously had led the composers' section within the Reich Music Chamber.[1] In one sense, West German participation in UNESCO symbolised the successful reintegration that was a principal objective of the re-education programme. At the same time, it pointed to the central failure of that programme: the problems with denazification. In 1953 a 'German Section' of UNESCO's International Music Council was set up. It included many who had played leading roles in musical life in the Third Reich, such as the musicologists Blume, Albrecht, Moser and Fellerer, and the composers Fortner and Egk. Representing the 'Working Group for Youth Music' was the former HJ composer, Gottfried Wolters, and representing the 'Association of

---

1   BAK B336/403, Sitzung des Vollzugs-Ausschusses am 13. September 1950, p. 5. Kater, who does not mention Egk's connection with UNESCO, notes the many other national and international honorary positions given to Egk after his denazification. See *Composers*, p. 30.

Music and Folk Music Schools' was former HJ music teacher Wilhelm Twittenhoff. The 'International Working Group for Youth and Folk Music' was represented by Fritz Jöde.[2] Today, it seems extraordinary that such a collection of compromised musicians should have been permitted to take on this representative function, but we must remember that in 1953, public knowledge of what these men had done before 1945 was limited. Such attention as there was at this time on this issue was focused on bigger fish, like Hans Globke, or on more notorious war criminals.

Within the Federal Republic, there was much for the western Allies to take pleasure in. Not only was the classical tradition still honoured, the Federal Republic had become the undisputed centre of the international avant-garde. The modernist composers of the 1920s were regularly performed, even in provincial towns, and on the radio. West German composers like Henze and Stockhausen had played a leading role in developing new musical idioms after 1949, and the festivals of 'new music' regularly held in Darmstadt, Baden-Baden, Cologne, and Donaueschingen attracted the most radical composers and performers from Europe and the Americas. '*Entartete Musik*' had returned with a vengeance. Even though there had been a resurgence of music publishing in the Federal Republic, there may also have been some quiet satisfaction amongst the wartime Allies that the pre-war German dominance of this field had been broken.

At a personal level, many of the relationships forged in the particular circumstances of 'Music Control' programmes in the immediate post-war years had become the basis for international networks. Many of these continued to be influential in the broader musical culture and infrastructure of the West in the 1950s and 1960s. One example is the friendship between the first British 'Music Supervisor' at *NWDR-Köln*, Ken Bartlett, and Hans-Werner Henze.[3] After 1947, Bartlett left the British Army to work for Schotts. Everett Helm, the American Music Officer in Hesse in 1948–49, was particularly active in supporting the Darmstadt Summer Schools, where some of his own music was performed.[4] He stayed in Germany when the American music programme was scaled down, working as a freelance composer and critic, and reporting for *Musical America*. In the former French Zone, Strobel's wide contacts with musicians exemplified the new internationalism. He invited John Cage and David Tudor to perform at Donaueschingen in 1954. Jack Bornoff, former 'Music Controller' in Hamburg, and John Evarts, Music Control Officer for Bavaria from 1946 to 1948, both worked for UNESCO in the 1950s. Nicolas Nabokov, after

---

2   BAK B106/299, 1. Generalversammlung der Deutschen Sektion des Internationalen Musikrates am 29./30. März in Köln. Moser's reputation as an anti-Semite and a Nazi is well known; Fellerer worked for the *Sonderstab Musik*; Wolters was blacklisted by the British in 1946; on Twittenhoff see Kater, *Composers*, pp. 120–22. Jöde exemplifies the trajectory of many German musicians in the first half of the twentieth century. He was active in the 'Youth Music Movement' of the 1920s, then in the HJ, before serving at the Office for Youth and Music in Hamburg from 1947 to 1952.

3   See Hans-Werner Henze, *Bohemian Fifths: An Autobiography* (trans. Spencer, London, Faber, 1998).

4   See Beal, "Negotiating Cultural Allies", pp. 112–16.

1950 the Secretary General of the Congress for Cultural Freedom was, of course, a tireless networker. In one of his memoirs, he highlights his close relationship in the early 1950s with Rolf Liebermann, the head of music at *NWDR-Hamburg*.[5]

A potentially sinister side of these informal networks was the spectre of CIA manipulation. The wide-ranging programmes of cultural sponsorship run covertly by the CIA in Western Europe during the 1950s have been debated since the late 1960s, and it is well known that various musical events, such as the Festival of Twentieth Century Music in Rome in 1954, the Berlin Festivals that were run from 1950 onwards, and tours in Europe by American orchestras, were partly supported by CIA money. It lies outside the scope of this book to explore in detail the links between avant-garde music and the CIA in the 1950s; elsewhere I have argued that the CIA had no great need to involve itself in the West German musical scene, as avant-garde music there was already so strongly supported by German authorities and by the Allied High Commissions. I have pointed, also, to the role played by Stuckenschmidt, who was, between 1950 and 1955, a salaried employee of the State Department, working as a 'Special Editor' for the *Neue Zeitung*, with a brief to promote American music in Germany. Stuckenschmidt was a friend of Nabokov's, and at his request spoke at the Rome Festival of 20th Century Music in 1954. Stuckenschmidt helped to plan the visit of Edgar Varèse to Darmstadt in 1950, and introduced colleagues like Eimert at the NWDR in Cologne to the music of John Cage.[6] Through these extensive personal networks, the music scene of the Federal Republic was prevented from slipping back into insularity and provincialism; eventually, as Amy Beal has argued, American experimental music came to play a dominating role in the 'new music' scene there, challenging established prejudices about America as a land without its own distinctive musical tradition.

This embrace of intermationalism is among the most significant changes brought about by the Allied programme of 'Music Control' in the western Zones of occupied Germany, and subsequently in the Federal Republic. Before 1945, there was a deeply rooted conviction of musical superiority in Germany, which had been exploited by the Nazis, and appropriated as part of their racial discourse. The French had identified this most clearly, and had recognised that to challenge this notion of musical supremacy was also to challenge Nazi racism. The Americans and the British, less coherently, had also recognised that the internationalisation of music in Germany was an important aspect of a broader programme of 're-education': such change had to be part of a wider shift in mentalities that was needed if Germany was to live in peace with the rest of the world. They had therefore similarly sought to challenge

---

5   Nabokov, *Bagázh*, p. 247. For more detail on Nabokov's role with the Congress of Cultural Freedom, see Saunders, *Who Paid the Piper?*; and Mark Carroll, *Music and Ideology in Cold War Europe* (Cambridge: Cambridge University Press, 2003), which focuses on the intellectual climate in France at the onset of the Cold War.

6   See Toby Thacker, '"Playing Beethoven like an Indian": American Music and Reorientation in Germany, 1945–1955', in Dominik Geppert (ed.), *The Postwar Challenge: Cultural, Social, and Political Change in Western Europe, 1945–1958* (New York and Oxford: Oxford University Press, 2003), pp. 365–86.

the idea of German musical supremacy by introducing music from other countries and traditions. We have seen that this process was not straightforward, and that the Americans, in particular, experienced difficulties, both of a practical nature, and in combating deeply ingrained German prejudices. There is no doubt that some German conservatives, and many of the older generation, deeply resented the imposition of what they regarded as a new orthodoxy after 1945; many of them clung privately to cherished views of 'German music' as something distinct from and superior to other musical forms. Politicians, officials and educators in the western Zones, and in the early Federal Republic, exhibited a curious mixture of genuine commitment and reluctant acquiescence in the support they gave to international modernism after 1945; no doubt many felt this was a repugnant duty forced upon them by alien occupiers. Some recognised it as an 'anti-fascist', and later an anti-Communist duty, but there were others who embraced the new internationalism wholeheartedly, and welcomed the avenue out of isolation and shame that it provided.

Albrecht Riethmüller has recently argued cogently that the doctrine of German musical supremacy lives on, and doubtless, in some quarters, not only in Germany, it does.[7] I have argued though, in the context of larger debates on citizenship and identity in twentieth-century Germany, that 1945 was a turning point in this regard, and that the Allied programme of 'Music Control' initiated a process that has seriously challenged this idea ever since.[8] This cannot be seen in isolation. It was part of a much larger shift, one which is still going on, from what Habermas has identified as a 'conventional identity', based on a sense of belonging to a territorial or national group, to a 'post-conventional identity', based on a much more complex and potentially challenging relationship with history.[9] If we relate this to music, it means a sense of identity based not on a presumption of a kinship with a national music, but on a recognition of the very notion of a 'national music' as something constructed and open to challenge.

This shift in Germany has not been smooth, continuous or unidirectional, but has moved at different speeds, and along different paths, amongst different parts of the population, sometimes being reversed and at other times moving rapidly forwards. The process continues as a now united Germany grapples with its position in the postmodern world. The French asserted after 1945 that the perception of German musical supremacy underpinned a broader claim to racial supremacy, but this demands qualification. For some Germans, particularly those involved in music, a

---

7   Albrecht Riethmüller, '"Is That Not Something for *Simplicissimus*?!" The Belief in Musical Superiority', in Applegate and Potter, *Music and German National Identity*, 288–304.

8   See Toby Thacker, '"Gesungen oder musiziert wird aber fast in jedem Haus": Representing and Constructing Citizenship through Music in Twentieth-Century Germany', in Geoff Eley and Jan Palmowski (eds), *Citizenship and National Identity in Twentieth-Century Germany* (Stanford: Stanford University Press, forthcoming).

9   See the discussion of these terms in Eric Santner, *Stranded Objects: Mourning, Memory, and Film in Postwar Germany* (Ithaca and London: Cornell University Press, 1990).

perception of musical supremacy was undoubtedly at the heart of a wider perception of human relations. For others, music may not in itself have been of such great significance. Equally, for many Germans after 1945, the Allied programme of 'Music Control' was not the most important or influential aspect of foreign occupation. It is clear, though, that music played an enormously important symbolic role in the re-education project, and in the transition from the dictatorship of the 'Third Reich' to the pluralistic society of the Federal Republic. In this sense, the internationalisation of music in post-war Germany can be seen to have made a significant and lasting contribution to the creation of a new society.

'Our Soviet Friends'

From the Soviet perspective, it makes more sense to ask how far their musical hopes for Germany in 1948 were realised by 1955. Their plans for musical reconstruction in 1945 were ill-defined, to say the least. Since they made their demand for a thorough politicisation of music in early 1948, though, they should have been well pleased with the results. Music in the GDR had been energetically developed by an intelligent and dedicated core of activists, who exploited some of the best living German musicians and ensembles to create an extraordinary fusion of traditional Lutheran choral singing, orchestral music and a new doctrine of 'contemporary realism'.

A comparison between the evolution of this musical culture and that of the Soviet Union itself in the period immediately after the Revolution in 1917 is revealing. Unlike the Soviet Union, the music of the GDR did not go through an experimental phase, but was plunged immediately into a theoretical orthodoxy of great rigidity. Particularly striking is the way that this orthodoxy was articulated and policed by the activist core within the SED, independently of the Soviet Union. There was, in the GDR's musical life, a kind of ritualised obeisance, expressed in exaggerated praise for Soviet performers and composers, and also in deference to Soviet judgement on sensitive musical issues. Thus, when Meyer and Eisler debated privately their views of Schoenberg in 1951, Eisler qualified his defence of his former teacher by saying: 'Our Soviet friends have the historic and moral right to speak clearly and sharply about such a great man as Schoenberg.'[10]

More significant, though, is the great scarcity of Soviet documents relating to music in the central SED archives, and the lack of reference in the German documents there to individual Soviet demands or recommendations. This independence is shown in the critical decision to prohibit further performances of the Brecht/Dessau opera *Lukullus* in March 1951, which, notwithstanding its implications for other areas of the arts like stage design and literature, set a clear *ne plus ultra* for composers. This decision was not pre-empted or suggested by the Soviets. The SED musicians, Meyer, Knepler, Notowicz and Goldschmidt, came to the decision to censor the

---

10   SAAdK, Hanns-Eisler-Archiv Korrespondenz, 113, Eisler to Meyer, 27 August 1951.

music independently, and were prepared to overrule esteemed colleagues on the matter. That included figures such as Eisler, who disagreed with them, and potential allies from outside the GDR like Hermann Scherchen, who had cooperated closely with Brecht and Dessau, and had already conducted the historic first performances of the opera before it was banned. Meyer and his colleagues, with their international connections, were at this time acutely conscious of the way this decision would be construed in the capitalist West – as an act of crude political censorship. Nonetheless, they took the decision to censor, and accepted the consequences.[11]

In the next four years, the SED musicians, the émigrés now working with old KPD fighters like Hartig and with new recruits like Pischner and Uszkoreit, had no need of supervision or encouragement from the Soviets. Even during the turbulent months after Stalin's death in March 1953, the SED musicians held firm. They used the structural and ideological repositioning of the Party after 17 June primarily to strengthen and extend their hegemony. By early 1954, they were arguably maintaining a stance of greater ideological purity than the Soviets themselves. It is fascinating to see how Meyer's group reacted to Kruschev's speech at the 20th Party Congress in Moscow in 1956. Anxiously, they met in Meyer's flat in Berlin with Paul Wandel to discuss the implications this had for music in the GDR, and agreed not to relax the demand for 'realism'.[12] In the next few months, they conducted a renewed ideological offensive.[13] After the revolution in Hungary, Notowicz travelled to Budapest to see what material and moral help the VDK could give to pro-Soviet Hungarian composers. In 1961, no fewer than five GDR composers wrote music to celebrate what Meyer called the 'necessary measures' of 13 August, that is to say the building of the Berlin Wall.[14]

No Soviet ideologue could have asked for greater commitment or more energetic engagement. And herein lay the seeds of the failure of the SED's musical ideology. Meyer, Knepler, Rebling and Notowicz, throughout the 1950s went further than the Soviets demanded. They also went further than their own convictions, pushed by their own idealism and dedication to the Party. They developed the SED's musical politics in a climate of Soviet anti-Semitism, xenophobia and narrow-mindedness that was actually profoundly foreign to them. At a number of levels, they were pushed into dishonesty and insincerity, becoming in the process habituated to a way of thinking that George Orwell had presciently characterised as 'doublethink'. The resulting

---

11   SAAdK Ernst-Hermann-Meyer-Archiv, 565, Ueber 'Das Verhör des Lukullus', 12 March 1951. In this document, Meyer suggests that Eisler agreed with himself, Notowicz, Knepler, and Goldschmidt. Knepler told me that Eisler did *not* agree with the decision to censor. Interview with the author, May 2001.

12   See SAAdK Hans-Pischner-Archiv, 1118, 'Meine Jahre im MfK', p. 25.

13   See the articles relating to this in the January, February, and March 1957 issues of *Musik und Gesellschaft*, above all Rebling's editorial 'Zwischen Dogmatismus und Modernismus', *MuG*, 1957/2, p. 66, and the transcript of Notowicz' speech to a VDK conference in February, 'Wo stehen wir heute?', *MuG*, 1957/3, pp. 129–134.

14   See SAAdK Ernst-Hermann-Meyer Archiv, 507, 'Warum waren Maßnahmen d. Reg. seit 13.8. nötig?'

tension is immediately apparent when reading SED documents about music from the 1950s, or a journal like *Musik und Gesellschaft* from the same period; it was, of course, apparent to many observers even then. It is undoubtedly the reason why the ideological music of the GDR was, and is, to this day, regarded with so much suspicion.

It is interesting to see how these tensions unravelled. Hartig died in 1962, and it is not known whether he reconsidered any of his acts since 1945 in his final years. Uszkoreit defected to the Federal Republic in 1975.[15] In the 1980s, Pischner wrote his memoirs, distancing himself from the worst excesses of Zhdanovism in the GDR's music, including the decision to censor *Lukullus*.[16] Rebling, in the 1990s, made an effort to disassociate himself from some of his most extreme pronunciations – notably the rabid article about music he wrote for the SED's theoretical journal *Einheit* in May 1953.[17] Ernst Hermann Meyer lived until 1988. Although as a composer his influence in the GDR waned after 1956, when younger composers turned increasingly to Eisler and Dessau for models, he played an important role in public life almost until the collapse of the GDR. In 1981, he was appointed a full member of the SED's Central Committee. The ceremony held in the State Opera in October 1988 to commemorate his life and work was one of the last set-piece expressions of GDR culture and ideology.[18] The nearest Meyer came to a public recantation was the following passage, written for a conference in 1981: 'Much has been spoken about a certain one-sidedness and impatience which dominated the cultural politics of the 1950s ... but the impatience and the exaggerations or injustices practised then lasted only a few years.'[19] We should remember that Meyer had in 1953 publicly called for the 'extermination' of the GDR's enemies.

Meyer's guarded reference in 1981 to 'exaggerations' and 'injustices' that lasted for 'only a few years' draws our attention to another significant point. By 1955, the GDR's attempt to construct a distinctive, German, socialist musical culture had largely failed. This failure could not be conceded then; indeed it could not be conceded fully until after 1989, but it is clear to us now. As we have seen, in 1948, the SED's musicians defiantly embarked on the construction of a musical culture that

---

15   Zur Weihen, *Komponieren*, p. 57, fn. 217.

16   Noting that he did not take part in the discussions about *Lukullus*, Pischner described the decision to ban the opera as 'musically, an absolutely mistaken judgement'. On the Zhdanov decree he wrote: 'Here stylistic means were made into the sole criterion for artistic judgement, and an unfruitful, absolutist crusade against atonality, dissonance, and disharmony was waged ... A difficult time of searching, and also of doubt began.' SAAdK Hans-Pischner-Archiv, 1118, 'Meine Jahre im MfK', pp. 50–53.

17   See zur Weihen, *Komponieren*, pp. 108–9. A draft of Rebling's article 'Situation und Perspektive unseres Musiklebens', dated October 1952, is in SAPMO-BArch DY 30/IV 2/9.06/284.

18   See 'Bewegende Trauerfeier für Genossen Ernst Hermann Meyer', *Neues Deutschland*, 14 October 1988.

19   SAAdK Ernst-Hermann-Meyer-Archiv, 304, Musik in der DDR von 1949 bis 1961 – Reinschrift VKM, November 1981.

would admit of no compromise with contemporary developments in the capitalist world. It rejected the trend towards dissonance, atonality and serialism, and the use of electronic instruments to generate new 'rationalised' sounds. It rejected an increasing specialisation, and demanded instead the abolition of the gap between performer and listener, calling for a new ideal of citizenship in which all would be active musicians. It rejected the idea of 'autonomous' music, and celebrated the connections between music and society. It demanded that composers identify with, and give expression to, the 'building of socialism'. It reconstructed music history, casting the 'great composers' as humanist pioneers who had sought to articulate the emancipatory instincts of the progressive classes of their time. Accepting a degree of censorship as a necessary evil, the GDR attempted to prevent the performance of westernised popular music, and to create a 'socialist' or 'realistic' popular music in its place. In the creation of this new culture, the GDR unashamedly challenged the liberal conception of music as 'apolitical' and used the state apparatus to 'guide' and 'control' the musical life of the country. The period between August 1951 and June 1953, when *Stakuko* was given responsibility for this regulation, can be identified as the most intense phase of conflict between the SED's ideals and the pressures from the capitalist West.

With the benefit of hindsight, it is clear that although the SED never openly or fully abandoned its ambitious programme, it gradually accepted ever more compromise, and turned from rejection of western influences to a policy of co-option. We have seen how this was reluctantly done with dance music; this created a pattern that was followed as successive waves of Anglo-American popular music came to the GDR. By the 1970s, the GDR's Academy of the Arts even had a 'Rock Music Section'. As early as 1957, GDR's Radio Berlin was broadcasting a talk on 'Developments in Electronic Music'. By the 1960s, it was supporting its own 'new music' groups, and publicly making a virtue of sponsoring music that ten years previously had been condemned as 'formalist', 'cosmopolitan' or even as 'manifestations of degeneration'.[20] Similarly, although efforts to write 'realist' music continued after 1955, we can see now that the effort to create a new 'national', 'realist', and popular music, exemplified in the party oratorios and cantatas of the early 1950s, had failed. We need to make an exemption for one area. The GDR had set out to construct a musical culture in which all citizens would be active as performers and listeners, and to break down the traditional barriers that had previously restricted involvement with 'serious music' to an educated middle class. It was by no means totally successful in this, but it has been generally conceded, even by critics of the GDR, that more of the working classes there did perform and listen to opera and traditional concerts than in the Federal Republic.

Georg Knepler discussed these questions with me recently in Berlin, shortly before his death. Knepler's formative years as a young adult were spent in Vienna – one of the great centres of German-speaking musical culture before 1938 – and

---

20   See Frank Schneider, *Momentaufnahme: Notate zu Musik und Musikern in der DDR* (Leipzig: Philipp Reclam jun., 1979).

he became a close friend of Meyer's in Britain in the 1930s. In 1946, he returned to Austria, but from 1949 committed himself unreservedly to the SED; during the 1950s, and long after, he could be relied upon to support the Party line. More recently, Knepler witnessed the collapse of the GDR, and the consigning of its culture to the dustbin of history in a re-united Germany. Knepler told me that the ideals he and Meyer had worked for in the GDR were good, but that the means used were frequently wrong. He highlighted as errors a whole range of decisions, from such broad policies as the restrictions placed by the GDR on its citizens travelling abroad, to such specifically musical issues as the repression of jazz in the 1950s, and the SED's support for so many opera houses. The Zhdanov decree, he said, had been 'a catastrophe'. Knepler also discussed Meyer with me in great detail. He said that he had spoken with Meyer's eldest daughter after her father's death in 1988. Meyer apparently said to her, in the last weeks of his life, 'I have made a mistake'.[21]

Fifty Years On

Where do the two musical cultures stand now, fifteen years after the *Wende*? On the surface, that of the Federal Republic appears to have triumphed completely. The GDR's music, along with its other institutions and ideals, has almost completely disappeared. The SED's musical organisations, such as the VDK and the *Kulturbund*, were disbanded in 1990. *Musik und Gesellschaft* ceased publication at the same time. The fading luxury of opera houses in towns like Chemnitz is a last physical reminder of the SED's commitment to high culture. The material documenting the activities of *Stakuko*, the MfK, and the VDK was subsequently transferred to the Federal Archive, where most of it is now open to researchers. The VDK's Music Information Centre, which includes many historic sound recordings, was moved to the German Music Archive in Zehlendorf. The Academy's huge collection of workers' songs is still housed at the Robert-Koch-Platz in Berlin. Tourists, and those in search of *Ostalgie*, can rifle through the flea markets of Berlin for old *Amiga* and *Eterna* records, or for fading copies of the GDR's literature on music. As the GDR's recording industry was so backward and incompetent in the early 1950s, recordings from that period are particularly difficult to find, even in specialist second-hand record shops in Berlin.

The outcome of decades of studied avoidance of GDR culture are certainly apparent outside Germany, notably in Britain – paradoxically the country which contributed so much to the GDR's musical culture.[22] Until very recently, a scholar in Britain interested in early GDR music would have been able to hear a few pieces by Eisler on CD, but would have had to visit the National Sound Archive in London to hear more. Even in a great national library like the Bodleian in Oxford, there

---

21   Interview with the author, May 2001.
22   See my essay, '"Something Different from the Hampstead Perspective": An Outline of Selected Musical Transactions between the British Left and the GDR', in Stefan Berger and Norman La Porte (eds), *The Other Germany: Perceptions and Influences in British-East German Relations, 1945–1990* (Augsburg: Wißner-Verlag, 2005), pp. 211–24.

are no copies of *Musik und Gesellschaft* from before 1957.[23] The BBC, which despite recent changes, still maintains a national radio station dedicated to what the Germans call 'serious music', never broadcasts music composed by SED activists. It is difficult to believe that these absences are purely accidental. They result from a Cold War determination to avoid any engagement with Marxist culture.[24] The situation is slowly changing in Germany. There are one or two record companies that have issued recordings of GDR music from the 1950s, and in 2004, RCA started to issue its huge *Musik in Deutschland 1950–2000* series, accompanied by a thorough documentation. This has now made recordings of much previously unheard music from the early Cold War period available to listeners in Germany and beyond.[25] There has, in recent years, been a growth of historical interest in the Communist societies of Central and Eastern Europe resulting from the opening of archives, and from a perception that these societies may have been more than pale reflections of the Soviet Union. There are academic researchers currently working on aspects of the GDR's music in Russia, Poland, Britain, and the USA, as well as in Germany.

There is one exception to this long-established picture of neglect: the GDR's performance of the classics. This is now a safe area of GDR culture to revisit, as it can be presented as something entirely independent from or even in active opposition to SED-inspired culture. As record companies and radio programmers jostle for market shares and niche audiences, they have realised that many of their archive recordings from the 1950s, for all their technical shortcomings, are of interest to connoisseurs today. There has been a spate of recently issued recordings from this period, and the exceptional quality of GDR performance of the classics has been noted. BBC Radio 3 has recently broadcast several performances of Beethoven, Haydn, and other classical composers recorded by the Dresden State Orchestra in the early 1950s.[26] The quality of choral singing from Leipzig and Dresden at this time is still admired by specialists, however much approaches to performance have changed. As the deeply ingrained prejudices and preconceptions of the Cold War gradually recede, musicians and audiences may get more opportunities to hear the SED's music and to judge it for themselves.

---

23   There are, in contrast, complete collections of several West German musical journals from the early 1950s in the Bodleian Library.

24   Ironically, Meyer himself sent a tape of the *Mansfelder Oratorium* to the British Peace Committee, which made efforts to get it heard by 'several of the leading people in the musical world'. SAAdK Ernst-Hermann-Meyer-Archiv, Korrespondenz bis 1951, Duncan-Jones to Meyer, 19 July 1951. From other letters in this archive it is clear that a recording of the *Mansfelder Oratorium* was played to a small audience in Britain in 1951, and again in early 1952.

25   For fuller details see www.deutscher-musikrat.de/mid/.

26   Perhaps the BBC had seen the letter sent by Willibald Roth from the Detmold Music Academy to Hartig in 1953: 'Send the Dresden State Orchestra as an ambassador to the Federal Republic, and you will have a great propaganda success for the GDR.' SAPMO-BArch DR 1/286, Roth to Hartig, 14 June 1953.

What of German musical culture since 1990? At first glance, it seems to be thriving. The casual observer or visitor to any German city today would be struck by the number and variety of musical performances on offer to the public. The music scene there is strikingly international. Former British music officers like Brian Dunn cannot have imagined, in 1945 or 1946, that the Berlin Philharmonic's principal conductor would in future be British, or that British musicians like John Eliot Gardiner and Nicholas McGegan would be seen in Germany as leading interpreters of Bach and Handel. Even the ghosts that dogged the German jazz scene and the place of popular music in German culture have been laid to rest. German towns, which after 1945 seemed like fortresses of reaction when Music Officers gave talks on modern American music, now host jazz festivals, and Germany has become a centre for the latest developments in electronic dance music. The old lines between *E-Musik* and *U-Musik* have become ever more blurred.

The vagaries of public reception mean that knowledge and appreciation of post-war West German composers has changed. Of the composers who dominated West German music between 1945 and 1955, only Orff is well known outside Germany today. Fortner and Egk are almost unheard of, although Hartmann is enjoying something of a revival. Some, like Pepping, are known in Germany, but not beyond. Many others, like Blacher, Tiessen, and Rufer, have disappeared almost without trace. The avant-garde, that is to say Henze and Stockhausen, has its place in cultural mythology, even if its actual music is very little known. Henze's opera *Boulevard Solitude*, premiered in Hamburg in 1952, which the SED called 'Boulevard of Darkness', was recently revived in London, and broadcast on BBC Radio 3.[27] This avant-garde has been condemned for taking contemporary music into a cul-de-sac, and in a way nothing symbolises this better than the fate of the NWDR's original electronic studio in Cologne, where Stockhausen worked. The studio is now unused, and one by one, the technicians who could operate it have died. The renamed WDR is not sure what to do with this piece of musical and technological history. Perhaps the studio will end up like the Bavarian Radio studio now exhibited in the German Museum in Munich, its bulky oscilloscopes, tape recorders and sine wave generators looking like something from a *Quatermass* film from the same period.

What of the legacy of Nazism, which was omnipresent in German musical culture after 1945? In one sense, the direct confrontation with Nazism in German music has passed: those who were active in musical life between 1933 and 1945, and had connections with Nazism, have died, or retired from public life. The controversies which occasionally surface in Germany now, like that around the conductor Christian Thielemann, have a slightly contrived air.[28] There is not the urgency that once attached to the continued public prominence of Furtwängler, Gieseking or Karajan.

---

27   Henze, the SED conceded, was 'astonishingly talented in the representation of ugliness in his musical language'. Karl Schönewolf, 'Boulevard der Finsternis', *MuG*, 1952/4, pp. 144–5, quote from p. 144.

28   See Steven Moss, '"What has C sharp minor got to do with fascism?"', *The Guardian*, 4 January 2000.

In another sense, though, the confrontation is only just beginning. The long years of silence and denial have only recently been broken, and there are still many myths to be exploded, many deliberate omissions to fill, and distortions to correct. The groundbreaking work of recent historians has raised as many new questions as it has answered. The culture of denial that developed in both Germanys after 1949 has created new layers of deception, which need to be stripped away.

Perhaps the most bizarre aspect of this is how the Allies themselves contributed, and still contribute, to this culture of denial. This culture depended for its success on a suppression of evidence. To examine how it gained ground after 1949, and was spread from Germany to the English-speaking world, we need to look at the fate of the archival records, which alone might reliably underpin scholarly analysis of the connections between music and Nazism. There are two collections of particular importance here. The first is that of the documents of the Nazi Party itself, which were captured in 1945 by the Americans. These documents include not only the central and regional card-indexes of the NSDAP, which provide evidence about individual Party membership, but also the records of many NSDAP associations, and government bodies like the Reich Research Council and the Reich Education Ministry, which sponsored research in the Nazi period. Significant groups of NSDAP records, which would have exposed many musical connections, like those of the HJ, did not apparently survive the war. The second critical collection of documents was that of the Reich Chamber of Culture. As we know, the British discovered this archive in Berlin in 1945, and used it over the next three years for denazification. During this period, the staff involved attached correspondence and reports about individuals to the existing personnel files, in a rather haphazard way. By 1949, therefore, when the British decided that these files should be made available to other 'Allied nations' that had an interest in them, they constituted not only a valuable source of information about the Nazi era, but also about post-war denazification processes – particularly those of the British and Americans. In 1949, the collection was transferred to the Berlin Document Center, run by the Americans, where it joined the other captured NSDAP collections.

Despite many reservations, mainly about the practical difficulties of storage and preservation, the Reich Chamber of Culture archive, complete with many attached British and American documents, was kept at the Berlin Document Center for the next forty years. In 1955, a new collection of some 28,000 British 'screening reports' on 'personalities in the public information media in the former British Zone of Germany' was added.[29] During the 1950s and 1960s, if private researchers were granted access to the RKK files, the attached post-war British and American documents were personally removed by the Center's Director, and 'secured in a locked cabinet' in his office, to be re-attached once the documents were returned by

---

29   I am grateful to Astrid Eckert for this information. A fuller account of the postwar fate of captured Nazi archives is given in her *Kampf um die Akten. Die Westalliierten und die Rückgabe von deutschem Archivgut nach dem Zweiten Weltkrieg* (Stuttgart: Steiner, 2004) .

the researcher.[30] The vast collection of material in the Berlin Document Center was put on microfilm, which was stored in the American National Archive; the original documents were returned to the custody of the Federal German Republic in 1994, but even the custodians of this material have only a limited understanding of it. When I enquired about the 28,000 British 'screening reports' added in 1955, I was told that the Federal Archive knew nothing about these. If they still exist as a discrete collection, they await detailed scrutiny. The American National Archives have helpfully indicated that amongst their microfilm collections of documents relating to the former Reich Chamber of Culture there are many postwar British documents, but states that 'we have no means of accounting for or identifying a discreet series of 28,000 items'.[31]

Thus, much vital information about the post-war investigations into individual musicians has been kept secret. The extensive documentation of the British occupation of Germany in the National Archive in London says very little about the denazification of musicians. All documents relating to individuals have been stripped from the French files in Colmar, and access to them has to be secured from the Ministry of Foreign Affairs in Paris. Within Germany itself, personal protection laws mean that access to many *Spruchkammer* files is limited. Many other documents that might illuminate these matters are in private hands, and not open to researchers. As a result, it is still very difficult to find out about the actions of individual musicians in Germany between 1933 and 1945, and also to establish how much post-war Allied investigators knew about them.

Much of the information on denazification presented in this book is garnered from individual documents which appear to have ended up in the wrong file, or to have been overlooked when other similar documents were removed, either to be destroyed or kept secure from prying eyes. In some cases, handwritten marginalia or allusions to other documents have provided the only evidence of investigations that were conducted, or that facts long considered unknown to the Allies were in fact known to particular investigators. Clearly, after 1949, the western Allies did not want this can of worms opened. It would not have been helpful to have permitted or encouraged investigations of connections between individual musicians and musicologists and Nazism – particularly at a time when the cultural life of the Federal Republic was being reconstructed as an apolitical sphere. We should be clear that the culture of denial relating to Nazism and music was, therefore, not a purely German construction. It was in fact, after 1949, actively aided and abetted by the British, French and Americans. There was, of course, a similar process in the East. The Soviets did not capture such significant collections of Nazi-era records in 1945, but they did find enormous amounts of compromising material – not least

---

30   British and US Documents in the Reichskulturkammer files of BDC, undated. National Archives, College Park, Maryland, RG 242, BDC Administrative Records, BDC Directorate Files, 1976-94, Box 1. I am grateful to Astrid Eckert for this reference.

31   Amy Schmidt, Archivist, Modern Military Records, National Archives at College Park, personal correspondence, 23 October 2001.

thousands of cultural artefacts, including musical instruments, manuscripts, books, and other documents looted by the Rosenberg organisation and stored in eastern Germany, away from British and American bombing. It is impossible to know with any precision how much archival material relating to Nazi Germany is still in the former Soviet Union.

It is in this sense that a genuine engagement with the issues of music, Nazism and denazification is now only beginning. The researchers who have started to explore previously closed or unknown archival sources have opened up areas for future work. To give just two examples: Willem de Vries has explored the activities of Rosenberg's *Sonderstab Musik* in Western Europe, causing great scandal in Germany. What will emerge from similar researches into musical plundering in Eastern Europe? Pamela Potter has hinted at the continuities in German musicology after 1945, and it is clear that this is a fruitful area for further research. Both Potter and de Vries have raised questions about the wartime origins of that monument of post-war German musicology, *Musik in Geschichte und Gegenwart*, and it is unlikely that these questions will go away. Nor is it clear why the Nazi affiliations and precise activities of individual musicians should be protected. In no meaningful sense are these matters any longer *sub judice*. Nor is there any consistency here. Material reserved by one archive, or protected by law there, may be openly available elsewhere. Nazi affiliations and activities, both greater and smaller, are in many other cases open for historical debate. A recent issue of the English language journal *German History* carries one article exploring the case of Ilse Koch, wife of the commandant of Buchenwald, and another which analyses Nazi affiliation and support in Oberammergau, naming ordinary villagers who were Party members and officials.[32] Why, apart from reasons of personal convenience, should a composer, conductor, musician, or musicologist be more privileged than any of them?

It might be argued that there has been enough raking through the ashes. Successive generations in Germany have wrestled in different ways with their 'unmasterable past'. Many would argue that no useful purpose is served by ever more detailed and obscure enquiries into collaboration and complicity with Nazism, whether these are conceived as judicial enquiries to determine issues of guilt or innocence, empirical investigations to uncover institutional and personal histories in the Third Reich, or in the wider sense of developing a postconventional or postmodern sense of German (and larger European) identity, as explored by many theorists, artists and historians since 1945. As long as this last project remains unfulfilled, two images of music will insistently push to the forefront of debate. The first is the ubiquitous presence of music in the 'Third Reich'. It is, after all, difficult to imagine Hitler's Germany without music, even if that music is imagined stereotypically as either Wagner, the *Horst-Wessel-Lied*, or the tragic pieces of Beethoven and Bruckner that decorated

---

32   See Alexandra Przyrembel, 'Transfixed by an Image: Ilse Koch, the "Kommandeuse of Buchenwald"', *German History*, 19:3 (2001), pp. 369–99, and Helen Waddy, 'Beyond Statistics to Microhistory: The Role of Migration and Kinship in the Making of the Nazi Constituency', *Ibid.*, pp. 340–68.

Nazi ceremonies and consoled concentration camp commanders at the end of the working day. Music, with its indefinable associations, is indelibly associated with all aspects of Nazism.[33]

As for a post-war German identity, or any German identity for that matter, how can it be imagined without music? We have seen how important Bach was in the reconstruction of a symbolic order in both the Federal Republic and the GDR in 1950. Stronger and more pervasive as a symbol is the image, so powerfully developed by Edgar Reiz in his *Heimat* films, of the postwar avant-garde. It is not coincidental that this abstract music has always served as a symbol – again poorly defined – for a reconstructed German spirit, held in opposition to both the materialism and artistic reaction of the Federal Republic and the bureaucratic state tyranny of the GDR.[34] If, though, we locate Darmstadt within these two political contexts, should we not mention that Darmstadt was also dominated initially by artists who had worked for the Nazis?[35]

In 1943, Hermann Hesse's novel *Magister Ludi* was published in Zurich. It subsequently came to be better known as *Das Glasperlenspiel*, and later in the English-speaking world as *The Glass Bead Game*. Hesse's book, portraying an austere future society, Castalia, was read after 1945 by influential German musicians on both sides of the 'Iron Curtain'. Musicians as ideologically opposed as the avant-gardist Stockhausen and the harpsichordist and Deputy Minister for Culture Hans Pischner have testified to the profound impact it had on their thinking. Hesse imagined a society in which music played a central role:

> ... there exists an ancient and honourable exemplar for the attitude of our own culture towards music ... we recall that in the legendary China of the Old Kings, music was accorded a dominant place in state and court. It was held that if music throve, all was well

---

33   One thinks in this context not only of the presence of music in so many accounts, by both perpetrators and victims, of the concentration camps, but also of the salient role that music has played in many cinematic representations of the Holocaust. The opposition of the sublime music of Bach or Beethoven to the horror of genocide has become an enduring symbol of the paradoxes of Nazism, and in some extensions of this, of 'modernity' more generally.

34   This convoluted statement in Borusio and Danuser is representative of the many which hold that Darmstadt represented an oppositional tendency in the early Federal Republic, and that its existence, therefore, signified something important about the West German state: 'Especially in a time of East-West confrontation, or rather during the so-called "Cold War", politically, and not merely in terms of cultural politics, the Darmstadt Summer Schools represent also directly through their opposition to the prevailing cultural currents of the Adenauer era the freedom of this form of state.' Borio and Danuser, *Im Zenit der Moderne*, *Band I*, p. 26.

35   This is not discussed in the latest English-language contribution to debate on Darmstadt, Gesa Kordes, 'Darmstadt, Postwar Experimentation, and the West German Search for a New Musical Identity', Applegate and Potter, *Music and German National Identity*, pp. 205–17.

with culture and morality and with the kingdom itself ... if music decayed, that was taken as a sure sign of the downfall of the regime and the state.

Hesse's future society had abandoned any attempt to compete with the past, recognising the period between the fifteenth and the eighteenth centuries as the supreme age of musical achievement: 'we have renounced – on the whole, at any rate – trying to vie creatively with those generations'. [36] Later, he wrote: 'We consider classical music to be the epitome and quintessence of our culture, because it is that culture's clearest, most significant gesture and expression.'[37] While we can identify the post-war musical cultures of both East and West Germany with aspects of Hesse's vision – both, notably, supported and revered the seventeenth- and eighteenth-century composers so esteemed by Hesse – there is something more distinctly Castalian in the austerity of the GDR's approach. Its high-minded promotion of Bach, Handel and other early composers, its cultivation of what are now called 'authentic' styles of performance, its emphasis on scholarship, and its horrified rejection of jazz, rock and sentimentality, accord with Hesse's ascetic vision. We know that Hesse was publicly identified with the pluralism and clericalism of the West, and certainly not with the Party regime of the East, but the SED's approach to music did have some correspondence with Hesse's values.

This is the most significant feature of the early GDR's musical culture. While the Federal Republic moved, unwillingly perhaps, into postmodernity – that is, towards a recognition of difference and a breakdown of traditional understandings of nation and culture – the GDR tried to create a 'national', 'socialist', culture that had its own distinct values, and in which music was of central importance. Ernst Hermann Meyer provides an interesting and revealing testimony. Here was a man who had built a successful reputation in Britain as an academic and a broadcaster. All his close relatives in Germany had been murdered by the Nazis. He had married an Englishwoman, and could have stayed in Britain and pursued a secure and potentially fruitful career there after 1945. He chose, instead, to return to the Soviet Zone of Germany, and to commit himself to the building of a new society. In the early years of the GDR, Meyer was constantly busy, composing, writing and giving advice to diverse organisations on matters musical. He found time to keep in touch with old friends from his time of exile, frequently describing in glowing terms the pleasure of working in a society where music was considered so important. He wrote to one, now in Mexico, in December 1952: '... I can only say that here in our German Democratic Republic, all the dreams, which one had as a young man, and all of the plans which one made then, are being fulfilled. ... We [musicians] are a real factor in national life here.'[38]

In their own way, the occupiers of Germany, between 1945 and 1949, also shared Hesse's conviction that music, along with the other arts, was essential to a healthy

---

36   Hesse, *The Glass Bead Game*, p. 30.

37   *Ibid.*, p. 40.

38   SAAdK, Ernst-Hermann-Meyer-Archiv, Korrespondenz 1952 M, Meyer to Mayer-Serra, 23 December 1952.

society. They too had a commitment to high culture that went largely unquestioned. We have seen how they eschewed the promotion of jazz. In this, they had much in common with the German musicians and politicians whom they allowed to work on the reconstruction of music in Germany after 1945. They also imposed a set of values that demanded tolerance and a commitment to freedom of artistic expression. In the west of Germany, these values were written into the constitution of 1949 and, although at times with reluctance, have been embedded in social attitudes since. By 1955, the exposure to not only contemporary international composers but also to jazz, swing and bebop was starting to erode the previously hard frontier in Germany between 'serious music' and 'entertainment music'. If a central feature of postmodernity is the dissolution of previous centres and a resultant coming to terms with differing categories of otherness, then in musical terms the post-war period may be seen in Germany as its onset. We can see a lingering effort in the GDR after 1955 to cling to the values of an older world, but the monastic conviction of the early years had gone. For along with the certainties of modernism had gone the conviction that a society was measured by, and understood through, its music. It is impossible to imagine a book like Hesse's carrying anything like the same resonance after 1955.

The officials, musicians, and soldiers who instituted 'Music Control' in Germany after 1945 certainly did not have a vision of postmodern diversity at the forefront of their minds when they first set up their offices in the semi-ruined cities of Germany, but they challenged the certainties which had underpinned music under Hitler and before. Previous writers have stressed the continuity between the post-war German music scene and that under Hitler. It is not hard to find striking examples of such continuity in terms of the people who dominated that scene, the music they played and they way they understood it. How could it have been otherwise? While not minimising the strength or significance of musical continuities before and after 1945, the onset of Allied occupation clearly represents a fissure in the musical history of Germany. The post-war period, and its extension in the GDR until 1989, can be seen as a transition, partly enforced, partly welcomed and partly resisted from within. In the early twenty-first century, when even the collapse of the GDR seems to have occurred in a different era, that transition period seems far distant. The ten years after Hitler's death and the end of the 'Third Reich' are probably the last time when music really mattered in Germany.

Bibliography and Sources

(1) UNPUBLISHED SOURCES

Bundesarchiv, Außenstelle Berlin

Abteilung Reich (ehem. BDC)
Reichskulturkammer

Abendroth H, RKK 2300/0001/05
Blume F, RKK 2703/0020/33
Butting M, RKK 2003/0011/17, RKK 2300/0021/20, RKK 2701/0003/11
Dammert U, RKK 2703/0037/31
Eimert H, RKK 2101/0262/14
Gieseking W, RKK 2300/0053/14, RKK 2702/0004/09, RKK 2703/0068/22
Jochum E, RKK 2300/0085/16, RKK 2667/0014/57,
    RKK 2702/0006/12, RKK 2703/0108/08
Keilberth J, RKK 2302/0052/14
von Knorr L, RKK 2703/0122/45
Konwitschny H, RKK 2703/0127/27
Müller E, RKK 2101/0872/06
Ramin G, RKK 2215/0008/33, RKK 2300/0147/15, RKK 2701/0015/69
Schmidt-Isserstedt H, RKK 2236/0095/04, RKK
    2702/0010/44, RKK 2703/0241/46
Wüst P, RKK 2300/0218/17

Ministerium für Kultur (DR 1)

Hauptabteilung Musik
7, 20, 34, 40, 41, 49, 66, 80, 81, 111, 141, 154, 161, 178, 212, 213, 215, 219,
    230, 232, 232a, 236, 237, 241, 243, 286, 288, 291, 323, 335, 340, 383, 462

Staatliche Kommission für Kunstangelegenheiten
240, 5831, 5843, 5934, 5943, 6133, 6137, 6192

Staatliches Rundfunkkomitee (DR 6)1

Stiftung Archiv der Parteien und Massenorganisationen der DDR im Bundesarchiv, Außenstelle Berlin

SED (DY 30)

Beschlüsse Politbüro
IV 2/2/ … 44, 54, 55, 73, 76, 98, 102

Abteilung Kultur des ZK
IV 2/9.06/ … 70, 202, 279, 284, 285, 286, 287, 291, 293, 294

Kaderfragen
IV 2/11/v. 710, 2626, 5404, 5433

Protokolle der Sitzungen des Sekretariats des ZK
J IV 2/3/... (Reinschriftprotokolle)
067, 070, 074, 115

J IV 2/3 A/... (Arbeitsprotokolle)
51, 53, 57, 98, 152

Kulturbund der DDR (DY 27)
38, 46, 213, 215, 249, 315, 433, 702, 841, 911, 1083, 1180, 1281, 1404, 1530, 1567, 1568, 1599, 2751

Stiftung Archiv der Akademie der Künste, Berlin

Ernst-Hermann-Meyer-Archiv
205, 228, 304, 309, 385, 386, 308, 316, 319, 329, 419, 431, 439, 475, 507, 516, 565, 608, 631, 632, 633
Korrespondenz bis 1951

Hans-Pischner-Archiv
651, 658, 681, 682, 740, 839, 840, 847, 874, 1114, 1115, 1116, 1117, 1118

Hans-Heinz-Stuckenschmidt-Archiv
33, 470, 471, 472, 473, 474, 476, 477, 478

Hanns-Eisler-Archiv
Korrespondenz: 71, 113, 118, 119, 120, 121, 122, 131, 134, 376, 412, 413, 414, 415, 416, 801, 814, 818, 823, 824, 860, 874, 1146, 1147, 1148.
2152 (Tonband 02)

Heinz-Tiessen-Archiv
Korrespondenz: Db 1450–Kasten, Wilhelm Pieck, Deutscher Bachausschuß, Max
  Butting, Kulturbund zur demokratischen Erneuerung Deutschlands.

Max-Butting-Archiv
11.I.b.1, 11.I.b.2
11.IV.27, 11.V.27
II Korrespondenz: Mappe 1: 1920–1945
                           Mappe 2: 1952–1956
                           Mappe 12: Korrespondenz VDK und Büro für
                           Urheberrecht

BBC Written Archive, Caversham

RCONT 1, Ernst Hermann Meyer, Artist, File 1: 1931–1962
RCONT 1, Ernst Hermann Meyer, Composer, File 1: 1942–1962
RCONT 1, Ernst Hermann Meyer, Copyright, File 1: 1937–1952

By country; Germany:
E1/737, 738, 739, 753/1, 753/2, 753/3, 753/4, 755, 756, 757, 758/2, 769, 802,
E15/81, 87

Music:
R27/68
R46/503
R47/121/1

British Library, London

Alan Bush Papers

**Centre des Archives de l'Occupation Française en Allemagne et en Autriche,
Colmar**

Archives de l'Occupation française en Allemagne, Mission Culturelle en
  Allemagne
Direction Générale des Affaires Culturelles
AC 28/2
AC 332/1
AC 486/3
AC 490/7, 8
AC 501/3

AC 505/3, 8
AC 508/5
AC 519/2, 3
AC 524/2
AC 526/2
AC 528/5
AC 594/5, 7
AC 595/8
AC 596/1
AC 600/4, 5

Affaires Culturelles
AC 827/3

Relations Intellectuelles et du Livre
AC 845/4
AC 857/5
AC 919/13, 14
AC 939/4
AC 1035

Berlin, Groupe Française du Conseil de Contrôle
Division de l'Information
Caisse 102/3
Caisse 107/3
Caisse 108/1, 2, 3
Caisse 113/4
Caisse 131/3, 5, p. 5

Archives Orales
AOR 10/1a, 1b
AOR 15/1a

Nordrhein-Westfälisches Hauptstaatsarchiv, Düsseldorf

NW 60: Kultus Ministerium, Abteilung III, Kunst- und Kulturpflege
339, 348, 358, 805, 849, 851, 861, 871, 885, 891

BR: Bezirke Regierungen
1047, 24302

Stadtarchiv Düsseldorf

IV 1763, 2528, 2529, 5877
XXIII 431, 652
XXIV 1643
XXXIII 503

Stadtarchiv, Göttingen

III HL 52, III B 146, Sammlung 5: 'Bach-Fest 1950', Kulturamt Nr.189.

The National Archive (formerly the Public Record Office), London

Foreign Office (FO)

FO 371: General Correspondence, Political
46748, 55432, 55580, 55513, 55633, 55798, 55876, 64322, 64323, 70706, 70716, 76524, 76525, 84975, 84891

Control Office for Germany and Austria (COGA)

FO 898: Political Warfare Executive and Foreign Office Political Intelligence Department Papers
401

FO 936: German Section
124, 125, 290, 291, 292,

FO 938: German Section, Private office
134

FO 945: General Department
217, 905

FO 946: Information Services Department
8, 30, 57

Control Commission for Germany (British Element)

FO 1005: Records Library
739, 831, 832, 1803, 1943

FO 1010: Regional Commissioners, Lower Saxony Region

44, 45, 93

FO 1012: Regional Commissioners, Berlin
166

FO 1013: Regional Commissioners, Nordrhein-Westphalen
1895, 1903, 1904, 1912

FO 1030: HQ SHAEF, Special Echelon, and Military Government HQ
379, 380

FO 1032: Military Sections and Headquarters Secretariat
759B

FO 1049: Political Division
71, 84, 274, 485, 1095, 1877

FO 1050: Internal Affairs and Communications Division
337, 794, 1171, 1181, 1217, 1233, 1279, 1344, 1345, 1370, 1373, 1375, 1443

FO 1056: Public Relations and Information Services Group
20, 23, 26, 65, 76, 77, 147, 150, 151, 220, 253, 268, 296, 327, 330, 354, 438, 513,
517

Bundesarchiv, Koblenz

B105: Deutscher Städtetag, Verbindungsstelle Frankfurt/Main
2, 3, 4, 24, 192

B106: Bundesministerium des Innerns
119, 299, 1072, 1073, 1079, 1090,1326, 1327, 21457, 21462, 45000

B136: Bundeskanzleramt
479, 1904, 3008, 5815, 5899

B137: Ministerium für gesamtdeutsche Fragen
1850, 2305

B336: Deutsche UNESCO-Kommission
403

Z45 F: Office of Miltary Government, United States (OMGUS)

OMGUS Information Services Division, Film, Theater and Music Branch
5/244–1/27
5/244–2/18

OMGUS Information Services Division, Press and Publications Branch
5/245–1/25

OMGUS Information Services Division, C/F
5/260–2/4
5/261–3/22
5/264–1/9, 24
5/265–1/16

OMGUS Information Services Division, Director's Office
5/266–1/31
5/269–1/21

OMGUS Information Services Division, Radio Branch
5/349–1/5

OMGUS Control Office, Director's Office
5/362–1/6
5/364–1/7

OMGUS Control Office, Records and Statistics Branch
11/47–1/17

OMGUS, Office of the Director of Intelligence
7/34–3/1

Generallandesarchiv Karlsruhe

Office of Military Government, United States (OMGUS)
Control Office, Historical Branch
3/407–3/3

Office of Military Government, Wuerttemberg-Baden (OMGWB), Education and
    Cultural Relations Division
12/9–1/14

OMGWB, Information Control Division, Theater and Music Control Branch
12/89–3/5, 7, 8
12/90–3/1, 8

12/91–1/7, 9
12/91–2/7, 9, 10

OMGWB, Information Control Division
12/97–1/1
12/97–2/5

Spruchkammer records
465f/15, 465h/85, 481/398, 552/71, 552/80, 552/96

Westdeutscher Rundfunk-Historisches Archiv, Köln

4069, 4070, 4129, 4217, 4232, 5571, 5759, 7362, 9434, 9454, 9464, 10070, 10100,
   10289, 10365, 10659, 10929
D756, D836, D857, D883, D919, D1442, D1471

Institut für Zeitgeschichte, München

Dk 090.007, *Germany – Basic Handbook, Part II Administration* (1944)
Dk 190.011, Manual for the Control of German Information Services. 12 May
   1945.

Office of Military Government, United States (OMGUS)

OMGUS Allied Control Authority, United States Secretary,
2/96–2/8

OMGUS Civil Administration Division, Public Safety Branch,
3/166–1/13

OMGUS Historical Division,
3/428–3/12

OMGUS Control Office, Historical Branch,
5/38–1/29

OMGUS Information Control Division, Press Control
5/237–3/3

OMGUS Information Services Division, Reports Office,
5/242–1/8, 48
5/242–2/36

5/243–1/4

OMGUS Information Services Division, Plans and Directives Branch,
5/243–2/8, 17

OMGUS Information Services Division, Director's Office
5/244–1/11
5/246–2/5
5/265–1/2, 16
5/266–3/10
5/267–3/4
5/269–1/21
5/270–2/11
5/270–3/4

OMGUS Education and Cultural Relations Division, Education Branch,
5/301–3/9
5/310–3/6

OMGUS Information Services Division, Theater and Music Branch
5/347–3/2, 25, 27
5/348–1/8, 15
5/348–2/7, 13
5/348–3/4, 10

OMGUS Information Services Division, Motion Pictures Branch
10/18–1/6, 7

OMGUS Information Services Division, Policy and Program Branch
5/245–1/21

OMGUS Control Office, Director's Office
5/364–2/38
5/368–2/4

OMGUS Historical Division,
5/428–3/9

OMGUS Control Office, Civil Administration Division, Reports and Statistics
    Section
11/47–3/24, 25, 26

OMGUS Adjutant General
1945–46/79/4

1947/20/2
1948/139/2

Office of the Political Adviser (POLAD)
459/9
461/53
757/19

Bayerisches Hauptstaatsarchiv, München

Kultus Ministerium
Mk 50129, 51335, 51340

Office of Military Government, Bavaria (OMGB), Intelligence Division, Culture
and Education, General
10/066–1/045

OMGB, Education and Cultural Relations, Cultural Affairs Branch, Music Section
10/048–1/1, 3, 4, 5, 7, 8, 9

(2) INTERVIEWS

Jack Bornoff, December 2000
Georg Knepler, May 2001
Sylvia Armit, May 2001
Klaus Meyer, October 2001

(3) PUBLISHED SOURCES

Abusch, Alexander and Gemkow, Heinrich (eds), *... einer neuen Zeit Beginn:
Erinnerungen an die Anfänge unserer Kulturrevolution* (Berlin and Weimar:
Aufbau, 1981).
Adorno, Theodor, *Prisms* (trans Weber and Weber, Letchworth: Garden City Press,
1967).
Adorno, Theodor, 'What National Socialism Has Done to the Arts', *Gesammelte
Schriften, Band 20:2, Vermischte Schriften II* (Frankfurt-am-Main: Suhrkamp,
1986), pp. 413–429.
Adorno, Theodor, 'Die gegängelte Musik', *Gesammelte Schriften, Band 14,
Dissonanzen; Einleitung in die Musiksoziologie* (Frankfurt-am-Main: Suhrkamp,
1990), pp. 51–66.

Allihn, Ingeborg, '"Verwürzelung in Deutscher Stammesart". Das Reichs-Bach-Fest 1935', Bach-Archiv Leipzig (ed.), *Leipziger Beiträge zur Bach-Forschung* (Hildesheim: Olms, 1995), pp. 199–209.

Amos, Heike, *Auferstanden aus Ruinen ... Die Nationalhymne der DDR 1949 bis 1990* (Berlin: Dietz, 1997).

Amos, Heike, *Die Westpolitik der SED 1948/49–1961. 'Arbeit nach Westdeutschland' durch die Nationale Front, das Ministerium für Auswärtige Angelegenheiten und das Ministerium für Staatssicherheit* (Berlin: Akademie Verlag, 1999).

Annan, Noel, *Changing Enemies: The Defeat and Regeneration of Germany* (London: HarperCollins, 1995).

Applegate, Celia and Potter, Pamela (eds), *Music and German National Identity* (Chicago and London: University of Chicago Press, 2002).

Arbeitsgemeinschaft für Musikerziehung und Musikpflege (ed.), *Zur Notlage der Musikerziehung und Musikpflege* (Kassel, 1953).

Autorenkollektiv, *Sammelbände zur Musikgeschichte der Deutschen Demokratischen Republik, Band V: Musikgeschichte der DDR 1945–1976* (Berlin: Verlag Neue Musik, 1979).

Bach-Archiv Leipzig (ed.), *Leipziger Beiträge zur Bach-Forschung* (Hildesheim: Olms, 1995).

Badstübner, Rolf and Loth, Wilfried (eds), *Wilhelm Pieck – Aufzeichnungen zur Deutschlandpolitik 1945–1953* (Berlin: Akademie-Verlag, 1994).

Baring, Arnulf, *Uprising in East Germany: June 17, 1953* (trans. Onn, New York and London: Cornell University Press, 1972).

Bausch, Hans (ed.), *Rundfunk in Deutschland, Band 3, Rundfunkpolitik nach 1945. Erster Teil 1945–1962* (Munich: Deutscher Taschenbuch Verlag, 1980).

Bausch, Ulrich, *Die Kulturpolitik der US-amerikanischen Information Control Division in Württemberg-Baden von 1945–1949* (Stuttgart: Klett-Cotta, 1992).

Bayerisches Staatsbibliothek (ed.), *Karl Amadeus Hartmann und die Musica Viva: Essays, bisher unveröffentliche Briefe an Hartmann, Katalog* (Munich: Piper, 1980).

Beal, Amy, 'Negotiating Cultural Allies: American Music in Darmstadt, 1946–1956', *Journal of the American Musicological Society*, 53:1 (2000), pp. 105–139.

Berman, Russel, 'Adorno's Politics', in Nigel Gibson and Andrew Rubin (eds), *Adorno: A Critical Reader* (Oxford: Blackwell, 1992), pp. 110–131.

Johannes-R.-Becher-Archiv der Deutschen Akademie der Künste zu Berlin (ed.), *Erinnerungen an Johannes R. Becher* (Leipzig: Reclam, 1968).

Joachim-Ernst Berendt, *das jazzbuch* (Frankfurt-am-Main and Hamburg: Fischer, 1953).

Betz, Albrecht, *Hanns Eisler: Political Musician* (trans. Hopkins, Cambridge and New York: Cambridge University Press, 1982).

Beveridge, William, *An Urgent Message from Germany* (London: Pilot Press, 1946).

Bidwell, Paul, 'Reeducation in Germany: Emphasis on Culture in the French Zone', *Foreign Affairs*, 27:1 (October 1948), pp. 78–85.

Blake, David, 'The Reception of Schoenberg in the German Democratic Republic', *Perspectives of New Music*, 21 (1982–83), pp. 114–137.

Borio, Gianmario, and Danuser, Hermann (eds), *Im Zenit der Moderne – Die internationalen Ferienkurse für Neue Musik Darmstadt 1946–1966* (Freiburg im Breisgau: Rombach, 1997).

Boughton, Rutland, 'Russian and British Censorship', *The Musical Times*, 89 (May 1948), pp. 153–4.

Boyd, Malcolm (ed.), *Composer Companion to J. S. Bach* (New York and Oxford: Oxford University Press, 1999).

Brabazon, James, *Albert Schweitzer* (London: Gollancz, 1976).

Brennecke, Dietrich, 'Max Butting – Die Musik und die Menschen', *Sinn und Form*, 1968/4, pp. 1345–1368.

Brooke, Caroline, *The Development of Soviet Music Policy, 1932–1941* (PhD thesis University of Cambridge, 1999).

Broszat, Martin and Weber, Hermann (eds), *SBZ-Handbuch: staatliche Verwaltungen, Parteien, gesellschaftliche Organisationen und ihre Führungskräfte in der Sowjetischen Besatzungszone Deutschlands 1945–1949* (Munich: Oldenbourg, 1990).

Bührer, Werner (ed.), *Die Adenauer-Ära. Die Bundesrepublik Deutschland 1949– 1963* (Munich: Piper, 1993).

Burckhardt, Jakob, *Weltgeschichtliche Betrachtungen* (ed. Rudolf Marx, Stuttgart: Alfred Kröner Verlag, 1969).

Burghardt, Max, *Ich war nicht nur Schauspieler: Erinnerungen eines Theatermannes* (Berlin and Weimar: Aufbau, 1976).

Burrin, Phillippe, *Living with Defeat: France under the German Occupation 1940– 1945* (London: Arnold, 1996).

Burton, Humphrey, *Leonard Bernstein* (London: Faber and Faber, 1994).

Burton, Humphrey, *Menuhin: a life* (London: Faber, 2000).

Butting, Max, *Musikgeschichte die ich miterlebte* (Berlin: Henschelverlag, 1955).

Calico, Joy Haslam, '"The Karl Marx of Music": Hanns Eisler Reception in the United States after 1947', Maren Köster (ed.), *Hanns Eisler: 's müßt dem Himmel Höllenangst werden* (Hofheim: Wolke Verlag, 1998), pp. 120–136.

Carpenter, Humphrey, *Benjamin Britten: A Biography* (London: Faber, 1992).

Carpenter, Humphrey, *The Envy of the World: Fifty Years of the BBC Third Programme and Radio 3 1946–1996* (London: Weidenfeld and Nicolson, 1996).

Carroll, Mark, *Music and Ideology in Cold War Europe* (Cambridge: Cambridge University Press, 2003).

Cerny, Jochen (ed.), *Wer war wer, DDR: ein biographisches Lexikon* (Berlin: Ch. Links, 1992).

Chamberlin, Brewster (ed.), *Kultur auf Trümmern. Berliner Berichte des amerikanischen Information Control Section Juli–Dezember 1945* (Stuttgart: Deutsche Verlags-Anstalt, 1979).

Clare, George, *Berlin Days 1946–1947* (London: Macmillan, 1989).

Clay, Lucius, *Decision in Germany* (London: Heinemann, 1950).

Clemens, Gabriele, *Britische Kulturpolitik in Deutschland 1945–49. Literatur, Film, Musik und Theater* (Stuttgart: Franz Steiner, 1997).

Clemens, Gabriele (ed.), *Kulturpolitik in besetzten Deutschland 1945–49* (Stuttgart: Franz Steiner, 1994).

Clemens, Gabriele, 'Die britische Kulturpolitik in Deutschland: Musik, Theater, Film und Literatur', Gabriele Clemens (ed.), *Kulturpolitik in besetzten Deutschland 1945–49* (Stuttgart: Franz Steiner, 1994), pp. 200–218.

Craft, Robert, *Stravinsky: Selected Correspondence*, **3**, (London and Boston: Faber, 1985).

Culshaw, Edward, 'The Realist Creed', *The Monthly Musical Record*, February 1950, pp. 41–44.

Davis, Edith, 'British Policy and the Schools', Arthur Hearnden (ed.), *The British in Germany: Educational Reconstruction after 1945* (London: Hamilton, 1978), pp. 95–107.

Deissler, Dirk, *Die entnazifizierte Sprache: Sprachpolitik und Sprachregelung in der Besatzungszeit* (Frankfurt-am-Main: Peter Lang, 2004).

Deutschen Sektion der Internationalen Gesellschaft für Neue Musik e.V. (ed.), *Neue Musik in der Bundesrepublik Deutschland; Dokumentation 1957/8* (Frankfurt-am-Main, London, and New York: Peters, 1958).

Dibelius, Ulrich and Schneider, Frank (eds), *Neue Musik im geteilten Deutschland: Dokumente aus den fünfziger Jahren* (Berlin: Henschel, 1993).

Dickens, Arthur, *Lübeck Diary* (London: Victor Gollancz, 1947)

Dietrich, Gerd, *Politik und Kultur in der Sowjetischen Besatzungszone Deutschlands (SBZ) 1945–49: mit einem Dokumentenanhang* (Bern: Peter Lang, 1993).

Dräger, Hans-Heinz and Laux, Karl (eds), *Bach-Probleme: Festschrift zur Deutschen Bach-Feier Leipzig 1950* (Leipzig: Peters, 1951).

Eckert, Astrid, *Kampf um die Akten. Die Westalliierten und die Rückgabe von deutschem Archivgut nach dem Zweiten Weltkrieg* (Stuttgart: Steiner, 2004).

Eisler, Hanns, *Gespräche mit Hans Bunge: Fragen Sie mehr über Brecht* (Leipzig: Deutscher Verlag für Musik, 1975).

Fark, Reinhard, *Die mißachtete Botschaft: Publizistische Aspekte des Jazz im soziokulturellen Wandel* (Berlin: Spiess, 1971).

Fischer, Uwe, 'Nationale Bedeutung der deutschen Bachfeier', *National Zeitung*, 4 August 1950.

Freymann, Richard, review of Friedrich Blume, *Wesen und Werden deutscher Musik* (Bärenreiter, 1944), *Music and Letters*, 28 (1947), pp. 279–280.

Fröhner, Rolf (ed.), *Wie stark sind sie Halbstarken? Beruf und Berufsnot, politische, kulturelle und seelische Probleme der deutschen Jugend im Bundesgebiet und in Westberlin* (Bielefeld: von Stackelberg, 1956).

Gerhard, Anselm, 'Musicology in the "Third Reich": A Preliminary Report', *The Journal of Musicology*, 18:4 (Fall 2001), pp. 517–543.

Gibson, Nigel and Rubin, Andrew (eds), *Adorno: A Critical Reader* (Oxford: Blackwell, 1992).

Gienow-Hecht, Jessica, *Transmission Impossible: American Journalism as Cultural Diplomacy in Postwar Germany 1945–1955* (Baton Rouge: Louisiana State University Press, 1999).

Gimbel, John, *The American Occupation of Germany: Politics and the Military, 1945–1949* (Stanford: Stanford University Press, 1968).

Glaser, Hermann, *Kulturgeschichte der Bundesrepublik Deutschland, Band 1: Zwischen Kapitulation und Währungsreform 1945–48* (Munich: Carl Hansen, 1985).

Glaser, Hermann, *The Rubble Years: The Cultural Roots of Postwar Germany 1945–1948* (New York: Paragon House, 1986).

Glaser, Hermann, von Pufendorf, Lutz, and Schöneich, Michael (eds), *So viel Anfang war nie: Deutsche Städte 1945–1949* (Berlin: Siedler, 1989).

Godman, Stanley, 'The Bach Exhibition at Göttingen', *Musical Times*, 91 (December 1950), p. 485.

Golèa, André, 'The Opera in West Germany after 1945', Paul Schallück (ed.), *Germany: Cultural Developments since 1945* (Munich: Hüber, 1971), pp. 110–126.

Grabs, Manfred (ed.), *Hanns Eisler: A Rebel in Music. Selected Writings* (trans. Meyer, New York: International Publishers, 1978).

Gulyga, Alexander, 'Ernst Busch 1945', *Sinn und Form*, 1968/4, pp. 1370–1383.

Hamel, Fred, 'Schwingt freudig euch empor', *Musica*, 8 (1954), pp. 448–449.

Hansen, Mathias (ed.), *Komponieren zur Zeit: Gespräche mit Komponisten der DDR* (Leipzig: Deutscher Verlag für Musik, 1988).

Hartmann, Günther, *Karl Straube und seine Schule: "das Ganze ist ein Mythos"* (Bonn: Verlag für Systematische Musikwissenschaft, 1991).

von Hase, Hellmuth (ed.), *Jahrbuch der deutschen Musik 1943* (Leipzig: Breitkopf und Härtel, 1943).

Häusler, Josef, *Spiegel der neuen Musik, Donaueschingen: Chronik, Tendenzen, Werkbesprechungen* (Kassel: Bärenreiter, 1996).

Heider, Magdelena, 'Kulturbund zur demokratischen Erneuerung Deutschlands', Martin Broszat and Hermann Weber (eds), *SBZ-Handbuch: staatliche Verwaltungen, Parteien, gesellschaftliche Organisationen und ihre Führungskräfte in der Sowjetischen Besatzungszone Deutschlands 1945–1949* (Munich: Oldenbourg, 1990), pp. 714–734.

Heimann, Thomas, 'Vom Lebensweg des Jazz. Notizen zu einem umstrittenen Dokumentarfilm der DEFA', *Das Jahrbuch der DEFA-Stiftung*, 2000, pp. 229–240.

Heister, Hanns-Werner and Stern, Dietrich (eds), *Musik 50er Jahre* (Berlin: Argument-Verlag, 1980).

Heister, Hanns-Werner and Klein, Hans-Günter (eds), *Musik und Musikpolitik im faschistischen Deutschland* (Frankfurt-am-Main: Fischer, 1984).

Henke, Klaus-Dietmar, *Die amerikanische Besetzung Deutschlands* (Munich: Oldenbourg, 1996).

Hennenberg, Fritz, *The Leipzig Gewandhaus Orchestra* (Leipzig: VEB Edition, 1962).

Henze, Hans-Werner, *Music and Politics: Collected Writings 1953–81* (trans. Labanyi, London: Faber, 1982).

Henze, Hans-Werner, *Bohemian Fifths: An Autobiography* (trans. Spencer, London: Faber, 1998).

Henze-Döhring, Sabina, 'Kulturelle Zentren in der amerikanischen Besatzungszone: der Fall Bayreuth', Gabriele Clemens (ed.), *Kulturpolitik in besetzten Deutschland 1945–49* (Stuttgart: Franz Steiner, 1994), pp. 39–54.

Herbst, Andreas, Ranke, Winfried, and Winkler, Jürgen (eds), *So funktionierte die DDR. Band 3, Lexikon der Funktionäre* (Hamburg: Rowhlt, 1994).

Herf, Jeffrey, *Divided Memory: The Nazi Past in the Two Germanys* (Cambridge, Massachusetts, and London: Harvard University Press, 1997).

Heribert, Henrich (ed.), *Blacher Boris, 1903–1975: Dokumente zu Leben und Werk* (Berlin: Henschel, 1993).

Hermand, Jost, *Kultur im Wiederaufbau. Die Bundesrepublik Deutschland 1945–65* (Munich: Nymphenburger, 1986).

Herz, John, 'The Fiasco of denazification in Germany', *Political Science Quarterly*, 63:4 (December 1948), pp. 569–594.

Hesse, Hermann, *The Glass Bead Game* (Harmondsworth: Penguin, 1977).

Theodor-Heuss-Archiv (ed.), *Theodor Heuss. Der Mann, das Werk, die Zeit. Eine Ausstellung* (Stuttgart, 1967).

Heyworth, Peter, *Otto Klemperer: His Life and Times* (Cambridge: Cambridge University Press, 1996).

Hinkel, Hans (ed.), *Handbuch der Reichskulturkammer* (Berlin: Deutscher Verlag für Politik und Wirtschaft, 1937).

Hinrichsen, Max (ed.), *Hinrichsen's Musical Year Book, Vols. I–VII, 1944–1950* (London: Hinrichsen Edition, 1944–1950).

Hofmann, Erna and Zimmerman, Ingo (eds), *Begegnungen mit Rudolf Mauersberger* (Berlin: Evangelische Verlagsanstalt, 1964).

Hofmeisters Jahresverzeichnis: Verzeichnis sämtl. Musikalien, Musikbücher, Zeitschr., Abbildungen u. plast. Darstellungen, die in Deutschland u. in den deutschsprachigen Ländern erschienen sind / begr. von Friedrich Hofmeister, **87**, 1938 (1939) – **91**, 1942 (1943).

Hopp, Annemarie and Warneken, Berndt (eds), *Feinde, Freunde, Fremde. Erinnerungen an die Tübinger Franzosenzeit* (Tübingen: Universitätsstadt Tübingen, Kulturamt, 1995).

Janik, Elizabeth, '"The Golden Hunger Years": Music and Superpower Rivalry in Occupied Berlin', *German History*, 22:1 (2004), pp. 76–100.

Jefferson, Alan, *Elisabeth Schwarzkopf* (London: Gollancz, 1996).

Johnson, Eric, *The Nazi Terror: Gestapo, Jews, and Ordinary Germans* (London: John Murray, 2002).

Kappelt, Olaf, *Braunbuch DDR: Nazis in der DDR* (Berlin: Reichmann, 1981).

Kater, Michael, *Different Drummers: Jazz in the Culture of Nazi Germany* (New York and Oxford: Oxford University Press, 1992).

Kater, Michael, *The Twisted Muse: Musicians and their Music in the Third Reich* (New York and Oxford: Oxford University Press, 1997).

Kater, Michael, *Composers of the Nazi Era: Eight Portraits* (New York and Oxford: Oxford University Press, 2000).

Kater, Michael and Riethmüller, Albrecht (eds), *Music and Nazism: Art under Tyranny, 1933–1945* (Laaber: Laaber Verlag, 2003).

Kaufmann, Michael, *Orgel und Nationalsozialismus. Die ideologische Vereinnahmung des Instruments im "Dritten Reich"* (Kleinblittersdorf: Musikwissenschaftliche Verlags-Gesellschaft, 1997).

Kerouac, Jack, *On the Road* (Harmondsworth: Penguin, [1957] 1972).

Klingberg, Lars, *Politisch fest in unseren Händern; musikalische und musikwissenschaftliche Gesellschaften in der DDR* (Kassel, Basle, London, New York, Prague: Bärenreiter, 1997).

Klingberg, Lars, 'Neue Bachgesellschaft und DDR', Bach-Archiv Leipzig (ed.), *Leipzig Beiträge zur Bach-Forschung* (Hildesheim: Olms, 1995), pp. 141–167.

Köster, Maren, *Musik–Zeit–Geschehen. Zu den Musikverhältnissen in der SBZ/DDR 1945 bis 1952* (Saarbrücken: Pfau, 2002).

Kruse, Brigitte, '"...Die Ferne wird nah, und die Nähe bleibt fern...": Exil in Großbrittannien im Spannungsfeld von englischer und deutscher Kultur – Ein Annäherungsversuch', Joachim Braun, Heidi Tamar Hoffmann, Vladimír Karbusický (eds), *Verfemte Musik: Komponisten in den Diktaturen unseres Jahrhunderts* (Frankfurt am Main: Peter Lang, 1997), pp. 321–332.

'La Vie Musicale sous l'Occupation', *Journal du Vingtième Siècle* (February 2000), pp. 142–143.

Lauter, Hans, *Der Kampf gegen den Formalismus in Kunst und Literatur, für eine fortschrittliche Deutsche Kultur: Referat von Hans Lauter, Diskussion und Entschließung von der 5. Tagung des Zentralkomitees der SED vom 15.–17. März 1951* (Berlin: Dietz, 1951).

Laux, Karl, *Die Musik in Rußland und in der Sowjetunion* (Berlin: Henschelverlag, 1958).

Laux, Karl, *Nachklang. Rückschau auf sechs Jahrzehnte kulturellen Wirkens* (Berlin: Verlag der Nation, 1977).

League of Culture for the Democratic Regeneration of Germany (ed.), *The League of Culture in Berlin: A Memorandum* (Berlin: Aufbau-Verlag, 1948).

Leonhard, Wolfgang, *Die Revolution entläßt ihre Kinder* (Cologne: Kiepenheuer and Witsch, 1955).

Leukert, Berndt, 'Musik aus Trümmern. Darmstadt um 1949', *Musik-Texte: Zeitschrift für neue Musik*, 45 (July 1992), pp. 20–28.

Levi, Erik, *Music in the Third Reich* (Basingstoke: Macmillan, 1994).

Lindt, Lotte (ed.), *Bruno Walter: Briefe 1894–1962* (Frankfurt-am-Main: Fischer, 1969).

Luther, Wilhelm Martin, *Johann Sebastian Bach: Documenta* (Kassel: Bärenreiter, 1950).

Maase, Kaspar, *BRAVO Amerika: Erkundungen zur Jugendkultur der Bundesrepublik in den fünfziger Jahren* (Hamburg: Junius, 1992).

Manifest des Kulturbundes zur demokratischen Erneuerung Deutschlands (Berlin: Aufbau-Verlag, 1945).

Marchall-Reiser, Johanna, *Findbuch zu Beständen des Bundesarchives. Band 70. Ministerium für Kultur. Teil 1. Staatliche Kommission für Kunstangelegenheiten, 1951–1954. Bestand DR 1* (Koblenz: Bundesarchiv, 1999).

Martens, Stefan (ed.), *Vom "Erbfeind" zum "Erneuer": Aspekte und Motive der französischen Deutschlandpolitik nach dem Zweiten Weltkrieg* (Sigmaringen: Thorbecke, 1993).

Matheson, Lynn, '"Ein Thema hat ungefähr so viele Möglichkeiten wie ein Mensch": Zur Beethoven-Rezeption Hanns Eislers', Maren Köster (ed.), *Hanns Eisler: 's müßt dem Himmel Höllenangst werden* (Hofheim: Wolke Verlag, 1998), pp. 107–113.

Mayer, Hans, *Gelebte Musik. Erinnerungen* (Frankfurt am Main: Suhrkamp, 1999).

Melrose, Georgiana, *A Strange Occupation* (Ilfracombe: Stockwell, 1988).

Menuhin, Yehudi, *Unfinished Journey* (London: MacDonald and James, 1977).

Merritt, Anna and Merritt, Richard (eds), *Public Opinion in semisovereign Germany: The HICOG Surveys 1949–1955* (Urbana, Chicago, and London: University of Illinois Press, 1980).

Meyer, Ernst Hermann, *Kontraste, Konflikte: Erinnerungen, Gespräche, Kommentare* (Berlin: Verlag Neue Musik, 1979).

Meyer, Michael, *The Politics of Music in the Third Reich* (New York: Peter Lang, 1991).

Ministerium für Auswärtige Angelegenheiten der DDR (ed.), *Um ein antifaschistisch-demokratisches Deutschland. Dokumente aus den Jahren 1945–1949* (Berlin: Staatsverlag der DDR, 1968).

Mitchell, Donald, *Britten and Auden in the Thirties: The Year 1936* (London: Faber, 1981).

Mitchell, Donald and Reed, Philip (eds), *Letters from a Life: The Selected Letters and Diaries of Benjamin Britten 1913–1976,* vol. 2 1939–1945 (London: Faber and Faber, 1991).

Monod, David, 'Internationalism, Regionalism and National Culture: Music Control in Bavaria, 1945–1948', *Central European History*, 33:3 (2000), pp. 339–368.

Monod, David, *Settling Scores: German Music, Denazification, and the Americans, 1945–1953* (Chapel Hill and London: University of North Carolina Press, 2005).

Moss, Steven, '"What has C sharp minor got to do with fascism?"', *The Guardian*, 4 January 2000.

Muck, Peter, *Einhundert Jahre Berlin Philharmonisches Orchester: Darstellung in Dokumenten* (Tutzing: H. Schneider, 1982).

Müller, Erich, 'Das Judentum in der Musik', Theodor Fritsch (ed.), *Handbuch der Judenfrage. Die wichtigsten Tatsachen zur Beurteilung des jüdischen Volkes* (31st edition, Leipzig: Hammer Verlag, 1932), pp. 323–333.

Müller, Erich, 'Das Judentum in der Musik', Theodor Fritsch (ed.), *Handbuch der Judenfrage. Die wichtigsten Tatsachen zur Beurteilung des jüdischen Volkes* (36th edition, Leipzig: Hammer Verlag, 1934), pp. 324–334.

Nabokov, Nicolas, *Old Friends and New Music* (London: Hamish Hamilton, 1951).

Nabokov, Nicolas, *Bagázh: Memoirs of a Russian cosmopolitan* (London: Secker and Warburg, 1975).

Naimark, Norman, *The Russians in Germany: A History of the Soviet Zone of Occupation, 1945–1949* (Cambridge, Massachusetts and London: Belknap Press of Harvard University Press, 1995).

Niemann, Konrad, *Ernst Hermann Meyer – für Sie porträtiert* (2nd edition, Leipzig: Deutscher Verlag für Musik, 1989).

Ortmeyer, Benjamin, *Argumente gegen das Deutschlandlied. Geschichte und Gegenwart eines Lobliedes auf die deutsche Nation* (Cologne: Bund-Verlag, 1991).

Paddison, Max, 'Immanent Critique or Musical Stocktaking: Adorno and the Problem of Musical Analysis', in Nigel Gibson and Andrew Rubin (eds), *Adorno: A Critical Reader* (Oxford: Blackwell, 1992), pp. 209–233.

Page, Tim and Page, Vanessa (eds), *Selected letters of Virgil Thomson* (New York and London: Summit Books, 1988).

Peyser, Joan, *Boulez: Composer, Conductor, Enigma* (London: Cassell, 1977).

Pike, David, *The Politics of Culture in Soviet Occupied Germany 1945–1949* (Stanford: Stanford University Press, 1992).

Poiger, Uta, 'Rock 'n' Roll, Female Sexuality, and the Cold War Battle over German Identities', *Journal of Modern History*, 68:3 (1996), pp. 577–616.

Poiger, Uta, *Jazz, Rock, and Rebels: Cold War Politics and American Culture in a Divided Germany* (Berkeley, Los Angeles, and London: University of California Press, 2000).

Pommerin, Reiner (ed.), *The American Impact on Postwar Germany* (Oxford: Berghahn, 1995).

Pommerin, Reiner (ed.), *Culture in the Federal Republic of Germany, 1945–1995* (Oxford: Berg, 1996).

Potter, Pamela, *Most German of the Arts: Musicology and Society from the Weimar Republic to the end of Hitler's Reich* (New Haven and London: Yale University Press, 1998).

Potter, Pamela, 'Blume, Friedrich', *New Grove Dictionary of Music and Musicians* (London, 2001), **3**, pp. 739–41.

Prieberg, Fred, *Musik im NS-Staat* (Frankfurt-am-Main: Fischer, 1982)

Prieberg, Fred, *Musik und Macht* (Frankfurt-am-Main: Fischer, 1991)

Prieberg, Fred, *Trial of Strength: Wilhelm Furtwängler in the Third Reich* (trans. Dolan, Boston: Northeastern University Press, 1994).

Przyrembel, Alexandra, 'Transfixed by an Image: Ilse Koch, the "Kommandeuse of Buchenwald"', *German History*, 19:3 (2001), pp. 369-399.

Raab Hansen, Jutta, *NS-verfolgte Musiker in England – Spuren deutscher und österreichischer Flüchtlinge in der britischen Musikkultur* (Hamburg: von Bockel, 1996).

Ramin, Charlotte, *Günther Ramin. Ein Lebensbericht* (Freiburg-im-Breisgau: Atlantis, 1958).

Rieple, Max, *Musik in Donaueschingen* (Constance: Rosgarten, 1959).

Riess, Curt, *Berlin Berlin 1945–1953* (Berlin: Non stop-Bücherei, 1953).

Rudorf, Reginald, *Jazz in der Zone* (Cologne: Kiepenheuer and Witsch, 1964).

Rühle, Jürgen, *Das gefesselte Theater* (Cologne and Berlin: Kiepenheuer and Witsch, 1957).

Sadie, Stanley (ed.), *New Grove Dictionary of Music and Musicians* (London: Macmillan, 1980).

Sadie, Stanley (ed.), *New Grove Dictionary of Music and Musicians* (Second Edition, Oxford: Grove, 2001).

Santner, Eric, *Stranded Objects: Mourning, Memory, and Film in Postwar Germany* (Ithaca and London: Cornell University Press, 1990).

Schallück, Paul (ed.), *Germany: Cultural Developments since 1945* (Munich: Hüber, 1971).

Schebera, Jürgen, *Hanns Eisler: Eine Biographie in Texten, Bildern, und Dokumenten* (Mainz: Schott, 1998).

Schieffer, Hans-Hubert and Müller, Hermann, *Neue Musik in Düsseldorf seit 1945* (Cologne: Dohr, 1998).

Schivelbusch, Wolfgang, *In a Cold Crater: Cultural and Intellectual Life in Berlin, 1945–1948* (Berkeley, California, and London: University of California Press, 1998).

Schmidt, Roderich (ed.), *Ludwig Doorman: Ein Leben für die Kirchenmusik. Erinnerungen, Gespräche, Briefe, Berichte* (Göttingen: Deuerlich'sche Buchhandlung, 1988).

Schmidt-Joos, Siegfried, *Geschäfte mit Schlagern* (Bremen: Carl Schünemann, 1960).

Schneider, Frank, *Momentaufnahme: Notate zu Musik und Musikern in der DDR* (Leipzig: Philipp Reclam jun., 1979).

Schwartz, Boris, *Music and Musical Life in Soviet Russia 1917–1970* (London: Barrie and Jenkins, 1972).

Schweitzer, Albert, *J. S .Bach* ([1911] trans. Newman, Boston: Bruce Humphries, 1962)

Shdanow, Andrei, *Über Kunst und Wissenschaft* (Berlin: Dietz, 1951)

Skelton, Geoffrey (ed.), *Selected Letters of Paul Hindemith* (New Haven and London: Yale University Press, 1995).

Solti, Georg, *Solti on Solti: A Memoir* (New York: Knopf, 1997)

Sozialistische Einheitspartei Deutschlands (ed.), *Protokoll der Verhandlungen der 2. Parteikonferenz der Sozialistischen Einheitspartei Deutschlands, 9. bis 12. Juli 1952 in der Werner-Seebinder-Halle zu Berlin* (Berlin: Dietz, 1952).

Spotts, Frederic, *Hitler and the Power of Aesthetics* (London: Pimlico, 2003)

Stackelberg, Karl-Georg (ed.), *Jugend zwischen 15 und 24: Untersuchungen zur Situation der deutschen Jugend im Bundesgebiet. Erste Untersuchung* (Hamburg: Jugendwerk der Deutschen Shell, 1953).

Stackelberg, Karl-Georg (ed.), *Jugend zwischen 15 und 24: Untersuchungen zur Situation der deutschen Jugend im Bundesgebiet. Zweite Untersuchung* (Hamburg: Jugendwerk der Deutschen Shell, 1955).

Starr, S. Frederick, *Red and Hot: The Fate of Jazz in the Soviet Union 1917–1980* (Oxford: Oxford University Press, 1983).

Steiert, Thomas, 'Zur Musik- und Theaterpolitik in Stuttgart während der amerikanischen Besatzungszeit', Gabriele Clemens (ed.), *Kulturpolitik in besetzten Deutschland 1945–49* (Stuttgart: Franz Steiner, 1994), pp. 55–68.

Steinweis, Alan, *Art, Ideology, and Economics: The Reich Chambers of Music, Theatre, and the Visual Arts* (Chapel Hill: University of North Carolina Press, 1993).

Stiftung Archiv der Akademie der Künste (ed), *Zwischen Diskussion und Disziplin: Dokumente zur Geschichte der Akademie der Künste (Ost) 1945/1954 bis 1993* (Berlin: Henschel, 1997).

Saunders, Frances Stonor, *Who Paid the Piper? The CIA and the Cultural Cold War* (London: Granta, 1999).

Söhngen,Oskar, *Die Wiedergeburt der Kirchenmusik* (Kassel: Bärenreiter, 1953).

Stuckenschmidt, Hans-Heinz, *Schöpfer der Neuen Musik: Portraits und Studien* (Frankfurt-am-Main: Suhrkamp, 1958).

Stuckenschmidt, Hans-Heinz, *Zum Hören Geboren: Ein Leben mit der Musik unserer Zeit* (Munich: Piper, 1979).

Thomson, Virgil, *Music right and left* (New York: Holt, 1951).

Thacker, Toby, 'The fifth column: dance music in the early GDR', in Patrick Major and Jonathan Osmond (eds), *The Workers' and Peasants' State: Communism and Society in East Germany under Ulbricht 1945–71* (Manchester: Manchester University Press, 2002), pp. 227–243.

Thacker, Toby, '"Playing Beethoven like an Indian": American Music and Reorientation in Germany, 1945–1955', in Dominik Geppert (ed.), *The Postwar Challenge: Cultural, Social, and Political Change in Western Europe, 1945–1958* (New York and Oxford: Oxford University Press, 2003), pp. 365–386.

Thacker, Toby, '"Liberating German musical life": The BBC German Service and planning for Music Control in Occupied Germany, 1944–1949', in Charmian Brinson and Richard Dove (eds), *'Stimme der Wahrheit': German-language broadcasting by the BBC, Yearbook of the Research Centre for German and Austrian Exile Studies*, 5 (2003), pp. 77–92.

Thacker, Toby, '"Anleitung und Kontrolle': Stakuko and the Censorship of Music in the GDR, 1951–1953', in Beate Müller (ed.), *Censorship and Cultural Regulation in the Modern Age* (Amsterdam and New York: Rodopi, 2004), pp. 87–110.

Thacker, Toby, '"Renovating" Bach and Handel: New Musical Biographies and the Building of Socialism', in Jolanta Pekacz (ed.), *Musical Biography: Towards New Paradigms* (Aldershot: Ashgate Publishing, 2006), pp. 17–41.

Thacker, Toby, '"Gesungen oder musiziert wird aber fast in jedem Haus": Representing and Constructing Citizenship through Music in Twentieth-Century Germany', in Geoff Eley and Jan Palmowski (eds), *Citizenship and National Identity in Twentieth-Century Germany* (Stanford: Stanford University Press, forthcoming).

Tiessen, Heinz, *Wege Eines Komponisten* (Berlin: Akademie der Künste, 1962).

Tippett, Michael, *Those Twentieth Century Blues: An Autobiography* (London: Pimlico, 1991).

Untersuchungsausschuß Freiheitlicher Juristen (ed.), *Ehemalige Nationalsozialisten in Pankows Diensten* (Berlin: no publisher given, 1965).

Vansittart, Robert, *Black Record: Germans Past and Present* (London: Hamish Hamilton, 1941).

Verband Deutscher Komponisten und Musikwissenschaftler, Musik Informationszentrum (ed.), *Komponisten und Musikwissenschaftler der Deutschen Demokratischen Republik* (Berlin: Verlag Neue Musik, 1965).

Verband der Komponisten und Musikwissenschaftler der DDR (ed.), *Chronik des Verbandes der Komponisten und Musikwissenschaftler der DDR 1951–1980* (Berlin: Zentralinstitut für Musikforschung, 1981).

de Vries, Willem, *Sonderstab Musik: Music Confiscations by the Einsatzstab Reichsleiter Rosenberg under the Nazi Occupation of Western Europe* (Amsterdam: Amsterdam University Press, 1996).

Vetter, Walther and Meyer, Ernst Hermann (eds), *Bericht über die wissenschaftliche Bachtagung der Gesellschaft für Musikforschung Leipzig, 23. bis 26. Juli 1950* (Leipzig: Peters, 1951).

Waddy, Helen, 'Beyond Statistics to Microhistory: The Role of Migration and Kinship in the Making of the Nazi Constituency', *German History*, 19:3 (2001), pp. 340–368.

zur Weihen, Daniel, *Komponieren in der DDR: Institutionen, Organisationen und die erste Komponistengeneration* (Cologne, Weimar, and Vienna: Böhlau, 1999).

Weissweiler, Eva, *Ausgemerzt! Das Lexikon der Juden in der Musik und seine mörderischen Folgen* (Cologne: Dittrich Verlag, 1999).

Weisz, Christoph (ed.), *OMGUS-Handbuch: Die amerikanische Militärregierung in Deutschland 1945–1949* (Munich: Oldenbourg, 1994).

Werth, Alexander, *Musical Uproar in Moscow* (London: Turnstile Press, 1949).

Westdeutscher Rundfunk Köln (ed.), *Zwanzig Jahre Musik im Westdeutschen Rundfunk. Eine Dokumentation der Hauptabteilung Musik 1948–1968* (Cologne: Westdeutscher Rundfunk, 1968).

Willett, Ralph, *The Americanization of Germany 1945–49* (London: Routledge, 1989).

Willis, Frank Roy, *The French in Germany 1945–1949*(Stanford: Stanford University Press, 1962).

Wilson, Elizabeth, *Shostakovich: A Life Remembered* (London: Faber and Faber, 1994).

Witkin, Robert, *Adorno on Music* (London and New York: Routledge, 1998).

Wulf, Josef, *Musik im Dritten Reich. Eine Dokumentation* (Gütersloh: S. Mohn, 1963).

Zintgraf, Werner, *Neue Musik 1921–1950: Donaueschingen, Baden-Baden, Berlin, Pfullingen, Mannheim* (Horb am Neckar: Geiger-Verlag, 1987).

Zuck, Barbara, *A History of Musical Americanism* (Ann Arbor: UMI Research Press, 1980).

(4) Selected Articles and Reviews, as Cited in Footnotes, from the Following Newspapers and Journals

Amerikanische Rundschau
Aufbau
Bach-Jahrbuch
Berlin am Mittag
Berliner Zeitung
Bonner Rundschau
British Zone Review
Das Buch
Der Kurier
Der Ruf
Der Spiegel
Die Aussprache: Mitteilungsblatt für die Mitglieder und Freunde des Kulturbundes zur demokratischen Erneuerung Deutschlands
Die Neue Zeitung
Die Musikforschung
Die Welt
Encounter
Frankfurter Allgemeine Zeitung
GMZF, Commandement en chef Français en Allemagne, Témoignages et Interrogatoires
Göttinger Tageblatt
The Guardian
Hannoversche Neueste Nachrichten
Hier spricht London. Programmheft des Europäischen Sendedienstes der BBC
Hör Zu!
Journal Officiel du Commandement en Chef Français en Allemagne

Junge Welt
Karlsbader Tages Zeitung
Kirchenmusikalische Mitteilungen
La France en Allemagne
La Revue de la Zone Française
Les Nouvelles d'Allemagne
L'oeuvre culturelle française en Allemagne
Melos, Zeitschrift für neue Musik
Military Government Information Bulletin (United States)
Mission Militaire pour les Affaires Allemandes, Articles et Documents
Mission Militaire pour les Affaires Allemandes, Bulletin d'Information
Mitteilungen des deutschen Städtetags
Monthly Report of the Control Council for Germany (British Element)
Musica
Musical America
Musikblätter
Musikleben
Musik und Gesellschaft. Arbeitsblätter für soziale Musikpflege und Musikpolitik
Nacht-Express
National Zeitung
Neue Auslese
Neue Rhein-Zeitung
Neue Zeitschrift für Musik
Neues Deutschland
New York Herald Tribune (Paris Edition)
Official Gazette of the Control Council for Germany
Pariser Zeitung
Picture Post
Réalités Allemandes
Revue de la Zone Française
Sinn und Form
Sonntag
Tagesspiegel
Tägliche Rundschau
Telegraf
The Stars and Stripes Magazine – Weekly Supplement
Time
Unser Tag
Volksstimme
Wiesbaden Post
Zentralblatt der DDR

Index